DAVID LODGE

David Lodge's novels include *The British Museum is Falling Down* (1965), *Changing Places* (1975), for which he was awarded the Hawthornden Prize, *How Far Can You Go?* (1980), which was Whitbread Book of the Year, *Small World* (1984), which was shortlisted for the Booker Prize, *Nice Work* (1988), which won the Sunday Express Book of the Year Award, *Thinks . . .* (2001), *Author, Author* (2004) and, most recently, *A Man of Parts* (2011). He has also written stage plays and screenplays, and several books of literary criticism, including *The Art of Fiction* (1992), *Consciousness and the Novel* (2002) and *Lives in Writing* (2014). His works have been translated into more than thirty languages.

He is Emeritus Professor of English Literature at the University of Birmingham and continues to live in that city. He is a Fellow of the Royal Society of Literature, was awarded a CBE for services to literature and is also a Chevalier de l'Ordre des Arts et des Lettres.

## ALSO BY DAVID LODGE

### Fiction

### Criticism

### Essays

### Drama

### Autobiography

DAVID LODGE

# Writer's Luck

A Memoir: 1976–1991

VINTAGE

1 3 5 7 9 10 8 6 4 2

Vintage
20 Vauxhall Bridge Road,
London SW1V 2SA

Vintage is part of the Penguin Random House group of companies
whose addresses can be found at global.penguinrandomhouse.com

Penguin
Random House
UK

First published in Vintage in 2019
First published in hardback by Harvill Secker in 2018

penguin.co.uk/vintage

A CIP catalogue record for this book is available from the British Library

ISBN 9781784708078

Printed and bound in Great Britain by Clays Ltd, Elcograf S.p.A.

Penguin Random House is committed to a sustainable future
for our business, our readers and our planet. This book is made
from Forest Stewardship Council® certified paper.

MIX
Paper from
responsible sources
FSC
www.fsc.org
FSC® C018179

For Jonny Geller

# FOREWORD

The Foreword to my previous volume of autobiography, *Quite a Good Time to Be Born: A Memoir 1935–1975*, published in 2015, concluded:

> This memoir describes how I became a writer,
> principally of prose fiction and literary criticism,
> beginning with the early experiences and influences
> that fed into my work later, and it covers what is, at
> the time of writing, the first half of my life, up to the
> age of forty. I hope to write another book about the
> second half, in added extra time.

The book you hold in your hands, however, covers not the next forty years of my life, but just fifteen of them. There were two reasons for this change of plan. One was the greater availability of data about the middle period of my life, and the second was what I hope is the inherent interest of this material. The narrative of my early life as a child and youth was necessarily based mainly on personal memories, supported by a precious but tantalisingly meagre collection of letters, photographs and other documents. It wasn't until the 1970s that I began to fill a succession of bulky folders and boxfiles with letters both personal and professional. As time went on and my activities as a writer expanded I also kept occasional diaries and other documents relating to particular projects or journeys. This archive has enabled me to recall all kinds of details about my professional and private life which I could never have summoned up from unaided memory. But trawling through the middle period of my life with a net of finer mesh added weight to the catch and imposed a slower tempo on the narrative than the first memoir, and therefore a shorter time span. The focus is still the same, primarily on my work as a writer, with occasional digressions into personal and family life; but the professional life became increasingly full of incident as I combined an academic career with writing novels and, after retiring early from university teaching, began writing stage plays and screenplays as well.

The seventies and eighties were exciting decades for both literary criticism and the literary novel in Britain. Traditional approaches to teaching and writing about literature in universities were challenged by new ways of reading texts and thinking about language. The Booker Prize and similar competitive awards sponsored by big business made the literary novel an object of interest to the mass media, and more lucrative for successful authors than before. I observed and participated in both these developments, and they are the subject matter of much of this book. For several reasons, of which the digitalisation of information and its transmission is probably the most important, the conditions under which literature is produced, circulated and financed have changed since then, generally for the worse as far as authors are concerned. I hope this detailed account of a writer's life in those more buoyant times will have some documentary value, and that readers of my novels will be interested to trace the ways in which they were conceived and developed. When I told Tom Rosenthal, who published my novels at Secker & Warburg between 1975 and 1984 and was a good friend thereafter, that I was going to write an autobiography, he said immediately, 'You'll need three books.' I am not sure whether I shall write a sequel to this one, but if I do it will perforce have a different, and more selective, structure.

'Writer's luck' is a phrase usually applied to good fortune, and I certainly consider myself lucky to have published my most popular novels in a period when there was something like a boom in literary fiction in Britain. The phrase can also apply to the discovery of a promising subject – for instance, when Thomas Keneally walked into a leather goods shop in Los Angeles one day to buy a briefcase and got chatting to the proprietor, who proceeded to tell him about Oscar Schindler. Without that chance encounter there would have been no *Schindler's Ark*. I haven't had a gift as astonishing as that, but there are many moments recalled in these pages where chance played a crucial part in inspiring or facilitating some important element in a work of fiction. The words 'lucky' or 'fortunately' appear quite frequently in this book. So, to a lesser extent, do 'unlucky' and 'unfortunate', for the possibility of disappointment and frustration for reasons outside one's control is inherent in all artistic activity. My experience of that is recorded here too.

In the course of a long career I published occasional accounts of my experiences in newspapers, magazines, collections of essays and introductions to reissued novels. I have drawn on these sources where it seemed appropriate and I have not hesitated to use their words, either in quotation or integrated into the narrative, when I could not think of better ones. What is written when the memory of an event is still fresh is likely to give a more accurate and expressive account of it than something composed long afterwards.

D.L., September 2017

# 1

*Quite a Good Time to Be Born: A Memoir 1935–1975*[1] ended with a brief glance forward to a book I published some years after the memoir's terminal date, a novel about

> the great changes that had taken place during that period
> in Catholic belief and practice, including my own. In the
> process of researching and writing *How Far Can You Go?*
> my faith had been demythologised, and I had to recognise
> that I no longer believed literally in the affirmations of
> the Creed which I recited at mass every Sunday, though
> they did not lose all meaning and value for me. But that
> is a subject, among others, for another book.

This conclusion was described by one reviewer as 'a bombshell' – presumably because there were few hints in the preceding pages of my harbouring fundamental theological doubts. I presented myself there as someone who had had a rather narrow and shallow Catholic education which nevertheless informed and stimulated my early

[1] Henceforward this title is referred to as *QAGTTBB*.

attempts at creative writing. These were also influenced by the work of Catholic authors like Graham Greene and Evelyn Waugh whose vision was essentially anti-humanist, privileging the supernatural drama of sin and salvation over the secular pursuit of material progress. My passage into adult life and its challenges, coinciding with a revolution in the Church triggered by the election of Pope John XXIII and the Second Vatican Council which he convened, transformed me into a liberal Catholic, supporting the modernisation of the Church in its organisation, liturgy and teaching, especially on the issue of birth control; but I did not consciously question the fundamental articles of the Creed or ask myself in what sense I actually believed in them until I started thinking about writing a novel that would reflect the extraordinary transformation of Catholicism that had occurred since the early 1960s.

I wrote once: 'A novel is a long answer to the question, *What is it about?*' The fundamental challenge for a novelist is to find the appropriate form for that answer, something which entails not just the invention of a story and its characters but all sorts of decisions about such matters as the point or points of view from which the story is told, the treatment of time, and verbal style. From its inception I decided this novel must have a large number of characters of more or less equal importance, with no central character or characters as in most novels, so that the full spectrum of attitudes and responses to the changing Catholic scene could be displayed. I also decided that the time span of the narrative should run from the early 1950s to the time of writing it in the late 1970s. Both these choices suggested that the dominant voice of the novel should be an intrusive authorial narrator, who would summarise and comment on the action and move it rapidly forward in time and history.

A fundamental distinction in the theory and practice of narrative literature is between 'telling' and 'showing' what happens in a story. Modern literary fiction generally favours the latter, either by using the technique of free indirect style, which fuses the authorial narrator's voice with the inner voice of a character's consciousness, or by having a character narrate the story in the first person. Both methods simultaneously 'tell' what happened and 'show' how it was subjectively perceived. The omniscient authorial narrator who describes, comments on and interprets the characters and their actions is a convention especially associated with the classic realist fiction of the nineteenth century, and was shunned as old-fashioned by most literary novelists in the first half of the twentieth. But in the 1960s a number of novelists began to get new effects from this narrative method by deliberately drawing attention to its artificiality. It was a feature of writing identified as 'postmodernist' – breaking away from the smoothly integrated showing and telling favoured by novelists in the forties and fifties but without reverting to the innovative methods of the great modernist writers earlier in the century like James Joyce and Virginia Woolf: stream-of-consciousness monologues, mythical allusions, overt symbolism and fractured syntax. John Fowles's *The French Lieutenant's Woman*, Muriel Spark's *The Prime of Miss Jean Brodie* and Kurt Vonnegut's *Slaughterhouse-Five* were three novels of the sixties I admired and wrote about as a critic, excited by the different ways their authors occasionally or repeatedly broke the illusion of reality they had created by drawing attention to how it was done. It was a technique that I thought would be appropriate to the novel I was preparing to write. In the first chapter ten students attending a weekday morning mass are rapidly introduced, and then recapitulated by an authorial narrator:

> Ten characters is a lot to take in all at once, and soon
> there will be more, because we are going to follow their
> fortunes, in a manner of speaking, up to the present,
> and obviously they are not going to pair off with each
> other, that would be too neat, too implausible, so there
> will be other characters not yet invented, husbands and
> wives and lovers, not to mention parents and children,
> so it is important to get these ten straight now. Each

character, for instance, has already been associated with some selected detail of dress or appearance which should help you distinguish one from another. Such details also carry connotations which symbolise certain qualities or attributes of the character. Thus Angela's very name connotes Angel, as in Heaven and cake (she looks good enough to eat in her pink angora sweater) and her blonde hair archetypecasts her as the fair virtuous woman, spouse-sister-mother-figure, whereas Polly is a Dark Lady, sexy seductress, though not really sinister because of her healthy cheeks and jolly curls . . .

Academic critics began to call this kind of novel 'metafiction', fiction which is partly about its own processes as well as about imaginary characters and events. Although as an effect it was not entirely new (it goes back as far as Laurence Sterne's *Tristram Shandy* in English fiction), to make it the dominant element in a novel is always a risky procedure, apt to irritate and alienate some readers. But I felt that as well as enabling me to handle a great chunk of human experience in a small textual space, it reflected the risks my characters were taking in their personal lives as a result of questioning aspects of the faith in which they had been brought up. The question that gives the novel its title is first quoted as one with which boys at a Catholic school teased the old priest who 'took' them for religious instruction, *'Please Father, how far can you go with a girl, Father?'* Sexual behaviour is certainly a key moral issue for the characters, but the phrase acquires a wider relevance as the story proceeds.

Father Austin Brierley, the diffident and repressed curate who celebrates the mass they attend as students in the first chapter, is radicalised first by being exposed to demythologising biblical scholarship, and later by publicly opposing the papal Encyclical of 1968, *Humanae Vitae*, which reaffirmed the Church's teaching against contraception. Suspended by his bishop on this account, he is supported by a movement of progressive laity called Catholics for a Changing Church (based on the actual Catholic Renewal Movement I described in *QAGTTBB*) to which several of the characters belong. He attends their 'agapes', meals hosted by different couples in turn, imitating the chaste love feasts of the early Christians, at which wholemeal bread is broken and passed round with cheap wine in a single cup or bowl in commemoration of the Last Supper, accompanied by New Testament readings and discussion. With Fr Brierly present:

> a certain theological ambiguity hung over these
> occasions. Was it a real Eucharist, or wasn't it? . . .
> To some this was a crucial difference, to others it
> was a relic of the old 'magical' view of the sacraments
> which they had renounced . . . Austin himself declared
> that the idea of a special caste exclusively empowered
> to administer the sacraments was rapidly becoming
> obsolete . . . So they stood upon the shores of Faith and
> felt the old dogmas and certainties ebbing away rapidly
> under their feet and between their toes, sapping the
> foundations upon which they stood, a sensation both
> agreeably stimulating and slightly unnerving.

This last image echoes a bleaker passage in Matthew Arnold's great poem 'Dover Beach'.

> The Sea of Faith
> Was once, too, at the full, and round earth's shore
> Lay like the folds of a bright girdle furl'd.
> But now I only hear
> Its melancholy, long, withdrawing roar,
> Retreating, to the breath
> Of the night-wind, down the vast edges drear
> And naked shingles of the world.

In 1984, several years after I wrote my novel, a television programme and associated book entitled *Sea of Faith*, by Don Cupitt, the Anglican Dean of Emmanuel College, Cambridge, prompted the formation of a movement or network of sceptical Christians and interested agnostics and atheists which adopted the Arnoldian phrase as its name. Its principles may be summarised as follows: religion is a creation of human consciousness and human culture. God did not create man – it was the other way round. The concept of a transcendent deity denoted by the word 'God' in religious discourse is without foundations and no longer commands the assent of thoughtful people in the modern world, where truth is established by scientific method. Nevertheless religion, especially Christianity for those who have been brought up in it, is or can be a cultural and spiritual force for good. Its rituals and ethos deserve to be kept up. There is something Cupitt called 'the religious requirement' (and Matthew Arnold more eloquently 'the eternal not ourselves that makes for righteousness') which should be obeyed for the sake of civilisation.

Predictably this position attracted criticism and ridicule from orthodox Christians and dogmatic materialists alike, but in me it struck a sympathetic chord, and in later years, when asked about my religious beliefs, I would sometimes describe myself as a 'Sea of Faith Catholic', although I never had any personal contact with the movement. The practice of religion, especially Catholic Christianity if that happens to be the tradition in which you were brought up, can be a useful stimulus to thinking seriously about fundamental questions which don't go away if you simply ignore them, questions formulated by the philosopher Kant which the radical Catholic theologian Hans Küng cited at the beginning of his book *On Being a Christian*, some of which I used as the epigraph to *How Far Can You Go?*

What can we know? Why is there anything at all? Why not nothing?

> What ought we to do? Why do what we do? Why and
> to whom are we finally responsible?
> What may we hope? Why are we here? What is it all
> about?
> What will give us courage for life and what courage
> for death?

The Creed and the Catechism had their answers of course, but like many others I found them increasingly difficult to accept in a literal sense. I decided that the language of religion is essentially metaphorical or symbolic and therefore comparable to literary language, which creates a virtual reality always open to variable interpretation. On this basis I continued to immerse myself once a week in that discourse by attending Sunday mass, saying the responses, reciting the Creed, singing the hymns, listening to the scriptural readings and the homilies, but with increasing awareness of the cognitive dissonance between what was said or what I said in response, and what I actually believed or did not believe. There were personal, familial reasons for persevering. My wife Mary's faith is deep and strong and not essentially intellectual. I did not wish to disturb it or place a barrier between us by questioning it; and I wanted my children to have a religious upbringing, so that they should know what it offered before they decided for themselves whether to continue with it, and would acquire some knowledge of the Christian elements in our cultural heritage. So it was not until a few years ago that I stopped going to mass regularly and publicly declared, when asked, that I was no longer a 'practising Catholic'. But how that came about, and worked out, does not come within the time frame of this book.

I started writing *How Far Can You Go?* in 1977, having spent some time previously making notes on subjects like the lives of nuns, modern biblical scholarship, liberation theology and the

11

surprising emergence of a Catholic charismatic movement. In the same year I published a book of academic criticism, *The Modes of Modern Writing: Metaphor, Metonymy, and the Typology of Modern Literature*, the writing of which had largely occupied me in the early seventies while *Changing Places* was making its painfully slow progress towards publication in 1975. The success of that novel did not weaken my commitment to the dual career of creative writer and academic critic, and in fact I published a novel and a book of criticism alternately for many years to come.

Criticism, like literature itself, has a periodic need to renew and refresh its methods, partly in response to new developments in writing, and partly in order to find new meanings in familiar texts. In the late sixties and early seventies something called 'structuralism' exerted a growing influence on academic criticism and the humanities generally. It was a way of analysing literature and all forms of cultural production from surrealism to striptease, by identifying the systems of signification they used rather than by responding intuitively to their surface effects. Its lineage was Continental European and went back to the first decades of the twentieth century. One of its father figures was the linguist Roman Jakobson, who came of age in the fertile intellectual and artistic climate of post-Revolutionary Russia and ended his career in the United States. But the news about structuralism came to Britain and America in the 1960s primarily from Paris, where a brilliant generation of critics and theorists, of whom Roland Barthes was the pace-setter, challenged academic orthodoxy under the banner of the *nouvelle critique*. They had in common with the British and American exponents of the New Criticism a focus on the literary text as a verbal object to be elucidated by analysis rather than by reference to the historical and biographical circumstances of its composition, but the French approach was more theoretical, abstract and deductive.

I am aware that some of my readers will not be much interested in literary and linguistic theory, and indeed their eyes may have already begun to glaze over at the mention of the word 'structuralism'. If so, they may prefer to skip the next few pages, although this kind of intellectual activity was an essential part of my life for many years and therefore cannot be omitted from a record of that life. It also fed into several of my novels in various ways. One of the most successful readings I have given from my fiction is the scene in *Nice Work* when the young feminist lecturer Robin Penrose gives a structuralist analysis of a poster advertising Silk Cut cigarettes to the incredulous and scandalised managing director of an engineering company whom she is shadowing. I could never have written it if I had not first written *The Modes of Modern Writing*.

As the teacher of an undergraduate course at the University of Birmingham called Comparative Critical Approaches and convenor of a weekly seminar for postgraduates on critical theory and methodology, I naturally took an interest in the work loosely bundled together under the label of structuralism, strange and difficult as it often seemed. The cryptic, declarative style of Roland Barthes' *Writing Degree Zero*, for instance, one of the first examples of the *nouvelle critique* translated and published in Britain in 1967, was a shock to someone used to the reader-friendly conversational style of British criticism, while I found the same author's *Elements of Semiology*, its title deceptively suggestive of a beginner's guide, almost incomprehensible. I did however remember from that discouraging experience an intriguing reference to Roman Jakobson's distinction between metaphor and metonymy which seemed worth following up when my friend and former Birmingham colleague Malcolm Bradbury asked me to contribute an essay on 'The Language of Modern Fiction' to a Penguin symposium called *Modernism* which he was co-editing. My starting point in trying to generalise about the language of novelists who wrote in very different styles was something I had often observed in reading early twentieth-century fiction, namely that the prose of the great modernists such as Henry James, James Joyce and Virginia Woolf was notable for an abundance of metaphor, whereas the representative writers of the 1930s such as

Christopher Isherwood, George Orwell and Graham Greene, who were consciously reacting against the older generation, preferred simile to metaphor when using figurative language derived from resemblances between things otherwise different. Barthes' reference led me to a paper by Jakobson entitled 'Two Aspects of Language and Two Types of Aphasic Disturbances', first published in 1956, which revealed a much more fundamental and illuminating distinction: between metaphor and simile on the one hand, opposed to metonymy and synecdoche on the other.

All four words belong to the terminology of classical rhetoric and everybody who has a GCSE in English knows (or ought to know) what the first two mean. The third and fourth are less familiar, though speech and writing are saturated with them. Metonymy substitutes an attribute of a thing, or an adjunct or cause or effect of a thing, for the thing itself, while synecdoche substitutes part for whole, or whole for part. In the proverbial phrase 'the hand that rocks the cradle' the word *hand* is a synecdoche signifying 'mother' and *cradle* is a metonym for 'baby'. These rhetorical figures can of course be combined with metaphor. In a sentence which I made up for illustrative purposes, 'A hundred keels ploughed the deep', the synecdoche *keels* is a part of a ship signifying the whole vessel, *ploughed* is a metaphor derived from a perceived similarity between the movement of a ship through the sea and the movement of a plough through the earth, and *deep* is substituted for sea because depth is one of its attributes. The similarity between keels and ploughs could have been expressed in the form of a simile, such as 'A hundred keels cut through the sea like plough blades', but not so elegantly. It might work for one ship, but applied to a hundred of them it summons up a rather grotesque image of a fleet of ploughs at sea. This is an indication that simile is more tightly bound to context than metaphor, which was precisely why the realist writers of the thirties favoured it over metaphor.

What is the point of these substitutions? They call attention to the referents by transforming a literal descriptive word or phrase into something that needs a little more effort to decode. They are ways of 'defamiliarising' (a very useful structuralist term) an item in a discourse. 'A hundred keels ploughed the deep' is a figurative transformation of the dull referential sentence 'A hundred ships crossed the sea'. Such metaphors and metonyms can become clichés, and then their effect is weakened because they require no conscious decoding. The creative writer is constantly challenged to find fresh ways of describing the world by using rhetorical figures of speech like metaphor and simile, metonymy and synecdoche.

Traditionally the second, third and fourth of these tropes had been regarded by grammarians as variations on the first because they all substitute a figurative description for a literal one, but Jakobson saw the two pairs as structurally different, metaphor/simile being based on similarity, and metonymy/synecdoche on contiguity (e.g. a keel is not like a ship, it is part of a ship) and he applied this distinction to all discourse, including the fractured speech of people suffering from aphasia, and indeed to all forms of cultural production:

> The development of a discourse may take place along two
> different semantic lines: one topic may lead to another
> either through their similarity or their contiguity. The
> metaphorical way would be the more appropriate term for
> the first case and the metonymic for the second. In normal
> verbal behaviour both processes are continually operative,
> but careful observation will reveal that under the influence
> of a cultural pattern, personality and verbal style, preference
> is given to one of the two processes over the other.

The universal applicability of the theory captivated me. Cubist painting is metonymic (an assemblage of parts) and surrealist painting metaphoric (combining images belonging to quite different contexts). The cinematic close-up is metonymic (or more exactly synecdochic, part representing the whole) while cinematic montage of the kind invented by Eisenstein (e.g. soldiers being

15

gunned down spliced with cattle being slaughtered) is metaphoric. Condensation and displacement in Freudian dream analysis are metonymic, symbolism (usually sexual) metaphoric. The theory is one of *dominance*, and the beauty of it is that it can be applied differently at different levels of generality. Thus poetry (verse composition) is dominantly metaphoric, emphasising phonological and rhythmical similarities as well as semantic ones, and prose is dominantly metonymic, connecting one topic to another according to their contiguity in space and time or logic; but there is poetic prose (in Virginia Woolf's work, for example) and prosaic poetry (in Philip Larkin's) in which the language is used contrary to generic convention for specific effect.

I was particularly struck by Jakobson's comment on the realistic novel as a genre, because it offered a way of accounting for the effectiveness of this kind of writing in terms of form rather than content, a project I had attempted with limited success in my first critical book, *Language of Fiction*. He says:

> Following the path of contiguous relationships, the realistic author metonymically digresses from the plot to the atmosphere and from the characters to the setting in space and time. He is fond of synecdochic details. In the scene of Anna Karenina's suicide Tolstoy's artistic attention is focused on the heroine's handbag.

The importance of circumstantial detail, what Henry James called 'solidity of specification', in creating the illusion of reality in novels is generally recognised, but in Jakobson's perspective it can be seen as not merely an observant element in prose fiction, but also an expressive one. His remark about Anna Karenina's red handbag made me revisit the scene with a fresh eye. A detail like that is a kind of synecdoche representing the multiplicity of items in her dress and appearance which would take pages to describe in full, and by being selected in this way and referred to more than once it gathers quasi-metaphorical associations and connotations without disturbing the realistic rendering of the situation. Anna's choice of colour is expressive of her character: red is a colour associated with passion and blood and adultery (as in 'scarlet woman' and the scarlet letter of Hawthorne's tale). But a handbag is also a woman's most important accessory, one essential to the conduct of her everyday life, and when the weight of the bag on her arm hinders Anna from throwing herself under the first truck of the train, slowly passing her as she stands on the platform, it is as if life gives her a last opportunity to refuse death. She is reminded of her hesitation at the moment of plunging into the sea to bathe, and '*for an instant life passed before her with all its past joys. But she did not take her eyes off the approaching second truck.*'

What had started as an article on style in modern fiction rapidly grew into a book of ambitious scope which, though predominantly focused on the novel, also dealt with poetry and drama, and other cultural phenomena, applying Jakobson's theory in close analysis and comparison of a wide range of texts. To give some continuity to the argument I returned repeatedly to several different descriptions of the same subject – execution: the report of a hanging witnessed by a *Guardian* journalist, Michael Lake; George Orwell's putatively autobiographical essay 'A Hanging'; Arnold Bennett's use in *The Old Wives' Tale* of a public execution by guillotine as the setting for a crisis in his heroine's life; Oscar Wilde's poem *The Ballad of Reading Gaol*; and the surrealistic hanging scene in William Burroughs's *The Naked Lunch*. Surveyed in that order they illustrate the continuum that extends from the metonymic to the metaphoric poles of writing.

I finished the book late in 1975, and sent it off to my agents, Curtis Brown, where Andrew Best was now exclusively handling academic and educational books, for onward transmission to Routledge & Kegan Paul who had published my two previous works of literary criticism, and Cornell University Press who had published the second of them. I was confident that Routledge would accept *The Modes of Modern Writing*, and even more so when Andrew informed me in February of the New Year that Cornell had received very favourable reports on the MS and were ready to publish it in collaboration with Routledge. But at the beginning of March I had a letter from him with 'the somewhat astonishing news' that Routledge had rejected the book, and that he had sent it to Edward Arnold, who had promptly accepted it. I was annoyed that he had acted without consulting me, but Arnold was a respected academic publisher and made a reasonable offer, which I accepted. Cornell teamed up with them. Nevertheless Routledge's rejection continued to rankle until I discovered that it was the result of an internal blunder which they tried, too late, to undo.

At about that time Jim Boulton, Head of the Birmingham English Department, put my name forward for a personal chair, i.e. a professorship not connected to an established post. The proposal was approved, and I gave my inaugural lecture as Professor of Modern English Literature in December 1976. Entitled 'Modernism, Antimodernism and Postmodernism', it was a highly condensed version of *Modes*. The industrial strife that would give rise to the following year's 'winter of discontent' was already extensive enough to cause power cuts, and I remember that the lecture theatre was freezing and many in the audience kept their overcoats on, but their reception was warm.

*The Modes of Modern Writing* was published in the autumn of 1977 and received numerous reviews in academic journals on both sides of the Atlantic, most of them favourable. Its reception in the British quality press, where such books were still occasionally reviewed, was more mixed. Up till that point the methods of teaching and writing about English literature in British universities had been divided between historical scholarship and the evaluative interpretation of texts by 'close reading', and sometimes there were clashes between these two schools of thought. But now the battle lines were being redrawn by the impact of structuralism. Some close readers like myself welcomed the explanatory power of its ideas, but others recoiled in dismay, and displayed something like panic at its increasing influence. Some of the reviewers who admired my commentaries on particular texts claimed that I didn't really need this theoretical apparatus and probably didn't really believe in it. A young don at Oxford, Peter Conrad, went further and wrote an extraordinary tirade in the *New Statesman* accusing me of perpetrating 'vengeful decreation' on literature: 'The nasty thrill with which Mr Lodge announces that he has reduced novels to figments of language "defamiliarising" (his word) the world we know and exterminating character, alerts us to the aggressive dislike of literature criticism of this kind often betrays . . . English empiricism, it seems from this book, has lost its nerve and . . . capitulated to the deconstructing, obfuscating hierarchs of what Mr Lodge calls the "*nouvelle critique*" . . . Things have come to a pretty pass.' I wrote a letter to the *New Statesman* identifying five of his assertions about my book which were precisely opposite to the truth, and concluded: 'Things have come to a pretty pass indeed, when something like this passes for a review.' Peter Conrad did not reply.

'Defamiliarising' was of course not my word, but a term used by Viktor Shklovsky, one of the Russian Formalist critics who flourished in the 1920s, and was attributed to him in my book. It's a translation of the Russian *ostranenie*, literally 'making strange'. Shklovsky wrote:

Habitualisation devours objects, clothes, furniture, one's wife and the fear of war . . . Art exists to help us recover the sensation of life; it exists to make us feel things, to make the stone *stony*. The end of art is to give a sensation of the object as seen, not as recognized. The technique of art is to make things 'unfamiliar', to make forms obscure, so as to increase the difficulty and duration of perception.

This seems to me the best answer ever given to the question 'What is the use of art?', at least as far as the verbal and visual arts are concerned (music offers a different challenge to aesthetics). It was implicitly a defence of the radical innovations of modernism, but it applies to the great art, and the good art, of all periods.

In the course of time, as structuralism turned into post-structuralism, and then became a hugely inflated field of multidisciplinary academic discourse about culture and society referred to simply as 'Theory', I myself became troubled by the obfuscatory jargon it employed – often, it seemed, designed to mystify rather than enlighten the reader, and thus demonstrate the writer's privileged access to the truth. But criticism cannot do entirely without jargon. To analyse language in use, you need a metalanguage, and it seemed to me in the 1970s that the metalanguage employed by Jakobson and later critics in the structuralist tradition like Tzvetan Todorov, Gérard Genette and Roland Barthes justified itself by its usefulness in answering the questions posed by Gertrude Stein which I used as the epigraph for *The Modes of Modern Writing*: 'What does literature do and how does it do it. And what does English literature do and how does it do it. And what ways does it use to do what it does.' *Modes* did not pretend to be a book for 'the general reader', but it had a long life as such publications go, remaining in print for more than thirty years, and was reissued by Bloomsbury Academic in 2015.

I spent the summer term of that year, 1977, as Henfield Fellow in Creative Writing at the University of East Anglia, Norwich, taking unpaid leave of absence from Birmingham. Malcolm Bradbury had suggested I apply for this one-term appointment and no doubt exerted his influence in my favour. The Fellowship was associated with the MA programme in Creative Writing which he and Angus Wilson (who then had a part-time post at UEA) had founded in 1970, and Malcolm was now its sole Director.

When he and I were students in the 1950s, and for most of the 1960s when we were lecturers, there was no degree course in Creative Writing at any British university. Now there are very few universities which do not offer the subject at undergraduate and/ or postgraduate level, and very few younger published writers who do not have such a qualification in their CV. The growth of Creative Writing as an academic subject, and its acceptance as a normal way of preparing to become a professional novelist, poet or playwright, is one of the most striking developments in contemporary culture, the effects of which are still difficult to assess. For centuries writers had learned their craft individually, by reading or listening to the work of others, by imitation, adaptation and experiment. Suddenly it seemed natural to do your apprentice work as a member of a group of students under the tuition of a master in whatever form interested you. Why did that happen?

The expansion of higher education, first in the USA and later in the UK, had something to do with it. In America, where a larger proportion of the 18-plus age group went to college than in Britain, and writers, in an always insecure profession, found teaching on a temporary or permanent basis a congenial 'day job', Creative Writing was established as an academic subject much earlier. It is hard to think of any significant American writer of the post-war period who was not at some point a student or teacher of Creative Writing (and often both). The same development occurred much later in Britain because there was a more deep-seated academic resistance to the concept here (as there still is in most Continental European countries) on the grounds that successful literary creation depends on innate personal faculties that cannot be taught and cannot be objectively assessed. They certainly could not be assessed within the structure of the traditional British BA degree by a set of three-hour examinations, and it was only when our universities began to move towards a modular course system that it became feasible to incorporate Creative Writing into the curriculum. An element of intellectual rigour was introduced into the subject by requiring students to give an analytical account of the genesis and composition of their work when submitting it. Creative Writing now justifies its place in the humanities as a discipline which trains the mind like any other subject and does not necessarily have a vocational application. Without being entirely convinced by that claim, I believe that creative writing exercises should have a place in every undergraduate degree course in English, because they enhance students' critical understanding of the process of literary composition. But a majority of the students who choose Creative Writing as a postgraduate degree or as the major part of an undergraduate degree have literary aspirations of their own.

The UEA course under Malcolm's direction gave a crucially important impetus to the phenomenon in Britain, and if it was not quite the first of its kind it was soon the most successful and influential. It thrived because from an early stage in its history it produced graduates who went on to make their mark as published writers. In the first year's intake there was only one student – but he was Ian McEwan. Kazuo Ishiguro and Rose Tremain soon followed in his footsteps, and a steady stream of other young writers who got their work published soon after graduating. New programmes in Creative Writing sprang up all over the country, but UEA has remained the most coveted place to pursue it, under the direction of other authors following Malcolm's retirement. Its website currently lists several hundred alumni whose work has been published, including many names well known to readers of contemporary fiction.

The duties of the Henfield Fellowship were light: to run a writing workshop one evening a week open to candidates from the local community as well as the University, to invite the occasional visiting speaker, and to be available for a few hours each week to talk to individual students. Otherwise the Fellows were free to get on with their own work. There was a modest stipend and free accommodation was provided in a small flat on the campus. It seemed an ideal opportunity to get on with the novel about Catholics I had just started, free from teaching, exam marking and domestic responsibilities. To make the most of it I agreed with Mary that I would spend the whole term on the UEA campus, rather than commuting back and forth, and she generously accepted the extra burden this would entail for her. Indeed she claims she positively encouraged me to do so, knowing what a preoccupied, irritable and unrewarding partner I was when getting a new novel under way. Since our six months in Berkeley in 1969 I had received frequent invitations to be a visiting professor at various American universities which I had to turn down, sometimes regretfully, because we didn't wish to disturb the children's education, so I looked forward to a change of academic environment while still remaining within easy reach of home if needed. And it certainly was a change.

UEA was one of the first of the 'new universities' that were built in the sixties and seventies in response to the report of the government-appointed Robbins Committee which called for a massive expansion of higher education in Britain, and it was one of the most successful in attracting talented staff and bright students. These institutions were usually located in pleasant pastoral sites on the outskirts of historic towns and cities, built from scratch on the American campus model, with ample residential accommodation for students. The striking architecture of UEA was the work of the Corbusier-influenced Denys Lasdun, who put all the teaching and research accommodation into a single curving concrete unit half a mile long, with elevated walkways giving access to the various departments and service roads underneath, while the accommodation blocks were terraced ziggurats, like blunt pyramids. It looked rather like a futuristic city from a science fiction illustration plonked down on the flat fields at the edge of Norwich. The architecture wasn't to everyone's taste, but it certainly made a statement: this is going to be a new kind of university.

A considerable number of them were built in various regions of the country. It was an expensive way of boosting the number of university graduates in a system almost entirely funded by the state, for universities are costly institutions to build and equip with adequate libraries and laboratories and study-bedrooms. Arguably it would have been more economical to build fewer of them, investing more in expanding existing urban universities, and encouraging students to attend their local ones, as they commonly did on the Continent. But the Oxbridge model of residential university education, which runs so deep in the psyche of the British establishment, prevailed. The University of Kent at Canterbury even had several 'colleges' on its site, between which staff and students were distributed. The new universities were however very popular. Academic staff welcomed the opportunities to initiate new subject areas, courses and research projects, and bright student applicants were also attracted by these features.

To me, a mature man temporarily separated from his family and a university embedded in a big industrial city, the UEA students seemed to inhabit an enclosed world. The campus contained almost everything they needed – shops, a bank, a post office, a medical centre, a counselling service, places to eat and drink – and many who lived on campus never left it from the beginning of term to the end. Every evening some form of entertainment was available. Feature films were shown for a negligible admission charge in the lecture theatres in the evenings (and I took advantage of them). At the weekends there were rock concerts and dances in venues from which the thud of bass notes and the wail of guitar riffs emanated and vibrated on the night air, though the young people in their flared trousers, cheesecloth shirts and maxi dresses called them not 'dances' but 'bops', knowing nothing of the bebop of the fifties – jazz that was listened to, not danced to – from which this term must have somehow been derived. Youth culture ruled the campus, and at its centre, in the student union building, there was a room full of pinball machines which was never unoccupied in my observation.

If the Bradburys had not been at hand I might have been very lonely. Malcolm was on study leave that term, but working from home. I was given his office to use for my weekly 'office hours', with his nameplate still on the door, no doubt encouraging the growing tendency of the world to confuse us and the authorship of our books. He and Elizabeth occupied a handsome Queen Anne dower house in a quiet cul-de-sac close to the centre of Norwich. I spent most Sundays with them and their two boys, Matthew and Dominic. They had bought a modern cottage near the coast with a bigger garden than the Norwich house and we practised (rather than played) a decorous form of cricket on the lawn there after lunch, or went for a walk on a nearby beach. Mary and I had often stayed with the family, and as a result we acquired a circle of acquaintance in Norwich and beyond, including Chris Bigsby and his wife Pam, and Anthony and Ann Thwaite, all of whom remained lifetime friends. Chris was Malcolm's colleague in American Studies and became the leading authority on Arthur Miller, and his official biographer. In their early years at UEA he collaborated with Malcolm on various writing projects including comedy scripts for radio and a TV play, *The After Dinner Game*, so in a way he filled the place I had occupied in Malcolm's life when he was at Birmingham, while Pam, a clinical psychologist, became a close friend of Elizabeth as Mary had been. The Thwaites we had known before we knew the Bradburys, through mutual friends at Birmingham. Anthony was a versatile and witty poet in the 'Movement' vein, a close friend of Philip Larkin and later editor of his letters, who supported himself working in radio, journalism and publishing. Ann wrote highly praised literary biographies, of Edmund Gosse and A.A. Milne among others. They were (and remain) a lively, hospitable couple who lived in a millhouse beside a stream deep in the country about 10 miles outside Norwich, where they entertained a wide range of literary friends, sometimes in large and bibulous parties. East Anglia attracted many writers as a place to live, property being cheaper there than in the Home Counties, and several of them were employed in the University's expanding writing programme.

*

I had arrived at UEA with a draft of the first chapter of *How Far Can You Go?* (though it did not yet have a name) in my briefcase, and I spent the first week revising and polishing it to my satisfaction. Then I found myself uncertain how to proceed. There were so many characters, and so much of their lives to cover. What should happen to them and how was I going to interweave their stories? For a while, I was stuck. I have found this often happens in the early stages of writing a novel: you get to a point when you have to make some major decisions that will place constraints on the development of the story, and you hesitate to commit yourself. All the options seem to have potential drawbacks. You may begin to lose faith in the project. I spent an unhappy second week brooding ineffectually on this problem in my silent flat, or while perambulating the muddy banks of an artificial lake the University was in the process of creating. I began to think the whole idea of trying to write a book while away from my usual habitat was a bad one. The breakthrough came when I thought of making the second chapter about the characters' initiation into sex, or in the case of two of them, one who became a nun and another who was homosexual, their abstention from it. The first chapter was entitled 'How It Was' and I decided to call the second one 'How They Lost Their Virginities'. What reader could resist the lure of that? Since the characters were practising Catholics this theme in most cases entailed dealing with their courtships and marriages, thus moving the story briskly along in time as I desired. The chapters that followed all had the same kind of heading – 'How Things Began to Change', 'How They Lost the Fear of Hell', 'How They Broke Out, Away, Down, Up, Through, etc.' I had not got very far in the sequence by the time I returned home, but it was enough to make me confident of finishing the book, though it took me nearly two years to do so, because of all the other things I was doing: teaching, supervising, reviewing, travelling on professional business and playing my part in family life.

# 2

Like most English parents Mary and I had to grapple with our country's stratified and politically disputed education system, a task rendered more complex for us by the circumstance that as practising Catholics we were under some pressure to send our children to Catholic schools. Most Catholic primary schools, like most C of E ones, perform well and we did not hesitate to send Julia to the nearest Catholic primary in Harborne after we returned from our first trip to America. But we moved to Northfield a year later and had to place her in the corresponding school in that parish. The readjustment to a new school was made more difficult for her because the Harborne one had adopted the Initial Teaching Alphabet, a method of teaching reading with a simplified spelling system for two years which the pupil then exchanged for the normal alphabet. Hailed by educationalists in the 1960s, ITA later fell into disfavour because of the difficulties pupils experienced in making the transition to normal spelling, and it was eventually abandoned. Julia thrived on the method and had soon used up most of the school's available storybooks in ITA, but she only had one year of it, and struggled to adjust to the normal alphabet when she transferred to Northfield. Later we discovered that she was dyslexic, which exacerbated the problem, though at that time the Birmingham Education Authority, like most others, refused to recognise the condition and would make no special allowances for her in examinations and assessments.

Choosing, or attempting to choose, secondary schools for one's children in Birmingham was a complicated and often stressful process for families. The city had resisted the nationwide comprehensivisation of grammar schools in the early 1970s and a group of them remained under the generic name of 'King Edward's', operating their own 11-plus examinations. If you put your child in for them, and they failed the exam, you forfeited your right to name a preference for a state comprehensive and had to take pot luck. That didn't concern us, however, as we were Labour voters and believed in comprehensive education. Mary had taught in a comp herself and planned to do so again when she had qualified as a school counsellor. Within walking distance of our home there was a very good one in Northfield called Shenley Court, to which many members of staff at the University sent their children, and we enrolled Julia there.

To reassure the parish clergy Mary undertook to teach her Catholic doctrine at home, along with two other girls in the same position, and was given a textbook for the purpose. Not thinking much of it, she devised a project for the three girls, to design a book for our Down's son Christopher, then aged about eight, which would convey to him the basic facts of the Catholic faith, and they responded enthusiastically. Chris accompanied us to mass every Sunday. He seemed to respond to the ritual, liked going up to the altar with us for a blessing from the celebrant when we took communion, and was eager to receive the sacrament himself. 'I want body,' he would say, echoing the words of the consecration, 'This is my body, this is my blood'. In due course a liberal-minded priest of the parish agreed that he could make his First Communion without having to go to Confession.

Christopher had a good sense of what constituted naughtiness but to introduce the idea of sin would have been inappropriate. Historically such children were sometimes called 'innocents' in Christian societies.

Shenley Court school did pretty well by Julia although, perhaps influenced by the fact that her parents were both arts graduates, they did not encourage her to build on her aptitude for biology by taking another science subject, so she did several O levels in arts subjects where her dyslexia was a handicap – not in reading (she devoured books) but in writing, especially spelling. She got an A grade in O Level English Literature in which misspelling was not penalised, but only a B in English Language. In the sixth form she did well in Biology and Computer Science, which Shenley Court enterprisingly offered in the dawn of the digital age, and before long the development of the personal computer with word processing software would enable her to overcome the handicap of dyslexia. But to gain admission to the BSc degree course in Biology at Southampton University she had applied for she needed another A level, which she obtained in Chemistry at a local college of further education after leaving school, while working part-time as a lab assistant at Aston University in the city centre. This job was offered to her by the Professor of Microbiology there, Mike Brown, one of a circle of liberal Catholic friends Mary and I had in Birmingham, when he heard of her situation, and it proved a very useful 'gap year' for her.

Julia obtained a 2.1 honours degree in Biology at Southampton in 1982, well before the era of grade inflation made this achievement commonplace. Mary and I went down there for her graduation, and brought her home, where we discovered that she had no idea of what she wanted to do by way of a career. The impact of Mrs Thatcher's monetarist economic policies on job prospects for graduates was already manifest, discouraging Julia from looking for employment. There was a period of some months, worrying to her parents, when she spent a lot of time at home reading and watching television, and not doing much else except some voluntary work for the Campaign for Nuclear Disarmament to which she was committed. This however happened to be a cause also supported by Mike Brown and as a result of a chance conversation with him one day he offered her a temporary post as a research assistant at Aston and later recommended her for a studentship to study for a PhD in Microbiology, which she obtained in 1987. In the same year she was appointed to a post-doctoral fellowship in the School of Biochemistry at Birmingham University, having deliberately waited till I took early retirement from that institution before she applied. Later she was appointed to a lectureship in the school, and at this time of writing she is a Senior Lecturer and Head of Education for the School of Biosciences, an important managerial position, very happy and fulfilled in her career and a source of pride to her parents. Mike Brown's part in this success story was crucial, but his faith in her potential has been fully vindicated.

Julia's younger brother Stephen was also highly intelligent, with no dyslexia, and the headmistress of his primary school, a nun, suggested to us when he was in his last year that he should be put in for a scholarship at Birmingham's top school, King Edward's, Edgbaston, next door to the University, the flagship of the King Edward's group. It had been a state-aided 'direct grant' school, but when faced with the alternative of going comprehensive became an independent school offering a substantial number of scholarships. Although officially the Church urged Catholic parents to send their children to Catholic schools, it privately and somewhat hypocritically approved sending gifted youngsters to elite non-Catholic schools like KE. Mary and I thought it would be a betrayal of our principles to send Stephen to such a school even if he won a scholarship and, from the little we knew about it, doubted whether he would be happy there. There was a Catholic diocesan boys' grammar school quite near us, called St Thomas Aquinas, which was rumoured to be turning comprehensive in due course, but we did not investigate it, nor did we consider another Catholic comprehensive in the area (of which more in a moment). We wished to send Stephen to the same school as his sister, and it was his own preference. Since Julia had been admitted there, however, a 'catchment area' had been allotted to Shenley Court by the local education authority, the boundary of which ran between our house and the school, though they were only a mile apart. The form on which parents had to list their preferred schools stated that these must all be within the catchment area where they resided, but priority had always been given to siblings in allocating places in schools, and relying on this practice I made only one choice on the form, Shenley Court, with a letter attached giving our reasons. As I heard nothing in response I was optimistic of the outcome.

When the allocation of places was announced Stephen was assigned to Northfield Comprehensive, which drew most of its pupils from a vast troubled housing estate and was regarded as the worst secondary school in the area on every count. A former pupil recalled: 'Growing up, as I did, in 1970s Northfield I remember the school having a woeful reputation.'[1] Stephen was, understandably, almost in tears at the news, and I promised him that he would not be going to Northfield Comp whatever happened, but I appealed to the local authority in vain. The only acceptable alternative was St Thomas Aquinas, and we were lucky to have a friend who knew the headmaster, a layman like the rest of the staff, and arranged a meeting with him. We were sorry to learn that he was due to retire shortly, because he impressed us as a wise and humane man. He teased us a little for not considering his school earlier, but was sympathetic to our plight, and after

[1] Andy Doherty, 'Birmingham Roundabout' website, posted 16th March 2010.

interviewing Stephen found him a place, though the intake was officially full, to our great relief and gratitude.

St Thomas turned comprehensive a year or two later, and became mixed in due course. Mary served as a governor for several years and gave useful advice on the needs of girl students to the other (all male) governors. Coincidentally, the Head of English when Stephen joined the school, John Bartlett, had been a pupil some years behind me at my old school in London, St Joseph's Academy, where he claimed to have been in awe of me, though I had been unaware of his existence. He was appointed as the new headmaster of St Thomas, and the teaching of English declined after he ceased to be directly responsible for it. When Stephen was assessed as likely to get a C grade in English Literature at O level a few months before the exam, Mary began coaching him at home in that subject and as a result he scored an A. The science teaching in the school on the other hand was first class, with one particularly keen and charismatic teacher who inspired enthusiasm and devotion in his pupils, and Stephen and his school friends opted for science subjects in the sixth form. A group of them became very interested in astronomy and joined the Birmingham Astronomical Society. Stephen built his own 6" telescope single-handedly, a feat that impressed the father of one of his friends who was MD of a manufacturing company. The propensity of my two older children to specialise in science, which I had found so unappealing as a schoolboy myself that I dropped it as soon as possible, and of which I was still pretty ignorant, surprised me and caused me some regret since I couldn't share their enthusiasm as they progressed in their favourite subjects. On the other hand, being always fully occupied with my own work I was selfishly grateful to be absolved from 'helping with homework'.

Stephen obtained three A's in his A levels and was offered a place to do Physics at Cambridge, the most coveted place to study subjects known there as 'Natural Sciences', which of course delighted his proud parents. But a few weeks before he was due to go up to

Emmanuel College, where my former colleague at Birmingham Derek Brewer was now Master, he announced that he didn't want to go to Cambridge and he didn't want to study Physics. Instead he proposed to go with some friends who had been trying, without much musical knowledge or skill, to form a rock band, to house-sit a property in the Welsh mountains where they would hang out and practise. The reader will easily imagine the dismay this caused Mary and me. Naturally we tried to dissuade him, but it was soon evident that this was no whim, and we reluctantly respected and accepted his decision. Stephen belonged to a generation who were born just too late to participate in the heady first wave of the sixties counter-culture, but yearned to catch up. The natural sciences did not offer the expansion of human experience he was looking for, and the ambience of Cambridge as he briefly encountered it when he was interviewed there had not appealed to him. The rock group never had a public existence, though a musician who associated with the house-minders in Wales played later in a successful band called the Housemartins. Stephen travelled in Europe, worked on two kibbutzim in Israel, came back to England to enrol for a BA in Politics at Newcastle, and graduated with a 2.1. He travelled around the world, worked for a year in Australia, came home via a spell in Central America, took a career aptitude test which indicated he was suited to law, and enrolled for a law conversion course at Newcastle Polytechnic. He was named 'Most Meritorious Student' at the end of his first year, and achieved First-class Honours in his final examinations. In due course he became a solicitor in Birmingham specialising in social justice legal aid work, and was involved in several important judicial reviews. He is currently employed by the Equality and Human Rights Commission in London.

In the mid-eighties the notorious Northfield Comp was closed down and merged with Shenley Court. Combined with the exclusion of able middle-class pupils from outside the catchment area, this resulted in a gradual decline in the morale and quality of education at Shenley Court, which eventually became a failing school requiring 'special measures', an outcome which would have been unthinkable when we sent Julia to it. There was a Catholic co-educational comprehensive school in south-west Birmingham named Blessed Humphrey Middlemore after one of the Forty English Martyrs of the Reformation period, whose history was even sadder. It was formed in 1966 out of two secondary modern schools in the older, poorer inner-city part of Edgbaston north of the Hagley Road, with many pupils from broken and chaotic homes, and accommodated in a new building in middle-class Harborne. It quickly acquired a reputation for low academic achievement and bad behaviour both inside and outside the school, and even the most loyal middle-class Catholic parents were reluctant to send their children to it. We came to know the school well because several of our friends in the Catholic Renewal Movement had taught there from its beginning, as did Mary herself as a teacher-counsellor from 1974. Her counselling skills were badly needed, and she was often required to speak for pupils at juvenile courts. The teachers at 'Blessed Humph', as it was familiarly called, were mostly able and dedicated, and had a remarkable *esprit de corps*, but they could not overcome the systemic flaws in the original foundation, and the best of them moved on to higher appointments elsewhere. Student numbers dwindled to the point where the school became unviable and in 1982 it was closed and demolished, only sixteen years after it had opened, to be replaced by a residential cul-de-sac called Humphrey Middlemore Drive.

Readers of *QAGTTBB* will recall that a similar fate overcame my own grammar school, St Joseph's Academy, Blackheath, when long after I was a pupil there it became a Catholic boys' comprehensive with a catchment area that included Lewisham, one of the most socially troubled boroughs in London. As the years passed it became a failing school with a bad local reputation and, after several unsuccessful efforts to reform it, was demolished and replaced in 2007 with a co-educational 'Academy' in the New Labour sense of the word. This remedy seems to have been successful, but in my memoir I described the sorry last decades of what had once been a school that had sent many students from a broad social base on to higher education as 'a sadly familiar story of unintended consequences in the implementation of an educational policy that claimed to be progressive'. In a long and otherwise sympathetic review of my book in *Prospect* magazine, the distinguished social historian David Kynaston regretted that I did not recognise the greater good achieved by the abolition of the socially divisive distribution of children between grammar schools and secondary modern schools at 11-plus, and that I said nothing about the even more malign effect of private education on equality of opportunity in British society.

In retrospect I regret the choice of the word 'claimed' because the motive for comprehensivisation *was* socially progressive, and probably far more people have benefited from its positive effects than have suffered from its negative ones. That presumption was one reason why Mary and I supported it in principle and, up to a certain point, in practice. In practice few educated middle-class parents will ask their children to suffer for their own principles; so we sent Julia to a good comprehensive but rescued Stephen from a bad one, pulling strings to get him into an acceptable alternative. A successful comprehensive school depends on having a student body with a broad spectrum of intellectual ability and social background, and a curriculum which allows for different levels and types of achievement. Where they survive, as in Birmingham, grammar schools cream off able students who might otherwise provide the leaven in local comprehensive schools and, as I have shown, the bureaucratic imposition of catchment areas can be even more damaging.

As to private schools, especially those still perversely called public schools, I think my novels, especially *Ginger, You're Barmy*, convey a critical view of their influence on British social and cultural life. Of the schools themselves I have little personal experience. In fact I have been inside only two of them. Some time in the sixties I was invited by a housemaster at Shrewsbury School (the alma mater of some of the founders of *Private Eye*) to speak to a group of his students one evening about Jane Austen. Out of curiosity, and as it was no great distance to drive from Birmingham, I accepted. It was a small gathering in the teacher's living room, and I saw little of the rest of the school, nor can I recall anything about my talk or its reception. What I remember about the occasion is that I received no offer of reimbursement for my car mileage and not even a letter of thanks afterwards from the teacher. I declined future invitations to speak at public schools, of which I received several over the years. They usually offered to pay travel expenses, though never a fee. One was from a group or society of senior pupils at Eton, and I was surprised to see my brief handwritten reply, in which I declined, offered for sale some years later in a catalogue. I felt, and sometimes said as much in my replies to such invitations, that I did not wish to take time out of a busy life to enhance the experience of pupils who were already receiving a very privileged education. The truth is that I never felt comfortable speaking in schools, but occasionally I would do so in comprehensives with which I had a personal connection.

My second visit to a public school was much later than the first, and of a very different kind. Over the last decade or so the Graham Greene Birthplace Trust has staged an annual Festival devoted to his work at Berkhamsted School, where he was a pupil when his father was headmaster. The Festival, held during the school holidays, attracts a variety of people – writers, academics and ordinary readers – interested in the novelist's life and work. One year I gave a talk about the literary influences on his writing, and in the course of the weekend I was given a guided tour of the school, including the rooms which were once occupied by the Greene family and are separated from the dormitories, corridors and classrooms of the school by a green baize door which frequently crops up in Greene's writing. To say he was unhappy at Berkhamsted is an understatement. As the headmaster's son he was regarded by other boys as a potential spy and victimised. In his travel book about Mexico in the 1930s, *The Lawless Roads*, he recalled his schooldays thus:

> In the land of . . . stone stairs and cracked bells
> ringing early, one was aware of fear and hate, a kind
> of lawlessness – appalling cruelties could be practised
> without a second thought; one met for the first time
> characters, adult and adolescent, who bore about them
> the genuine quality of evil.

The young Greene was so miserable at Berkhamsted that he flirted with suicide in the game of Russian roulette, and ran away to live rough on the local Common for some days. As Norman Sherry revealed in the first volume of his biography, Greene eventually broke the schoolboy code and named his chief persecutor, who was expelled, passing on to the future novelist a lifelong fascination with the theme of betrayal. His situation was unusual, of course. Not all public school boys suffered as much as he did, and many claim to have enjoyed, or at least benefited from, the experience. But I have not read any novel of literary merit which has changed my opinion that sending children to boarding school at a young age, unless there is some pressing practical reason, is unnatural and sometimes cruel, and that single-sex education in boarding schools is apt to cause psychosexual problems in personal life later, as well as providing temptations and opportunities to paedophiles.

The critic and Oxford professor John Carey, who is almost my exact contemporary, and attended what was obviously a very good London grammar school, much better than mine, asserts in his memoir, *The Unexpected Professor* (2015), that if most grammar schools hadn't been abolished in the 1970s they would have improved to such an extent that they would have seen off the independent schools eventually by offering just as good an education free. This seems to me an unlikely scenario, but even if it had happened it would still have left open the question of what kind of education to provide for those who didn't qualify for the enlarged grammar school sector, which is where the pre-comprehensive system largely failed.

As things are, it is undeniable that the best independent schools offer an education that is beyond the reach of schools in the state system, and some of them, like King Edward's in Birmingham, are day schools which allow their pupils to lead a normal family life. King Edward's Boys in Edgbaston stands proudly opposite the main entrance to the University, an impressive and immaculately maintained redbrick building with extensive playing fields behind it, and a sister school for girls nearby. I have passed it countless times but never been inside. Once I was asked to speak there, but declined, giving my usual reasons. I could easily have made a more informal visit, but I didn't. Perhaps I feared to stir up possible feelings of regret. For I sometimes wonder, especially when reminded of the limitations of my own education – its failure to give me any competence in the sciences, modern languages or music – whether we were right to deny Stephen the chance of going to KE, and whether he would have benefited from the superior education it offered. He would have been a contemporary there of Jonathan Coe, whose novel *The Rotters' Club*, inspired by his schooldays, suggests that Stephen would not have felt out of place there. A pointless speculation, of course. If he had gone to KE his life would have taken a completely different path. Among other things he would not be happily married to Una, whom he met on the Newcastle law course, or have their two charming and gifted daughters, who adore him.

*

The education of our Down's son Christopher presented a different challenge to Mary and me from those we faced in relation to Julia and Stephen. As I explained in *QAGTTBB*, he was fortunate to be born at a time when attitudes to Down's people were changing for the better and the state had recently recognised that they were educable in special schools. He was especially fortunate living in Birmingham where the provision of special education was very good. He also had the advantage of having a mother who was a trained teacher, and of being our youngest child, with two older siblings to stimulate him and no younger one to overtake him, so that he grew up with great confidence in his own abilities. Indeed, he was sometimes overconfident, occasionally escaping from the rather insecure side garden we had instead of a back garden to explore the neighbourhood. At the age of about six he was brought home by a neighbour who spotted him on a nearby railway embankment.

Every stage in his development was slow, and completed much later than if he had been a normal child, but gradually he learned how to speak, how to walk, how to use a knife and fork, how to tie his own shoelaces. He attended the same admirable nursery school as his brother and sister and this helped him to make the transition to a junior Special School for children with Moderate Learning Difficulty that was only a mile from us, where he learned to read and write. From there he went to a Special secondary school, Victoria School, which at that time took both physically and mentally handicapped pupils. It was superbly equipped and staffed and we could not speak too highly of it. Among other achievements they taught him to swim, for he had completely lost the confidence he had as a water-winged infant, and later he did a monitored one-mile swim.

As time went on, educating children like Chris in special schools fell out of favour. Instead they are now usually placed in ordinary schools, with teaching assistants helping them in the classroom. The aim is admirable – to integrate them into the community and accustom normal children to their existence – but Mary and I were unconvinced that this policy was educationally as effective as dedicated special schools, and we remain grateful that good ones were available to Chris in Birmingham in the crucial years. He was always a very confident boy and achieved a considerable level of independence – learning to use public transport to travel to school, for instance – and we attribute this in part to the fact that he never felt inferior or out of place in his peer group; in fact he was usually at the top of it. He benefited of course from belonging to an educated and articulate family, and considering his IQ rating in the low 60s as an infant he became remarkably able in speaking and reading, perhaps due to genetic as well as environmental factors. Capable of quite witty repartee, he would make speeches at family celebrations, and learned to plan his own TV viewing (which we rationed for all our children) from the *Radio Times*. He was addicted to soaps and popular dramas, and the family next door to us in Northfield would sometimes invite him round and watch him watching *Dallas* on their set, so entertaining was his total engagement. Later he was devoted to the James Bond movies, saw them all on their first release and again on video, and assembled a considerable library of books about Bond and the film actors who played the role, until he was almost up to *Mastermind* standard on the subject. He was timid in some respects – he hated heights, was uncomfortable on steep staircases and escalators, and would only ride bicycles several sizes too small for him. But from infancy onwards Chris was exceptionally at ease with animals and they with him. It first struck me when he was five years old, but still a toddler by normal standards of development. We were on holiday in Switzerland, renting an apartment in a chalet in Morgins, a winter ski resort in the mountains above Lake Geneva. We lost sight of Chris in the garden one day and after a brief but anxious search found him sitting placidly, upright and cross-legged on the grass, beside a large Alsatian. Mary, who had had a bad experience in childhood with such a dog, was alarmed at this sight, but it was obvious that the animal was calmly enjoying Chris's company until, very gently, we led him away. I can't help wondering if there is something in his condition which has this effect on animals.

We chose Morgins for that holiday because our college friends Martin and Jeswyn Jones had a chalet there, Martin being currently employed in Geneva. They had several children by now and our two families got on well together, but I found I did not really like mountains, beautiful as they are to look at from a distance. When the clouds came down on the slopes above Morgins, as they not infrequently did, blotting out the sun, draining the colour from the landscape and imparting a damp chill to the air, I succumbed to what John Ruskin called 'Mountain Gloom' and eloquently analysed in a famous chapter of *Modern Painters*. To escape it we often drove down the twisting road to Montreux where it always seemed sunny and warm beside the lake, and where I lived in hope of one day glimpsing Vladimir Nabokov, perhaps returning from a butterfly hunt with net in hand to the Montreux Palace Hotel where he and Vera lived in their last years.

In the years that followed we had several family summer holidays in Connemara, a stretch of the west coast of Ireland which runs from north of Galway Bay to south of County Mayo. It has mountains – a symmetrical row of them called the Twelve Bens – but nobody lives on them as far as I know. They are essentially a scenic frame for a low-lying landscape of turf and rock, reeds and water, rimmed by broad beaches washed by Atlantic rollers. It is a place of incomparable beauty when the sun is out, but you have to accept a variable quota of days when the air consists mainly of fine rain. We would not have thought of it as a holiday location if Mary's sister Margaret and her husband Ioan had not owned a cottage there. Ioan went on to have a distinguished academic career in English and Welsh studies at the Universities of Warwick and Aberystwyth, and was Dean of the Arts Faculty at the latter institution before he retired; but his real passion was, and still is, building: restoring, renovating, extending and modernising dwellings of various kinds and sizes, doing much of the physical work himself. This is one of several respects in which we are antithetical in character, for as soon as I could afford it I gave up all forms of DIY domestic maintenance and employed professional experts for the purpose. One of the earliest of Ioan's projects was to render habitable the shell of an Irish smallholder's cottage which he and Margaret discovered in the course of a holiday in the west of Ireland some time in the 1960s at a place called Cashel in Connemara (not to be confused with the more famous Cashel in Tipperary) situated at the innermost point of an elongated bay. The cottage, one of the last dwellings on the road that leads out of the hamlet towards the open sea, consisted simply of four stone walls when they bought it freehold for not much more than a hundred pounds. Ioan put a roof on it, and over the years that followed extended and improved the property as a holiday home for his growing family. It is now, I understand, a spacious and comfortable modern house, but when we first saw it in the mid-seventies it still consisted mainly of one large, rather dark room, with peat smouldering in the open fireplace, much as it had been in the time of its former occupants.

On that first Connemara holiday we rented a modern bungalow about half a mile from the Williams' cottage, but in subsequent years we stayed at a hotel called the Seals Rock in the charming fishing port of Roundstone, about half an hour's drive from Cashel. The hotel was well named because on a fine summer evening you could sometimes see from its front garden a group of seals swimming past with their snouts out of the water. It belonged to the O'Toole family and was a somewhat ramshackle residence in those days. If you opened a casement window too forcefully it might come off its hinges in your hand. The walls of the partitioned bedrooms were thin and the springs of the beds when you turned over sounded like a quartet of percussionists tuning up. When we were amorously inclined Mary and I spread a quilt on the floor. The food was acceptable though not brilliant. But the ambience of the hotel was hospitable to children, and one of the O'Tooles' was a Down's boy, so we felt at ease there. Superb beaches were within easy reach, sparsely populated even in August. The sand was clean and golden, and the Gulf Stream warmed the sea. But there were days when it rained from dawn to dusk, and then all you could do was take the car and drive to the main town, Clifden, or to a gift shop with a café near Renvyle which advertised its attractions with the scrupu-lously qualified claim 'Possibly the Finest Gift Shop in the West', a phrase which became a family joke. It was a long journey from Birmingham to Connemara – up the M6 to Liverpool, a night ferry to Dublin sleeping in a cabin, and a day's drive across the waist of Ireland to Galway. But we went back several times because when you got there you had a real sense of being on holiday, in a place with an utterly different and more relaxed tempo of life from busy, crowded England. Even the farmers in Connemara didn't seem to get up until nine or ten in the morning.

In 1978 however, we had a different kind of summer holiday. Ioan had a rubber dinghy with outboard motor, and later a small boat similarly equipped which he used to fish for mackerel, and this gave me the idea that if Julia, Stephen and I learned to sail a dinghy it would greatly enhance our holidays in Connemara. Accordingly I booked a week's introductory course with a sailing school in Salcombe, Devon, preceded by another week in a hotel near Boscastle on the north coast of Cornwall. I had supervised an MA student working on Thomas Hardy's novel *A Pair of Blue Eyes*, which is set in that spectacular and romantic landscape and has many connections with Hardy's courtship of his first wife. I had conceived the idea of writing a television dramatisation of the story. It seemed to me that Hardy had a very cinematic way of placing human figures in landscape, and there was one scene in particular in *A Pair of Blue Eyes* which cried out to be filmed, when the heroine rescues one of her two rival suitors, who is clinging perilously to the edge of a high cliff, by stripping off all her Victorian underclothes and making a rope of them. We had a most enjoyable week exploring the location of this story in and around Boscastle before moving on to Salcombe for the sailing course.

We stayed in a hotel, Mary spending the days onshore with Christopher, while Julia and Stephen, then aged eighteen and sixteen, did the course with me. They told me later in life that they hated every minute of it, and I didn't enjoy it much myself. None of us had any previous experience of, or natural aptitude for, sailing, and such courses inevitably generate a competitive atmosphere which is depressing to the less adept, so we felt more and more marginalised as the week progressed. It ended with a race in the course of which we ran aground on a sandbank and had to be towed off. We did however learn the rudiments of dinghy sailing, and I was determined to apply this knowledge on our next holiday in Connemara. The following summer (having had no sailing practice in the meantime) I rented a Mirror-Class dinghy from a supplier in Birmingham, a very basic boat built of wood, so heavy that Stephen and I only just managed to lift it on to the roof rack of our Ford Cortina estate, and drove it all the way to the west of Ireland. (As I write this I wonder at my commitment to such a foolish and laborious project.) I had divided the holiday into two parts: one week at a hotel at Renvyle, a beautiful part of the coast at the north-west extremity of Connemara, and a week in a rented bungalow near the Williams' cottage in Cashel. Julia, now old enough to be independent, had wisely arranged some other kind of holiday for herself, so Stephen and I were the only sailors.

The first week was wet and windy and Renvyle is much more exposed to the Atlantic weather than Cashel or Roundstone. It could not have offered more different or more challenging conditions than the sheltered Salcombe estuary. Stephen and I made an attempt to launch our boat from the beach and were soon beaten back by the Atlantic rollers. A photo survives, taken by Mary, of the enormous empty beach under a threatening sky, and in the middle distance our boat lying on its side in the shallows with Stephen and I stooped forlornly over it like survivors of a shipwreck. The weather did not improve enough that week to encourage us to make another attempt, but I thought that Cashel Bay, being a long inlet from the open sea, would offer more favourable conditions. The weather also improved, and on an encouragingly sunny day we got our dinghy into the water, and set sail. At first all went well. A strong breeze from off the shore filled the sail, and we sped along at an exhilarating pace – much faster than anything we achieved at Salcombe. This, I thought, is the real thing at last. Then I became aware that around us and ahead the waves were flecked with crests of white foam that in some cases were caused not by the wind but by the projection of rocks. A collision with one of these at the speed we were going could hole and sink the boat, which was already taking a good deal of water over its characteristic blunt prow. Stephen and I both wore life jackets, and he was a strong swimmer, but I was not, and by this time we were well down the bay, and at some distance from either shore. Scanning the land I could see no sign of any person who might observe us if we got into difficulties; nor was there another craft to be seen on the water. I pointed out the rocks to Stephen, and said: 'This is too dangerous, I'm going back.' I managed to turn the boat round without capsizing it and tacked back to our starting point, so I suppose some of the Salcombe training had stuck. We dragged the boat out of the water, put it on the roof of the car, and I never sailed in it, or any other dinghy, again.

In fact Mary and I have not been back to Connemara since, and it wasn't because of the sailing debacle. Julia and Stephen were getting too independent to relish a traditional family holiday of the kind we had enjoyed there. And towards the end of our week in Cashel something happened which, in retrospect, broke the spell the place had over us. We were sitting in the garden of our bungalow in the late afternoon looking out over the bay when we heard on my portable radio the news that Lord Mountbatten, one of his twin grandsons aged fourteen, and a local youth aged fifteen employed as a boat boy had been killed when a bomb planted by the IRA exploded on their yacht at Mullaghmore, County Sligo. Sligo is some way north of Connemara, but its coastal landscape has the same kind of enchantment, as I remembered from my attendance at the Yeats Summer School back in 1961, and this violent, cowardly and callous crime seemed a violation of everything we valued in the extreme west of Ireland: its beauty, its tranquillity, the slow, easy-going rhythm of life there. I believe that, without consciously articulating the thought, both Mary and I felt afterwards that we had experienced Connemara at its best, and had no urge to return there, though our children and grandchildren have done so and enjoyed themselves.

# 3

During the years when we took our family holidays in Connemara I also made several professional trips to countries in Continental Europe and further afield which could be described as working holidays. They were usually arranged in my university vacations or periods of study leave, so did not interfere with teaching duties. Most of them were organised by the British Council, usually in response to requests from foreign countries, and known as Specialist Tours on which one lectured at several universities. Being both a published novelist and an academic specialising in modern literature and critical theory, and able to speak in both capacities, I was very eligible for this work, as was Malcolm Bradbury. One was not usually paid for it, though occasionally a university would offer an honorarium. But the Council arranged the travel, and paid a reasonable per diem allowance which was seldom used up because of the hospitality provided by one's hosts. As well as affording opportunities to meet scholars in one's own field, it was a great way to see the world free of charge, staying in decent hotels, being shown around interesting foreign cities by knowledgeable escorts who spoke fluent English, and eating in restaurants which at that date were superior to their British equivalents, at least on this side of the Iron Curtain. These travels also yielded material for future novels. Occasionally, if the dates coincided with school holidays and we could make arrangements for the children to be looked after, I managed to include Mary in such trips, paying only for her travel. In 1973 she accompanied me for the first week of a tour in Austria visiting Innsbruck, Salzburg, Graz and Vienna before she had to fly home while I carried on to Linz alone. It was the first time either of us had seen any of these places.

I regretted that I was not able to take her with me on a more leisurely tour of Italy in the spring of the following year. It was my first visit to that country and I prepared for it by learning a little basic Italian from a BBC book and LP record for beginners. My itinerary began in Naples, and continued to Rome, Florence, Bologna and Milan. The journey to Naples entailed a change of planes at Rome. Here a security alert required passengers on the second flight to identify themselves and, if requested, open their luggage which was spread out on the tarmac beside the plane. This exercise delayed our departure considerably, and it was late at night when we landed in Naples. I took a taxi to my hotel through what seemed a sinister city of shadows and sparse street lighting, with rough-looking men and short-skirted prostitutes gathered round fires made of tyres and refuse burning on street corners. They stared, balefully or hopefully according to gender, as my car passed rattling and bumping over cobbles and potholes, confirming the stereotype of Naples as a hotbed of crime and vice which I had acquired from the media. Eventually the taxi deposited me at a large hotel on what appeared to be the city's waterfront, though I could see little of it in the pitch-dark night. I scurried into the lobby, checked in with the night porter and fell into bed in a vast high-ceilinged room. When I woke the next morning I drew the curtains on a scene of legendary beauty – the Bay of Naples, with the calm sea in its arms, reflecting a blue and cloudless sky.

The British Council representative in Naples had left a note for me in the hotel. To my surprise he did not propose to meet me until the following day, when he would take me to lunch, and invited me to amuse myself in the meantime. I took a hydrofoil to Capri and spent an enjoyable day exploring the island. While eating lunch on a restaurant terrace I got talking to a young Japanese mathematician who spoke English. He was attached to the University in some capacity, and we kept each other company for the rest of the afternoon. The next day the British Council rep, a middle-aged expat of few words, took me to lunch as promised, escorting me through the crowded crooked streets, festooned with drying laundry, of the old quarter, and I discovered for the first time how delicious authentic *antipasti* and the rest of Italian cuisine can be. So passed the second day. I never discovered whether it was by accident or design that I was given such an extended period of acclimatisation. On the third day I gave my lecture at the University to a large number of students on a topic chosen by members of staff because it interested them, and I had an uneasy impression that it went over the heads of my audience. In fact it was also well above their level of competence in English, as I realised when I finished and one of the teachers spoke at length to the students in Italian, evidently summarising my discourse for their benefit.

My remaining lectures were more successful, but the Italian university system, from the impressions I received during the tour, seemed very strange. There were, for instance, no written examinations, only oral ones. The student accumulated credits towards a degree by presenting herself (most of the students doing English Literature were female) whenever she felt ready for inter-rogation on some part of the syllabus by one or two members of the teaching staff, which might take place in an office shared by several others chattering away at the same time. Those who made it to the final stage were however required to write a short dissertation to qualify for a degree, and in time my own work became quite a popular subject for this purpose. Some years later

I turned up at my office in Birmingham one morning to find an Italian youth squatting on the floor outside. He had been told to write a dissertation on my first novel, *The Picturegoers*, which by then was out of print, and had come to ask if he could borrow a copy. I lent him one to photocopy in the University's library.

I had an interesting long weekend in Rome, thanks largely to Maurice Dodderidge, who was Director of the British Council there, one of the organisation's plum positions. There was a personal connection between us because Mary knew him and his family, who were Catholics and lived in Broxbourne just a mile or so from her home in Hoddesdon. Maurice was an exceptionally nice man but he put himself out especially for my sake, introducing me to two British writers who were living in or near Rome whose work I knew well and admired: Muriel Spark and Anthony Burgess. They too were Catholics, though of very different kinds. Muriel Spark, brought up in a Jewish family of lukewarm religious allegiance, was a convert in adulthood who found the Catholic metaphysical world picture intellectually satisfying and imaginatively stimulating but practised her adopted faith in an idiosyncratic fashion. (She was, for instance, irregular in mass attendance and always arrived too late to hear the sermon.) Anthony Burgess was a cradle Catholic who lost his faith as a sixth-former at Xavier College in Manchester, run by an order of teaching brothers and much like the De La Salle school I attended in London. He subsequently embraced a rackety freethinking bohemian lifestyle but his imagination remained saturated in Catholicism, like the apostate James Joyce whom he revered. In his best-known novel, *A Clockwork Orange* (1962), the problem of evil posed by violent criminality is addressed in terms derived from the dispute between Augustine and Pelagius about the concept of original sin. These two novelists were both key figures in leading British fiction into the period of postmodernism. Muriel Spark rejected the dominant realism of English fiction in the 1950s from the very beginning of her career as a novelist with an exhilarating mixture of supernaturalism, meta-fiction and satirical wit in novels like *The Comforters* (1957) and *Memento Mori* (1959) and later in black comic variations on classic crime fiction, *The Driver's Seat* (1970) and *Not to Disturb* (1971). Anthony Burgess's early work was essentially realistic in technique, having an affinity with Kingsley Amis's social comedies, but increasingly he too experimented boldly with the novel form, exploiting and pastiching different fictional subgenres – the crime thriller, the biographical novel, the dystopia – and inventing new kinds of narrative voice. *A Clockwork Orange*, set in the future after a Russian occupation of Britain, is written in an Anglo-Russian argot which the reader picks up (with the aid of a glossary at the back) in the process of reading.

At a supper after my lecture Maurice seated me next to Muriel Spark, and she invited me to a party in her grand apartment the following evening, seeming to be a quite different person on each occasion. I have described these two intriguing but slightly baffling encounters elsewhere.[1] At the first she was demure, self-effacing, deferential to my academic status; at the second she was the glamorous hostess, superbly gowned and coiffed, moving regally among her guests, and I did not exchange more than a few words with her. Later she wrote warmly to thank me for something I had written about her work and gave me an open invitation to visit her in the rustic home in Tuscany to which she had moved, but I never found an opportunity to do so, or perhaps I should say that I didn't make an effort to find one. I had a feeling that Muriel Spark was someone I would prefer to know through her books. She had a reputation for being unpredictable in personal relations and she certainly caused my friend Martin Stannard, her authorised biographer, an immense amount of frustration and anxiety by first giving him carte blanche and then blocking the

[1] 'A Tricky Undertaking: the biography of Muriel Spark', *Lives in Writing* (2014), pp. 64–65.

publication of the book until after her death because she disagreed with his treatment of her troubled relationship with her son.

Anthony Burgess was a much more genial and transparent character. At the time I was in Rome, he was living with his second wife Liana and their son Andrea in Bracciano, an ancient town in the hills about 20 kilometres outside Rome overlooking a picturesque volcanic lake. Maurice kindly drove me there one morning and we spent a pleasant hour or two chatting and drinking on a balcony with Anthony and enjoying the splendid view. He was a loquacious host, but I made no notes of the occasion, and all I distinctly remember of what he said was that his reason for moving out of Rome was a fear that his son might be kidnapped. I had reviewed several of his novels over the past ten years, and he had reviewed my second novel, *Ginger, You're Barmy*, a circumstance which can cause some awkwardness when writers meet, but there was none in this case. His main criticism of *Ginger* – that it attributed too much importance to the tribulations of National Service in the army – was entirely understandable coming from a veteran of the Second World War, and he had softened his verdict by predicting a bright future for me as a novelist. My reviews of his novels had been mostly positive, and I could claim some credit for having called *Inside Mr Enderby* (1963), which he published under the name of Joseph Kell, 'a little masterpiece' in *The Spectator*, without knowing that he was the author. The prolific Burgess adopted this nom de plume when his publishers warned him he would not be taken seriously if he published more than one novel in the same year, and amused himself by writing a favourable review of *Inside Mr Enderby* for the *Yorkshire Post*, where he was a regular fiction reviewer at the time. Humourlessly they sacked him from this post when the secret of Joseph Kell's identity was revealed, but he was never short of such employment.

He was an extraordinary writer, a kind of genius, publishing more than thirty novels and as many non-fiction books about literature, linguistics and other subjects, in an unstoppable stream.

He made a shortened version of James Joyce's *Finnegans Wake* with commentary, in a noble effort to coax readers to attempt that formidable text. He wrote poetry, stage plays and screenplays (inventing a language for Stone Age men and women in the French feature film *Quest for Fire*) and the book and lyrics of a musical version of *Cyrano de Bergerac*. He was also a composer of some two hundred and fifty works of music. Birmingham University, in whose Extra-Mural Department he had worked between 1946 and 1950, gave Anthony an Honorary D.Litt. in 1986, and I had the pleasure of looking after him during his visit. He always had something knowledgeable to say about the academic specialisation of any member of staff to whom I introduced him, in whatever department or faculty. On his last evening a section of the Birmingham Symphony Orchestra gave the first performance of his latest musical composition, a piece for brass ensemble, in the Central Library's auditorium.

I met him occasionally after that in London. The last time was in 1992 when we did a joint event promoting our latest books in the South Kensington branch of Waterstones – his was a book about the English language called *A Mouthful of Air*. He told me privately that he had just been diagnosed with lung cancer and the prognosis was not good. This was not surprising news as he was addicted to cheroots and was defiantly smoking one as he spoke, but it had understandably lowered his spirits. Like the trouper he was, however, he entertained the audience with his usual wit and fluency. He died at the end of the following year. Perhaps he wrote too much, too fast, and arguably he never produced a flawless masterpiece – even *A Clockwork Orange* is compromised by having different endings with opposite meanings in the British and American editions – but he made up for his books' imperfections with the fecundity of his invention, the breadth of his intelligence, and his stylistic virtuosity. It is good to know that there is an International Anthony Burgess Foundation in his home city of Manchester to assert and celebrate his greatness.

*

In the autumn of 1975 I was asked by the Council to do a tour in the south of France visiting the Universities of Toulouse, Montpellier, Aix-en-Provence and Nice, lecturing on Jane Austen's *Emma*. It sounded an attractive itinerary, and I accepted. I was asked to speak about *Emma* because it was a set text for the *Agrégation* that year, the competitive national examination for candidates of postgraduate status who hope to obtain one of the limited number of new appointments available as teachers at the top *lycées* or as junior lecturers in universities. I was well qualified for this task, since I had written an introduction to the standard text of *Emma* published by Oxford University Press in 1971, and three years previously I had edited a selection of criticism about this novel from the time of its publication to the present day in Macmillan's Casebook series. I remember that my literary agent at that time, Graham Watson, tried to dissuade me from doing this book, believing that it would involve a lot of work for little financial reward. But *Emma* was my own favourite novel by Jane Austen, and I sometimes named it as my favourite novel by anyone, so I relished the task of tracing the history of its reception. Furthermore it was the novel by Austen most often prescribed as a set text in higher education, and both JA and HE were booming. The Casebook did very well, being reprinted in an extended form in 1972 to take into account the rise of feminist criticism, and Graham sportingly wrote to me confessing that he had been wrong. I still receive a trickle of royalties from that Casebook.

I became a little bored with giving my *Emma* lecture in one university after another in the same week, but an unexpected feature of this tour provided some diversion. My first engagement was in Toulouse. At that time the University was distributed among buildings in the centre of the city as it had been for centuries (it has since moved to a campus on the outskirts). I gave my lecture in the afternoon, and in the early evening I walked from my hotel to the restaurant where a group of the senior staff were gathered for dinner. On my way I passed a cinema which, I was surprised to see, was showing *Deep Throat*. This film and its star Linda Lovelace had received enormous media attention since its release in America in 1972, being the first movie with hardcore pornographic content to be publicly shown in New York and other American cities, and its story was well known: the heroine has difficulty achieving orgasm until her doctor discovers that her clitoris is located in her throat, after which she finds sexual fulfilment by fellating a series of grateful men while the doctor disports himself in more orthodox fashion with his nurse. The film was banned in Britain, and I thought I would take this opportunity to see it. The dinner started and ended at a conveniently early hour, and I assured my hosts that I could find my own way back to the hotel. As I approached the cinema I saw a crowd of young people milling about outside in an excited and hilarious mood, waiting for admission, and I joined them. It seemed to be as novel and transgressive an experience for them as it was for me. *Deep Throat* turned out to be a light-hearted movie which used montage to juxtapose close-ups of carnal intercourse of various kinds with the clichés of mainstream cinema for sexual ecstasy, shots of fireworks exploding and waves breaking on the shore (another example of the binary opposition between metonymy and metaphor to add to my collection). The comic nature of the film's fantastic premise was perhaps what allowed it to get into the public domain in some places, for pornography whether visual or written does not usually arouse laughter intentionally. Nevertheless, any frank depiction of sexual congress will have a powerful effect on a viewer unaccustomed to it. When the film began with a shot of a naked woman sitting on top of a kitchen appliance with her legs wide apart and a man knelt to perform cunnilingus on her, the youth slouched in his seat in the row in front of me suddenly straightened up like a released spring, as if his entire body had had an erection. I was aroused myself, if less demonstratively, in the course of the film.

I discovered later that I had arrived in France at a time when either the censorship of films had been relaxed or cinema owners had decided to challenge the existing code, and hardcore porn films were being exhibited widely. I went to two more on my tour, one in Montpellier and another in Aix, seizing the opportunity to extend my knowledge of the sexual revolution, though not unaware of the irony of pursuing this research in the evenings while lecturing on one of the most chaste and reticent novelists in the English literary canon by day. I don't recollect anything from the first of these cinematic experiences except a short film in which a pair of diminutive blonde-haired identical female twins jointly pleasured a Popeye-lookalike sailor with an enormous penis, to a hornpipe musical accompaniment. The last film I saw, entitled *L'Essayeuse*, was more serious, and had some artistic pretensions. A young blonde who sells lingerie to men to give to their wives while having wild sex with them, falls in love with one of her clients. His wife, not knowing of this relationship, pays the blonde to demonstrate how to act out the sluttish behaviour her husband seems to desire, which sets up a series of increasingly depraved episodes involving both women. The last scene of the film is an orgy which takes place in a steamy bathhouse. The camera pans to take in a convoluted chain of naked men and women, some on their feet, others on their hands and knees, each connected to an orifice or organ of the body in front of them, groping, moaning and writhing in polymorphous abandon. Finally the camera turns aside to show two naked grey-haired women, with sagging breasts and wrinkled skin, sitting on the floor at a distance, and one says to the other as she gazes at the spectacle, '*J'ai peur.*' Only the French could make a porn film that ends with the line, 'I am afraid.'

This film provoked widespread protest from family organisations and religious groups in France, and in 1976 it was judicially condemned and the original negative was burned. Subsequently a stricter censorship of films was applied and hardcore movies were banned from public cinemas in France (though the development of videotape would soon make this method of distribution redundant). Not long afterwards I read a brief report in the

*Guardian* that Isabelle Bourjac, who played the wife in *L'Essayeuse*, had committed suicide. It is difficult not to connect this act with the notoriety of the film. *Deep Throat*, in spite of its playful high spirits, also turned out to have a dark side, when its star Linda Lovelace revealed in an autobiography that she had been coerced into performing in it by her controlling husband. She became a born-again Christian and campaigner against pornography.

Pornography is not without social usefulness. It may give solace to those who for one reason or another are unable to experience sexual intercourse, it is of assistance to sperm donors, and it may have a positively liberating effect in some circumstances. A priest of my acquaintance told me that one of his parishioners claimed that persuading his wife to watch a 'blue movie' with him had saved their marriage. But its availability needs to be controlled by scarcity and shame, because it easily becomes addictive, as I discovered on my journey through the south of France in 1975. Since those days pornography, often in extreme forms, has become omnipresent and instantly accessible from the internet on computers, tablets and smartphones, with calamitous effects, especially on the young.

This was brought home to me recently when I watched a Channel 4 TV documentary about sex education in secondary schools. A Dutch expert in the field was invited to a British mixed comprehensive school in Yorkshire to see if she could improve the attitude and understanding of 15–16-year-old pupils with regard to sex. A liberated and enlightened lady whose style of teaching was to be totally frank and unshockable, she was perceptibly shaken when the boys spoke casually in the mixed class about 'jissing' (i.e. ejaculating) on to girls' faces. There may have been an element of unfounded bravado in this, but their assumption that this practice was quite normal was disturbing. They could only have learned about it from internet porn. (I first encountered this item in the erotic repertoire myself in a funny, shocking but entirely unpornographic short story by Martin Amis first published in

1981, called 'Let Me Count the Times'.) By the end of the televised sex education experiment the teacher had succeeded, it appeared, in making the boys more respectful and the girls more assertive towards the opposite sex, but whether these effects will survive continued exposure to internet porn must be doubtful.

The British Council Specialist tour was not the only way for a suitably qualified academic to see the world from the 1970s onwards. Increasingly the international conference provided further opportunities, facilitated by the rapid expansion of commercial air travel. If you were invited to deliver a paper in your subject area at such a conference you could usually get a grant from your university to cover your expenses; and sometimes a foreign association of university teachers of English would invite you to be a guest speaker at their annual conference, and then they would pay the expenses. Sometimes the British Council sent a group of specialists to such a conference if it was considered important. In the spring of 1980 I went to Turkey with such a group to a conference in Ankara, and we moved on afterwards to give lectures in Istanbul. Both parts of this trip would provide locations and prompt ideas for a future novel.

At the end of 1978 I was invited to the Big Daddy of all such gatherings, the annual convention of the Modern Language Association of America, which was a memorable experience for more reasons than one. The 'MLA', as the event is known familiarly to American academics, was held in those days between Christmas and the New Year in a big city on either the East or the West Coast. In 1978 it ran from 27th–30th December, in New York. I was invited to contribute a short paper to a panel on the concept of 'period' in literary history, for which the MLA was willing to pay for my airfare and accommodation. By happy chance (or perhaps it wasn't chance, perhaps in the US as well as the UK we were by now tagged as a kind of double act) Malcolm

Bradbury was also invited to give a paper at the convention, and it was a pleasing prospect to have each other's company for this trip. To complete its attractions, my friend Donald Fanger, Professor of Russian at Harvard, invited both of us to join him and his family on New Year's Eve in the Boston suburb where they lived, and to stay on for a few days. Since the Fangers' houseroom was limited, it was arranged that I would stay with them and Malcolm with other mutual friends, Martin and Carol Green.

To ensure that Malcolm and I would have adjoining seats on the flights I offered to obtain our tickets, and did so at a branch of American Express which had opened on the Birmingham campus (a sign that academic travel was a growing market). We met by arrangement at Heathrow – it was Terminal 3 in those days for all intercontinental flights – and joined the line to check in for the 13.30 Pan Am flight to Kennedy airport, which because of the time zone difference would get us there comfortably in the afternoon. I handed over my passport to the check-in clerk, who flipped through it several times. 'You don't have a valid visa,' he said.

*WHAT?* I was astonished, incredulous, stunned, shocked and dismayed in quick succession as I struggled to grasp the truth. I had not noticed that the ten-year employment visa I had obtained at the time of my stint at Berkeley had expired. It was a humiliating and stupid oversight. I could not travel to New York, and the whole eagerly anticipated trip seemed about to dissolve like a dream. The Pan Am clerk was sympathetic, and said he could put me on the same flight next day if I got myself a new visa in time. 'Will the American Embassy be open today?' I asked. He assured me that it would be, but pointed out that there was no other Pan Am flight to New York that day. 'Can I transfer this ticket to another airline?' Not normally, was the discouraging answer. I decided that I would try to get a visa anyway, and pay if necessary for the first available flight to New York. I said farewell to a disappointed Malcolm and took the Tube back to central London, carrying my suitcase, and sweating in the overcoat I was wearing for New York temperatures. Oxford Street was crowded with shoppers looking for sale bargains in the big stores. I stopped in one to get new passport photos from an automatic machine, as I was sure I would need them, before hurrying to the embassy in Grosvenor Square. It was open and fortunately not very busy. I made my request, filled in the forms, and sat and waited for about four hours until my name was called and I was handed my passport with the new visa.

I dashed into the one-way street beside the embassy and hailed a taxi. An Indian family tried to get in through the opposite door but I shooed them away, and ordered the driver to take me to Heathrow as quickly as possible. It was early evening when we got there and Terminal 3 was relatively quiet. The departures board showed one last flight to New York, by British Airways, at 2200 hours. The Pan Am desk was deserted apart from a single female official, who was desultorily tidying the desks. I threw myself on her mercy and explained my plight. Could she authorise the transfer of my ticket to BA? She could. She would. She did. Blessing her, I hurried to the BA desk. The flight was full on paper, but there was a little group of standby passengers hoping for no-shows. I joined them, and after a tense couple of hours we were all issued with boarding passes and checked our luggage. With one bound (well actually it had been several bounds) I was free of the knots I had tied myself in.

Our flight benefited from a tail wind, according to the captain, and got to New York in record time. The immigration area in the Kennedy terminal, laid out like a cattle pen, was almost empty and I was whisked through. The driver of the yellow cab I took drove as if he was trying to break a record, with no need for encouragement from me. The result was that I entered the foyer of the Hilton Hotel in mid-town Manhattan at about 8 p.m. New York time. I felt it had been the longest day of my life, and it wasn't over yet. Most astonishing of all – there was Malcolm, in the foyer, chatting to a group of people with his overcoat on and his suitcase at his feet. He laughed in astonishment when I greeted him. 'How on earth did you get here?' he demanded. When I explained he said, 'You did well,' and patted me on the shoulder in an almost fatherly way. 'But you look as if you only just got here yourself,' I said, which turned out to be almost the truth. The Pan Am flight had been delayed by an hour and a half. The immigration queues at Kennedy had been long. He had got talking to a group of other British conferees and joined them in taking a bus into Manhattan instead of a cab; and not realising that his VIP status entitled him to check in at a special desk, he was waiting for the long line which stretched from the main Reception desk into the street to diminish.

Recovering from the disastrous start to my trip had put me into a euphoric mood to enjoy the extraordinary event that was the MLA. Some ten thousand academics had converged on two gigantic hotels in Manhattan (not all of them actually staying in one, of course, as Malcolm and I were) to attend lectures and panel discussions on every conceivable literary and linguistic subject from 'Old English Riddles' to 'Faulkner Concordances', from 'Lesbian-Feminist Teaching and Learning' to 'Problems of Cultural Distortion in Translating Expletives in the Work of Cortázar, Sender, Baudelaire and Flaubert'. The programme was laid out in a book as thick as the telephone directory of a small town, listing 600 different events running concurrently, thirty at a time, from 8.30 in the morning to 10.15 at night. Those that involved the stars of the profession took place in huge ballrooms with audiences of over a thousand, but people at less prominent events were fickle and might leave halfway through to try the one next door if there was audible applause or laughter from it. But that was only one level of conference activity. There were also caucus meetings and cocktail parties and cash bars and business meetings for various specialist groups. Above all, the MLA was a place to meet people: old friends and old enemies, people whose books you had reviewed, or who had reviewed yours, people you

61

might hire, or who might offer you a job. Some senior professors spent most of their time at the MLA interviewing young hopefuls in their bedrooms. And it was likely that other, more intimate bedroom meetings were being arranged. After Malcolm had delivered his talk a woman engaged him in conversation and invited him to spend the night with her. 'People only come to this circus to get laid,' she assured him, as he struggled to find a polite way of declining. My own talk, 'Historicism and Literary History: Mapping the Modern Period', was well received, though nobody tried to seduce me afterwards. I was sufficiently entertained by everything else that was going on, and arranging to have breakfast, lunch or dinner with old friends from Brown and Berkeley. I was especially pleased to see Stanley and Adrienne Fish again, though Stanley had left Berkeley and was now at Johns Hopkins in Baltimore, a step up towards fulfilling his ambition to be the highest-paid professor of English in America.

Every MLA convention has a particular, though by no means exclusive, theme, and that year it was Modernism and Postmodernism. On the first morning the biggest of the Hilton's ballrooms was packed for a session on Postmodernism with three well-known speakers: the Arab-American literary theorist Ihab Hassan, who was one of the first to apply the concept to contemporary writing; Julia Kristeva, the Bulgarian-French feminist poststructuralist critic; and Christine Brooke-Rose. I was personally acquainted with this lady. Born in 1923, she had produced by this time a substantial *oeuvre* of fiction and criticism, and would add to it substantially in the rest of her long lifetime, which she spent partly in England and partly in France. In 1968 she moved from the former to the latter to take up a professorial appointment at the radical university of Paris Vincennes. She took a sympathetic interest in the work of Alain Robbe-Grillet and other exponents of the *nouveau roman*, translating some of their books, but continued to be a presence in the British literary avant garde in the 1970s with her own novels, full of postmodernist metafictional devices and language games, and wrote academic criticism in the structuralist and poststructuralist modes.

In 1977 it was Birmingham's turn to host the annual Conference of University Teachers of English (UTE), and I volunteered to organise it with the help of my colleague Ian Small. I had been impressed by an article Christine Brooke-Rose had recently published, wittily entitled 'The Squirm of the True', about Henry James's famously ambiguous ghost story, which prompted me to think that she would be an interesting guest speaker who might entice our colleagues in other universities to give up three days of their Easter vacation to attend the conference. Ian agreed.

Although we were able to offer only travel expenses and accommodation in the University's Staff House, she accepted our invitation, and I was responsible for looking after her. She flew from Paris to Birmingham, where I met her at the airport. She wrote to me in advance, 'How shall we recognise each other?' and answered her own question with a description of her planned attire as meticulously detailed as anything in Robbe-Grillet's novels:

> I am medium height (5'7") with short blonde hair
> (shortish with fringe). Will be wearing black trousers
> and, if mild, a yellow raincoat top, ¾ length, if cold, a
> black fur coat with grey fox collar. But may just wear
> a black, tan striped cardigan & carry the coat. I think
> I'll wear my black velvet cap, that is probably the most
> distinctive.

She was at this time teaching part-time at Vincennes while living in the country outside Paris, alone except for occasional visits, she told me, 'by my lover'. The way she referred to this person, somehow implying that every attractive single lady of a certain age would have one, struck me as the quintessence of French sophistication, and the relentless specificity with which she had prepared me to recognise her made me apprehensive that she

63

would be a rather demanding guest. But she was not. Our conference, like most of its kind in Britain, was a small and unglamorous affair, taking place in one of the University's halls of residence, and attracting only about seventy-five participants, but if she was disappointed she did not show it and seemed pleased to be part of the event. I never felt completely relaxed in her presence, because I was not as familiar with her work as I ought to have been and as she assumed I was. I do not remember what she spoke about, but that goes for most of the many lectures I have heard in my life, and I believe hers was well received. We parted on amicable terms, expressing mutual pleasure in her visit.

*The Modes of Modern Writing* was published about six months later, and I put her name on a list of people to receive advance copies from the publisher. I soon received a letter from Christine complimenting me handsomely on the book, making two criticisms on technical points, and then continuing:

> I do, however, have a more personal complaint, which I hope won't sound peevish. It is not meant to, I assure you, for I have become quite philosophical on this odd state of affairs. And that is, you don't once mention me, either as critic or as writer. I'm used to it now, after 20 years, but immensely puzzled.

It was an immensely long letter, typed in single spacing on both sides of a foolscap sheet, a *cri de coeur*, a catalogue of complaints about being ignored by British academic and journalistic critics, her ideas borrowed without acknowledgement, her novels misunderstood, misrepresented or simply ignored. I read this letter with increasing discomfort, for I was keenly aware that Christine was perfectly justified in complaining that I had not made any reference to her novels in the final chapter of my book, which was on Postmodernist Fiction, since they were obviously eligible for inclusion by virtue of their formal and linguistic experiment.

The simple reason was that I hadn't read any of them when I finished *Modes* and sent it off to my agent, some months before I thought of inviting Christine to speak at our conference and started belatedly to acquire some knowledge of her work. I felt free to confess this in reply to her letter because at the end of it she suddenly abandoned the tone of an embittered victim and said disarmingly, '*Well, that's enough complaint. And I who complain haven't read your novels! That's the way it goes, life speeds by, one can hardly keep up.*' On the basis of these mutual *mea culpas* we were able to draw a line under this contretemps. Or so I thought.

I was unaware that Christine was speaking at the MLA until I got to New York and studied the programme of events. Her presence gave the forum on Postmodernism a special interest for me, but the topic was interesting to a great many delegates, and I could only find an unoccupied seat towards the back of the hall. I regretted this until Christine began to speak and quite soon uttered some very disparaging remarks about *The Modes of Modern Writing*, and then I was glad to be sitting among strangers well back from the platform. It seemed that she had not after all forgiven me for ignoring her work in my book. Later in the day somebody who recognised me and knew Christine well told me that she was distraught and refusing to leave her room, having learned that I had been present in the audience for her talk. She had had no idea that I was at the MLA. I asked my informant to assure her that I was not seriously upset or offended, which was true. I completely understood her continued resentment, and how embarrassed she would be by having unwittingly exposed it to me so publicly.

There was a vase of red roses in my hotel room, placed there by the organising committee to welcome me to the convention. I took one out, dried and trimmed the stalk, and attached it to a brief note telling her I was more amused than offended by the episode, and bade her think no more about it. This I gave to Reception to deliver to her. We patched up our friendship in subsequent correspondence, but we did not meet again.

In September 1984 she sent me a copy of her latest novel, *Amalgememnon*, inscribed, '*For David, whom I should have put into this as a fleeting character, tit for tat. With love, Christine.*' *Small World* was published earlier that year, but she was not the model for any of the characters, so I assumed she meant she had resisted the temptation to take satirical revenge for my neglect of her work in *The Modes of Modern Writing*. The affectionate conclusion of the inscription, however, indicated that she bore no real grudge. In the latter years of her life Carcanet Press ensured that her old and new work was kept in print, and it attracted more attention, but she was always chiefly famous for not being famous. '*Christine Brooke-Rose, brilliant and neglected*' was the heading of a *Guardian* obituary article when she died in 2012.

Readers of *Small World* will recognise the MLA convention in New York I have described as the setting of that novel's penultimate chapter and narrative dénouement. It ended with a VIP champagne reception on the penthouse floor of the Hilton, to which Malcolm and I were invited, and later I contrived a brief Hitchcockian appearance for both of us among the guests at the fictional party. The young hero, Persse McGarrigle, also present, has his glass refilled

> in an absent-minded fashion by a shortish, dark-haired
> man standing nearby with a bottle of champagne in
> his hand, talking to a tallish dark-haired man smoking
> a pipe. 'If I can have Eastern Europe,' the tallish man
> was saying in an English accent, 'you can have the rest
> of the world.' 'All right,' said the shortish man, 'but I
> daresay people will still get us mixed up.'

In 1978, when the action of my novel takes place, Malcolm was writing his novel *Rates of Exchange*, about a fictional eastern

European communist state called Slaka, which he published in 1983; and though I had not started *Small World*, it wouldn't be long before I did.

The morning after the MLA ended we took the train to Boston to see in the New Year with Donald and Margot Fanger, their family and friends. It was a jolly occasion, but the icing on the cake of this trip for me was that Donald, knowing I had written a book inspired by the linguistic theory of Roman Jakobson, and having been a colleague of the great man at Harvard, had thoughtfully arranged for the three of us to have breakfast together before my return to England later the same day. It took place at the Hyatt hotel overlooking the Charles River, a new and trendy structure having a large atrium with real trees growing inside it and glass elevators. It also had a revolving restaurant at the top, but we breakfasted in a more modest one on the ground floor. I recall I had Eggs Benedict for the first time on Donald's recommendation, and enjoyed them. Roman Jakobson ate more sparingly. Small in stature, neatly dressed in suit and tie, he was then aged eighty-three, physically frail but mentally alert. He smiled as he shook my hand and said he was glad to meet the author of *The Modes of Modern Writing*. Two years earlier he had thanked me for '*your very interesting book*' when I sent him a copy – these words handwritten on one of the customised postcards he used to acknowledge such gifts, which were evidently numerous. I later discovered that I had misrepresented one element of his seminal paper, 'Two Aspects of Language and Two Types of Aphasic Disturbances', in my book. I corrected this in the second edition published in 1979, sending a copy to Jakobson. He thanked me on another customised postcard for '*the new, improved edition of your fundamental Modes*', a conative message which gave great pleasure to the addressee, to use Jakobson's own linguistic terminology. At the breakfast I apologised once more for my error and took the opportunity to mention what appeared to me a more serious misrepresentation of his metaphor/metonymy distinction by a guru of poststructuralism, the psychoanalyst Jacques Lacan, in one of *his* seminal papers, 'The Insistence of the Letter in the Unconscious'. In a brief reference to Freud's terms for the different ways in which dreams are structured, Jakobson had identified both 'condensation' and 'displacement' in the dream-work as metonymic substitutions, as opposed to what Freud called 'symbolism', which is based, like metaphor, on similarity between dissimilars (e.g. long pointed objects as phallic, openings as vaginal). Lacan however, though referring to Jakobson's work, identified 'condensation' with *metaphor*, in opposition to the metonymic 'displacement', and made no reference to 'symbolism'. I asked Jakobson if he agreed that Lacan seemed to have either misunderstood the distinction between metaphor and metonymy, or revised Jakobson's formulation without acknowledging it. The old man smiled and nodded an ambiguous assent but made a deprecating gesture as if to indicate that it didn't bother him, and perhaps it didn't at this late stage of his life. He was glad that his ideas were still in circulation, but evidently he didn't want to be drawn into any further controversy about them. At some later point in the conversation he said that if he had his life over again he would like to devote himself to a more thorough investigation of aphasia.

Some two years later, on 24th July 1982, I received a telegram from his wife Krystyna, with a three-word message: 'ROMAN IS DEAD'. I had not been in touch with him since our meeting in Boston, and was unprepared for this news. I was touched that Mrs Jakobson, whom I had never met, had taken the trouble to inform me personally, and I felt all the more fortunate to have met him, thanks to Donald's initiative.

# 4

One of the great perks and privileges of academic life, which compensated for the fact that one was paid less than comparably qualified people in other professions, was the sabbatical, traditionally one year in seven of paid leave from teaching and administration, allowing recipients to concentrate on their research and recharge their intellectual batteries. By this stage in my career it had been replaced at Birmingham by 'study leave' of one term's duration every three years, and I qualified for this in the summer term of 1979. I took the opportunity to accept invitations to two conferences in June which were of interest to me and conveniently scheduled to run consecutively: the James Joyce Symposium in Zurich, and a conference on 'Narrative Theory and the Poetics of Fiction' split between the Universities of Tel Aviv and Jerusalem.

The Symposium is held every few years, usually in a city associated with Joyce, and timed to coincide with the anniversary of 'Bloomsday', 16th June 1904, the day during which the action of Joyce's novel *Ulysses* takes place. Zurich was an appropriate venue for one of the earliest of these events because Joyce wrote much of that novel when he took refuge there during the First

World War, and he died and was buried there early in the Second. He boasted that he had put into this book 'so many enigmas and puzzles that it will keep the professors busy for centuries arguing over what I meant', and so far it seems that his confidence was justified (though just to make sure of retaining the professors' interest he wrote another book, *Finnegans Wake*, which is even more densely encoded). Joyce has probably attracted more scholarly attention internationally than any other modern writer, in a period of rapid expansion in higher education when literary criticism became an academic industry in need of texts on which to demonstrate its various kinds of expertise. As D.H. Lawrence's star sank in the literary firmament, Joyce's rose, and his work was particularly amenable to criticism that belonged to the schools of structuralism and poststructuralism. Even so, I was impressed by the numbers of those who registered at the University of Zurich in the afternoon of Monday 11th June, and by the well-known names among them. We were all bussed to a civic reception at the other side of the city, and I found myself strap-hanging next to a tall tousled-looking man who introduced himself as Hugh Kenner, a Canadian who had made his career mainly in the USA, a brilliant critic of Joyce, Ezra Pound, Samuel Beckett and several other major modernist writers. We chatted on the journey, and I learned later that he was born stone deaf and managed conversations by lip-reading, which impresses me even more in retrospect, having suffered significant hearing loss myself later in life. Whether he was able to lip-read the speeches of welcome by various Zurich dignitaries, I didn't discover. The city takes a genuine pride in its association with Joyce, and one speaker, who was in charge of its excellent tram service, imaginatively acclaimed him as the 'Bard of Trams', on the strength of Leopold Bloom's approving comment on this method of transport on his way to the funeral of Paddy Dignam in a horse-drawn carriage: '*another thing I've often thought is to have municipal funeral trams like they have in*

*Milan, you know. Run the line out to the cemetery gates and have special trams, hearse and carriage and all.'*

American or American-based Joyceans were the largest single group of the conferees: the second semester had just come to an end in the States and a grant-assisted trip to a conference in Zurich was a convenient way to start a European vacation. Among the names on the programme familiar to me were Ihab Hassan, J. Hillis Miller, A. Walton Litz, Robert Scholes and, intriguingly, Marilyn French, the author of a bestselling feminist novel, *The Women's Room*, and also, I discovered, a college teacher who had written a book on *Ulysses*, and was down to speak on a panel entitled 'The Joyce of Sex'. (Joyceans favour punning titles in homage to the master whose last book was written in a language consisting almost entirely of puns.) There were many European and British academics present whose work I knew, and several whom I had encountered before on my travels. Those in the British contingent whom I met for the first time included Colin MacCabe, soon to be at the centre of a famous academic controversy in Cambridge, and Maud Ellmann, daughter of Richard Ellmann, Joyce's definitive biographer, following in her father's footsteps as a lecturer in English at Southampton. The wine at the civic reception ran out quickly, so I went with some of my old and new acquaintances to the James Joyce Pub on Pelikanstrasse, a popular gathering place throughout the conference. It is a replica of an Irish bar, selling draught Guinness and other appropriate liquid refreshment, with furnishings and fittings taken from the bar in Jury's Hotel in Dublin when it was demolished, and transported to Zurich by devotees of *Ulysses*.

I kept a rough diary of my six days in Zurich from which it is clear that I thoroughly enjoyed the exchange of ideas with other Joyceans in both the formal sessions and private conversations. There was something exhilarating in the phenomenon of all these people from all over the world congregating like pilgrims in the city of Zurich to discuss and pay homage to the work of

71

a single author. But whereas medieval pilgrims took months to reach their destinations on foot or horseback, we had travelled for only a day or two, shot through the air in tubes of steel from country to country and continent to continent; and we would soon disperse, but with every expectation of bumping into each other again before long at another conference. I wrote in my diary, *'More and more I think that air travel has revolutionised the academic world, made it a global campus – a novel there, if Malcolm doesn't write it first.'*

I was adapting Marshall McLuhan's metaphor, 'the global village', for a world shrunk by the speed of modern communications, and I discovered in Zurich that I was now quite well known on the global campus, as both critic and novelist. It was pleasing, of course, to be frequently complimented by readers of *The Modes of Modern Writing* and/or *Changing Places*, but the city itself contributed a great deal to my euphoric mood. *'I like it more and more,'* I wrote. *'Birmingham is a junk heap in comparison.'* Beforehand I had associated Zurich exclusively with banks, and I vaguely expected it to look and feel like the City of London or Wall Street. It is of course utterly different from both, a charming low-profile city of harmonised period and modern architecture on a human scale, with a calm and civilised ambience which seemed to extend to every level of life, high and low. In the principal art gallery, superbly appointed and lit, I discovered a stupendous collection of Impressionist and Post-impressionist art which put Birmingham's municipal Museum and Art Gallery into the deepest shade. My modest hotel, chosen at random, from which I walked to the gallery was on the edge of the red light district, where prostitutes were allowed to ply their trade, but in a very Swiss way, standing patiently on the street corners, just one per corner, and all looking clean and wholesome even if dressed in minuscule skirts and skimpy tops, though some of them wore smart cocktail dresses, or floaty kaftans, appealing to more refined customers.

Marilyn French would no doubt have taken a less detached view of this spectacle if she had observed it, which was unlikely because, as I discovered, she was staying at the Waldorf in a posher part of town. Although I missed her participation in the conference programme, I did get to meet her on its penultimate evening. There was a party given by a publisher to which I went with many others, and I left at the same time as Marilyn, Bob Scholes, a professor at Brown University and author of influential books on narrative literature (including *The Fabulators*, which had prompted the title essay of my book *The Novelist at the Crossroads*), and a young woman, a former graduate student of Bob's, who was currently based in Paris, sitting at the feet of various intellectual celebrities there. I had met them together before, when Marcia (not her real name) gave me an amusing account of a lecture given by Jacques Lacan to some two hundred auditors. He came into the room, the chatter of the audience died into an expectant hush, and he shuffled his papers for ten long minutes before saying: 'Why is there not a third sex?' Then he relapsed into silence again, and began to transcribe some diagrams on to the blackboard, but having failed to do this to his satisfaction, abruptly announced that the seminar was '*terminé*' and departed, leaving his question unanswered. Or perhaps that was the answer.

Marilyn invited us to have a nightcap in her hotel room, where she had a bottle of whisky, and although it was getting late we accepted. But as soon we got inside the room Bob Scholes, a big, genial, bearded man, announced that he just *had* to sleep and Marilyn invited him to crash on her bed, which he promptly did. She was then fifty years old, blonde, elegantly coiffed and plump of figure, and at the height of her fame. *The Women's Room*, published two years earlier, sold twenty million copies and was translated into twenty languages, but success hadn't changed her pessimistic view of the damage patriarchy had done to women. We talked for well over an hour, mostly about

73

feminism, a conversation dominated by Marilyn. As the only male awake I felt I had to tread delicately, and so evidently did Marcia, who had a more nuanced view of relations between men and women than our hostess, but refrained from challenging her directly. I recorded in my diary: '*An odd conversation. Marcia obviously wanted to make friends with Marilyn (partly no doubt because she is famous) without being willing to pay the full price Marilyn was demanding, which would have been complete acceptance of her particular brand of feminism. Marilyn's observations constantly sounded phoney and rehearsed without actually being so – I think she is quite honest and sincere.*' The conversation livened up somewhat when Marcia enterprisingly asked Marilyn how she chose her clothes, and volunteered the information that she herself took the advice of a former lover, and was actually wearing a rather mannish shirt he had given her. Soon afterwards Bob woke up and we departed, slinking guiltily past the night porter – the Waldorf had a rule against guests in bedrooms after midnight. I thought later that it would make an effective first scene in a play to have three people talking in a hotel bedroom and what appears to be a heap of quilts and clothes on the bed suddenly erupts to reveal an unsuspected fourth character who has been asleep underneath it (or perhaps awake and listening).

I haven't written that play, but several years later I discovered that our extended and rather dull conversation had had an unsuspected subtext. I never met Marcia again, but at another conference several years later I met Bob Scholes, and we recalled that evening in Zurich. To my astonishment he told me that Marcia had been strongly attracted to me during the conference and was hoping to further this interest over Marilyn's whisky in the Waldorf bedroom, but she had been intensely frustrated by the way the evening developed, with Bob unavailable to distract Marilyn or prevent her from keeping the conversation dourly focused on the subjection of women, marginalising me. I had not been conscious of any amorous element in Marcia's friendliness, though for my own part I did describe her as '*attractive*' when first mentioning her in my diary, and on this second occasion wrote: '*She is tall, very slim, long-limbed, nice smile, perfect teeth, petite pinched nose, soft waved hair. Good sense of fun – an amusing way of*' There the entry breaks off tantalisingly in mid-sentence like the last chapter of Sterne's *A Sentimental Journey* – but without the same implied sequel.

If Marcia's reference to 'a former lover' was a subtle hint to me of her availability should I be interested, I missed it, not being on the lookout for such opportunities. There were plenty on the conference circuit, as I became increasingly aware, and it was not surprising. Where else are men and women, far from home and spouses, more likely to meet attractive members of the opposite sex with the same passionate intellectual interests as themselves? Such affairs would figure largely in the conference novel that was germinating in my head, and transgressive sexual behaviour is a major topic in most of the novels that followed. Indeed I am sometimes accused of being excessively preoccupied with it. But as I often say, my perspective on the sexual revolution which happened in my lifetime has always been that of a war correspondent, not a participant. Occasionally journalists try to test the authenticity of this stance. The late Lynda Lee-Potter of the *Daily Mail* interviewed me over lunch at the time of the publication of *Therapy* in 1995, and asked me boldly if I had ever had any affairs. If I had answered that it was none of her business, I might have given the impression that I had something to hide, so I said, no, I hadn't. I said I had met women with whom I could imagine having a fulfilling relationship, but 'one makes a choice' and I had made it in favour of fidelity.

There were several reasons for this, including certainty that Mary was equally committed to the principle and would never tolerate anything else, and the responsibility that we shared for our children, especially Christopher. The conditioning of my Catholic upbringing also no doubt played a part, though I no longer believed that I would put my immortal soul in jeopardy if I committed adultery. But I claim no special virtuousness for my behaviour. The fact is that I am constitutionally monogamous, like my father. I value the emotional security of a marriage made on the traditional contract, and have not found that desire is extinguished by it. I am never comfortable when telling a lie even for trivial social reasons, and would be quite incapable of the systematic deception that an adulterous affair entails, but it is not difficult to imagine what both the excitement and the stress of such experience would be like. In fact it seems to me that it would be difficult to describe it effectively in a novel if it were based on personal experience without one's spouse suspecting something, certainly a spouse as perceptive as Mary; and perhaps the forced nature of much erotic writing in contemporary fiction is partly the consequence of the writers having to suppress more authentic sources of inspiration for this reason.

The critic Mark Lawson, who has generally been a friend to my work, noticed Lynda Lee-Potter's interview and teasingly accused me in another newspaper of 'inverted hypocrisy', giving the impression of familiarity with sexual adventure while secretly being an uxorious husband. I plead guilty to a measure of uxoriousness, but not to pretending to be more immoral than I really am. A novel is a novel and the 'implied author' of the text is not identical to the person who wrote it but has another self in the real world. That is not to say that my novels have no autobiographical sources – of course they do, like most novels that purport to represent the real world. But in works of fiction facts are modified, transformed, heightened, and sometimes inverted for artistic reasons. When readers identify things in my novels that they presume must be autobiographical but which in fact I invented, or vice versa, I am always pleased.

*

The conference in Israel to which I went straight from Switzerland was as memorable as the Zurich symposium, though quite different in character and in various ways more strenuous. The political situation there was different from what it is today. The Israeli government's treatment of its Palestinian citizens was not the festering issue that it is now, the Intifada was some way off in the future, and Israel and Egypt had signed a peace treaty, brokered by the USA, in the previous year. But other neighbouring Arab countries were still hostile, embittered by losing two wars in the last two decades, and Israel was on permanent alert. Several other conferees had taken the same flight as mine, including two who had been at the Joyce Symposium, and security procedures at Tel Aviv airport were exhaustive and exhausting, our identities carefully checked and luggage thoroughly searched before we were allowed through the exit doors and met by our hosts. The Sabbath had ended and the shopping streets through which we were driven were thronged with people in short-sleeved, chain-store casual clothes, like Birmingham's Bull Ring on an exceptionally hot day. Our hotel was not luxurious, but it was adequate and had a decent swimming pool, which we couldn't wait to plunge into.

Among the latest arrivals I was glad to see Allon White, one of the two cleverest students I had taught at Birmingham. (The other was Patricia Waugh, who was in the same third-year tutorial group as Allon, and is currently a professor at Durham University.) There were just under fifty participants in the conference, divided between foreign guests and Israelis, roughly in a two-to-one ratio. Hosted jointly by the Universities of Tel Aviv and Jerusalem, it was due to relocate to the latter halfway through the programme, to appease rivalry between the institutions and to give the foreign guests an opportunity to see the historic city; but it was essentially the brainchild of Professor Benjamin Hrushovski, Head of the Department of Comparative Literature and Poetics which he founded at Tel Aviv. A Lithuanian born in

1928, he managed to survive the war and was among the first illegal immigrants to enter Israel after it. Having read *The Modes of Modern Writing* he had written to me asking if he could add my name to the masthead of the journal *Poetics Today* which he published from Tel Aviv, and as it was a purely honorary position, I agreed. But when he asked me later to give a public lecture as well as a paper at the conference, I couldn't very well refuse. He had also asked me about Allon White, whom he was interested in recruiting for his department, and I told him truthfully that he was one of the most promising young critics in Britain. But Allon made his career at the University of Sussex, writing with rare elegance and clarity on a broad spectrum of topics in the field that was beginning to be known as Theory. Exceptionally clever, he was also a remarkably nice person. Alas, his life was cruelly cut short by leukaemia, and he died in 1988 at the age of only thirty-seven, greatly mourned by his friends and colleagues.

As it was a small, elite conference, at which everybody attended every session, we soon became a unified group, or rather two groups, the home team and the visitors. The Israeli academics, with the exception of the suave and smiling Hrushovski, seemed different from the Jewish intellectuals I had met in America – more earnest, less witty, and although always courteous to the visitors, ferocious in argument with each other. The programme was absurdly crowded. Every participant had been asked to send to the organisers in advance a copy of their paper, to be distributed to all the others before the event, so that each session could consist of a brief summary of the paper by its author, followed by questions and observations from the audience. This procedure is a good one in principle, but as usual several participants had not submitted their papers in time, or had revised them since doing so, or took too much time summarising them, and so the programme tended to get more and more behind schedule as the day wore on. There were eight to ten papers a day, with titles like 'A Theory of the Impossibility of a Theory of the Literary Text', 'Isotopic Organization and Narrative Grammar' and 'The Inflatable Trope as Narrative Theory: Structure or Allegory'. Israel was experiencing a heat wave. We were crammed into a low-ceilinged room only just big enough to contain our number, with air conditioning that was barely adequate, and at the end of the day we tumbled out of it, exhausted, sweating, and gasping for a drink and a swim. Then we went out into the city in groups to eat at one of the many open-air restaurants in Tel Aviv, some of them set up on the street pavements, serving delicious Middle Eastern food in the warm Mediterranean night.

On the evening of the second day this relief was almost intolerably delayed by an official reception at Tel Aviv University, an address by the Rector, and two public lectures, one by me entitled 'Ambiguously Ever After: Problematic Endings in English Fiction' and the other, 'What is Semiotics?', by Umberto Eco, of the University of Bologna, who had joined the conference late. He was not yet the world-famous author of *The Name of the Rose*, which was published the following year. I was acutely conscious that the last thing my fellow conferees wanted to do that evening was to listen to two academic lectures, back to back. Their misery was compounded by the fact that the air conditioning in the auditorium was obviously not working, because the atmosphere was stifling. Even the 'public' members of the audience soon began to wilt. The chairman of the evening took Eco and me aside and begged us not to take more than 45 minutes each to deliver our lectures. With an effort, editing as we went along, 'We did it!' as Umberto said triumphantly to me at the end of his lecture, with perspiration pouring down his face into his beard. He seemed to have enjoyed the challenge and had delivered his lecture *con brio*.

When you go to a conference of this kind you always feel a certain tension as you wait for your turn to speak, but as I had given both my paper and my lecture by the end of the second day, I felt free to relax and enjoy the rest of the event. In our precious off-duty hours something like a party spirit developed among some of us, inspired and encouraged by Mieke Bal of the University of Utrecht. She had quickly made friends with another conferee, Susan Suleiman, who was then attached to a college in California, but not long afterwards moved to Harvard where she had a distinguished career as Professor of French and Comparative Literature. Together they befriended me, and in the case of Susan the friendship has been long-lasting. Professional engagements brought her to England from time to time, and me to Cambridge, Mass., and we are regular correspondents. Mieke Bal too went on to have a distinguished academic career, in the Netherlands, publishing books on an impressively wide range of cultural subjects, but I saw her only once again after the Israel conference. It was years later in America, and I scarcely recognised her. I described her in my Israel diary as '*blonde, voluptuous, dressed in semi-diaphanous silk or cotton dresses and smocks, with matching hair ribbons and plastic pop jewellery – butterflies, cakes, ice cream cones etc.*' In America she was blade-thin, short-haired, and austerely dressed, but what had prompted this transform-ation I never discovered.

After three days the conference 'went up to Jerusalem'. The biblical phrase became a reality as our bus climbed steadily, the road lined on each side by burnt-out trucks treated with preservative paint and placed there to commemorate the blockade of Jerusalem in 1948. Soon after arriving we were given a walking tour of the Old City, plunging into labyrinthine alleys lined with stalls selling kaftans, leather goods, jewellery and sweetmeats that, I opined in my diary, '*could give you dysentery just looking at them*'. We visited the Church of the Holy Sepulchre looked after by Greek Orthodox priests, one of whom pressed saccharine holy pictures and miniature crucifixes on us in return for donations. The place resounded with the noise of restoration work, and had no religious atmosphere. In fact most of the Holy Places we saw in Jerusalem and on later excursions outside were a disappointment to me. Bethlehem was perhaps the worst, the main square a bazaar of tawdry devotional objects, the shrine of the Nativity full of flashlight-popping tourists.

On the last day there was an excursion by coach, first to Masada, site of the fortifications under siege by the Roman army in AD 70, which ended in the mass suicide of the Jewish defenders. Tourists reach it by a vertiginous cable car ride. We concealed our misgivings by joking that the progress of narratology would be seriously retarded if the cable snapped, which was hard on Mieke Bal who was genuinely terrified. We proceeded to Jericho, a sad disappointment, and then to the Dead Sea which was fun – floating effortlessly in the soup-like water, followed by a mineral-rich mud bath. The prone barrel-chested figure of Umberto Eco encased in black mud, save for his head and beard, was a sight to remember. Back in Jerusalem Mieke, quite recovered from the trauma of the cable car, led a party of those who were up for it to a discotheque at the Hilton. It was something I had never done in Birmingham, though Birmingham had dozens of discotheques and Jerusalem seemed to have only two, of which the Hilton's was the more exclusive and expensive, where we danced incongruously among the city's gilded and smartly dressed youth. The next day the conferees dispersed, except for those of us who had signed up for an optional three-day tour of Israel which included the Jordan Valley, a delicious swim in the Sea of Galilee, an illuminating stay at a kibbutz run on the traditional communitarian model, and visits to the historical sites of Acre and Caesarea.

In *Small World* Morris Zapp organises a conference on 'The Future of Criticism in Jerusalem' which (until Philip Swallow apparently contracts legionnaires' disease) is a huge success because '*there is just one paper a day actually delivered by its author early in the morning. All the other papers are circulated in Xeroxed form, and the remainder of the day is dedicated to "unstructured* discussion" of the issues raised in these documents, or in other words to swimming and sunbathing at the Hilton pool, sightseeing in the Old City, shopping in the bazaar, eating out in ethnic restaurants and making expeditions . . .' This totally fictitious event was intended as a climactic example of '*the appeal of the conference circuit: it's a way of converting work into play, combining professionalism with tourism, and all at someone else's expense. Write a paper and see the world!*' It suited my fictional purposes to exaggerate the hedonistic character of Morris Zapp's conference, but I always feel a twinge of remorse when I re-read this travesty of the real one. In spite of the flurry of sightseeing at the end, it was a hard-working, serious and rewarding intellectual event. As always there were some dud papers, but the general standard was high, and the engagement of the participants intense. One paper, by Anne Banfield of Berkeley, aroused so much interest and disagreement that we voted to schedule an additional session to continue the debate. Admittedly that was on the first day of the conference, before the gruelling nature of the programme had fully sunk in.

## 5

The late seventies and early eighties were years of professional advancement and widening horizons for me, but over the same period illness and mortality took a heavy toll on the previous generation of my family. In 1976 my uncle John, who had been suffering from what he thought was back pain, was diagnosed with terminal lung cancer. When the specialist broke this bleak news to my aunt Lu she decided that John should not be told, and instead he was informed that the pain he was experiencing was caused by shingles. He was however ill enough to need care in a private sanatorium in Knokke-le-Zoute, the resort on the Belgian coast where they lived in retirement, and I accompanied my mother to visit him. We travelled by train and boat to Ostend where Lu met us with her car. She had been devastated by the diagnosis and was irrationally angry with the doctors who insisted that there was nothing to be done except palliative care. Lu was I think an atheist, while John was a long-lapsed Catholic, and both were strongly anticlerical. Unable to invoke the consolations of religion, she used the fiction of 'shingles' to spare him the knowledge that his plight was hopeless. I doubt whether he was deceived. I was shocked when I saw him in his room in the sanatorium, thin and haggard, moving with difficulty between his bed and the bathroom, his dressing gown drooping from his bowed shoulders. He had always taken a pride in his appearance and physique, and enjoyed challenging sports like sailing and gliding, and it was distressing, especially to Mum, to see him brought low by disease. I visited him again on my own during our brief stay in Le Zoute, and he said to me at some point, 'I've been a bloody fool in my life, Dave.' He had been a habitual cigarette smoker, and I assumed he was referring to that, but he may have been regretting other things done or not done in the past.

Not long afterwards I returned to Knokke-le-Zoute to attend his funeral – alone, because Mum, who was getting increasingly frail, was not equal either physically or psychologically to making this second journey. John and Lu had a wide circle of friends, including her relatives, so it was a big bourgeois funeral with a great display of expensive wreaths vying with each other to demonstrate the mourners' status and grief. Lu tactfully advised me on the choice of one to represent John's British family. She told me that when he was near the end of his life she had been asked by the sanatorium if he would like to see a priest, and when she put the question to him, he nodded; so like many a lapsed Catholic he received the last sacraments. I was pleased, knowing that this would be a great consolation to his sisters. In consequence a Catholic priest officiated at the funeral, though it was a simple service, not a requiem mass. I observed that when one of the cars conveying mourners drew up at the cemetery the occupants emerged coughing in a cloud of smoke, caused, one of them told me, by a cigarette stub smouldering in the vehicle's over-filled ashtray – a mishap which to a novelist's eye had a black comic appropriateness in the circumstances, and which I later incorporated in a funeral scene in How Far Can You Go?

*

Mum, who was now seventy-four, had given up some time ago a part-time clerical job in the library of Goldsmiths' College in New Cross, which she had greatly enjoyed for the pleasant company of the staff and the interest they took in the publications of her son. She no longer made occasional visits to us in Birmingham, and led a sequestered life at home with Dad, who became increasingly worried by her mental deterioration and loss of weight. In the autumn of 1977 she was admitted to King's College Hospital and was also referred to the Maudsley, London's premier psychiatric hospital. The Maudsley diagnosed depression, though they were not certain, and King's College more confidently determined that she had mild Parkinson's disease. In fact she was suffering from both conditions.

When I informed her sister Eileen in Hawaii of Mum's sad state she immediately recognised the symptoms of depression from episodes in her own life: *'almost identical to mine, all the same symptoms – the lassitude, the tiredness, the lack of interest in anything, the constant depression – so that I can understand just what hell she is going through.'* I had wondered in my own letter whether this propensity was inherited, since I knew that Adèle Murphy, my maternal grandmother who died when I was an infant, had suffered from depression, and Eileen emphatically agreed. *'You are quite right. I am convinced that we all inherited this unfortunate trait . . . Our mother had two breakdowns and each time had to be sent away to a mental hospital for approximately a six-month stay . . . I am sure, too, you knew that John had a breakdown a few years after he was married and had to go away. He received the "Shock Treatment" which apparently was effective.'* I knew vaguely that my uncle John suffered some kind of nervous breakdown at that time but not the seriousness of it, nor did I have any idea that my grandmother had spent such long periods in a mental hospital, for Mum seldom spoke of her parents. Eileen added: *'the weakness is definitely on the maternal side, because I can relate other instances in my mother's sister's family. There has been no trace of any such weakness in my father's siblings and their offspring.'* These revelations and Eileen's shrewd analysis of them (*'In every case it seems to indicate an inability to cope with setbacks, not from mental weakness per se'*) had uncomfortable implications for my own tendency to overreact to setbacks with anxiety and depression, of which I am more conscious now than when I read Eileen's remarkable letter. I was saddened to learn that what she identified as her own *'first lapse into depression'* was precipitated by the reunion with her two siblings in Hawaii in 1969, in which I had had a hand. She was already sinking into a depressive state when they arrived, and so far from being the happy occasion she had anticipated, it was perceived by her as a disaster for which she was chiefly responsible. *'I became burdened with guilt and remorse, dwelling on the fact that I had not given them the happy time I had planned. Everything seemed to go wrong . . . I felt terrible on the morning they left, they didn't realise I'm sure what a state I was in, but I couldn't believe they could go off and leave me – it was devastating and I felt I had no-one to turn to.'*

In fact they did realise what a state she was in, though they concealed it from me at the time. This depression lasted two years, in the course of which Eileen was treated by a psychiatrist, and her brother John wrote a letter to the doctor, which he copied to me, giving a detailed account of Eileen's disturbing behaviour while they were with her, in the hope that it would be useful. By one means or another Eileen recovered from the depression, and in the letter of 1977 she said, *'I really think this is one of the happier periods of my life. All my projects and interests I find so enjoyable and no two days are alike.'* She was supporting herself mainly by babysitting for the tourists in the Waikiki hotels – with her beautiful manners and classy British accent she must have seemed like a reincarnation of Mary Poppins to these families – supplemented by some investment income and an occasional day's work as an 'extra' in the long-running TV series *Hawaii Five-O*. She wrote: *'I cannot think of any other place where I could lead such an interesting, full and diversified life, and still in one of the most delightful places to live.'*

Mum came out of hospital and her condition seemed to improve as a result of the drugs she was given, but she was very thin and lacking in energy and became increasingly dependent on Dad's loving care. I did my best to visit them when I was in London on business, and she always managed a rare smile for me and took an interest in my professional and family news, but each time I returned to the house in Brockley, it seemed to me that she had faded a little more, like a photograph. The house, however, still looked almost exactly as it had done when I left it to get married. I could have helped them financially to modernise the house, or to move to a more comfortable one, but it was far too late for either of them to contemplate such upheaval.

Dad's mother, my much-loved Nana, was living contentedly, as she had done since Pop died in 1969, in a little apartment of her own in a house in East Dulwich belonging to her niece Hilda and her partner, Stan. They were unable to marry because Stan could not obtain a divorce from some previous union – a fact known to their close acquaintances but never mentioned. At some point I cannot now identify, Hilda and Stan revealed that they wanted to retire to the seaside, and were willing to take Nana with them. This precipitated an uncharacteristic anxiety crisis in Nana. She did not want to leave her cosy apartment with its proximity to Dad and Mum, and to me too since I used to take opportunities to visit her when I was in London; but she could not live alone, and clearly she could not move into Millmark Grove where Dad already had his hands full. She became so seriously disturbed that she was admitted to a psychiatric hospital where, after all other treatments had failed, she was given electroconvulsive shock therapy and miraculously cured. Two of my relatives benefited from a medical procedure that would soon be regarded as dangerous and oppressive. Nana returned home serene and cheerful, Hilda and Stan heroically agreed to stay on in East Dulwich for her sake, and their three lives continued as before.

By the autumn of 1979 Eileen was depressed again, and with some reason. The trigger was a sudden fall in the US stock market which greatly reduced the value of her investment income. She lived in Waikiki, Honolulu's beach resort, in a rented apartment the cost of which was likely to be increased, and she was afraid she would not be able to afford it. I took the opportunity offered by yet another conference, at the beginning of November that year, to visit her briefly and give her some support. It was a symposium entitled 'The State of the Language' organised by the English Speaking Union in San Francisco, and my participation came about through an article I published in *Encounter* in 1978, entitled 'Where It's At: The Poetry of Psychobabble'. I had been contributing regularly to this magazine ever since Frank Kermode, who was co-editor with Melvin Lasky, had asked me to review a clutch of books about H.G. Wells published in 1966, his centenary year. In the following year it was revealed that *Encounter* had always been covertly funded by the CIA. Frank, who had been kept entirely ignorant of this fact when he accepted the editorial position, understandably felt betrayed by Lasky and resigned, but I continued to write for *Encounter*. The CIA's motives for subsidising the magazine were to demonstrate what quality journalism was like in a free society, in contrast to equivalent publications in the Soviet bloc, and it seemed to me to do this admirably in spite of the underhand methods of the sponsors. I always read the magazine with pleasure and instruction, and never experienced the slightest politically motivated attempt to influence my own contributions. For much of this time the literary editor I dealt with was my friend Anthony Thwaite, who from 1973 became co-editor of the magazine. I valued the fact that *Encounter* gave its contributors plenty of space, so that it was worth taking the trouble to write a piece that could later be collected in a book – as several of mine were.

I suggested the 'Psychobabble' article to Anthony myself. Someone had sent me a novel called *The Serial* by an American writer, Cyra McFadden, which was a satirical portrait of the affluent, self-obsessed people who lived in Marin County, on the other side of the Golden Gate Bridge from San Francisco. Readers of my previous memoir may recall our enjoyable family excursions to its attractions, like the little port of Sausalito and Stinson Beach, when we were living in the city in the summer of 1965. *The Serial*, so called because it was originally serialised in a Marin County alternative newspaper, is a kind of soap opera about crises and conflicts in the personal relationships of Marin folk as expressed in their characteristic dialect, which may be illustrated by the following quotation:

> 'Harvey and I are going through this *dynamic* just
> now, and it's kinda where I'm at. I haven't got a lot
> of psychic energy left over for social interaction. So
> whatever it is, maybe you should just run it by me right
> here. Off the wall.'

It was another American writer, R.D. Rosen, who a little later gave this kind of speech a name, in his *Psychobabble: Fast Talk and Quick Cure in the Era of Feeling*, which Cyra McFadden herself endorsed. She was quoted as saying that conversations conducted in psychobabble 'make any exchange of ideas impossible, block any attempt at true communication; substitute what Orwell called "prefabricated words and phrases" for thought'. Though *The Serial* works brilliantly as satire on the behaviour of a particular social group by exaggerating their dependence on this vocabulary, I questioned her denunciation of the vocabulary itself. Most of the language we use in speech is 'prefabricated' inasmuch as we don't coin the words and rarely invent the phrases we use in normal speech. Colloquial slang, of which psychobabble is an example, is generated to overcome the deadening monotony of simple referential discourse, until it itself becomes too familiar to perform that function, when it either disappears or is absorbed into the received lexicon. And it seemed to me that the very success of psychobabble, which quickly spread across America from the West Coast, suggested that it had some stylistic appeal to its users which would be worth analysing. Examining the vocabulary of the characters in *The Serial* – *coming from, coming down, where it's at, get down, get centered, get it on, get to, get off on, get together, hang in, blow away, run by, upfront, off the wall, spaced out, etc.* – I concluded that psychobabble is a metaphorical type of slang, which presents experience primarily in terms of the movement and organisation of matter in space:

> Human existence is seen as a process of incessant
> change, readjustment and discovery – no one's
> condition is static or fixed. This is ultimately a very
> optimistic world view of a characteristically American
> kind, since it banishes ennui and promises that no
> evil will be permanent. It also tacitly allays the fear of
> death by avoiding metaphors drawn from organic life,
> in which change means eventual decay. Its model of
> experience is drawn from physics, not biology – the
> individual is pictured in terms of energy and mass,
> moving about in a curiously timeless space . . .

Soon after this article appeared my Berkeley friend Lenny Michaels wrote to say he had read it and wanted me to write something on the same theme for a book he was co-editing with Christopher Ricks called *The State of the Language*, which was to be published by the University of California Press in association with the English Speaking Union, and launched at the San Francisco Symposium. It seemed to me a surprising collaboration, and Lenny was deviating from his editorial brief since Ricks was supposed to commission the British contributors, and Lenny the American ones. I said he was welcome to reprint the article but I couldn't write a new one. Most of the book's contents were new essays by a variety of distinguished authors, but there were a few previously published articles, including mine, and I was invited to take part in the Symposium.

One of its sponsors was the British entrepreneur Freddie Laker, who pioneered low-cost air travel from 1966 onwards and in 1977 started his Skytrain operation between Britain and America. He generously provided free travel for three of the Brits who attended the conference – the critic and Cambridge professor Christopher Ricks, the art critic Marina Vaizey and me. I was seated next to Ricks, whom I had met once before, but so briefly that he did not recall it. He was two years older than me and had by this date established a reputation as an outstanding critic and scholar in the field of English Literature. He had been educated and later taught at Oxford, was appointed to a professorship at Bristol University at the age of thirty-five, and moved to Cambridge in 1975. As I mentioned in *QAGTTBB*, he had reviewed *Ginger, You're Barmy* sympathetically in 1962 in the *New Statesman*, but neither of us had reviewed the other's work since then, perhaps because, as regards criticism, his interest was focused mainly on poetry and mine on prose fiction. I was aware however that he was hostile to the growing influence of structuralist and poststructuralist criticism on literary studies, and that he would probably disapprove of my attempt in *The Modes of Modern Writing* to combine some of those methods and concepts with the kind of interpretative close reading of texts typical of the British and American New Criticism, of which he was a brilliant exponent. Ricks also had the reputation of being emotionally volatile. Our conversation on the journey was sparse and somewhat wary, and I can recall only one thing he said, at its outset. As the DC10's engines rose to a high pitch at the end of the Gatwick runway, straining against the brakes, and the plane suddenly surged forward to take off, he said: 'I love this moment – the sheer power – like a punch in the small of the back', a phrase I used later in *Small World*. Marina, seated on the other side of the aisle, was jollier and I was glad of her company on the long journey, which entailed a stop at Bangor, Maine to refuel and clear immigration, and a change of planes at Los Angeles to get to San Francisco. At the end of the day I fell gratefully into bed, in a luxurious room in the Mark Hopkins Hotel overlooking the Bay.

I had negotiated eight days' leave from Birmingham, from Tuesday 30th October to Tuesday 6th November. Wednesday was for long-distance travellers to recover and be entertained by the hosts. The Symposium was held on the Thursday and Friday. To justify the length of my absence in term-time I had arranged to give a talk or reading at Berkeley on the Monday, so that I could make a flying visit to Eileen in Honolulu at the weekend. On the day after my arrival I walked into the first travel agency I found and booked flights. Then I took a stroll to remind myself, after a ten-year absence, of the civilised ambience of San Francisco, and later mingled with the other conferees in and around the Mark Hopkins. It was an interesting gathering, with other Brits besides the Laker-sponsored trio. The most famous of them was Alistair Cooke, whose weekly *Letter from America* was probably the longest-running talk programme ever broadcast by the BBC. Among the distinguished academics was Randolph Quirk, who had been a lecturer at University College London when I was an undergraduate, and was now Quain Professor there, and Director of a ground-breaking Survey of English Usage. Christopher and Lenny, as editors, moderated most of the panel discussions, and the former began the opening session, entitled 'Where Is Our Language Going? Are We Getting It Right?' provocatively by circulating Philip Larkin's poem 'This Be The Verse', with its decorum-busting first line, '*They fuck you up, your mum and dad*', less familiar and more shocking to some Americans in the audience than to the Brits.

One of the American participants, John Simon, a drama and film critic based in New York, commented: 'I don't give a flying fuck whether people speak in the right tone, but I do care about grammar and syntax.' He quickly established himself as the Symposium's prime defender of 'correct English', a concept rejected by most modern linguists like Quirk, who regard change in living languages as inevitable and unstoppable. One of the cherished causes of linguistic conservatives is to preserve the distinction between *disinterested* (meaning objective, unbiased) and *uninterested* (meaning not interested). In common speech and increasingly in writing the former word is often used as if it were synonymous with the latter. In his contribution to the closing session of the Symposium, Randolph Quirk said the attempt to preserve *disinterested* as a term of approval was bound to fail because English words beginning with the prefix *dis* were always emotively negative, and to prove his point he recited a long list – '*dislike, disapprove, disappoint, distress, disgust,*' etc. John Simon, who was on the panel, said: 'Looking at the woman I love in the audience, I think of one of the most beautiful words in the English language: *disrobe.*' For perhaps the only time in his life, Randolph could think of no effective riposte, and stared blankly ahead as the audience erupted in laughter and applause.

When Lenny first wrote to me about contributing to *The State of the Language* he asked me if I knew that Stanley Fish, who had first brought us together at Berkeley in 1969, had recently split up with his wife, Adrienne, and was now living with another woman. I didn't know, and was surprised and sorry, as one usually is when it happens to friends, but in this case with an extra twist that only novelists experience. I had created the character of Morris Zapp partly out of certain attributes of Stanley recognisable to all who knew him, but I invented a fictional history for Zapp which had no parallels in the life of Fish, one of them being a matrimonial breach between Morris and his wife Desirée, brought to a head by his infidelity with their babysitter. It is to disguise the humiliating separation demanded by Desirée that Morris Zapp, to the surprise of his American colleagues, agrees to exile himself for six months to unfashionable Rummidge University on an exchange scheme. But now there *was* a parallel between the lives of Stanley and Adrienne Fish and Morris and Desirée Zapp. Life had imitated art. I felt uncomfortable about this coincidence, fearing that some readers of the novel familiar with its source material would infer that I had consciously anticipated the breach between the Fishes, whereas it had always seemed to me that they were as firmly married as Mary and I.

It was less of a surprise that not long afterwards Lenny told me he had split up with his wife Priscilla, and was living with a young poet whom he had met when she was a student at a summer school where he was teaching. It had been obvious to Mary and me in Berkeley in 1969, when we saw a lot of Lenny and Priscilla, that there was considerable friction between them. Unlike Stanley and Adrienne they had always seemed antithetical types, Priscilla blonde, willowy, reserved and quietly spoken, Lenny dark, tense, mercurial, declamatory. In due course they divorced, sharing custody of their two boys, and Lenny married the poet, Brenda, though I did not meet her until 1981.


Glanced at on a small-scale map Honolulu did not look all that far from San Francisco, but the Pacific is a very big ocean and I discovered that it would be a five-hour flight. Looked at rationally, at least through British eyes, it was absurd to travel nearly five thousand miles there and back for a short weekend, but Eileen appreciated the effort, and flying then was much less of a hassle than it is now. It was the first of four visits I made to Hawaii between 1979 and 1990, and I will have more to say about the place later. On this occasion I did little more than talk to Eileen and let her show me something of Waikiki. She had a comfortable air-conditioned apartment with a pleasant outlook from its balcony, though she drew my attention to a lot that was being prepared for a high-rise building which would take light away from her. The apartment was about ten minutes from the beach, where she introduced me proudly to a little group of friends whom she joined there nearly every day. I was very conscious of being a kind of surrogate son to her, the son she never had and never would have. I had brought a pair of swimming trunks with me and enjoyed a dip in the warm, milky swell of the sea. In the evening she took me to her favourite Chinese restaurant where the tables were arranged on little platforms above ponds filled with water lilies and carp.

We talked incessantly, about family, about John's death and Mum's illness, about her past life, about my career, about her depression and its causes. It was a relief to her to express the anxieties which she concealed from her friends. The imminent construction of the high-rise building next to hers was an ominous sign of the growing property boom in Waikiki, and she knew it was only a matter of time before her rent would be increased beyond her means. The thought of having to find a cheaper apartment, probably in some less attractive location, filled her with panic. I suggested that she should start looking at possible alternatives now, before the matter became urgent, and I offered to give her some financial help myself. She resisted the idea at first, but I pointed out that she had told me I was the only legatee of her will, so that unless she died a pauper it would be a kind of loan, and later I made covenanted contributions to her income.

Eileen wrote to me after I got back home, thanking me for making the effort to spend just thirty-six hours with her, adding: '*And thank you Mary, too, for encouraging David to do so.*' I was glad to show this to Mary, for I felt spasms of guilt at having had a year full of such interesting travel without her, even though she didn't like flying and I usually had to persuade her to accompany me when opportunities arose.

# 6

A few days after my return home from Hawaii, the proofs of *How Far Can You Go?* arrived in the post, always an eagerly awaited and slightly anxious event in an author's life. So much of the act of writing consists of reading, and re-reading, what one has written, trying to read it as if one had not written it in order to assess its effectiveness, and then revising it if that seems appropriate. The gaps between the various stages of a book's production assist this process. Each change in the physical appearance of a text – from handwritten manuscript to typescript, from typescript to printed proof, and from that to the first finished copy of the bound book – defamiliarises the text to some degree for the writer, and allows him or her to see previously unperceived flaws to be remedied and new possibilities for improvement, until the last stage – the first printed and bound edition – when it is too late to change anything.

That is a simplified description of the physical evolution of a book as it was in the pre-computer age. When my early novels were published I received galley proofs before page proofs – long strips of paper which the writer could emend substantially without creating problems for the printers. For James Joyce this was an essential part of the creative process, and he was notorious for making innumerable changes and additions to the texts of *Ulysses* and *Finnegans Wake* while they were in galleys. But fairly early in my own career publishers began to skip the galley proof stage and set the author's typescript (usually still termed the manuscript or 'MS') immediately in page proofs, which meant that extensive additions and deletions could upset the pagination and be expensive to incorporate. Publishers' contracts usually specify the percentage of emendations, excluding printers' errors, above which the author must bear the cost. The page proofs of a novel by a friend of mine contained a long paragraph which had been printed twice by mistake and he was begged to compose a passage of entirely superfluous description exactly long enough to fill the space left when the duplicate paragraph was deleted. Nowadays with computer software a writer can effortlessly produce the simulacrum of a printed book from the very first draft, and much of the defamiliarising effect of the traditional process has been lost, though that advantage is greatly outweighed by the physical ease of editing and revising text on a computer. And there is a real difference, which assists revision, between reading text on a screen and reading it on pages of A4. For me, and I imagine for other authors who are not still wedded to their pens and/or typewriters, writing now consists of putting words on a screen, printing them out, reading them, making emendations, deletions and additions, and returning the revised text to the screen for, in due course, further reworking. I use a lot of paper.

Another way for an author to measure the effectiveness of work in progress is to show it to others and invite comments. I never did this until much later in my career, and then very rarely, fearing that I would get different or contradictory reactions which would disturb and distract rather than help me in continuing with the book. But it is undoubtedly a strain to be the only reader of a novel in progress, often for years, when you are longing to get some reaction to it. Mary was always the first to read my novels when they were finished, and before I sent them to agent and publisher. We had an agreement that she could veto anything to which she strongly objected, but she never invoked it. This didn't stop her from making critical observations, which I took seriously and often acted on. The spouses of novelists can easily become the object of intrusive and prurient interest from readers, but Mary had a forceful way of dealing with comments from those who assumed, because some elements in a novel are probably auto-biographical in origin, that everything in it must be. I remember someone at a party getting a crushing response when he said to her, 'I did enjoy that bit in *The British Museum is Falling Down* where you dried David's underpants under the grill.' It was an incident which I had in fact pinched from someone else's life, mentioned in a newspaper or magazine. The man at the party wrote to me later saying, 'I enjoyed meeting your wife. She bites.' *How Far Can You Go?* contained more material with analogues in our own lives and friends' and relatives' lives than the earlier novel, and I was a little apprehensive when I finished it and gave it to her to read. She didn't really like it – mainly, I think, because of the ironic perspective in which it viewed Catholicism – but she didn't find fault with it as a novel.

My agent Graham Watson, who was the next person to read the manuscript, in May 1979, didn't like it much either, mainly because of my metafictional authorial asides. He wrote a chilly letter in which the only positive sentence was the first, 'You have had a good go at the Pope', and he continued: 'I am sure you are wrong in your personal interpolations. I think there is a certain element even of arrogance in referring back directly to your earlier novels.' Fortunately for my morale my publishers were enthusiastic. John Blackwell said it was 'brilliant' and

Tom Rosenthal wrote me a long letter to warm any writer's heart. 'It is a dazzling performance . . . a tour de force . . .' I valued his praise all the more because he wrote 'as not only a non-Catholic, but as someone who has a fairly jaundiced view about all religions'. To make the recent history of the Catholic Church interesting to non-Catholics of all kinds (Tom himself was a secular Jew) had always been to me the primary challenge of this novel.

Later that summer Graham told me that he was going to retire soon and proposed to hand me over to another agent at Curtis Brown, Mike Shaw, whom I did not know. Mike took me to lunch and congratulated me on the new novel, which he had read with interest and appreciation sharpened by the fact that he was an active member of the Church of England, which had been experiencing moral and theological controversies analogous to those in the Catholic Church over the same period. Thus began a professional association which lasted till Mike's retirement twenty-four years later, and a friendship with him and his wife Marian which continued after it. As his retirement party witnessed, he was greatly cherished by all his clients for his personal warmth and cheerfulness and his understanding of the neurotic anxieties of authors, as well as his professional skill in negotiations with publishers. Graham had always done his best for me according to his lights, and I was fortunate to be represented by the senior director of the agency, but he didn't really understand my commitment to a twin career as academic and novelist, or appreciate that the security of the first occupation freed me to take artistic risks in the second. He probably felt justified in his opinion of *How Far Can You Go?* when it was rejected in turn by four American publishers to whom he submitted it, but when the UK paperback rights were sold to Penguin before publication for what was considered a good advance his attitude warmed and he wrote to say he was looking forward to reading the finished book 'for pleasure'. He received the news about the Penguin sale when lunching with Tom Rosenthal, whose enthusiasm no doubt had something to do with this change of heart. The leisurely and bibulous publisher's lunch is an institution that has fallen into disfavour since the financial crises of the twenty-first century, but it had its uses. Tom also entertained Bernard Levin, then the lead fiction reviewer of the *Sunday Times*, to lunch before *How Far Can You Go?* was published, and in due course the newspaper carried a glowing review by Levin of a novel which might not otherwise have attracted his attention. Tom had the reputation of being rather parsimonious with advances, but he was generous with his time and energy in promoting his authors.

Another piece of luck was that a former tutorial student of mine, John Archer, who was working in BBC television at this time, was given a new series called *The Book Programme* to produce, in the first of which he featured *How Far Can You Go?* shortly after it was published. John had been an undergraduate in the Birmingham English Department in the early 1970s, a tall, curly-haired lad from rural Warwickshire, with a laid-back manner and an engaging smile, who managed to convey his appreciation of my teaching without the least tincture of fawning. One evening he phoned me up at home and invited me to come round to his bedsit in Moseley to listen to an LP he had just acquired, The Who's *Quadrophenia*. He was entranced by it and thought I should hear it. Even in the relaxed relations between staff and students that had developed since the sixties this was quite a surprising invitation, but I accepted and drove round to his bedsit. I had probably mentioned to him my interest in jazz and vocal music in the folk-blues tradition, and he wanted to introduce me to the latest thing in rock. I listened to the album with interest (though I enjoyed Pink Floyd's *Dark Side of the Moon*, which he also played for me, rather more) and was grateful for the initiation. Now he was proposing to do me a much bigger favour.

\*

Thirty-odd years later I had scant memories of this TV programme, except that the other participants were Joseph Heller, author of *Catch-22*, Margaret Drabble and Malcolm Bradbury. But I was still occasionally in touch with John Archer, who had moved to Scotland to work in television and more recently in documentary filmmaking, and was now running a small production company called Hopscotch, so I asked him if he could refresh my memory of the occasion and its format. This he was glad to do. Each instalment of *The Book Programme* focused on a different literary genre, starting with the Novel, and the participants discussed it with reference to their own recent work. *How Far Can You Go?* and Heller's novel *Good as Gold*, just out in paperback in the UK, were the two books under review in our programme. Margaret Drabble and Malcolm were there to give their views on each of these novels respectively, before all four of us engaged in a general discussion of the novel as a form and our own practice. The presenter was Robert Robinson, a familiar figure on television in this role. As well as giving me this information, John mentioned that he could probably obtain a DVD of the original recording from the BBC's archive. I begged him to try, and it arrived not long afterwards.

Viewing it was an extraordinary experience. I have often been surprised to read in interviews with well-known actors that they never watch their early work in films or TV drama, but now I understand. It is disconcerting suddenly to see yourself as you were at a distant time in the past – in my own case thirty-five years previously – not in a still photograph, but breathing, gesturing, speaking. I never possessed a film camera or camcorder, and if I had I would have been behind it, not in front of it, so there is no home-movie footage of myself. The televised programme was an authentic fragment of the life that I have been painstakingly trying to describe in words in this book and its predecessor, and viewing it brought back in detail an event of which I had only a hazy memory. It began with a wide shot of the five of us sitting in an arc with me in the middle, followed by Robert Robinson speaking to camera about the device of deliberately pointing out the fictionality of events in *How Far Can You Go?* – for example, the accidental death of a young child of one of the married couples in the story – which I had described in a manner to make them seem real and appropriately moving. Why would a novelist deliberately break the illusion he had created, Robinson asked. Instead of seeking my answer at once, he observed that Joseph Heller did the same sort of thing in *Good as Gold* and invited Malcolm to comment on that book, to which Heller replied. So far I had not said a word, and was reduced to looking thoughtful in the occasional shots that appeared on the screen, but these were hypnotically interesting to me.

I was then aged forty-five, but looked considerably younger, partly due to the luck of the genetic draw from both sides of my family, and partly no doubt to the BBC's make-up department. I was wearing a fawn corduroy suit from Austin Reed, and a Beatles hairstyle, a helmet of fine hair combed forward over brow and ears, and my features seemed eerily smooth and well-fleshed, free of the flaws and blemishes that I now see every morning in the shaving mirror: the scars of a tricky operation to remove a basal cell skin cancer from one of my nostrils, age-spots and defunct pimples, the thinning of my lips and the way they turn down at each side of the mouth to become furrows in the cheeks reaching almost to the jawline. Except for reading I did not need glasses in 1980, which allowed my eyes to add expression to my words when I eventually spoke; and I spoke rather well, it seemed to me, with very few of the 'erm's' and 'I think's' which punctuate the interviews that I give these days. Also, it appeared that I was not yet suffering from significant hearing loss, with none of the anxiety that tends to show on the faces of people thus afflicted, as they strain to hear something of importance in a conversation.

Margaret Drabble, only four years younger than me, also looked amazingly youthful on the programme, sitting erect on her swivel chair, radiating health and vigour and confidence in a simple but elegant blue dress. I had not met her before, but I had written a distinctly tart review of her generally well received debut novel, *A Summer Bird-Cage*, published in 1963 when she was in her early twenties. In due course she became a friend whom I called 'Maggie', but neither of us ever referred to this review and I often wondered whether she had forgiven me or had forgotten it or not even noticed it. Anyway she had every reason to disregard it, having published seven more novels by 1980, including *The Millstone* which was one of the seminal feminist novels of the period. She briskly summarised *How Far Can You Go?*, said that it contained a lot about sex in the lives of the characters and not much about their work, but was clever and cool and often very funny. Joseph Heller, by far the oldest of the writers, with a mop of grey curls, responded to the first point by saying that for the protagonists of his last two novels sex *was* work.

Some interesting differences in attitude and practice emerged between us four novelists. I spoke about the way the form one chose to embody a novel's basic idea would determine the content to a considerable extent. Margaret portrayed herself as an instinctive writer, who avoided self-consciousness about technique, and made up alternative fictional versions of the life she was leading herself, so that the action of the novels tended to have the same time span as they took to write. Heller said he had only had three ideas for a novel in his life, and had written one about each of them. Malcolm said it took him as much as ten years to write a novel, citing *The History Man* as an example, and that his own depression at that period of his life had given the novel its disillusioned tone – at which point he turned to me and said, 'like the treatment of sex in your novel – you make sex seem as depressing as the Black Death'. The others chuckled, but the camera caught me reacting with a jerk of the shoulders, as if stung – which was how I felt. It was true that I described the disappointments, frustrations and absurdities in the sexual lives of my characters, caused for most of them by their Catholicism, but it seemed an unduly gloomy reading of my book. Shortly afterwards, however, Malcolm wrote me a letter which mended matters between us:

> I was feeling particularly low and miserable that day, as I largely have since getting back from China, which I found a rather amputating experience. I'm sorry about the remark about the Black Death. I wanted on the one hand to say something amusing, feeling the programme was getting a bit over-solemn; I was also trying to get through to a discussion about the treatment of sexuality in your book and in modern writing which somehow couldn't get through the chat. I thought your performance was excellent and very strong, like the book itself.

Malcolm had been on a British Council tour in a China which was still recovering from the repressive regime of Chairman Mao. It entailed long journeys by train on which he was accompanied by an interpreter-guide, and it particularly troubled him that this person had to sleep and eat in appalling conditions while he himself enjoyed luxurious but lonely accommodation in first class. 'An amputating experience' is a characteristically vivid phrase which I never forgot.

In the summer of the previous year we had both been involved in another British Council enterprise: a seminar which every summer brought together a select group of about fifty foreign academics, writers, journalists and publishers in a Cambridge college for one week in July, listening to and questioning an impressive procession of British novelists, poets and playwrights, who gave readings from their work and answered questions about it. Malcolm chaired the event that year and continued to do so for many years afterwards, during which time I participated in most of them. On that first occasion I read from the opening pages of *How Far Can You Go?*, which I had just finished writing. It was the first time I read from my work to a sizeable audience, and it was a challenging one. A number of the auditors, probably from more conservative cultures, were uncomfortable with the text's explicit references to subjects like masturbation, and to its ironic treatment of religion, though others were impressed and amused. In future I was more careful in choosing what to read and often edited the text for the purpose. Poetry readings had been around for a long time, but it was only in the 1980s that public readings by novelists became common in bookshops and at literary festivals. It was part of a revolution in the promotion, circulation and reception of literary fiction that had many other constituents, the most important of which was probably the Booker Prize.

The invention of the Booker Prize, awarded to the best novel of the year by a British, Irish or Commonwealth writer, is usually credited to the publisher Tom Maschler, senior editor at Cape, who proposed that Britain should have something like the prestigious French Prix Goncourt, which had been going since the beginning of the century, to stimulate public interest in new literary fiction. The two prizes are however quite different in organisation. The Goncourt is awarded by a standing committee of academicians, and is widely suspected of favouring a few Parisian publishers who publish the work of several of them, whereas the Booker has a new panel of judges each year, which gives protection against corruption but makes for erratic and controversial verdicts. The

Goncourt is worth a paltry nominal sum but the winner is sure of enormous sales. The Booker's sponsor was a large company with many financial and commercial interests and a conveniently appropriate name, which began by providing a cash prize of £5,000 for the winner and steadily increased this sum to keep pace with inflation and the growing prestige of the prize. (It now stands, with a different sponsor, at £50,000.) The Booker judges issued a shortlist of six candidates several weeks before the winner was announced, when each of the unsuccessful writers received a small monetary prize as well as benefiting from the associated publicity. The Booker Prize had an uncertain start but in the course of the 1970s it gradually attracted more attention, mainly on account of controversies associated with it (as when John Berger donated half of his prize to the Black Panthers), and established itself as a feature of the British literary scene. But it didn't make its winners rich and famous until the 1980s.

Up till then the judges had secretly decided on the winner at the same time as they issued the shortlist, and there was always a risk that the result would leak out; but in 1980 they met again to choose the winner on the day scheduled for the announcement, which was made at a black-tie banquet in the Guildhall. The change of procedure made bookmakers willing to take bets on the outcome, and this generated great media interest even though a comparatively small amount of money was actually wagered. When you have 'favourites' and 'outsiders' a literary prize becomes a horse race and a drama. In 1980 the shortlist included two titans of contemporary British fiction, William Golding and Anthony Burgess, and the competition between them attracted a lot of media attention and public interest. Golding, who attended the banquet, was awarded the prize for *Rites of Passage*; Burgess, who was waiting at the Savoy Hotel in evening dress to accept it for *Earthly Powers*, if summoned, was disappointed.

*How Far Can You Go?* was published in late April of that year and was widely reviewed, mostly favourably, sometimes very favourably, and often at considerable length. Inevitably it crossed my mind that it might be a contender for the Booker shortlist (in those days there was no longlist) but I wasn't surprised or more than fleetingly disappointed when it was passed over. What was a surprise, and a very gratifying one, was a telephone call from Tom Rosenthal, shortly after the Booker reached its climax in October, to tell me that I had won the Whitbread Best Novel Prize, to which I had given no thought at all. Sponsored by the eponymous family-owned brewing company, the Whitbread was founded a few years after the Booker and on a more modest scale. At this time it offered three awards, for best novel, best biography and best children's book of the year, each worth £2,500. The judges in 1980 were Nicholas Bagnall, literary editor of the *Daily Telegraph*, John Rae, author of children's books and one-time Head of Westminster School, and Penelope Mortimer, novelist, journalist and ex-wife of the celebrated writer and barrister John Mortimer.

It so happened that in 1980 the organisers, no doubt imitating the competitive element of the Booker, decided to add a higher level to the prize: one of the three category winners would be nominated 'Whitbread Book of the Year', to which an additional prize of £2,500 was attached. When I discovered what the other books in contention were, I felt, without having read them, that I had a decent chance of winning it. One was David Newsome's biography of the Edwardian don and man of letters A.C. Benson, based on his copious diaries, which though highly praised by reviewers seemed a subject of limited appeal. The other was *John Diamond*, a novel for young readers by Leon Garfield. He had already won many prizes with books of this kind but it seemed to me that the genre placed a writer at a disadvantage in competing for a general literary prize. All three of us were asked to keep the information of our involvement confidential until the prizes were announced. John Blackwell wrote a characteristic letter of congratulation: 'I'm inexpressibly pleased by the news whereof we may not yet speak . . . This is exactly the wrong time, of course, to remind you of the fine spoonerism attributed to Rachael Heyhoe-Flint – "Titbread's Wankard".

The prizes were awarded, not at a black-tie banquet in the Guildhall, but at a luncheon in the comfortably furnished cellars of the Whitbread brewery in the City of London, on Tuesday 11th November. Mary, who was now a teacher-counsellor at Blessed Humphrey Middlemore school, was not able to accompany me to the event because she had a high-priority engagement there on the appointed day. Happily I was able to invite Dad to be my guest in her stead. He was in need of such a break: looking after Mum was becoming more and more demanding, and at the same time his mother, my beloved Nana, relapsed into a worse mental state than before, and had to be hospitalised again. The Whitbread presentation was a great treat for Dad, and if he had been in the habit of dining out he could have done so later on the story of how the chairman of the company, Mr Samuel Whitbread, drew him a tankard of the brewery's best draught bitter before lunch. At the meal Dad sat between me and Tom Rosenthal, who relished his reminiscences of the music business and always asked me about him afterwards. I already knew I had won the Book of the Year award, for a photographer had told me discreetly at the press conference which preceded the lunch, but I kept the information to myself and enjoyed the food. When it was my turn to say a few words on receiving the prize, I said it was the high point of my writing career to date, and I meant it.

Afterwards I met Penelope Mortimer and thanked her for choosing my book as best novel and Book of the Year. I discovered to my surprise that she was appointed sole judge of the latter. What I knew of her and her work, which was not a great deal, made her enthusiasm for *How Far Can You Go?* also surprising. She was well known, via the media and her transparently autobiographical novel *The Pumpkin Eater*, for her stormy marriage with John Mortimer, which began when she was pregnant by her previous, recently divorced husband, and produced several other offspring before they divorced in 1971. I wondered that she was able to empathise with the burdened consciences of my earnest Catholic characters, but she said in the printed statement which each of the judges issued to explain their decisions: 'The novel I hoped to find had to teach me something about contemporary life that I didn't already know, and be thoroughly entertaining in the process . . . David Lodge's novel achieved all this and a great deal more . . . With this ambitious, compassionate and supremely readable novel he moves into the big league.'

I kept in touch with Penelope after the prize-giving, and she invited us to dinner that summer in her cottage in the Cotswolds near Moreton in Marsh. When we arrived on a bright sunny evening she was working in the fine garden, ablaze with flowers, which we discovered was her own creation and principal pastime. But the dinner was already prepared, and a bottle of Sancerre chilled. (It was my introduction to this esteemed dry white – at home in those days we drank a cheap medium-dry plonk made in Austria but bearing a French name, Hirondelle.) Penelope was then about sixty, and the stresses of her life had left their traces on her striking and much-photographed features. I had enjoyed John Mortimer's dramatic work on stage and television since the 1950s, when Mary and I saw his very first play *Dock Brief*, and would have been inclined to prompt Penelope's views on this aspect of his career if she had made any reference to their marriage, but she didn't give me that opportunity. She did however mention being visited regularly by her grown-up children, including a daughter who had a young Down's child, and I had little doubt, as she spoke about this grandchild, that it was a factor in her very positive response to *How Far Can You Go?*, which treated that subject in one of its plot-strands.

In her prime Penelope had been a very successful novelist and short-story writer, and one of the few British authors regularly published in the high-paying *New Yorker*, but at the time when we met her she seemed to be rather anxious about her income

109

from writing. She had a new novel in progress, but confided that she would probably accept a commission to write a book on a surprising subject, the Queen Mother, because she needed the money. The novel, her last, appeared in 1983. Entitled *The Handyman*, it was a deft fictional synthesis of her own present situation and past reputation, about a conventional sixty-year-old woman suddenly widowed, who retires to the country and encounters a number of seriocomic challenges involving the eponymous handyman and a neighbour who is a once-famous woman novelist with an outrageous past. I didn't read the Queen Mother book but was not surprised to learn that it caused some consternation to her publishers when she delivered it, and controversy when it appeared, but it evidently made a refreshing change from the usual sycophantic royal biography, as one would have expected. Although we saw Penelope again, giving her a meal when she was in Birmingham, both parties let the connection go eventually, mutually aware perhaps that we didn't have enough in common to sustain a real friendship, but I remained immensely grateful to her for giving an invaluable boost to my career as a novelist. She left the Cotswold cottage eventually and spent the last years of her life in London in a small house with a smaller garden, well looked after by her large family, according to her agent Giles Gordon, who wrote an evocative obituary in the *Guardian* when she died in 1999.

At the end of the proceedings in the Whitbread cellars, Dad and I were driven in a limousine to London Bridge station to take the train to Brockley. It was a dull, chilly November afternoon and almost dark by the time we reached Millmark Grove, but our spirits were still warmed by my success and the hospitality we had received. We looked forward to telling Mum all about it. There were however no lights on in number 81 as we approached, nor when Dad opened the front door. We found Mum cowering in her usual upright armchair in the small living room at the back of the house, visible only by the light coming in through the French windows from the streetlamps above the back garden fence. When Dad switched on the ceiling light and she saw us she blinked and gave a feeble smile, but could not explain why she was sitting in the half-dark. Dad had arranged for somebody to come into the house and sit with her for a few hours, but they had evidently had to leave before we returned. I was shocked by how much her condition had worsened since I had last seen her. Her arms were pitifully thin and her hands trembled, but she also seemed mentally confused, unable to take in what we told her about the prize-giving. After a while she rallied somewhat, but in those first few moments I realised her condition was now very serious. It was a sad end to a day of celebration.

I went back to Birmingham later that evening. The next day the *Guardian* and other newspapers carried the story of the prize, and soon messages of congratulation began to arrive, with a less enthusiastic one from my daughter Julia, now studying Biology at Southampton University, who liked to conceal her connection with me and my novels as much as possible. Fortunately I had just sent her a cheque. 'It almost makes up for you getting your name in the paper and drawing attention to yourself again,' she wrote. One of the longest and liveliest of these epistles was from Barbara Wall, the mother of Bernard Bergonzi's wife Gabriel, and of Gabriel's sister Bernadine, members of a very literary Catholic family mentioned in *QAGTTBB*. Bernard and Gabriel, living in Warwick where Bernard taught at the University, were good friends whom we saw regularly for Sunday lunch at one house or the other, and through them we met Barbara, who was a delightful person and, writing under her maiden name of Barbara Lucas, a skilful exponent of the English novel of middle-class manners with a Catholic slant. She happened to hear the news of the prize on the BBC radio arts programme *Kaleidoscope*, which carried an interview with me recorded after the lunch, and wrote next day:

All your couples were a generation younger than me,
but far more scrupulously worried about contraception
than were Bernard (my Bernard, Bernard Wall) and
me. We used French letters, as we called them in our
old-fashioned way, after our first two had been born.
Bernard didn't think this was wrong (at least I don't
think he did – after all Coventry was being coventrated
[sic] and bigger sins were being committed in Europe as
a whole, not I admit, that this exculpates the individual)
but I in a funny kind of way did, so went to confession
for us both. But the thing about Bernard and me is that
we used to talk about GOD the whole time, whereas
your chaps don't seem to worry much about God and
trying to be holy (pace Angela, I think she does . . .).
I do congratulate you from the bottom of my heart.
Each character is so vivid, and the whole Zeitgeist so
brilliantly portrayed. The only chap who's absent one
feels, is God, except with Angela, Angela is holy.

This strikes me now, reading it again some thirty-five years later,
as a very interesting and shrewd comment on the novel. The
different attitudes regarding birth control Barbara described,
between Catholics of her class and generation and mine and
Mary's, was illuminating. But she had also discerned what I was
only dimly becoming aware of: that I was not innately spiritual,
that my faith was the product first of conditioning, and then of an
intellectual and philosophical commitment, and when the foundations of the latter came to seem increasingly rickety, the faith
began to drain away.

I received many letters from Catholic readers of my own generation endorsing the representative accuracy of my fictional story.
One lady, writing from Tunbridge Wells in 1981, listed twenty-
three separate events or situations in the novel which corresponded
to things which had happened to her or members of her immediate

family. She concluded, 'Your book will be of tremendous historical importance, to show what it *was* really like.' The Jesuit Rector of the Catholic University of Leuven in Belgium, whom I had met when judging a doctoral dissertation there, reviewed the novel in a Dutch newspaper, and wrote to me personally to say that the chapter which dealt in an almost essayistic way with the *Humanae Vitae* controversy was the best thing he had read on the subject. But some conservative Catholics were displeased.

A few years after the novel's publication I received a letter from Chris Walsh, a lecturer in the English Department of St Mary's College, Twickenham, a Catholic college of education affiliated to London University which is now a university in its own right. He declared himself a fan of my work, and asked if I would give a talk to the students at St Mary's and allow him to interview me for the college literary magazine, *Strawberry Fair*. He enclosed a specimen copy which impressed me with its quality and the distinction of some of the extramural contributors. I often heard references to St Mary's in Catholic circles, and knew that it occupied the neo-Gothic castle which Horace Walpole, author of *The Castle of Otranto*, had built for himself, but I had never visited it, and took this opportunity to do so. Chris Walsh was a congenial host and skilful interviewer, and when I read the published transcript I thought it was the best interview I had given up to that point in time. After the tape recorder was turned off, Chris told me that *How Far Can You Go?* was a set text in a course on contemporary British fiction at the college, and very popular with the students; but the father of one of them had got hold of the novel and been very shocked that his daughter was required to read such a heterodox and sexually explicit book at a Catholic institution. He made a formal complaint to the college, demanding that the book be withdrawn from the curriculum; and when this was politely refused he took his case to the Cardinal Archbishop of the Westminster diocese, Basil Hume, who to his great credit declined to anathematise my novel. The father subsequently withdrew his daughter from the college.

# 7

For Dad, the excitement of the Whitbread Prize presentation must have seemed as fleeting as the apparition of a shooting star on a black night. At the turn of the year the two most important women in his life were both seriously ill. Nana had been moved to Bethlem Royal Hospital, a mental hospital that was historically descended from the notorious Bedlam lunatic asylum, but now affiliated to the Maudsley and King's College hospitals and situated in West Wickham on the southern rim of London. I visited her there twice, accompanied by Mary on the first occasion. She was in bed, propped up with pillows, looking frail but calm and pleased to see us, though she responded only to me, and Mary was doubtful whether Nana had recognised her. I made the second visit in January on my own and it was a poignant and distressing experience. I thought she recognised me, but the smile that used to light up her face when she greeted me did not appear, and conversation was difficult. Reports about how our children were doing, which had always aroused her interest in the past, made no impression. She rambled and groaned and sighed and shook her head at any suggestion that she would get better.

The hospital staff told me she was suffering from an intestinal problem as well as severe depression, but they did not propose any surgical intervention for the former. It seemed to me that Nana had clearly had enough of life and wanted only to die, as she did not long afterwards – peacefully, we were glad to hear from the hospital – on the 20th of January, at the age of ninety-two.

She was a lady of innate human goodness, whom I loved as a child and in adulthood, and it saddened me that, having lived a long and challenging life with admirable resilience, she should have suffered mental illness at the end of it. This feeling was not relieved by her funeral, which was a dismal affair, on a damp, cold January day. There were few mourners – the faithful Hilda and Stan of course, and a handful of other relatives of Nana's – and I remember very little about the occasion except that the Honor Oak Crematorium did its best to add to the gloom. It was never lovely to look upon, and at that time a strike of municipal workers was affecting maintenance, so the precinct of the chapel was littered with rotting wreaths and bunches of decaying flowers from previous funerals because there was no one available to clear them away.

Not long afterwards Mum took a turn for the worse, and was admitted to the Maudsley again, where they diagnosed that she now had pneumonia. In fact she nearly died, but she survived the crisis and remained in a stable but fragile condition. She was in good hands, and it was a relief for Dad that he no longer had the responsibility of looking after her. I arranged for her to be visited by the Catholic chaplain to the hospital and to receive the sacrament that used to be called Extreme Unction but now, in the post-Vatican II era, the Sacrament of the Sick. I wrote to a friend at the beginning of March that it was not clear whether she would ever be able to return home, and later in the month I reported to Eileen that she seemed very weak and confused, and called me 'John', her dead brother's name. Some time ago I had arranged a complicated trip to America in mid-April, built around a short fellowship residency at Princeton University and entailing other lectures, meetings and visits in New York, Philadelphia, Baltimore, and Washington DC. Mary was invited to accompany me, and as the dates were mainly in the Easter holiday period she agreed to join me in Princeton. I had to tell all the people involved that my mother was gravely ill, and I might have to cancel the trip at short notice, which added an extra degree of anxiety to the situation.

On the 24th of March, not long after I had sent this message to the appropriate persons in America, Dad phoned to tell me, his voice husky with emotion, that Mum had died quite suddenly. I went immediately to London to consult with him about the funeral, and then to the Maudsley, where I had my last sight of my mother, laid out in a chill, dimly lit room in the basement. I was alone, and in the presence of a dead person for the first time in my life. She looked like a carved effigy of herself on the top of a tomb: the phrase 'the breath of life' acquired a new meaningfulness from its total absence. Her features, once so comely, were hollow and shrunken, the skin stretched tight over the bone. I stooped to kiss her forehead and its touch on my lips was as cold and unyielding as marble. What other thoughts went through my head I cannot recall. I did not weep. I never do.

So there was another funeral, which I helped Dad to organise, recruiting a priest from the parish church of St Mary Magdalene to officiate at the cremation. Honor Oak Crematorium had improved its appearance since Nana's funeral – the rotting wreaths and bouquets had been cleared up – but Julia, who accompanied us, was dismayed by the dreariness of the place and the minimal service. There were more mourners than on the previous occasion, but not a great many, because we had so few close relatives. Afterwards we had a reception in a private room at a local public house, and when the guests had departed, Mary and Julia and I went back to 81 Millmark Grove and stayed as long as we could with Dad before returning to Birmingham.

*

The ending of these two lives, so close together, saddened but did not depress me at the time, because I had so much else to occupy and distract me over the same period – not merely teaching duties, but commitments and developments in the wider world. John Archer had been sufficiently pleased with my contribution to *The Book Programme* to invite me to appear in January in the first of a new series he was producing, a regular review of recent television programmes called *Did You See?* Three guests with some expertise in the subject matter of one of the chosen programmes each led a discussion of it, after an illustrative clip had been shown, under the chairmanship of Ludovic Kennedy. He was a writer best known for books exposing miscarriages of justice, but also a skilful broadcaster with a personality perfectly suited to a talk show of this kind: relaxed and unassertive, setting his contributors at ease, but always intelligent and incisive in his comments and prompts. For my debut on this programme I had a stimulating combination of topics and fellow speakers. The other guests were Marina Vaizey, whom I knew from the 'State of the Language' symposium, reviewing a programme about Hieronymus Bosch, the fifteenth-century artist whose surrealist paintings of Heaven and Hell had fascinated me ever since I discovered them in youth; and Dr Anthony Clare, who would soon become famous for his BBC radio programme *In the Psychiatrist's Chair*, reviewing a documentary called *Facing Death*. I was asked to kick off the discussion of BBC2's four-part serial version of *The History Man*, about which I had plenty to say.

Because Malcolm wrote many TV screenplays later, people often assume that he must have adapted his own novel, but the BBC evidently didn't consider him sufficiently experienced at this stage to entrust him with the task. It was given to Christopher Hampton, a distinguished playwright as well as screenplay writer, who produced an excellent script that was very faithful to the original. But it wasn't a difficult task for him, because the novel itself is formally very like a film, consisting almost entirely of dialogue and objective impersonal description of people, places and things, with no access to what the characters are privately thinking and feeling such as novels usually provide. That is precisely what made Malcolm's novel so effective, since it required readers to make up their own minds about the motivation of the characters, especially the central one, the dynamic Marxist sociology lecturer at the new University of Watermouth, Howard Kirk, who believes his task is to forward the leftward march of history, a mission which also feeds his appetite for intrigue, control and sexual conquest.

*The History Man* was a TV hit, and attracted an enormous amount of media attention. The title became a proverbial phrase, and new applications and echoes of it (like Alan Bennett's *The History Boys*) continued to appear for many years afterwards. There were several reasons for the programme's great impact. Antony Sher, a little-known actor who had come to England from South Africa, was cast as Howard Kirk, initially to Malcolm's disappointment; but he seized the part, made it unforgettably his own and the springboard for a brilliant career. The serial also broke new ground for British television in the explicit representation of sex, not porn-style, but in a witty adult way, as when Kirk and his colleague Flora Beniform sit up in bed after intercourse, both naked except for Flora's horn-rimmed spectacles, open their diaries and try to find a slot in a busy term for their next assignation. Clive James, who was then reviewing television in the *Observer*, wondered whether it was right that men like himself should be permitted to feast their eyes on the opulent breasts of Isla Blair, who played Flora. The TV adaptation gave the novel a second lease of life and attracted many new readers, but the political climate had changed since it was written and first published in the early seventies. Then, it had satirised fashionable radical orthodoxies, but also exposed the weakness of liberal opposition to them; now it seemed to confirm all the prejudices of the Conservative Party triumphantly elected to government in 1979 under Margaret Thatcher. *The History Man* was frequently invoked in the media as evidence of the dangerous radicalisation of universities, and actually blamed later for the decline of sociology as a discipline. This reaction dismayed Malcolm, who respected sociology, disliked Thatcherism as much as militant Labour, and supported the SDP when it was formed in March 1981. The TV serial was set in the period of the original novel, with the appropriate clothes and furnishings, but it was not interpreted historically by most of the audience. It must also be said that Antony Sher's Howard Kirk was a totally amoral character, 'compulsively loathsome' in Ludovic Kennedy's words, whereas in the text there is an undercurrent of respect for his energy and intellect. It would seem that the producers had some misgivings about the serial's reception and tried to correct it by appending a footnote to the last episode, 'Howard Kirk Voted Conservative in the General Election of 1979', but that seemed highly implausible.

Meanwhile another conflict between radicalism and conservatism was being played out in the English Faculty of Cambridge University, in what came to be known as the 'MacCabe Affair'. I had met the chief protagonist, Colin MacCabe, at the Joyce Symposium in Zurich, as mentioned earlier, and subsequently reviewed his book *James Joyce and the Revolution of the Word* in an academic journal of small circulation called the *James Joyce Broadsheet*. It was a favourable review because I thought the book was a bold and original effort to bring the concepts of Continental poststructuralist criticism to bear on a key modern writer whose difficult work was usually taken as a challenge to traditional interpretative criticism. But such interpretation, MacCabe argued, tried to make the work conform to a notion of 'meaning' that it was precisely Joyce's aim to undermine. He was concerned 'not with representing experience through language, but with

119

experiencing language through a destruction of representation'. That was an aphoristic overstatement, but an interesting take on the later episodes of *Ulysses* and the whole of *Finnegans Wake*. In this way Joyce could be seen not as an art-for-art's-sake mandarin but a truly revolutionary writer. MacCabe had spent some time in Paris studying and listening to the stars of the French intelligentsia, and his intellectual interests were not exclusively literary, but embraced linguistics, politics, psychoanalysis and cinema, including contributions to the radical film journal *Screen*. He and some other young teachers in Cambridge, especially his friend Stephen Heath at Jesus College, who were similarly attracted by the new ideas about literature and culture emanating from Continental Europe, aimed to fertilise and invigorate from these sources the Cambridge English syllabus, which had not changed much since the days of I.A. Richards and F.R. Leavis.

In the academic year 1980–81 Colin MacCabe was a Fellow of King's College and in the last year of a five-year appointment as assistant lecturer in the University. It was the practice of the English Faculty to offer permanent positions to the best and brightest of the assistants at this stage, and to let the others go. Colin MacCabe's lectures were popular with students, and he had published a book and numerous articles. He was obviously a strong candidate for a permanent lectureship, but the committee delegated by the Faculty Board recommended that he should not be appointed to one of the few available. Such dubious decisions are not uncommon in academic life and there is no procedure to appeal against them, nor do they usually arouse interest outside the institution concerned. Colin could have continued teaching at Cambridge as a Fellow and waited until his case for a university appointment was irresistible. But in his view, and that of his supporters, his qualifications were demonstrably superior to those of the successful candidates, and he had been unjustly passed over by a Faculty Board numerically dominated by dyed-in-the-wool Leavisites and traditionalist scholars who were resistant to new ideas. Colin was of a combative disposition, and had several contacts in London journalism who knew how to generate public interest in the story he told them. Reports began to appear in the quality press about the dispute. A reading public which up till then had been bored or baffled by references to structuralism and poststructuralism and their impact on academia found the matter interesting when it was dramatised as a clash between personalities. Professor Christopher Ricks was cast as the leader of the anti-MacCabe faction, while Frank Kermode, who occupied the Edward VII Chair of English, was known to be sympathetic to MacCabe. This media exposure fanned the flames of controversy in Cambridge. Dons gave imprudent statements to the press, and libel writs were issued. Colin himself received one and counter-sued the complainant. The issue became national news, and then international news, as I myself witnessed.

When my review of Colin's book on Joyce was published in 1978 he had written to thank me warmly for it. Although I wasn't aware of his employment situation at the time, for him it was a valuable endorsement of his work from a respected source outside Cambridge, and from then onwards I was his friend. In the correspondence between us that followed he agreed to give a talk in the spring term of 1981 to the weekly seminar on new developments in Critical Theory which I ran, with the support of two colleagues, for postgraduates in the Birmingham English Department and interested students in some other departments. The appointed date was at a time when public interest in Colin's dispute with the Cambridge English Faculty reached a new peak. I was taking a tutorial while awaiting his arrival when the depart-mental secretary knocked on my door and, apologising for the interruption, said: '*Newsweek* is on the phone. They want to speak to Colin MacCabe.' *Newsweek!* I could hardly believe it: the reverberations of the MacCabe Affair had reached the other side of the Atlantic. When the protagonist himself arrived he was fizzing with the excitement and stress of his sudden fame. We put him up at home for the night, and Mary remembers him striding about with our phone pressed to his ear for much of the evening, chattering to his friends and media people about the latest developments. His talk at the seminar that afternoon – I think it was about the relevance of Plato to current thinking about language and representation, but I can't honestly remember – was probably not as coherent as it might have been, but that didn't matter. He was the man of the moment, and the room was packed with intent listeners. I preened myself a little on having brought him to Birmingham at that juncture.

At the eye of the storm was the English Faculty Board in Cambridge. Frank Kermode, who served on it *ex officio* but with no more power to affect the outcome of its deliberations than his single vote, gave a brief but eloquent account of what it was like at this time in the last chapter of his memoir, *Not Entitled* (1995). After much hesitation he had moved to Cambridge in 1973 from University College London where he was very happy, seduced as he admitted by the idea of capping his brilliant career by occupying the most prestigious Chair of English in the country, only to find that he had no power, no office and no secretarial assistance. At UCL he had chaired an open seminar for people interested in the new critical theories and practices, to which some of the most distinguished Parisian critics, including Roland Barthes, accepted invitations. He had been encouraged to think by some progressive members of the Cambridge English Faculty that it would be glad of his guidance in reforming their rickety syllabus, and dutifully set about this formidable task, but the conservative faction on the board persistently blocked his working party's proposals. When the MacCabe issue erupted, Frank inevitably became involved on Colin's side. He wrote later:

> It seemed to me plain that this man was being dealt
> with unjustly; against my will I was involved in a
> fight with opponents more determined than I. Useless

to recount all the complex manoeuvres, the dirty tricks,
the calculated rhetorical performances . . . It was not
. . . a lofty debate about rival literary theories, which
is how some students took it, and how the Sunday
papers mockingly reported it. It was certainly related
to the whole question of how literature should be
taught, especially in Cambridge; but intellectually the
disputation was feeble and rather disreputable, and the
argument ruthlessly *ad hominem*.

The affair generated so much acrimony and scandalous gossip
that eventually the University held an inquiry – known in its
own jargon as a 'Discussion', and chaired by the Vice-Chancellor
– into the state of the English Faculty, at which every member
of staff was entitled to speak. Its proceedings were recorded
verbatim in the University's *Gazette*. I obtained a copy from a
former Birmingham colleague who had moved to Cambridge,
and it is a fascinating read, a credit to the University's openness
to public scrutiny, but not flattering to one of its key departments. Needless to say the whole saga reinforced a conviction I
had long held, that my decision not to pursue an appointment
at Cambridge for which I had been invited to apply in 1967,
plunging me into obsessive regret for many months afterwards,
had been absolutely right.

The result of the Discussion was that a high-level committee
was formed to review the decision not to appoint Colin MacCabe,
which concluded that no miscarriage of justice had taken place.
So his enemies had won, but it was a pyrrhic victory. The English
Faculty was like a battlefield strewn with corpses, from which the
wounded of both sides limped away. Kermode resigned from his
chair and became a freelance critic and lecturer, Stephen Heath
emigrated to America, and Christopher Ricks soon went to America
too, though he cited domestic reasons for the move. As to the *casus
belli* himself, Colin MacCabe very soon became Professor and Head

of the Department of English at the new University of Strathclyde in Scotland, the youngest in the country to occupy such a position, so could claim to have won the battle in a sense. One of his first actions was to appoint a second professor in his department, and he asked me to be an external assessor for this position. So I met him again, and his partner Flavia, staying overnight with them in their cottage outside Glasgow, and thus began a friendship which has lasted till the present, in spite of the stresses of a collaboration which I shall describe in its place, and long intervals without contact. He has remained a man of strong opinions tempered by a lively sense of humour, and our occasional reunions, including Mary and Flavia, are always full of hilarity and argument.

Looking back on the 'MacCabe Affair' it must be acknowledged that with the passing of time I, Frank Kermode, Colin MacCabe himself, and many others on his side at the time, became disillusioned with the poststructuralist approach to literature, especially of the Deconstructionist variety, when it became a kind of orthodoxy which ambitious young scholars felt obliged to embrace and apply to literature in a jargon-heavy discourse of tortuous obscurity. But intellectual and creative progress is furthered by the rise of new ideas and their eventual decline, only what is permanently valid in them surviving. In 1981 the majority on the Cambridge English Faculty Board was out of sync with this rhythm.


At the Joyce Symposium in Zurich Walt Litz, Chairman of the English Department at Princeton, had asked me if I would accept something called the 'Whitney J. Oates short-term Fellowship' there in two years' time. The visitor had to give two public lectures on subjects of his choice and conduct two seminars to discuss them further, meet faculty and postgraduates informally and be generally fêted. There was a substantial honorarium. I said yes. Two years later, but less than three weeks after my mother had died, I flew to New York early in April to fulfil this engagement, to which several others had been added. But first I spent two nights in New York, partly in order to meet a new American agent acting for Curtis Brown, who had split with their partner, Curtis Brown New York. His name confusingly was James Brown. I was also to have lunch with some editors from Doubleday, who were interested in my work in spite of the indifferent reception of *Ginger, You're Barmy* when they published it back in 1965. They had passed on *Changing Places*, like every other American publisher to whom it was offered, but had perhaps revised their opinion since Penguin USA issued it successfully as a paperback original in 1978. They were hesitating about *How Far Can You Go?* and when they heard I would be passing through New York they asked to meet me.

I was booked to stay at the Royalton hotel in mid-town Manhattan. A friend had recommended it because it was inexpensive but conveniently located near Times Square and opposite the classy Algonquin, famous for its literary habitués since the 1920s. I didn't know how long ago my friend had last stayed at the Royalton, but I felt it must have declined steeply in the meantime when I checked in. The foyer was small and dingy, there was just one receptionist, who demanded advance payment in cash, and no one was available to carry my case and show me my room. The room itself at the back of the hotel lowered my spirits still further. It was clean, but shabby. The furniture, the carpets and the bed linen had a worn, exhausted look and the walls badly needed redecorating. The bath enamel was chipped and there were rust marks under the taps. But what most worried me was the array of various locks and bolts crudely attached to the inside of the door, as if accumulated in response to repeated attempts by thieves and thugs to break into the room. I spent an uneasy night there, waking up in the early hours from jet lag.

I was already depressed when I arrived in New York because I hadn't had time or peace of mind to grieve for my mother. A seedy hotel in New York was certainly not the place to start, nor was the busy schedule that lay ahead. When she died I could not suppress a feeling of relief that I would not have to cancel the whole trip at the last moment, as had seemed very possible, but I felt guilty at having this unuttered thought. So I was not in the right mood to make the most of my lunch with the Doubleday people. The venue was the fabled Four Seasons, probably the most expensive restaurant in the city at that time. I was seated at a round table in a circle of smart, friendly, sophisticated people in whose company I felt dull-witted and provincial. Invited to order first, I chose a conventional starter and main course from the menu and was disconcerted when everybody else ate from an enormous split-level platter of seafood, and nothing else. Some said flattering things about *How Far Can You Go?* and others regretted that it would be a hard sell in the US. I perceived that they wanted to find out what kind of novel I was planning to write next, and if it took their fancy they might take a punt on it. I hadn't told anyone about the subject of *Small World*, which was still at the notebook stage, and it didn't even have a title yet. I am always rather secretive about a new novel-in-progress, in case it shouldn't work out and have to be abandoned, or the idea be stolen by someone else. I told them it would be about academics, and hopefully funny, like *Changing Places*, but that wasn't enough to satisfy their curiosity or whet their appetite. We parted amicably but inconclusively.

I called at James Brown's office. He was friendly and courteous, but he seemed to me almost elderly, not quite my idea of a dynamic New York agent, and he hadn't yet read *How Far Can You Go?* so there was not much to talk about. I walked back to the Royalton, but couldn't face my bleak room, crossed the road and went into the Algonquin where I ordered a cup of tea in the lounge. It seemed such an attractive, civilised place that when I had finished my tea I booked myself into a very expensive room for the night and went back across the road to fetch my luggage and check out of the Royalton. The man on the desk seemed only mildly surprised, and did not of course refund me for the second night. I understand it has since been totally refurbished and turned into a chic boutique hotel with self-catering rooms.

The town of Princeton has its own railway branch line and is connected with the New York–Washington main line by a shuttle service. Arriving in this fashion is an appropriate introduction to a place which combines a sense of privilege with the ambience of a bygone age, made concrete in the elaborate Victorian neo-Gothic architecture of the campus and the perfectly preserved 1930s Nassau Inn where Mary and I were very comfortably accommodated. At first I was alone, because Mary's term had not quite finished when I had to leave England, but Walt Litz was an assiduous host who ensured that I was never left on my own for very long before and after my first lecture and seminar, introducing me to colleagues in the English Department and to some of the distinguished academics at Princeton's Institute of Advanced Studies, once the academic home of Albert Einstein.

It happened that the annual Gauss Seminars in Criticism were in progress at the time of my visit, a handsomely endowed series of talks given by distinguished visiting speakers in the humanities to a small, select audience. This year the visitor was Harold Bloom, a legendary figure from the Yale English Department. He was associated with the Yale Deconstructionists such as Paul de Man and J. Hillis Miller, but was in fact a totally idiosyncratic critic, opinionated and omnivorous, ranging over the whole canon of Western literature which he interpreted with entirely original theories and a jargon of his own that had a psychoanalytical and prophetic slant. The first book of his I had read was not one of his best, *Poetry and Repression: Revisionism from Blake to Stevens*, published in 1975. Martin Amis, who was then assistant literary editor of the *New Statesman*, had asked me to review it, encouraging me to be candid if I was not impressed – and I was not.[1] While I was eating dinner with Walt Litz in the Faculty Club on my second evening, a tall, stout figure stalked in with an entourage, paused and glanced around the room. It was Harold Bloom, and it seemed to me that his gaze focused balefully on me for a moment before he moved on to his table. I wondered if he had been told that I was another visitor on campus. I told Walt that I had written a distinctly unflattering review of Bloom's book, but I didn't suppose he would remember it. 'Harold remembers everything,' Walt said discouragingly. And it was true: Bloom's memory was prodigious. It was said that he knew all the poetry he wrote about off by heart, including the entire text of *Paradise Lost*, and for this reason gave no references for his numerous quotations, though I suppose some editor must have checked their accuracy. I kept my head down for the rest of the meal.

Mary arrived the next day. The University sent a car to Kennedy to meet her and bring her to the Nassau where I was waiting, and I embraced her with huge relief. Up till then I had managed to keep the depression attached to Mum's death and the experience in New York on ice, as it were, while I concentrated like an actor on playing the role of the visiting scholar. Now with someone to confide in, I was able to purge some of the bad feelings and take spontaneous pleasure in the rest of the trip. Mary had arrived in the afternoon, and after a few hours' sleep she was ready to join me for dinner in the Princeton faculty's favourite restaurant, with a group of the English Department's

[1] Sample passage from the review: 'It is not so much the jargon that annoys one, though it is tiresome enough, as the extraordinary vanity of the discourse, its assumption that we are interested not only in its conclusions but in every wavering thread of cogitation that leads up to them. It seems impossible to arrest the text, to stem the flow of words, to grasp a single point that can be simply understood, weighed and tested. Gradually one's mind goes numb.' I did read other books by Bloom later, notably *The Anxiety of Influence*, which were more rewarding.

PhD students. They were a bright, talkative bunch of intensely ambitious young people, and the evening gave me an insight into how carefully Ivy League universities like Princeton groomed and assisted their best students to get a footing on the first rung of an academic career – which none of these seemed to doubt they would achieve.

There was more hospitality the next evening in the form of a dinner party given by Joyce Carol Oates and her husband. A famously prolific novelist whose readers could hardly keep up with her growing *oeuvre*, she also managed at the same time to be the jewel in the crown of Princeton's Creative Writing programme. She was a striking figure with a pale oval face and huge eyes framed by dark curls, set above a long narrow white dress, who spoke quietly and economically. The other guests were Elaine Showalter and her husband English (an unusual first name made all the more memorable by the fact that he is a specialist in French literature). Elaine could not be more different from her friend Joyce: plump, exuberant, talkative. In 1978 she had published *A Literature of Their Own: British Women Novelists from Brontë to Lessing*, a stand-out book in the new wave of feminist criticism. I had met her before in London and invited her to give a lecture at Birmingham. She was then teaching at Rutgers University, but would shortly join Joyce at Princeton. Elaine and English were Anglophiles who made regular visits to England, where we would meet them frequently in the future.


Our next destination was Philadelphia, where I had been invited to give a lecture at the University of Pennsylvania (known colloquially as Penn) by Larzer ('Larry') Ziff, who was a senior professor there. He and his wife Linda put us up for two nights in their period town house in a tree-lined street in an older part of the city. We had first got to know them in 1969 during my spell at Berkeley, where Larry taught and wrote books about American literature and culture. A few years later the Oxford English Department introduced an American literature option into their syllabus and appointed Larry to run it, which he did very effectively for several years at the Lecturer grade, but eventually despairing of promotion he returned to America and the prestigious professorship which was his due. While they were in England Larry and Linda lived in a village outside Oxford and occasionally they invited Mary and me to visit them at weekends, which we were glad to do, for they were good company and it was always amusing to hear Larry's tales of the eccentricities of Oxford academia.

It was on one of those weekends that I met for the first time Richard Ellmann and his wife Mary, who were invited to dinner by Larry after he discovered that Ellmann was a great fan of *Changing Places*. Larry Ziff himself had been alarmed when he first heard that I had written a satirical campus novel set partly in a fictionalised Berkeley in which one of the main characters was called Morris Zapp, but was relieved when he read it and according to some reports went about Oxford afterwards chuckling to himself and accosting acquaintances to tell them, 'It's not about me, it's Stanley Fish!' Like Larry, Richard Ellmann (Dick to his friends) had had a distinguished career in America, teaching at Yale and Northwestern University, and writing outstanding biographies of Wilde, Yeats and Joyce before moving with his family to Oxford where he was Goldsmith Professor and a Fellow of New College. He was a critic I had revered and learned from ever since I was an undergraduate studying the Irish authors he specialised in, so I was very glad to meet him, and he proved to be a charming man.

Subsequently he twice invited me to be his guest at the New College Feast, an annual black-tie event when the Fellows and their friends consume a multi-course dinner and a vast quantity of expensive booze to celebrate the college's foundation. I also called on him at his house in St Giles on other occasions when business took me to Oxford, and once I climbed the stairs to Mary Ellmann's room where she occasionally received visitors, seated in an armchair. The Ziffs' dinner party must have been at that time one of the rare occasions when she ventured out for a social evening, for she was a chronic invalid and increasingly confined to her home. Earlier in life she had been a respected literary journalist, and her book of essays *Thinking About Women*, published in 1968 when second wave feminism had barely begun, anticipated some of the key ideas of later criticism in that mode. When they moved to England she wrote witty journalistic pieces about English life. I especially remember an article, in *Encounter* I think, harking back to an earlier visit to England when her children were young, describing their amusement when listening to a BBC radio programme called *Top of the Form*, a quiz competition for schoolchildren which I knew well from my own early years. What convulsed them was the upper-class accent and patronising tone of the quizmaster, and the crushing manner in which he informed the nervous contenders that they had given a wrong answer. The Ellmann children would mimic him, asking each other impossibly difficult questions, deriding the answers offered, and then fall about laughing. One of these children was Maud, whom I met at the Joyce conference in Zurich and later invited to speak at Birmingham, and another was Lucy, who won the *Guardian* Fiction Prize with her first novel, *Sweet Desserts*, in 1988 and has published several others since then. It was a brilliant literary family which seemed unfairly singled out for suffering by fate – first in Mary's long debilitating illness and then by Dick's later affliction with motor neurone disease. I remember reading with dismay the letter in which he informed me, without a trace of self-pity, of the diagnosis and the bleak prognosis. For some years Dick divided his time between Oxford and Emory University, Atlanta, but he and Mary both died in England, Dick in 1987, and Mary two years later. In 2001 I was honoured to give the Ellmann Lectures founded at Emory in his memory, published in *Consciousness and the Novel* in the following year.

*

We broke our journey to Philadelphia for a few hours in Baltimore, where Lenny Michaels, on leave from Berkeley, was a visiting teacher at Johns Hopkins, to have lunch with him and his new wife, Brenda, who was now a mother too, of a baby girl. In February he had sent me a long letter handwritten in green ink relating with gloomy relish various woes he had recently suffered, including flu, skidding off the road in a snowstorm, having the car stolen in New York, the chilliness of the Johns Hopkins faculty and administrative staff towards him, and the stresses of sharing custody of his two sons with Priscilla, who was living in Pittsburgh. Lenny's letters always emphasised misfortune: his prose style thrived on it. He was also nervously awaiting the reception of his first novel, *The Men's Club*, soon to be published by Farrar Straus and Giroux, and mentioned that it had just been accepted by Cape in England without seeming to be greatly encouraged by this. I wrote back that he should be very pleased because Cape was the ideal British publisher for his work.

Lenny met us at the railway station and drove us to the small modern house which he had found on the outskirts of the city. He seemed happy with his new wife and family, but Brenda looked so young beside him, and seemed so different in personality and background (she had been brought up in a God-fearing Protestant family in the South) that it was hard to believe the marriage would last. Before we left, he gave me a bound proof of *The Men's Club*, which I read on the remainder of our trip. It begins:

> Women wanted to talk about anger, identity, politics,
> etc. I saw posters in Berkeley urging them to join
> groups. I saw their leaders on TV. Strong, articulate
> faces. So when Cavanagh phoned and invited me to
> join a men's club, I laughed. Slowly, not laughing, he
> repeated himself . . . He and some friends wanted a
> club. 'A regular social possibility outside of our jobs
> and marriages. Nothing to do with women's groups.'

In fact it is more like a negative image of a women's group than a club. The narrator agrees to go to the first meeting, which also turns out to be the last, held at the house of Kramer, one of the seven members, most of whom are strangers to each other. They agree that each should tell the story of his life, which turns out to mean their relationships with women. Their tongues are loosened by liquor, and their stamina is fortified by raiding the kitchen for the lavish cold supper prepared by Kramer's wife for her women friends who are to meet in her house the following evening. The stories the men tell are funny, sad, bizarre and sexually explicit. They get increasingly drunk and violent, smashing things, howling like wolves and throwing knives at the living room door. At this point Mrs Kramer returns home. The denouement is brilliant. The whole book is brilliantly written. I read it with delight, and an envy for Lenny's use of language that is the highest compliment one writer can pay to another. It did very well in the US, but when it was published in Britain it sadly made little impression. It was reissued in 2017 by Daunt and much more favourably reviewed, but that was no consolation to Lenny.

Our last reunion on this trip was with Martin and Carol Green whom we knew well from the years Martin spent teaching in the Birmingham English Department, as described in *QAGTTBB*. He was now a professor at Tufts University, Boston, but at present on a sabbatical which he was spending in Washington DC, doing research for his current book. Martin always had a book in progress, being almost as prolific in non-fiction as Joyce Carol Oates was in fiction. We were with them for little more than 36 hours, but there was time for a perambulation round the Washington sights. It was April, the weather was warm and the city's famous cherry blossom was in bloom, which gave me premature hay fever. I remember the relief of entering the air-conditioned National Gallery of Art and being able to breathe normally for an hour or so. Some confusion about which of the two Washington airports we were departing from nearly caused us to miss our plane, but happily Carol got us to the right one just in time. It was a night flight, and in the early morning we had the surprising sight of England spread out beneath us blanketed with snow. The runways at Heathrow had been cleared but the unseasonable snowfall had had an all too familiar effect on the British railway network. When our taxi arrived at the entrance to Euston officials waved their arms and shouted that no trains were running in or out of the station. They advised us to try an alternative route from Paddington, so we did. The journey via Reading and Oxford in a packed train took about six hours – all in all it took us longer to get from Heathrow to Birmingham than it had taken us to get from Washington to London. But I had been gifted a great idea for the beginning of *Small World*.

Later in the summer of that year, 1981, *How Far Can You Go?* at last found an American publisher. Jim Brown, my new American agent, had sent it to William Morrow, an established New York imprint, and they made an offer which the senior editor there, Howard Cady, candidly admitted to Mike Shaw in a letter confirming the deal was 'picayune'. It was a word I had to look up, and Collins dictionary told me it meant 'of small value or importance; mean, petty', being derived from the name of a small Spanish-American coin. Morrow's position was that they were doubtful about the novel's sales prospects in the USA, but they admired my writing and wanted to have an option on my future work. I was in no position to turn down their offer, or to refuse the request attached to it – namely, that I think of a different title for the novel. Cady and his colleagues thought that *How Far Can You Go?* might confuse booksellers and put off potential readers who would associate it with 'How To Do It' manuals and psychological self-help books. I agreed reluctantly, because the phrase 'How far can you go?' runs like a refrain through the text of the novel, but I composed some alternative titles, of which *Souls and Bodies* was the agreed choice. The change of title later caused endless bibliographical confusion, and annoyance to American readers who had enjoyed *Souls and Bodies*, and purchased *How Far Can You Go?* in the British Penguin edition when they came to the UK, assuming that it was a different book. I never encountered a single American reader or bookseller who understood Morrow's objections to the original title.

*Souls and Bodies* got excellent reviews all over the USA when it was published in January 1982. Howard Cady's colleague wrote to me when forwarding a fresh bunch of cuttings, 'We have certainly never seen such consistently positive reviews, and in such quantity to boot.' Unfortunately the one significant exception was the most important and influential – the *New York Sunday Times Book Review*. It was written by the novelist (and later travel writer) Paul Theroux, who had had a Catholic upbringing himself, and wrote about it evocatively at the beginning of his semi-autobiographical novel *My Secret History* (1989). After spending some time in Africa, and writing about his experiences there, he married an English woman and settled in the 1970s in south-east London very near where I grew up myself. I remembered reading his thriller *The Family Arsenal* in 1977, about an anarchist terrorist cell holed up in Deptford, and being impressed by how well he had captured the character and atmosphere of that seedy and depressed borough.

Theroux made it clear that he didn't like my novel, which was his prerogative; but I resented his patronising tone and his complaint that the novel contained 'a culture-bound set of references that will ring no bells for the American reader' – citing as an example *Blue Peter*, the name of an immensely popular and long-running BBC television programme for children, named after a nautical flag that signals departure from port. Theroux must have known perfectly well that, whereas in the past American publishers re-set the texts of British novels and discreetly edited them to assist American readers (e.g. 'plimsoles' was changed to 'sneakers' in the Doubleday edition of my novel *Ginger, You're Barmy*), this was a luxury they could no longer afford, and they now reprinted the British texts, as we did American ones in the UK. This was actually a positive development, preserving the integrity of the author's work; and part of the pleasure and value of reading a book in a variety of English which is different from one's own is learning what unfamiliar expressions mean from their context. I wrote a letter to the *NYT Book Review* to this effect, which they published. It concluded: 'If a mentally handicapped child is sat down in front of the TV by her mother to watch something called 'Blue Peter' isn't it pretty likely that this is the name of a TV programme for children, rather than, say, a pornographic movie?' Tom Rosenthal, who subscribed to the *Times Book Review*, and knew that *peter* is US slang for penis, enjoyed the joke.

A rave review in that place can sometimes propel a book on to the newspaper's bestseller list, which is the US book trade's bible. *Souls and Bodies* did not figure there, needless to say, though some national magazines like *Newsweek* and the *New Yorker* reviewed it favourably, and *Time*, with the biggest circulation of all, proposed to run a feature review with photo. But there was a tight deadline. A photographer came to my house in Birmingham and kept a taxi waiting outside for an hour and a half with the meter running, before hurrying off to deliver the negatives to a courier who would take them to New York by Concorde. For a few days I was buoyed up by this glamorous scenario, but it all ended in anticlimax. Either the deadline passed, or editorial decisions changed, for the review and photo never appeared. Howard Cady told me this was a frequent occurrence at *Time*. The book probably did better than expected – he reported sales of just under 5,000 later that year, a decent figure by British standards; but it would have sold more if they had had more faith in the book, paid more upfront, promoted it more vigorously and made sure that it was available when the good reviews came out. 'Our main problem is getting books into the bookshops,' Cady admitted in a letter to me shortly after publication.

But I did not repine. I was cheered by the enthusiasm of the great majority of the reviews, and encouraged to take an important step which I had been meditating ever since winning the Whitbread prize: to become a part-time professor. That spring I made a formal request to the University to alternate a period of paid employment, including a teaching term, with an equivalent period of unpaid leave, and they agreed to this arrangement for a three-year trial period. They would save some money by employing a young academic to cover my teaching when I was away. At this time the Thatcher government's cuts in funding were beginning to bite, and all universities were struggling to reduce their salary bills. Nevertheless I'm not sure I could have made such a deal at any other British university. Now I had the time I needed to complete *Small World*.

# 8

Ever since I made that note in my Zurich diary about the 'global campus' I had been mentally nurturing the idea of a comic novel about academics going to international conferences, combining professional self-advancement with the pleasures of tourism and romantic dalliance. It would have a big international cast of characters, some of whom could be taken from *Changing Places*, including Philip Swallow and Morris Zapp, whose futures I had fortunately left completely open at the end of that novel. In the notebook I dedicated to this project I wrote down ideas for new characters, suitable locations, amusing episodes and situations, but for some time I was unable to see how they could all be connected in a unified narrative. I thought it might start at a depressed and depressing conference in the Easter vacation at a provincial British university. Rummidge would serve again as the setting for that, and to make life more uncomfortable for the conferees I would have an unseasonable snowfall blanket the campus. Then the novel would open out eventfully into the big wide world. But how? '*What could provide the basis for a story?*' I scribbled rather desperately in my notebook one day; and then just below, '*Could some myth serve, as in* Ulysses?' I was thinking of the way James Joyce used the mythical story of Homer's *Odyssey* as a structural model for his realistic rendering of the lives of modern Dubliners on a single day in 1904. And a little later, immediately below that, I wrote: '*E.g. the Grail legend – involves a lot of different characters and long journeys.*' I had found the solution to my problem.

I have described this breakthrough elsewhere,[1] and I cannot do so more concisely than by repeating it here:

> The Grail legend – the quest for the cup which Jesus
> used at the Last Supper – is at the heart of the myth
> of King Arthur and the Knights of the Round Table. I
> thought of it at that moment because I had just seen
> *Excalibur*, John Boorman's slightly over-the-top but
> highly enjoyable movie treatment of this material, and
> been reminded what a wonderfully gripping narrative
> it is. I saw an analogy, comic and ironic, between
> modern academics jetting round the world to meet
> and compete with each other for fame and love in
> various exotic settings, and the knights of chivalric
> romance who did the same things in a more elevated
> style assisted by poetic licence and magic. The Grail
> sought by the modern knights might be a Chair of
> Literary Criticism endowed by UNESCO, with an
> enormous salary and negligible duties. The volatile
> state of contemporary literary studies, with various
> methodologies (structuralist, deconstructionist, Marxist,
> feminist, psychoanalytical, etc.) challenging traditional
> scholarship and each other, would generate rivalry
> and conflict. I also thought of T.S. Eliot's great poem,
> *The Waste Land*, and its use of the Grail legend as

[1] Introduction to *The Campus Trilogy* (2011).

interpreted by the folklorist Jessie Weston, who saw
it as a displaced and sublimated version of an older
pagan myth about a Fisher King with a parched,
infertile kingdom. I saw connections here with various
kinds of sterility afflicting modern writers and literary
intellectuals. There might be an elderly, immensely
distinguished, unhappily impotent professor called
Arthur Kingfisher somewhere in the story . . .

With this inspiration my novel began to take shape. The hero
would be a young Irish academic, a conference virgin as well
as a literal one, who comes to the Rummidge event from the
University of Limerick (a fictitious institution, though somewhat embarrassingly a university with that name was established
some years later). I called him Persse McGarrigle: Persse recalling
the chaste knight Percival of Arthurian legend, and McGarrigle
because I liked the music of the McGarrigle sisters at that time –
though I was delighted to discover that the surname means 'Son
of Super-Valour' in Gaelic. One of the pleasures of writing this
book was finding such unexpected symmetries and correspond-
ences, which thickened the mix of motifs and echoes linking the
mythical and the modern. At the conference Persse is befriended
by Morris Zapp, who has flown in from California at the invitation
of Philip Swallow and shocks the conference with a lecture called
'Textuality as Striptease'; and he falls in love with a beautiful young
scholar called Angelica, who is pursued by several admirers but
proves as elusive as her namesake in Ariosto's chivalric romance
*Orlando Furioso*, possessor of a magic ring which she rubs to
make herself invisible to importunate males. I read this classic of
Italian literature in the Penguin translation as I began to plan my
novel, led to it by a lucky discovery in Birmingham University's
bookshop. This was a small facility which mainly stocked texts
prescribed for courses, but the Literature section carried a random
selection of scholarly books, and among them was *Inescapable*

*Romance: Studies in the Poetics of a Mode,* by Patricia A. Parker, published by Princeton University Press in 1979. I bought it, and it opened my eyes to a whole range of romance narratives in classic European literature, which one of the characters in my novel, Cheryl Summerbee, a check-in clerk at Heathrow airport, learns to distinguish from the debased modern form of the heroine-centred love story published by Mills and Boon to which she was previously addicted. 'Real romance,' she says, 'is full of coincidences and surprises and marvels and has lots of characters who are lost or enchanted or wandering about looking for each other, or for the Grail, or something like that. Of course they're often in love too.' When *Small World* was published it was subtitled *An Academic Romance*, in the double sense of being about academics and drawing on the academic rather than the popular concept of romance as a genre; and one of the two books to which I acknowledged a special debt in an Author's Note was *Inescapable Romance*. The other was *Airport International,* by Brian Moynahan, a documentary survey of modern air travel.

Patricia Parker was described on the jacket of her book as Associate Professor of English and Comparative Literature at the University of Toronto, and several academic readers of *Small World* who knew her told me that my heroine Angelica resembled her to such an extent that they assumed I knew her personally. In fact I met her for the first and only time a year after the novel was published, when I was passing through Toronto on my way to visit the University of Newfoundland. It was a brief meeting, which may have been at a bookshop signing arranged by Penguin Books, and I have no clear memory of it. Some months later Patricia sent me a warm invitation to spend a week and give a public lecture at the University of Toronto. She wrote that 'lots of people here have been enjoying *Small World* . . . and I feel it is such a honour to have in some way been part of that book', which I interpreted as a reference to my acknowledged debt to *her* book rather than any resemblance between herself and Angelica.

I wasn't able to accept the invitation, but I was relieved that she took pleasure in her association with my novel.

There was also a putative real-life model for my hero. I was occasionally asked by Irish readers if Pat Sheeran, a writer and critic who taught at University College Galway, was the model for Persse McGarrigle, as he apparently claimed. I prevaricated in response, though there was a smidgeon of truth in the assertion. Some time before starting to write *Small World* I attended the annual conference of university teachers of English, hosted that year by Bristol University, and there I met a likeable young lecturer from Galway whose name I soon forgot subsequently. Over a drink in the bar he told a group of us a droll story of going to a chemist's shop in the city centre that afternoon to buy a large quantity of condoms, which were then unobtainable in Ireland due to the Catholic Church's ban on contraception. He had experienced much embarrassment in making his purchase, due to the difficulty the female shop assistant had in understanding his accent, and he hers. This later inspired a farcical episode in *Small World*, when Persse, preparing to lose his virginity (as he hopes) to Angelica, buys a package of the baby food Farex instead of the Durex he requested. Pat Sheeran must have been the source of this episode, though nothing else in Persse's story, apart from his belonging to a small university in the west of Ireland, bears any relation to Pat's life and career. He was evidently a very popular lecturer at University College Galway and a lively creative presence on the Irish literary scene until his too early death in 2001. He published several books of fiction with his Polish wife Nina Witoszek, who wrote under the name of Nina Fitzpatrick, including a collection of stories, *Fables of the Irish Intelligentsia*. It won the prestigious and valuable Irish Times/Aer Lingus Irish Fiction Prize for Literature in 1991, but when it was discovered that the real Nina was not an Irish citizen, the prize was withdrawn and given to another novel. I felt a retrospective pang of sympathy when I read about that, for the writer's life is difficult enough without such unexpected reversals of fortune, and regretted that I never met Pat Sheeran again after our encounter in Bristol.

*Small World* is divided into five Parts. The first is set in Rummidge and establishes Persse, Swallow and Zapp as the three main characters whose adventures in the wider world provide the narrative continuity of the novel. Some minor characters were carried over from *Changing Places*, but my intention was that those three would become involved with a host of people from other countries whom I had to invent from scratch. I stalled at this point for some time, until I thought of introducing most of them in a long sequence in which they are shown doing various character-revealing things simultaneously, but in different time zones in different parts of the world. For some of those locations I drew on my own recent academic travels, and I accepted new invitations in the hope that they would yield more material and local colour for my work in progress.

In April 1979 I went to Genoa as guest speaker at the Italian equivalent of the British UTE conference. The airport is situated in a valley between mountains and a high promontory projecting out into the sea which planes must circumnavigate to land and take off, a challenging manoeuvre for pilots; and this association prompted me to make it the site of an alarming emergency landing for Philip Swallow which precipitates the commencement of his particular romantic strand in the novel. As previously noted, the MLA convention in New York at the end of the same year provided the stage for the novel's denouement, in which many mysteries are resolved and Persse's quest for Angelica appears to end. An earlier episode in this quest, which takes place in Hawaii, draws on my impressions of the place during my weekend there after the San Francisco Symposium and on another subsequent visit. In early April 1980 I went to Turkey with a group of colleagues sent by the British Council to attend an 'All-Turkey

Seminar on Contemporary English Literature and its Teaching' in Ankara, followed by several days in Istanbul where we gave lectures at two universities. I sent Philip Swallow on a similar trip: in dusty, smog-polluted Ankara he suffers comical humiliations of various kinds, but on his last day finds the lover he thought he had lost for ever and carries her off to Istanbul, which provides a suitably romantic backdrop for their reunion.

Private holidays could also feed into the work in progress. In the summer of 1981, after visiting my aunt Lu, the widow of my uncle John, on the Belgian coast, Mary and I spent a few days in Amsterdam. As well as visiting the Van Gogh Museum and other high cultural attractions we strolled through the red light district where prostitutes sit at their front windows in their underwear, a street which would figure in Persse's search for Angelica; and I discovered a luxury hotel in the city that incorporated a circular Lutheran chapel converted into a conference auditorium, which in the novel became a modern version of the Chapel Perilous in the Grail legend, where the Grail Knight fights a gigantic Black Hand – in my story a German professor who is hostile to Persse and always wears a black glove on one hand.

In the spring of 1982 Mary and I had one of our most enjoyable holidays, added on to another British Council specialist tour, this time in Greece. After I had done my professional stuff in Salonika and Athens, she flew out to join me in the latter city and we spent a week in a hired car, going first to Delphi and then exploring the Peloponnese, the former providing the perfect setting in the novel for an ambiguous prophecy about the fate of the UNESCO Chair, which is received by Philip Swallow from a sibyl-like female scholar first encountered at the Rummidge conference. We were fortunate to arrive in the Peloponnese simultaneously with the Greek spring. The weather turned warm, the snow was beginning to recede on the mountains, the wild flowers were blooming under the olive trees in the valleys, the seaside hotels and restaurants were just opening up for the season, and we stopped overnight when and where we fancied. We visited several famous ancient sites including Mistras, remnant of the medieval city that was once the flourishing capital of a Byzantine state, and the great theatre of Epidaurus where the cycles of classic Greek drama were originally performed. On a hillside at Mistras, as we were exploring the amazing fortifications, churches and monasteries, a few still inhabited but most in various stages of dilapidation, we came across an aged workman or caretaker digging the stony soil. We greeted him and he responded in some unintelligible Greek. 'We are English,' I said. His face lit up with a toothless grin. 'Ah, Engleesh!' he said. 'Thatcher!' I was impressed that her reputation had reached the ears of such a man in this remote spot. But later I wondered if perhaps he had known something we did not. While we were taking our holiday and out of touch with news, Argentina had invaded the Falkland Islands, and Britain was at war.

Later that year I contributed to *Authors Take Sides on the Falklands,* one of a series of books on international crises edited by Cecil Woolf and Jean Moorcroft Wilson, modelled on a famous compilation of 1937 about the Spanish Civil War. I wrote:

> I do not know how far I might have shared the
> feeling of outrage that seems to have swept the House
> of Commons, and most of the country, that fateful
> weekend. Returning a week later, and taking stock of
> the situation after initial dazed incredulity, I came
> to the conclusion that we should not have sent the
> Task Force, for the following reasons: 1. The enterprise
> was inherently very risky, and the repossession of
> the Falklands was not worth the loss of human life,
> especially British lives. 2. Even if we were successful in
> repossessing the islands, we could never defend them

indefinitely without an absurdly disproportionate investment of military capability. I still hold to that view as I write this, on the 8th June, with the British forces poised to retake Port Stanley, while feeling great admiration for the courage and resourcefulness with which they have conducted the campaign. If there had to be a war, it is obviously vital that we should win it, since our cause, it seems to me, is just.

In fact I had been completely caught up in the fortunes of the Task Force, and addicted to the radio and television news reports, sparse and carefully controlled though they were. My disaffection with the military as a National Serviceman was suppressed, and the patriotic emotions of my wartime childhood were revived. The French narratologist A.J. Greimas proposed that most narratives are basically of three kinds: their stories concern a journey away from and back to home, or the making and breaking of a contract, or the performance of a difficult and decisive action. The Falklands War, combining all three elements, had an imaginative and emotional appeal comparable to classical epics like the *Iliad*.

I did not mention in my contribution to *Authors Take Sides* the sinking of the *Belgrano*, which was, I came to think, a deed of doubtful legality. The rest of the piece surveyed various options for ending the dispute without further bloodshed, and came down in favour of a formal recognition of Argentinian sovereignty combined with a leaseback of the Islands to their British inhabitants. What I and most people failed to foresee was how quickly the military junta governing Argentina would collapse following defeat. And it surprised me as time went on that those in Britain, mainly on the left, who had opposed the war and continued to condemn it, failed to recognise that it had rid Argentina of an evil and oppressive regime which would have gained a long lease of life from victory and thus made a return to democratic government possible. Perhaps the saddest and most troubling fact of the war is that ninety-five British servicemen who served in it have subsequently committed suicide – nearly half as many as died in the campaign.

In the same month that the war ended, and relieved of anxiety on its account, I attended another James Joyce Symposium – a very special one, celebrating the 100th anniversary of Joyce's birth, and held in Dublin to coincide with Bloomsday. I gave a paper on 'Joyce and Bakhtin' alongside Colin MacCabe on 'Joyce and Benjamin' and Seamus Deane of University College Dublin on 'Joyce and Lukács'. But the academic programme was almost a sideshow to the plethora of performances, recitals, dramatisations and exhibitions related to Joyce's life and work. On Bloomsday itself, 16th June, actors representing characters in the novel and wearing clothes appropriate to 1904 appeared at various places in the city at the times when they appeared there in Joyce's text. At three in the afternoon a procession of horse-drawn coaches carrying the British Vice-Regent and his retinue in period costume drove through the streets of the city along the route described in the episode of *Ulysses* known as 'The Wandering Rocks'; while the Ormond Hotel, scene of the 'Sirens' episode, was mobbed as it sold Guinness at 1904 prices for several hours. And all through the day a local radio station broadcast a reading of the entire text of Joyce's novel, so that wherever you went you heard it coming out of open doors and windows, or inside pubs and restaurants, or from the lowered windows of cars. It was a magical, unforgettable experience to be in Dublin that day, and it inspired me later to invent a somewhat similar piece of street theatre in my novel – an enactment of T.S. Eliot's *The Waste Land* in Lausanne, the town on Lake Geneva where he wrote most of that poem, performed by actors dressed up as the personae, ancient and modern, who speak its lines.

Earlier that year I had been approached by the British Council to join a delegation to a conference on Modern British Literature to be held in Seoul in August, organised by the English Language and Literature Association of South Korea. It was the most ambitious event of its kind they had staged, and the Council was anxious to support it, so had persuaded a distinguished figure to lead the British contingent, Professor Randolph Quirk. His participation was an enticement for me, but I wondered whether it was really wise to give up more time in the precious long summer vacation for yet another foreign excursion. Mary had arranged to visit her sister Eileen in Canada in August, taking Chris with her, and I entertained visions of having the house to myself with hours of peace and quiet in which to get on with the novel. My young colleague Deirdre Burton, whose research field was linguistics and stylistics but who also had interests in women's writing and critical theory, had been invited to join the team going to Korea and accepted eagerly. One day she phoned me up to discuss the itinerary, which was to begin with an overnight stay in Hong Kong, and I told her I was going to drop out. 'You don't really mean that, do you?' she said, and after chatting with her for a while I changed my mind. Asia was missing from my knowledge of the global campus and this seemed a golden opportunity to fill the gap.

In the event Korea contributed very little to *Small World*. There is one Korean character, the young companion, secretary, masseuse and bedfellow of Arthur Kingfisher in the USA. Persse meets her in a plane on the way to Seoul to visit her family, and she gives him some tips on how to locate the conference Angelica is supposed to be attending there, but that's about it. The problem was not that the country was uninteresting, but it was curiously opaque to my Western eyes, with a middle class restrained by an elaborate, old-fashioned code of manners and a proletariat, as we observed them in Seoul, apparently dazed and confused by their sudden emergence from an agrarian peasant economy into an industrial consumerist one. There was nothing I observed that rang any bells with the themes and motifs of my novel. But when I committed myself to this long journey I had decided to make the most of it, continuing on around the world instead of returning home by the same route. I arranged to spend a few days in Tokyo to meet my Japanese translator Susumu Takagi, then to go to Hawaii to visit Eileen, and finally to a stopover in Los Angeles where Ruth apRoberts, a professor at the Riverside campus of the University of California, had offered to meet me at the airport and drive me to my hotel. She was a friend of Park Honan,[2] in whose house in Birmingham I had first met her, and we had corresponded since then. I had booked myself into the celebrated Beverly Hills in Hollywood, thinking it might be fun to send Persse there, as in due course I did.

Susumu Takagi, who taught English at a university in Tokyo, had introduced himself by airmail a few years before as the translator of *Changing Places*, appending a long list of questions about the meaning of English words and phrases in the text (like 'Y-fronts' and 'a bit of spare') that he found puzzling. I always answer translators' queries, because I have an interest in their work being accurate, but my correspondence of this kind with Susumu – he has translated most of my novels into Japanese – has been particularly copious. He is a very scrupulous translator, and in the practice of his craft often notices mistakes in the English texts of my novels that proofreaders including myself have missed. It was great to meet him in the flesh. He was a charming companion and guide to Tokyo, and helped me to buy a duty-free Sony Walkman cassette player, a fairly new device which seemed just the thing for long-haul flights, and yukatas for myself and Mary. These are deliciously soft and soothing cotton robes, one of which I found folded on my hotel bed when I arrived, and quickly became addicted to it. Tokyo fascinated me – outwardly just like a modern Western city but inhabited by people whose manners were entirely different. I was told that it was perfectly safe to walk about the streets at night and it seemed to be true. One hot

[2] My long association with the American Park Honan, whom I first met when we were postgraduates at University College London, and who subsequently became a colleague at Birmingham University, is described in *QAGTTBB*.

humid evening I went for a stroll through the streets off the Ginza, the entertainment quarter, and it began to rain, so I took shelter in a basement bar under the sign 'Pub', the only recognisable English word amid the neon dazzle of Japanese characters. Its clientele, however, were all Japanese. The bar staff didn't speak English, but with the help of a customer who spoke a little, I gathered that in order to get a drink I had to stand up and sing a pop song, selected from a menu which *was* in English, to a taped backing track. I chose 'Hey Jude' and was warmly applauded. When I got back to my hotel I lay on the bed laughing out loud at the memory and resolved to work this bizarre experience into the novel. I discovered next day from the British Council Representative that I had been performing *karaoke* (literally meaning 'empty orchestra'), a word and activity not yet known in Britain. I also learned from Susumu that the Japanese equivalent of the saying 'It's a small world' is '*It is narrow world*'. At the end of the novel Persse McGarrigle, now searching for Cheryl, the check-in girl who has displaced Angelica as the object of his desire, stands in front of a Heathrow departure flutter-board and wonders 'where in all the small, narrow world he should begin to look for her'. When I was in Los Angeles some years after the book was published, I glanced idly at the personal ads in the *LA Times* one day, and my eye was caught by this item:

DESPERATELY SEEKING Angelica. Last seen in
New York, MLA Convention '79. Have $12 left, after
that it's back to Limerick – Persse McGarrigle.

I have no idea who posted this poignant appeal.

When I got to Honolulu I found that Eileen was depressed again. Added to her financial worries was a sense that Waikiki had lost much of the charm which had originally persuaded her to settle there. As well as the relentless construction work of the developers (as Joni Mitchell sang, '*They paved Paradise and put up a parking lot*') the resort was becoming increasingly criminalised, and she had given up babysitting as a source of income because she no longer felt safe walking home late at night. She even spoke of returning to England for the remainder of her life, but I could not imagine her being happy there. I did my best to cheer her up, but it was a taxing task, and feeling the need to be on my own for a while I took a tourist excursion to a beach popular for snorkelling, with equipment provided. I covered up on the hot beach, but foolishly assumed I could not get sunburned while swimming. In fact snorkelling, which was new to me, exposes the back to the sun's rays, and I was badly burned, especially on the back of my legs. I was obliged to adopt a stiff-legged gait for the remainder of my travels, grateful to use the handle of a luggage trolley in the airports as a kind of wheeled Zimmer frame.

I made another academic visit to a foreign country in this period which did not leave any trace in *Small World*, but was one of the most memorable. In 1981 I went to Warsaw with a British Council-sponsored team to take part in an international symposium on 'The Quest for Identity in 19th & 20th Century English Literature'. It had been arranged at the beginning of that year but took place almost at the end of it, in early November, when the fate of Poland was in the balance. The flourishing independent trade union Solidarity, founded and led by Lech Wałęsa, was challenging the Soviet-backed Communist government with strikes and demonstrations, and Russia had responded by imposing a hard-line army general, Wojciech Jaruzelski, as Prime Minister. The consequence of the strikes was a drastic fall in the value of the Polish zloty and shortages of food and other basic necessities, severe enough to be widely reported outside Poland. The British party who made the journey included two friends of mine, Bernard Bergonzi and Barbara Hardy, Professor at Birkbeck

College London, and Ian McEwan whom I met for the first time on that occasion. We were warned in advance by the Council that commodities like coffee and soap were unobtainable in Poland, and informed that they would make very acceptable presents to our hosts. It was a hint which most of us took and we wondered as we gathered for the opening reception how to hand over these goodies gracefully. Our accommodation was in a small palace on the outskirts of Warsaw, a replica of the eighteenth-century original which had been destroyed in the war, like almost every other building of note in the capital, and due to a breakdown in the electric power supply there was no hot water. 'I brought plenty of soap, but the British Council didn't tell us to bring water,' I remarked to a lady from Poznań at the reception. 'Ah, Poland will always surprise you,' she said with a smile. 'By the way,' I added, 'would you like a bar of soap?' The offer lacked finesse to my own ears, but it was received with charming good humour. 'I promise you it will be the last bar of soap I shall use,' she said.

At the welcoming dinner, the ingredients for which must have been obtained with immense difficulty, the Rector of the University praised us for our 'courage' in coming to Poland in its present state, a compliment most us felt we scarcely deserved. The Poles of course were more aware of what was at stake, and outside the formal sessions of the symposium they talked about little else except the political crisis. In the city its impact on everyday life was very evident: long queues of cars outside garages and long lines of people outside shops with bare counters and empty shelves, waiting for supplies of petrol and food to be delivered. Underlying these frustrations and deprivations was a fear that the Russians would suppress Solidarity by sending in troops and tanks, as they had done in Hungary in 1956.

I had earned some royalties on the Polish edition of my first novel, *The Picturegoers*, in zlotys, which was a blocked currency, and I intended to claim them from the publisher and spend them while I was in the country. But the currency had lost much of its original value since *Kinomani* was published in 1966. My zlotys turned out to be worth only about £280 at the official rate of exchange and a fraction of that in reality, and I used them to buy a not very elegant necklace of bits of amber for Mary. *The Picturegoers* was the first, and for some years the only one, of my novels to be translated into a foreign language. The publisher, called Pax, was a Catholic organisation, which accounted for their interest in the book, but I discovered after it appeared that Pax was disapproved of by the Vatican, and regarded as compromised by many Poles, because it operated with the approval of the Communist state. The senior editor at the time of my visit, Marta, was charming, fluent in English and smart. She told me that she and her colleagues had 'reviewed' *How Far Can You Go?* but would not be publishing it, because my view of the Catholic Church was 'very different' from the Polish perspective. That was no surprise. I had seen the TV news pictures of the striking workers at the Gdansk shipyards hearing mass and going to Confession and communion in the open air in their thousands, and I was aware that the Church had become the spiritual focus of the Polish people's opposition to the domination of their country by Soviet communism, all the more fervently since the surprise election of their Cardinal Wojtyła as Pope John Paul II in 1978, an event with which I concluded *How Far Can You Go?* almost as it happened:

> The first non-Italian pope for four hundred and fifty
> years: a Pole, a poet, a philosopher, a linguist, a man
> of the people, a man of destiny, dramatically chosen,
> instantly popular – but theologically conservative . . . A
> changing Church acclaims a Pope who evidently thinks
> that change has gone far enough. What will happen now?

Well, we know what happened in the world at large: increasing tension and conflict between progressive sections of the Church and the Vatican, but Polish Catholics remained staunchly traditional, and Pax obviously identified with that stance. Photographs of John Paul were plentiful on the walls of the Pax offices. While we were discussing recent English fiction Marta showed interest in Anthony Burgess's *Earthly Powers* because the central character was a pope, but when I explained that he was portrayed as an active homosexual, she said wryly, 'No more questions.'

At the end of the Symposium the British participants either returned home or went their separate ways to other destinations in Poland. I took up a long-standing invitation to visit the University of Łódź, a word which looks as if it might be Polish for 'Lodge', but is in fact pronounced 'Woodge'. It is a manufacturing city and I was prepared for something rather grim but the centre is not unattractive, laid out in a grid of streets and boulevards lined with fine houses. Unlike Warsaw, Łódź sustained little damage during the war, but it had a dark history in those years. Before the war 30 per cent of the population was Jewish but very few of them survived it; and many from the surrounding areas were herded into the Łódź ghetto before being sent to Auschwitz and other extermination camps.

I was provided with an escort, a young teaching assistant at the University. She had spent two years in adolescence on a scholarship at Atlantic College in Wales, spoke perfect English, and yearned hopelessly to escape from Poland and the cramped life she could expect there. One day she took me to meet Dr M., a single lady and lecturer in the English Department at the University, in her tiny apartment. She prepared a three-course lunch for us which I ate guiltily, knowing what an effort it must have required to obtain the food. I wrote in my diary later:

> Dr M. is a fervent Catholic and patriot – to her the two
> things go together, and she seemed slightly disconcerted
> to learn that I am a Catholic too, almost as if she
> thought Catholicism was the special property of the
> Poles. The pontificate of Pope John Paul II has rather

encouraged this attitude. Our talk is polite but serious, with none of the jokes, evasions and qualifications that would characterise such a meeting between strangers in England. We discuss the crisis, the films of Wajda, Polish history, Catholicism, the Pope. Dr M. remarks that the liberal theologian Hans Küng's description of the Polish Church as 'authoritarian' was insulting. I introduce the subject of nuclear disarmament. 'Of course,' she says flatly, 'unilateral disarmament means death.' She concedes the difficulty of reconciling the use of nuclear weapons with Christian principles, but this is obviously a vaguer, more problematic issue to her . . . . To a British observer Poland is a looking-glass world in which many of the 'progressive' and 'conservative' positions in our own ideological discourse – on disarmament, on the economy, on religion, on Viet Nam, even on the Boy Scouts – are queerly inverted.

I returned to Warsaw and checked in for my last night to the Europejski, a pre-war grand hotel of slightly shabby splendour, where hard-currency whores plied their trade discreetly amid the potted palms. It was 11th November, Polish Independence Day.

This evening Solidarity has organized a huge procession from the Cathedral of St John in the Old Town to the Tomb of the Unknown Soldier, which faces the Europejski across a vast, barren square. Just after 7.00, X, a young lecturer at Warsaw University, calls at the hotel with a package for me to mail in England, and we go out into the streets to observe the demonstration. Large crowds have turned out to line the pavement and applaud the marchers – unions, Boy Scouts, and many other groups, some of them illegal, like the movement for an independent Poland . . . X and I go back to my hotel room

which overlooks the square and the floodlit tomb of the
Unknown Warrior. X telephones his wife and, standing at
the open window through which amplified speeches carry
to us, describes the scene to her like a war correspondent.
'She says there is nothing about it on the radio,' he says
to me. His eyes are bright with excitement. 'If you had told
me a year ago that such a demonstration could take place
in Warsaw, I would not have believed you.'

A month later, on 13th December, General Jaruzelski declared martial law, the leaders of Solidarity were arrested and imprisoned, and Poland entered a period of political repression which lasted until 1989.

After my visit to Poland I decided to introduce a Polish character into *Small World*. She was called Wanda Kedrzejkiewicelska (the Polish name with the most consonants that I was able to discover), a young lecturer at the University of Łódź specialising in British theatre of the absurd, which she finds not at all absurd, but a sombrely realistic analogue of life in Poland. I wrote a scene or two in which she is shown queuing for sausage for her husband's dinner, while reading *The Birthday Party* and, dreaming longingly of a promised invitation to a British Council summer school in Oxford; then I decided that the invitation would not materialise, and Wanda would spend the entire novel travelling about Łódź by tram in search of likely-looking food queues, poignantly excluded from the plot and all the fun the other characters are having. But her character refused to come alive, and I realised that the plight of the young Polish academics I had met, and of the Polish nation at large, was too grim for incorporation into my lighthearted satire on the global campus. So I cut her out of the story altogether, a decision which also had the advantage of avoiding trespass on Malcolm's fictional territory.

That trip did however make a useful contribution to my novel before I set foot in Poland. I flew to Warsaw from Heathrow on a Sunday, and arrived at the airport very early in order to explore its interdenominational chapel, which was mentioned in Brian Moynahan's book. I had a hunch that it would make a useful setting for a scene or two, and when I discovered that it was called St George's Chapel, with all the mythical and chivalric associations of that name, I knew I was in luck. It took me some time to find it, because no employee of the airport seemed certain where it was, but eventually I discovered it below ground level near Terminal 3: a fan-shaped space with a vaulted ceiling curved like the interior of a giant jet. Although it was officially interdenominational, the Catholics seemed to have taken it over: there was a statue of Our Lady against one wall, and a red sanctuary lamp glowed beside the altar. As I sat there, a priest wearing vestments came in. I asked if he was going to say a Catholic mass. He said 'Yes – do you want Communion?' I asked how long it would take. He said, 'As quick as I can make it.' He evidently had a plane to catch too. His rapid recitation of the liturgy was punctuated by burps of indigestion. I did not use this unromantic episode in the novel, but I did make use of the chapel's ambience and architecture, at once archaic and modern, and exploited the petition board at the back of the pews, where travellers pinned their handwritten prayers. One quoted by Moynahan, obviously from a distraught Irish girl in trouble, suggested a plot strand, and the board would also play a part in Persse's pursuit of Angelica.

Between 1982 and 1983 I was intermittently engaged on an interesting project in a form new to me: the television documentary. I was approached by Jim Berrow, a producer at Central, the independent TV company which then served the Midlands and had its headquarters in Birmingham. At that time he made documentaries for a weekly half-hour slot dedicated to subjects of regional interest, and he asked me if I would write and present a programme about Birmingham writers in the 1930s. He had got the idea from reading a recently published memoir, *As I Walked Down New Grub Street*, by the novelist and critic Walter Allen, who was born in 1911 and brought up in the working-class inner suburb of Aston, Birmingham. He was a scholarship boy who studied English at the city's University before beginning his career as a freelance writer, eventually moving to London like many other young men from the provinces with literary ambitions. I knew him mainly as a book reviewer for the *New Statesman* and author of *The English Novel: A Short Critical History*, a book widely read by several generations of students. The memoir which Jim passed to me contained intriguing information about other writers connected with Birmingham in the thirties. W.H. Auden's father was the city's Chief Medical Officer and his son grew up in Harborne, the adjoining suburb to Edgbaston. He wrote later in 'Letter to Lord Byron': '*Clearer than Scafell Pike my heart has stamped on/ The view from Birmingham to Wolverhampton*'. It's a sentiment likely to surprise most people who have travelled by train between those two cities, but as he explained in the next stanza, '*Tramlines and slagheaps, pieces of machinery,/That was, and is, my ideal scenery.*' That Auden's friend and collaborator Louis MacNeice was a lecturer in classics at the University from 1930 to 1936 was no doubt an incentive to return frequently to the family home at this time. There were several novelists and short-story writers in the region who attracted the attention of the London literati with their authentic descriptions of proletarian life and were known as 'the Birmingham Group', John Hampson being the best known. His first novel, *Saturday Night at the Greyhound*, was published by the Woolfs' Hogarth Press, and widely admired. Walter Allen was acquainted with Henry Green, whose posh family derived their considerable wealth from a Birmingham foundry, and who worked his way up in the firm from factory floor to director, using the experience to write his first novel, *Living*, arguably the best, and certainly the most original, work of fiction written about British working-class life between the wars.

Jim Berrow arranged for me to record a video interview with Walter Allen in his flat in north London. He had recently suffered a stroke, and his speech was slightly impeded, but he spoke with animation, candour and humour. Later I interviewed Reggie Smith, who grew up with Walter in Aston, and was a fellow student at Birmingham before making his career in the British Council and the BBC. He married the novelist Olivia Manning, who portrayed him unforgettably as Guy Pringle in her novel sequence, *Fortunes of War*. When I interviewed Reggie, he provided a vividly amusing account of the farewell party Louis MacNeice gave to his writer friends when he decided to move to London, an event which Reggie claimed 'went on for days'. He recalled the avant-garde theatre director Rupert Doone, who must have come up from London for the occasion, tossing a glass of vodka into the fire with a careless conversational gesture, causing a jet of flame to leap out and singe the trousers of the poet Henry Reed, another alumnus of Birmingham University, who later wrote one of the best poems to come out of the Second World War, 'The Naming of Parts'.

Louis MacNeice's flat was in a converted coach house and stables next to an Italianate Victorian villa in spacious grounds, called Highfield, the home of Philip Sargant Florence, Professor of Economics at the University of Birmingham, and his American wife Lella, a committed feminist, pacifist and pioneer in promoting birth control. Between the wars they made Highfield a refuge for several distinguished refugees from Nazi Germany, including Nikolaus Pevsner and the Bauhaus architect Walter Gropius. Other guests included Vera Brittain, Bertrand Russell, Julian Huxley, Margaret Mead and I.A. Richards. Lella was related by marriage to James Strachey, brother of Lytton and biographer of Sigmund Freud, who often visited with his family, and one might say that Lella and Philip created their own version of 'Bloomsbury' in Selly Park, Birmingham. The young William Empson, future author of the seminal *Seven Types of Ambiguity*, stayed at Highfield when he was expelled from the Cambridge college where he was a postgraduate research fellow, after his bedder reported that he had contraceptives in his room. Philip Sargant Florence hoped to get him a job in the English Department of the University and invited its head, Ernest de Selincourt, to tea with this design, but Empson blew his chances when De Selincourt (whom Walter Allen remembered as 'a stuffy old bore') asked him what he was reading and received the answer, 'Malinowski's *The Sexual Life of Savages*.'

We filmed a section of the TV programme in the flat once occupied by MacNeice, which was still in good shape. But both Philip and Lella were dead by this time and the house had fallen into a sad state of disrepair as local residents struggled to resist the attempts of property developers to buy it – ultimately in vain. Our video camera was probably the last to record the gay, brightly coloured murals of dancing couples that decorated the hall and some rooms. Not long afterwards the building was demolished and an executive housing estate obliterated all trace of the civilised life that had flourished there. Jim Berrow was as fascinated as I was by the story of Highfield, and given more time would have made another film about it. We called the one we did make *As I Was Walking Down Bristol Street*, adapting the first lines of an early Auden poem referencing the main road into the city centre from the west. I enjoyed the experience, and was grateful to Jim for coaching me in the art of writing and presenting documentary television. He is a man of many talents who did not remain for long in the employ of Central, but diversified into writing, lecturing and practising in fields in which he has expert knowledge: music, architecture and the preservation of historic church organs. At the time I met him he also flew his own light aeroplane for recreation. He offered to take me up in it as a passenger, but I declined. I did not doubt Jim's competence as a pilot, but I had the impression that small, privately owned planes crashed more often than big commercial jets, and I did not wish to increase my chances of dying before *Small World* was published.

*

I delivered the typescript of *Small World* to Secker in May 1983, which was later than I had predicted and too late for it to be published in that year; but Tom Rosenthal was pleased by the delay because he was about to publish *Rates of Exchange*, Malcolm's first new novel for eight years, and he didn't want us to be competing with each other once again for the same prizes, especially the Booker. Like every other publisher in London he was excited by the sudden rise in the public profile of this prize and its impact on reputations and sales. When he read *Small World* he 'loved it' and a contract was quickly drawn up. John Blackwell was equally delighted, but made a useful suggestion for improvement. He feared that the first chapter, describing the comical discomforts and fiascos of the Rummidge conference, would create an expectation that the whole novel would be a campus novel of a familiar type in the mode of *Lucky Jim*, and he suggested some kind of prologue which would signal the later opening out of the story thematically and geographically. I saw his point, and quickly wrote a prologue that borrowed the opening lines of Chaucer's *Canterbury Tales*, about the coming of spring, when '*longen folk to goon on pilgrimages*, only these days, professional people call them conferences'. John wrote in early August to report that enthusiasm was spreading through the stacked floors of 54 Poland Street, the tall narrow town house in Soho occupied by Secker & Warburg. Sales and Marketing were extremely positive, and 'the major difficulty now is getting the TS out of production and to the printer, as the entire department want to read it, and refuse to let it go until I've sent a spare Xerox'. John knew how, with a little exaggeration, to lift an author's spirits.

But mine seemed destined to go up and down unpredictably – like every writer's spirits, no doubt. Soon after Secker accepted *Small World*, Morrow – who had taken on *How Far Can You Go?* because they believed in my future as a writer – rejected it. Jim Brown had sent it confidently to Howard Cady, who returned the typescript to him with exceptional speed, as if he couldn't wait to be rid of it, with a covering letter, copied to me, in which he declared himself 'terribly disappointed and somewhat bewildered' by the novel. These words described exactly my own reaction to his rambling and emotional epistle, e.g.: 'Although happy endings are not essential, each one of the facets of the story involving suspense tends to end with a whimper and a sigh. Nothing works and nothing turns out to be worthwhile. Although I found it fascinating, there is too much of it and it is too deliberately disenchanting.' He devoted a paragraph to his father's career as a professor of English who always attended the MLA convention after Christmas, and to supplement his meagre income taught summer schools at several universities, including Berkeley, all through the Depression. It seemed to me that my carnivalesque satirical novel had somehow dishonoured the memory of his father, or else stirred up some repressed Oedipus complex, in Howard Cady's psyche. Jim Brown, who was equally astonished by the rejection, agreed with me. Cady himself evidently regretted the tone of his letter because he attached to it another one addressed to me personally, saying he wrote it on 'a bad day for me with all kinds of pressures', and his last word about the novel was 'may you soon prove that I am totally wrong about it.' Eventually I did, but it took some time.

Later that summer I received a dramatic and disturbing phone call from Eileen in Hawaii. She had come to England in the previous year to assess the advisability of returning permanently. Her cousin Lilian, and Lilian's daughter, Pat, a schoolteacher married to another, John, were virtually her only relatives in Britain apart from me. They lived comfortably together near Henley on Thames, were very fond of Eileen, and generously offered to help her settle near them. This was a great relief to me as Mary and I had no spare time or energy to devote to this task ourselves, and

Birmingham was not a place Eileen was likely to find congenial. The cousins found a private residential home for retired people fairly near them which agreed to take Eileen for a trial period of a month. She came in the autumn, and Mary and I visited her there one day and took her out to lunch. She had a bed-sitting room, but ate her meals communally, and had the use of a large lounge with upright armchairs which, like all such rooms in such places, gave an impression that time passed very slowly there. The building was a large villa, clean but old-fashioned and somewhat dingy in décor and furnishings, presided over by an authoritarian female manager, and its general ambience was cripplingly genteel. I immediately sensed that Eileen could not possibly be happy there, though she was tactful in her remarks about the place, not wishing to appear ungrateful to Lilian, Pat and John for all their efforts on her behalf.

It was not until she returned to Hawaii that she expressed in a letter to me the full depths of her unhappiness during her stay. It had been exacerbated by the fact that she was not feeling well at the time, suffering pain that was diagnosed as arthritis. The phone call I received in July 1983 revealed the real cause. She had been diagnosed with terminal abdominal cancer, and then unluckily had a fall and broke her shoulder. She spoke to me from the hospital where she was being treated, very distressed because she was sure she was dying and unable to do anything to settle her affairs. She asked if I could possibly come out to help her, and I said I would. I then phoned her doctor who told me that she might live for a year, but she had refused chemotherapy so it could be much less. I decided to go sooner rather than later and flew to Honolulu in mid-August, changing planes in Los Angeles. By now I was used to the eighteen-hour journey, and my previous acquaintance with Waikiki was helpful for this mission.

I stayed in Eileen's apartment and as soon as I had slept off the fatigue of the journey I hired the cheapest car I could find and went in search of her. She was no longer in the hospital but in what was described as a 'care home', i.e. the home of somebody who was making a little money by looking after convalescent patients whose insurance did not cover the cost of a proper nursing home – nor, in Eileen's case, a very high standard of care. I found her in a shabby bungalow in a run-down suburb of Honolulu, and we had an emotional reunion. She was overjoyed to see me, but in poor shape, weak and thin, with one arm still in a sling, lying under a sheet on a low bed in a scruffy room. She was chronically constipated from the pain-killing drugs she was taking, and had no appetite for the food her Filipino landlady provided. I promised to see her doctor as soon as possible and to insist that he came to see for himself that she needed to return to hospital. This was accomplished by the end of the next day. Her constipation was treated successfully, and she was allowed to remain in the hospital while I looked for the best nursing home she could afford without exhausting her savings before she died – a grimly delicate calculation.

I devoted several days to this quest, which took me to some deeply depressing institutions stinking of incontinence and abandoned hope, but I finally found one on the outskirts of the city which I thought would be acceptable – the staff were warm and friendly and the management inspired trust. I obtained power of attorney for Eileen – we signed the forms in the presence of a lawyer beside her hospital bed – and had meetings with her bank and stockbroker to sell her shares and consolidate her funds. I made arrangements for the termination of her lease on the apartment and disposal of her furniture and other effects. These appointments took me into downtown Honolulu where there was a small-scale imitation of Wall Street like a movie set, with tower blocks whose occupants wore suits and ties in their icily air-conditioned offices. My dealings with them were totally incongruous with the hedonistic pursuits of the tourists in Hawaiian shirts and flip-flops who swarmed over the beaches and pavements of Waikiki, and I could not be unaware of the ironies of my situation, helping an elderly Christian woman in pain to die as comfortably as possible, in a place dedicated to commercialised pleasure. Even as I went about my melancholy business in this setting, I thought that one day I might explore its thematic possibilities in fiction.

When I got back to the apartment in the late afternoon I usually refreshed myself with a swim in the small pool provided for residents, but one evening I put on a pair of swimming trunks under my shorts and drove to the beach instead, to a quiet stretch beyond the last big hotels, where only a few other people were scattered over the sand. After an enjoyable dip I dried off and sat down to watch the sun set over the calm sea. When I decided to put on my shorts I discovered that my keys – the car key, the apartment key, and the key to Eileen's safe-deposit box, all together on a key ring – were not in the pockets of the shorts, or in any other item of my clothing, so must have fallen into the soft dry sand when I changed. I rotated very carefully without moving from the spot, conscious that doing so might only cover the keys with more sand, but could see no sign of them in the small hillocks and hollows of the beach. I groaned aloud. The difficulty of replacing the keys didn't bear thinking about, and the merit of my efforts on Eileen's behalf would be cancelled out by the worry this mishap would cause her.

Soon it would be too dark to search, for the huge golden disc of the sun was now almost touching the horizon, its beams reflected in the surface of the sea. This gave me an idea. Looking down very carefully at where I was planting my feet for any sign of the keys, I walked straight down to the water's edge, some fifteen yards away, turned my back to the sun, squatted down and looked at the place where I had changed for my swim. I was aware of a couple of youths further up the beach watching me curiously. A yard or two to the right of my towel something glinted. When I stood up the gleam disappeared; when I squatted again it returned. Keeping my eye fixed on the spot, I walked to it and with indescribable relief plucked from the sand the protruding tip of Eileen's safe-deposit key and the key ring to which it was attached. A few moments later the sun disappeared beneath the horizon. I have no idea what inspired this ingenious recovery of the lost keys, for I am not of a practical and scientific turn of mind. Perhaps it was the buried memory of a similar feat in some adventure story read in boyhood. In due course the incident, somewhat elaborated, was incorporated into the novel which was already germinating in my mind.

Eileen's faith was a great help to her and I did not disturb it by voicing my private agnostic views, though we did discuss religion from time to time and she was by no means uncritical of the Catholic Church as an institution. I arranged for a priest to visit her regularly after I had gone, and made a phone call to a Catholic hospice organisation which was answered by a voluntary helper called Marian Vaught, who generously offered to do the same. When I came to the nursing home to say goodbye to Eileen the evening before I was due to fly home, a meeting I was dreading because we both knew we would never see each other again, she was eager to tell me of the wonderful woman who had visited her earlier that day, a tall, fair, gracious lady, wearing the long loose cotton dress Hawaiians call a *muu-muu*, who had spoken to her so kindly and comfortingly that she felt she had been visited by an angel. In consequence our parting was much less painful than I had feared. Marian Vaught was indeed a treasure whom I had been lucky to stumble on. She visited Eileen frequently and kept me in touch with her condition until she died, peacefully in her sleep, on the 15th of September, only a few weeks after she entered the nursing home. It was a merciful release from a situation that no amount of kindness could make tolerable for long. About two years later Marian and her husband came to England on a vacation that included a canal cruise on a narrowboat which brought them near Birmingham, and I was able to invite them to visit us and to thank Marian in person for what she had done for Eileen.

# 9

I have usually found that the most enjoyable period in the long process of producing a novel is in the interval, which can be as long as a year, between having it accepted by the publisher and bracing yourself for its imminent publication. Acceptance proves that your labour has not been wasted, but only the public reception of the book will show whether it is a success or failure or something in between, and is therefore awaited with growing tension as it approaches. The earlier part of this transitional period is dedicated to mostly agreeable and absorbing tasks like polishing and improving the text in collaboration with your editor, approving (and sometimes drafting) the blurb and catalogue copy, discussing the jacket design and so on. The more important the author becomes to the publisher, the more s/he is consulted about such matters. The jacket of *Changing Places*, my first book with Secker, was a disappointingly plain and cheap affair: pale yellow unlaminated paper that quickly became tattered and soiled in use, on which the author's name and title were printed in large red and blue letters, with the designation 'A Novel' at the bottom, oddly printed in silver. I don't recall being shown a rough of this cover before I saw it wrapped around the finished book, but in any case I would have hesitated to complain. Tom admitted to some embarrassment about it after the book's success, and from then onwards I always had approval, and often personal input, in the matter of jacket design. The cover of *How Far Can You Go?* featuring a Snakes and Ladders board was my concept, elegantly executed by an anonymous artist. I took a keen interest in this aspect of publishing, and suggested the main image or basic idea for most of the Secker jackets of my novels, while for the novella *Home Truths* I produced a sketch which was faithfully followed. The art director at Secker when *Small World* was in production was Gill Sutherland, then married to a fellow academic and friend, John Sutherland, and she took on board my suggestion that the artwork on the jacket should combine imagery of modern global travel with motifs from ancient myth and romance. The result was an ingenious treatment of the title in which the capital 'S' of the first word was drawn on a large scale and elaborately illuminated as in a medieval manuscript. Two naked maidens on a seashore, who might be sirens or sacrificial offerings to a dragon, shared the top curve of the 'S' with an image of Concorde in flight, while the bottom curve was occupied by a warrior on a galloping horse leaping over a typewriter keyboard, and other synecdochic details were packed into the frame around the letter. I was delighted with it.

The typescript of a novel in production has to be copy-edited, i.e. prepared for the printer by careful scrutiny, and correction where required, of grammar, spelling, punctuation, and referential accuracy. Nowadays this task is usually given to a freelance copy-editor, whose queries the author answers by email, but John Blackwell was an editor of a kind now almost obsolete, who undertook the entire process of overseeing and assisting a book's progress from typescript to print, including the time-consuming task of copy-editing, and he encouraged face-to-face consultation. I was always glad to have a reason to visit 59 Poland Street, which seemed more like the home of a delightfully eccentric extended family than the premises of a commercial business. At the rear of the ground floor, in an office made out of a conservatory, was Barley Alison, a legendary figure who had her own list of distinguished authors, including Saul Bellow, published as 'Alison Press Books' under the Secker imprint, but I did not get to know her and her eventful history well until some years later. On the first floor was Tom's office and I would glimpse him through the open door at his desk, in boldly striped shirt and red braces, booming down the line to New York or Sydney, with telephone in one hand while he signed letters brought by his secretary with the other. Further up the crooked staircase were other offices housing the various departments of the publishing process, with John's cosy attic at the top, full of tottering piles of books and manuscripts, and his assistant Alison's cubbyhole close by.

In November, when I was correcting proofs, I received a letter from John Batchelor, a former Birmingham colleague and currently Fellow of New College, Oxford, asking me if I was going to apply for the Goldsmiths' Chair of English Literature which had just been advertised by Oxford University. This was a prestigious chair, linked to a fellowship at New College, and had been occupied most recently by Richard Ellmann, who had decided to retire, so it was a reasonable assumption that the School of English would be looking for a successor specialising in the modern period. I thought I would be eligible, and after talking it over with Mary, I decided to apply.

That I took this step shows I was still wedded to the idea of a twin career, as novelist and academic. This was partly due to innate financial caution. I had never expected to earn enough money from writing fiction to support a comfortable lifestyle and provide for my family – in particular for Christopher, whose long-term needs were imponderable – and although I was doing well financially at the time, I did not feel confident of maintaining the same level of income from writing indefinitely. The £5,000 I had received from the Whitbread Prize was serious money in the early eighties, and it had emboldened me to negotiate the contract with Birmingham which gave me more time to write – and not only fiction. I still derived intellectual satisfaction from writing criticism, and I wanted to continue the rhythm I had settled into, of producing a novel and a critical book in alternation. The part-time arrangement I had at Birmingham was in many ways ideal for this purpose, but I had been in the same department for twenty-three years, and the repetitiousness of teaching in the same institution for so long was becoming wearisome. If I was ever going to move from Birmingham before I retired, wouldn't an Oxford chair be an excellent opportunity and a real change? Professorial duties were light: a modest number of lectures per academic year, some of which could be converted into seminars, and the supervision of postgraduate theses, but none of the personal tutoring of undergraduates which was the main work of most dons in English. Terms were short, vacations correspondingly long, Oxford as a city had numerous attractions as a place to live, and we had friends there. Our two older children had finished with school education and Christopher had nearly come to the end of the excellent provision Birmingham had offered in this respect. These were the factors which persuaded me to apply, and Mary acquiesced. The school where she had been a teacher-counsellor for eight years had closed down and she was exploring new career possibilities herself. I knew the job would attract a strong field of applicants, but I thought I had nothing to lose by applying. If memories of the stress I had suffered over the possibility of moving to Cambridge in 1966 occurred to me, I must have discounted them. So I posted my letter of application and CV.

At about this time my friend and colleague, Park Honan, who had joined the Department in 1968 as Lecturer in English and American Literature, and was now Reader, had also been feeling restive. When Leeds University advertised a new chair of English and American Literature he applied for it and asked me to be one of his referees. To his great delight he was appointed, and after a period of commuting, found a spacious early Victorian house on top of a hill in Leeds into which he and Jeannette moved, their three children having by now left home. Mary and Jeannette were close friends and particularly sad to be separated, but we promised each other to exchange regular visits in the years ahead.

Early in 1984 the publicity department began to take up more of my time. Secker's chief publicist was then Beth Macdougall, an enthusiastic and energetic lady, who arranged several press and media interviews for me around the book's publication at the beginning of April, including a featured interview in the *Guardian*, another with Hermione Lee for Channel 4 TV, and a talk on BBC Radio 3 in a series called *The Living Novelist*. The BBC's TV programme *Bookmark* proposed to preface its discussion of *Small World* with a filmed sequence in which I would be shown checking in at Heathrow on my way to a conference in some exotic location, with extracts from the novel read in voice-over. Heathrow would not co-operate, so the sequence was filmed at Manchester airport. A comely check-in clerk was asked to take the place of Cheryl Summerbee, but unfortunately she had no natural talent as an actress, and several takes of the simple scene were required, but I enjoyed the experience. To cap it all I was a guest on *Desert Island Discs*.[1] Some people have spent whole lifetimes hopefully compiling and revising lists of the eight pieces of music they would most like to listen to if stranded

[1] In case it is of interest my own choices were: 1. 'Chocolate Apricot', from the LP *A Different Kind of Blues* by André Previn and Itzhak Perlman. 2. Simon & Garfunkel, 'Dangling Conversation' from *Parsley, Sage, Rosemary & Thyme*. 3. Miles Davis, 'Concerto de Aranjuez' from *Sketches of Spain*. 4. Albinoni's *Adagio*. 5. Joni Mitchell, 'You Turn me On, I'm a Radio' from *Miles of Aisles*. 6. Monteverdi, the *Deposuit* from the Magnificat in Six Voices. 7. George and Ira Gershwin, 'A Foggy Day', sung by Ella Fitzgerald. 8. Edward Elgar, the 'Nimrod' movement from *Enigma Variations*.

on a desert island with a record player. My session was one of the last presented by its originator, Roy Plomley, before he retired and was replaced by other interviewers. He entertained me to lunch at the Garrick Club before the recording, as was his practice, and told me candidly that he had had time to read only one of my books. He had chosen *The British Museum is Falling Down*, I suspect because it was the shortest, but it gave me a good reason to make 'A Foggy Day' one of my discs. This was the first time in my life that I had received this kind of attention, and it was undeniably rather exciting. Nevertheless I awaited the general verdict of the reviewers on *Small World* with the usual degree of suspense.

In the previous year Malcolm had published *Rates of Exchange*, and I observed its reception with interest, especially in relation to the Booker Prize. He had himself been involved in its operation as chairman of the judging panel in 1981, an experience which impressed him with the power and glamour of the prize and made him dream of winning it himself one day. In that year the judges awarded it to Salman Rushdie's *Midnight's Children*, though Malcolm told me beforehand that he had personally favoured D.M. Thomas's *The White Hotel*. The competition between these two writers, Thomas and Rushdie, who were little known previously, both experimenting with types of magic realism alien to the English novel tradition, aroused almost as much media interest as that between the two veterans, Golding and Burgess, the previous year. *The White Hotel* was a fictitious case study of one of Freud's patients, mediated through poetic and hallucinatory erotic sequences, including a harrowing account of the Babi Yar massacre of more than 30,000 Jews by German forces in the Ukraine in 1941. It was disliked by the first British reviewers on its publication in the spring of 1981, but everybody in the literary world was talking about it when I was in New York and Princeton so I obtained a copy, and it seemed to me a powerful and original work. Soon its success in America filtered back to Britain, critics began to talk up its merits, and it became a strong contender for the Booker, though later Thomas was accused of borrowing too freely from Anatoly Kuznetsov's documentary novel *Babi Yar*. Salman Rushdie's success was a happier story, though it would have a fateful sequel in the long term.

In the following year the winner was Thomas Keneally's *Schindler's Ark*, which provoked another controversy, also connected with the Holocaust, as to whether it was really a novel, since it told, in a historical rather than a novelistic style, the true story of how the German businessman Oskar Schindler saved the lives of more than a thousand Jews in Nazi-occupied Poland by employing them in his factory. In fact it was first published in America as a work of non-fiction, but in Britain as a novel. I was then reviewing fiction regularly for the *Sunday Times*, and I concluded my piece on this book: 'Thomas Keneally has done marvellous justice to a marvellous story, and *Schindler's Ark* is well worth a literary prize. But perhaps it should be a prize for knowing when fiction could not improve on the facts.'

There was no generic ambiguity about Malcolm's *Rates of Exchange*. It was unmistakably a work of fiction, set in an imaginary East European Communist state called Slaka with resemblances to several Slavic and Balkan countries. I happened to be on a British Council tour of Yugoslavia in the spring of 1983 not long after it was published, and one day on a street in Zagreb my eye was caught by a music cassette entitled 'Slaka' in the window of a record shop. It had a picture on the box of a band of musicians in a rustic setting, wearing folk costumes and wielding large brass instruments. Slaka turned out to be the name of the band. I bought the cassette and listened to it on my Walkman that evening, highly amused by the ponderous *oompha oompha* music, which was just what one would expect Slakan music to sound like, and when I sent the cassette to Malcolm as a gift he was delighted with it. He had invented a detailed history for this country, and a language. The latter generates much of the novel's humour (brandy is *rot'vitti*, the state department store is MUG) as does the slightly fractured English of the educated Slakans whom the central character, an English academic called Dr Petworth, meets on his British Council tour of the country, where his name is subjected to ludicrous mutations, 'Petwert, Prevert, Pervert', etc. Superficially the linguistic jokes are at the expense of the Slakans, but in the end they emerge with more credit and dignity from the story than their English visitor, who fails to understand the complexities of living as an intellectual in a totalitarian state.

In America the crucially influential *New York Times Book Review* has the humane practice of circulating its reviews to publishers in advance of publication so that authors can be warned of a disappointing one or cheered by a favourable one and spared some suspense. In Britain the important reviews come out bunched together over a short period around the official publication date, and there is no way of discovering what they are like beforehand. You would probably see the first one in your daily or Sunday newspaper, and breakfast might be a queasy meal in consequence. Malcolm had heard that Martin Amis was reviewing *Rates of Exchange* for the *Observer* and was apprehensive, with reason. Amis was a role model for many younger British novelists, and also a very skilful writer of critical prose, and it was impossible not to see his witty put-down of Malcolm's novel as a challenge from a new literary generation against the preceding one. There was however an excellent review in the *Sunday Times* to compensate, and there were enough good ones subsequently to encourage Malcolm's hopes of being shortlisted for the Booker. To his great joy and relief he was shortlisted in September, though the bookies made him an outsider with the longest odds. Just before Judgement Day in October I sent Malcolm a postcard of the young James Joyce gazing quizzically into the lens of a camera (wondering, he recalled later, if the photographer would lend him five shillings) to wish him luck. To be the outsider, I told him, was a good position, because if you win the glory will be all the greater, and if you don't the disappointment will be milder.

The chairperson of the judges that year was the novelist Fay Weldon. Martyn Goff, the chief administrator of the prize, who would perform this function for more than thirty years, revealed in an interview in 2003 that, at their final session to choose the winner on the day of the award, the other four judges were divided evenly between J.M. Coetzee's *Life and Times of Michael K* and Salman Rushdie's *Shame*. This gave Fay Weldon the casting vote. But she was quite unable to decide between them, and changed her mind several times, reading passages aloud from each to compare their merits, as the clock ticked on to 6 p.m. when the result *had* to be conveyed to the PR staff, until she eventually chose Coetzee. Goff dashed to the phone in the room and delivered the message, pretending not to hear Fay say, 'Hold it a minute . . .' Thus are literary fortunes determined in the media-dominated modern world. The South African Coetzee was not well known in Britain, but he went from strength to strength subsequently, winning the Booker a second time with *Disgrace* in 1999, and the Nobel Prize in 2003. The judges knew that he would not be attending the banquet that evening, a decision which seemed very much in the writer's independent character, but made for a rather anticlimactic presentation ceremony. The prize was accepted by his British publisher – Tom Rosenthal, who was in the unusual position of having two novels in the shortlist of six. I was sure he would have preferred to see Malcolm going up to receive the prize for *Rates of Exchange*.

In those days the BBC devoted a long programme to live television coverage of the event on BBC2, including shots of the guests arriving, and then eating and drinking at the banquet tables, a panel of critics speculating about the result, and the presentation and acceptance speeches. Mary and I watched the whole thing of course, and I called Malcolm the next evening to commiserate and chat about the result. He sounded tired and in low spirits – not surprisingly. All the shortlisted candidates know, however much they discount their chances, that they will have to make a speech if they win, and most will take the precaution of preparing a few words for that eventuality. But to do that is to imagine oneself winning, which makes the experience of not winning all the more deflating, as I would discover myself in due course. But that wasn't what Malcolm meant when he said at the end of our conversation, with a wistful sigh, 'Well, now it's your turn.' He meant: now it's your turn to have a taste of all that excitement and publicity and drama if you're shortlisted. Though I made a self-deprecating response, the enthusiasm of everyone at Secker for *Small World* was encouraging. 'This is going to be the big one,' Tom Rosenthal assured me.

On Friday 16th March Claire Tomalin, the literary editor of the *Sunday Times*, wrote a letter to me: 'I am so sorry – we have a *very* unfavourable review of your new book (from Peter Kemp). I'm writing to warn you, because it may be slightly less horrible to know in advance.' This was kind of her, but unfortunately I did not receive the letter until the following Monday morning, a day after the review appeared. It was indeed a stinker, and a very long one. Kemp declared his admiration for my previous novels at the outset, and as chief fiction reviewer for the *Sunday Times* he was consistently favourable to several of my later books, but he simply hated the self-conscious literariness of *Small World*, and didn't have a single good word to say for it. It was the first review I read and therefore all the more demoralising. I read one more that Sunday, in the *Observer*, by Anthony Thwaite, which was wholly positive, but bad reviews always have more effect on the author than good ones, and the fact that Anthony was a friend made his count for less as an indicator of the book's likely reception. I waited for most of the other reviews to be sent to me by John Blackwell or Beth Macdougall, and those I saw in that first week were not encouraging. Blake Morrison was cool in the *TLS*, and when I peeped inside a copy of the *New Statesman* in W.H. Smith's on New Street station I found a contemptuous six-line dismissal of *Small World* which made me think that my hopes for this novel had been deluded.

The short film at the beginning of the BBC's *Bookmark* programme, showing me checking in at the airport, was quite amusing, but the discussion of the novel that followed, between three well-known figures from the literary world, began with a sourly disapproving verdict from Christopher Ricks. He said it was not an accurate description of academic life, and was indifferent to anything important about universities, with tired jokes that didn't make him laugh much, and in general was 'the work of a tired man'. Beryl Bainbridge, who looked rather intimidated by Ricks or the occasion, said timidly she had enjoyed it and had found it funny but thought it was over-long and many of the lit. crit. references went over her head. Fortunately Leo Cooper, publisher and husband of the writer Jilly Cooper, said it was a very funny book which had a good chance of being shortlisted for the Booker Prize, and several of the characters in it had reminded him slightly of Professor Ricks. Ricks did admit that the only occasion on which he met me was on a plane going to a conference, and I was reminded also of the Bristol UTE conference where I met Pat Sheeran. That conference featured a lecture by Ricks, who arrived one morning, having flown overnight from New York where he had delivered another (or possibly the same) lecture the previous day, hired a car at Heathrow and drove to Bristol just in time to perform a brilliant discourse on Samuel Beckett, and departed shortly afterwards to his next engagement: typical behaviour of a star of the global campus. John Blackwell wrote next day, 'We are thinking of putting out a contract on Christopher Ricks', and pretended similar malevolence towards Peter Kemp. But as cuttings from other newspapers began to flow in it became evident that favourable reviews greatly outnumbered the unfavourable, and there were several that could be called 'raves'. A.S. Byatt and Margaret Drabble each wrote one, a rare example of agreement between these sisters. Antonia Byatt's review in *The Times* contained a small but piquant example of writer's luck. In *Small World* Philip Swallow, whose wife is called Hilary, has a passionate affair with a woman called Joy, who resembles Hilary when she was younger and prettier. When he first meets her, Joy is wearing a dressing gown like one Hilary used to wear. In her review Antonia noted approvingly that the theme of identity and difference which runs through the whole novel, most obviously in the story of the two twins, was neatly encapsulated in the names of the two women, Hilary deriving from the Latin *hilaritas*, meaning 'joy'. I did not intentionally produce this pleasing symmetry. I called Philip's wife Hilary in *Changing Places* because it is an androgynous first name and at that stage of their marriage she was the dominant partner, or as people used to say, she wore the trousers. I gave Joy that name because when Philip falls in love with her he is in pursuit of what he calls 'intensity of experience', an essentially Romantic quest, with a capital 'R'. At the moment of consummation he exclaims 'Joy!' fusing the proper name and the abstract noun. I had no conscious knowledge of the Latin root of the name Hilary when I wrote the novel, but the play on words enriches the text and I gratefully appropriated it. It is a good example of what Roland Barthes called 'the text working' (rather than the author).

*Small World* appeared on the lower rungs of the *Sunday Times* bestseller list two weeks after publication, and I felt more cheerful about its prospects as I set off shortly afterwards for a sojourn in the Italian Lakes. It was my Harvard friend Donald Fanger who first told me, some time in the early eighties, about the Villa Serbelloni at Bellagio. It was acquired shortly after the Second World War by the immensely rich Rockefeller Foundation, who turned it into a luxurious conference centre and residential retreat for 'academics, artists, thought leaders, policymakers, and practitioners' (as its website states), mainly, but not exclusively, Americans. It is a palatial building which traces its history back to the fifteenth century, in an idyllic situation high above the village of Bellagio, on the steep-sided promontory where Lake Como and Lake Lecco meet and merge. Donald explained that you applied to be a resident for periods of four weeks' duration to work on a specific project. You were given a study, either in the Villa or in one of the gazebos scattered through the surrounding estate, and a spacious bed-sitting room in the Villa. The routine was like that of a traditional country house party, and applicants were encouraged to bring a spouse or partner. (It was said that one had twisted the arm of his recently divorced wife to accompany him, rather than jeopardise his chances by applying solo.) Every day there was a sit-down lunch, preceded by aperitifs on the terrace, with the alternative of a packed lunch for the more industrious residents, and in the evening a dinner, followed by civilised socialising in the drawing room. Donald and Margot had been guests there and had thoroughly enjoyed the experience. He said I should apply and kindly offered to be one of my referees. I needed no urging: I had just begun to make notes for *Small World*, and it seemed to me that the Villa Serbelloni would be the ideal place to work on it.

Spring and autumn were thought to be the best seasons to be there, and I accordingly applied to spend four weeks in April 1983, when Mary would have an Easter holiday from teaching and could join me for part of the time. But I was too late – the Villa was already booked up for that year. I was encouraged by the Foundation in New York to reapply for the following year, and did so, but by that time I had nearly finished writing the novel. Accordingly I changed the project I proposed to work on at Bellagio to something academic. I had recently accepted a commission from Walt Litz to contribute an essay on 'Form and Structure in Jane Austen's Novels' for a book called *The Jane Austen Companion* of which he was a co-editor, so I proposed to spend my time at the Villa Serbelloni preparing to write that piece. Re-reading Jane Austen's *oeuvre* in that setting would, I thought, be a very enjoyable and stress-free project. In due course I was accepted as a resident in April 1984, and I looked forward to the experience.

I could not, however, resist the temptation to anticipate it by incorporating the Villa Serbelloni into the story of *Small World* – it seemed such a quintessential example of the perks of the global campus that were available to its most successful denizens, and I thought I could get enough information from Donald Fanger to describe it accurately (which turned out to be the case). I decided to send Morris Zapp there. Looking down from the balcony of his suite at the pre-lunch aperitifs on the terrace:

> He surveyed the scene with complacency. He felt sure
> he was going to enjoy his stay here. Not the least of its
> attractions was that it was entirely free. All you had to
> do to come and stay in this idyllic retreat, pampered
> by servants and lavishly provided with food and drink,
> given every facility for reflection and creation, was to
> apply. Of course you had to be distinguished – by, for
> instance, having applied successfully for other, similar
> handouts, grants, fellowships and so on, in the past.
> That was the beauty of the academic life, as Morris saw
> it. To those that had, more would be given.

Morris is punished for his hubris by the plot, when he is kidnapped by Italian terrorists while jogging on the footpaths of the Villa's estate and held for ransom, but even so it was a passage that made me increasingly uneasy as the time approached for me to take his place in actuality, only a couple of weeks after *Small World* was published. When I was writing the novel I had not envisaged such a close contiguity between these two events. How would the custodians of the place and my fellow residents react when they heard about the novel? Would I stand accused of biting the hand that fed me? Would it be any mitigation that I had bitten before I was fed?

To my surprise and temporary relief I found that no one at the Villa had any idea that I was a novelist. The paperwork connected with my visit, including the list of current residents, had me down only as a professor of English Literature working on Jane Austen. (There was an additional irony in the fictional fact that Morris Zapp was 'a Jane Austen man'; indeed, he liked to think, *the* Jane Austen man.) It is not my habit to volunteer the information that I am a novelist, and I resolved to keep schtum on the subject in Bellagio. It so happened that there was no one among the other residents with an interest in contemporary fiction who might have recognised my name in that context. The only other literary scholar among them was a German-American professor of Comparative Literature at Washington University, Seattle, whose subject was the influence of Nietzsche on critical theory. His beautiful blonde wife was a professor of Germanic Studies at the same university, and after Mary joined me we played tennis doubles with them on the Villa's tree-shaded court. Mary, needless to say, was happy to follow my lead in making no reference to my novels in conversation with them and other residents. There were two rather jolly female Canadian professors of nursing who were collaborating on a book about life and death decisions in medical treatment, one of whom proposed as after-dinner entertainment that we should all collaborate in composing the scenario of a whodunnit called *Murder at the Villa Serbelloni*, and she was disappointed that I showed no enthusiasm for this exercise.

Then one day a resident went to Milan airport to meet his wife and returned alone (her flight was delayed) but with a Penguin edition of *Ginger, You're Barmy* in his hand which he had picked up from the airport's bookstall. He confronted me with it and accused me genially of hiding my light under a bushel. My cover was partly blown, but evidently nobody had heard of *Small*

*World*. I wondered how long I could keep the Villa's inhabitants ignorant of its existence. Twice during our stay there was briefly an influx of people from all over the world for small-scale elite conferences – one on 'Privacy' and another on 'The History of European Ideas' – with whom we mingled at dinner, and it seemed quite possible that one of them would have brought a copy of *Small World*, or a British magazine containing a review of it, to read on the plane. What I most feared was an arrival of the latest issue of the *London Review of Books* in the Villa's library, for I had noticed that they subscribed to it, and Frank Kermode had written to me that he was reviewing the novel for the *LRB*.

Our time at Bellagio passed very agreeably. The sun shone, the spring flowers bloomed, the Villa's huge estate invited walks which gave breathtaking views across the lakes, and we made a couple of excursions by boat to Como. I enjoyed revisiting Jane Austen's novels, and Mary was given a gazebo of her own to do some course planning for her teaching at a Further Education unit in Birmingham she had just joined. Nevertheless, I suffered a lingering sense of guilt, or bad faith, and occasional urges to confess my secret. At the end of our stay I shook hands with our hosts and fellow guests with it still intact, resolving that as soon as I got home I would write a letter to the Villa's chief administrator revealing all, and donating a copy of *Small World* to the library.

This I did, and both letter and book were received with great good humour. But towards the top of the heap of mail that awaited us at home was the latest issue of the *London Review of Books*, containing Frank Kermode's review. It was a very favourable one, which was no surprise because he had told me how much he admired the novel. What struck me most forcibly was the heading it had been given by some member of the editorial staff – by whom, I do not know, nor upon what whim, or with what telepathic insight into my own anxiety, for it was not the most obvious strapline for the review of a novel with so many exotic locations. It was entitled 'Jogging in Bellagio'.

## 10

A couple of weeks after our return from Bellagio, I received a letter from the Registrar of Oxford University:

> Dear Professor Lodge,
>   The electors to the Goldsmiths' Professorship of English Literature were glad to have the opportunity of considering your application. They have, however, appointed Mr E.L. Jones to the professorship and his election will be announced shortly.
>
>                                         Yours sincerely, A.J. Dorey

This was the first communication I had received from Oxford since I applied for the chair six months earlier, during which time I had given less and less thought to the matter, assuming that as I had not been called to an interview I was not in the running. It had also crossed my mind lately that the irreverent treatment of academia in *Small World* might have an adverse effect on my chances. But my immediate reaction when I read the letter was an ejaculation of surprise. Who on earth was Mr E.L.

Jones? I could not think of a likely candidate of that name, with no 'Professor' or 'Dr' prefixed to it. He was, I soon discovered, Emrys Lloyd Jones, Reader in English Literature and Fellow of Magdalen College, who had spent his entire academic career at Oxford, and like many dons of his generation had not bothered to acquire a PhD. He was a highly respected scholar specialising in poetry and drama of the Elizabethan and Jacobean periods, including Shakespeare, and by all accounts a very amiable man, but he was a surprising choice to succeed Richard Ellmann. He was married to another Shakespeare specialist, Barbara Everett, a Fellow of Somerville College, who also wrote criticism on modern literature. Coincidentally, she had written to me in February, though we had had no previous contact, to express appreciation of a selection of Ring Lardner's stories I had recently published with Dent, and also her enjoyment of *Changing Places*, for which I thanked her, neither of us knowing that I was competing with her husband for the same chair.

Not that there had been any competition in the usual sense. In those days each named chair of English at Oxford had a small standing committee of electors dedicated to it, with autonomous power to make appointments. I learned later, from various sources, that the Goldsmiths' committee of four, chaired by Rachel Trickett, Principal of St Hugh's College, had decided that they need not interview any outside candidates since there were two eligible insiders. They were however evenly divided in their preferences between these two, and so entrenched in their positions that the appointment was delayed for months, until eventually the Vice-Chancellor of the University was obliged to break the deadlock and decided in favour of Emrys Jones. I was told there was a great row in the Oxford English Faculty when the decision was announced, and the committee was criticised for appointing a Renaissance scholar rather than a modernist who would fill the gap left by Ellmann, especially in the supervision of postgraduates. In due course a new Readership in Modern Literature was created to make good this deficiency, to which Jon Stallworthy was appointed. I believe that these days they make professorial appointments at Oxford with a procedure more like that of other universities.

Writing to Mike Shaw about another matter shortly after receiving the Registrar's letter I said: 'I shan't, by the way, be moving to Oxford. They've made an internal appointment to the chair I told you about. This rather encourages me to emphasise more the creative side of my life.' As an Oxford graduate himself, in History, Mike had been supportive of my application, but as an agent he welcomed my response to the result. Since I had applied for the position, my career as a creative writer had developed more momentum and an enticing set of future possibilities. *Small World* was doing well in Britain, and had finally found an American publisher in Macmillan (which is independent of the British firm) and the senior editor there, Hillel Black, sounded genuinely enthusiastic in correspondence. This was followed by a good offer from the German publisher List for the same title, which would be my first appearance in that language. Meanwhile Secker had reprinted some of my earlier books with introductions by me, starting with *Ginger, You're Barmy* and *The British Museum is Falling Down*, and Penguin were issuing them in paperback at intervals. It was agreed that the new edition of *Out of the Shelter* would be re-set, erasing the memory of the deplorable Macmillan first edition, and I proposed to use this opportunity to revise the text substantially.[1] It was the only occasion on which I have done this, and in principle I disapprove of the practice, because it can weaken the imaginative unity of the original text, whatever its flaws, and confuse the record of a writer's development. But in this case I felt I had been pressured into cutting the original text too hastily, and I thought I could improve the novel without changing its essential character, restoring some cuts in

---

[1] The story of this edition is told in QAGTTBB.

the process and making some new ones. At about the same time, Channel 4 expressed interest in a film adaptation of this novel to be produced in collaboration with a German TV company, and in August they took an option on the book and gave me a contract to write a draft screenplay. These were the projects I intended to work on next, and I would not have been able to pursue them if I had been preoccupied with all the entailments of a move to Oxford. I realised that, if I had been offered the chair, it would have presented a much more difficult decision than it would have seemed when I applied, and as time went on I became more and more grateful that I had not been required to make it. Had I gone to Oxford, I'm sure I would have had a less rewarding (in every sense of the word) career as a writer.

Nevertheless the immediate effect of a new door being firmly shut rather than opened wide was somewhat deflating. A long letter I wrote to Lenny Michaels a few months later, bringing him up to date with my life, reflects my mood at this time:

As I think you know, I have been on a part-time contract with the University for the past three years. I have been flirting with the idea of becoming a fulltime writer, but Mary thinks I would disintegrate psychologically without a regular job and she may be right. I shall, I think, try to go half-time. I must admit that I am losing my zest for teaching as the years go by and I can't decide how much that is due to the fact that I have been in the same place so long. I think I told you that I had applied for a chair at Oxford which has very light duties, but I didn't get it ... There really isn't anywhere else where I could go in the British academic system that wouldn't mean more teaching and administration than I do now ... So I find myself turning more and more to writing for personal satisfaction. I'm also getting deaf, and my

boredom tolerance is diminishing, all of which makes
me increasingly unfitted for teaching.[2]

The temptation to become a full-time writer was strengthened after Tom Rosenthal rang me up late one afternoon in mid-September to tell me jubilantly that *Small World* had been shortlisted for the Booker Prize – not that I had any realistic hope of winning it, but to be in contention at the final stage was a considerable boost to my self-confidence. I had been sent a proof copy of J.G. Ballard's *Empire of the Sun* in May, and I was quite sure that it would carry off the Booker, as were most reviewers and commentators. This story about a young English boy who was separated from his expat parents in Shanghai by the Japanese when they occupied the city in 1941, and precariously survived internment until near the end of the war, was known to be based on Ballard's own experience. It was more realistic and emotionally involving than his previous novels, mostly dark dystopian fables about aspects of contemporary urban life which were greatly admired by younger writers like Martin Amis. Not only was I gripped and impressed by *Empire of the Sun* – I could see how perfectly it would fit the narrative appeal of the Booker Prize itself, bringing fame and fortune to a serious and original writer whose work had hitherto been a minority cult.

Tom Rosenthal told me who the other shortlisted candidates were: Julian Barnes, *Flaubert's Parrot*; Anita Brookner, *Hotel du Lac*; Anita Desai, *In Custody*; and Penelope Lively, *According to*

[2] I had recently been diagnosed with moderate high frequency deafness and issued with a National Health Service hearing aid for one ear, the first stage in a long process of gradually deteriorating hearing which required more and more sophisticated and expensive aids for me to function as a social being. As I have treated this subject extensively in a novel, *Deaf Sentence* (2017), I will not make more than passing reference to it in this book.

*Mark.* I read the Barnes and the Lively and press coverage of all the books in the interval before the prize was awarded, and did not revise my opinion that Ballard would win it. The bookmakers agreed. A few days after the shortlist was announced, Ladbrokes had *Empire of the Sun* a clear favourite at 6–4 – but to my pleased surprise *Small World* was second in the list at 3–1. Literary novelists of the past such as Henry James and Virginia Woolf would probably have been outraged at the idea of being treated like racehorses, but it was a crucial element in the publicity generated by the prize. In the weeks between the shortlist announcement and the award ceremony, the newspapers were full of articles about the six lucky authors (and we *were* lucky, for there were other eligible books which, with a different set of judges, might have filled some of the six places). The interval was designed to encourage readers to buy the books and form their own opinions, and in those early years of the revamped prize it was effective, helped by bookshop readings and signings of the shortlisted novels by their authors. Sales of *Small World*, published in March, had begun to tail off by late summer, but the shortlist prompted a new surge which doubled the total by the end of the year. (Later the Booker lost its unique influence on the market, and these days only the winner usually benefits significantly in terms of sales.) The announcement of the shortlist brought messages of congratulation from friends, including a characteristic letter from John Blackwell sent the next morning, enclosing some review cuttings from foreign newspapers: 'What do we learn from the enclosed? . . . That the Dutch for "castigate" is "op der hak nemen"; that the Swedish for "subtitle" is "underrubrik". These things do brighten the day. The announcement of the Booker shortlist brightens an entire year – nay, more. Only one man in England can conceivably be more pleased than Yours, John.'

The euphoria of all this attention and excitement was much reduced by a letter dated 24th September from Tom Rosenthal, beginning 'It is with great sadness that I have to tell you that in order to pursue other interests in publishing, I have decided to resign as Chairman of Secker & Warburg and will be leaving here at the end of this month.' It was a short letter, obviously sent to other Secker authors, and though he followed it up with a longer and more personal one, neither gave any hint of what the 'other interests' were. I gathered later that there had been serious disagreement between Tom and other members of the board of the Heinemann Group of publishers to which Secker then belonged, ending with his resignation. I was stunned by this turn of events, and its timing, for I had looked forward to attending the Booker banquet in Tom's company. He did his best to make up for my disappointment by inviting Mary and me to spend that day and stay the night with him and his wife Ann at their London home in Primrose Hill, but we both had commitments in Birmingham which made that impracticable, so we booked into a hotel.

Tom had been temporarily replaced as head of Secker by the Marketing Director, Peter Grose, and forfeited his place at the Booker banquet in the Guildhall. But he wangled an invitation to the event and sidled up to me during the pre-dinner drinks with a bizarre request: that if I won I should, in my acceptance speech, ask the guests to stand for one minute's silence in protest against a threatened imposition of VAT on books which was then in the news. He was entirely serious. I inwardly recoiled from this alarming proposal and I thought it was tactless of Tom to make it at such a moment, when I was already under sufficient stress. Fortunately we were summoned into the dining hall at that point so I did not have to refuse point blank. The Guildhall looked magnificent with its glittering chandeliers, ancient panelling and white napery, but I doubt if shortlisted authors in their dinner jackets and evening gowns ever really enjoy the dinner itself. Each one sits at a separate round table with his or her publishers, partner, agent, etc., like boxers with their seconds and trainers, surrounded by other tables occupied by literati, senior executives in the book trade, and representatives of the great and the good. TV cameramen roam the aisles peering here and there, and I was advised by a veteran of the occasion not to be caught eating as it invariably results in an unflattering shot. You also had to be careful not to drink too much, since there is always the possibility that you might win and be required to say a few words of thanks, and to stumble over them, or over the steps up to the podium, would be embarrassing.

At the end of the meal, after a brief interval, and in an atmosphere of rising expectancy there were speeches from Sir Michael Caine, the Chairman of Booker McConnell (the company's full name), followed by the chairman of the judges, who that year was the Oxford historian Professor Richard Cobb. This ritual speech is a description of the shortlisted books, which are already familiar to most of the audience, with praise distributed to each without revealing a preference for one of them. Then came Cobb's final sentence: 'The 1984 Booker McConnell Prize for fiction goes to . . .' As he paused tantalisingly, all eyes were focused on the Gollancz table where Ballard was sitting. But the TV people had been tipped off, and a camera caught the truly amazed – almost shocked – face of Anita Brookner as her name was announced, an image which was reproduced in several newspapers the next day. She had been a 6–1 outsider when the betting closed the day before.

Several people, including Malcolm, who was present as a member of the management committee, came up to our table afterwards and commiserated with me for 'losing' to a slighter book, an opinion generally shared by the Secker contingent. Not having yet read *Hotel du Lac* I could not honestly share their indignation, but I certainly felt more disappointed than I would have been if Ballard had won, and found some relief in accepting the general opinion. In fact I had been very impressed by Anita Brookner's previous novel, *Look at Me*, when I reviewed it two years previously in the *Sunday Times*, as I was reminded a little later that evening. One of the judges joined a small group of us drinking at the bar. He was Ted Rowlands, a Welsh Labour

MP, who had been appointed according to a practice which the Booker management committee later abandoned, of having one person on the panel who was outside the literary world, a kind of People's Tribune. He confided that one of the other judges, the Irish writer and journalist Polly Devlin, had swung the argument in favour of Brookner at the final meeting by reading out words of praise for *Look at Me* taken from my *Sunday Times* review, which were quoted on the back cover of *Hotel du Lac*. It was an ironic disclosure I could have done without at that stage of the evening.

Writing this account thirty years later I wondered what passage in my review had been quoted, so I looked it up in my files and decided it was probably the last paragraph.

> *Look At Me* is a good example of the excellence that contemporary British novelists can achieve by a conscious formal constraint. Like a tear trembling in an eyelid, it continually threatens to spill over into existentialist metafiction . . . but manages to stay – just – within the bounds of the English novel of sentiment and manners . . . If she should ever transgress those bounds the results would be interesting. Meanwhile I cannot praise too highly this novel's poise, perceptiveness and purity of style.

Although I did not keep up with Anita Brookner's formidable rate of production, very nearly a novel a year for twenty-odd years, I don't think she ever did transgress the limits of the well-made English novel of manners – and certainly not in *Hotel du Lac*. When I got round to reading it I enjoyed it, but thought it lacked the dangerous edge of its predecessor. She was however, in her own line, a very skilful artist, and in retrospect by no means an unworthy winner of the Booker.

Immediately after a Booker Prize is awarded there is always a flurry of speculation, rumours and leaks in the press about how the result was arrived at. As it happens, an unusually full and reliable report of the proceedings of the 1984 judging was published fourteen years later, though I did not find it myself until I was writing this book. One of the judges, Anthony Curtis, then literary editor of the *Financial Times*, who died in 2014 at the age of eighty-eight, wrote a quite detailed account of their deliberations in his memoir, *Lit Ed* (1998). He listed twenty-five novels, out of well over a hundred submitted, which he and the other judges – Cobb, Ted Rowlands, Polly Devlin and the Oxford don and poet John Fuller – reduced to a long list (though it wasn't known as such or made public then) of twenty-five arranged in alphabetical order, beginning with Amis, Kingsley for *Stanley and the Women* and Amis, Martin for *Money*. The media would have been delighted with a contest between father and son, but neither book was shortlisted. According to Curtis, 'Cobb's guillotine came down sharply . . . on any mention of Martin Amis's *Money*.' He was apparently shocked and disgusted by Amis's rhetorically brilliant, mordantly satirical account of the squalid and humiliating adventures of a young would-be filmmaker jetting between England and America, and it would seem that neither Curtis nor the other judges felt strongly enough to defend it. When I read *Money* later I had no doubt that its exclusion from the shortlist was a great injustice, and that it would have been deserving of the prize. It confirmed Martin Amis as the stylistic leader of the younger generation of British novelists, and it is still arguably his finest achievement.

According to Curtis, when the judges agreed the shortlist there was a general consensus among them that Ballard was the likely winner. But when they gathered four weeks later for the final meeting, sentiment had subtly shifted. In the meantime two people who had been interned in Shanghai during the events described in *Empire of the Sun* wrote to *The Listener*, where it had been reviewed, to say that it bore no resemblance to what actually happened there. It also became known that Ballard had not in fact been separated from his parents at that time. *Empire of the Sun* did not pretend to be anything other than a work of fiction inspired by personal experience; but these revelations had the effect, for some readers, of undermining the authenticity of the story to some degree. Curtis admits that this may have contributed to a cooling of the judges' admiration for the book, and after re-reading all the shortlisted titles some shared Fuller's view that *Empire of the Sun* was damagingly overwritten in places. *Hotel du Lac* was brought forward in contrast as a formally perfect novel and obtained general support – except for Curtis. He recalled: 'I admired *Hotel* but it was not my choice . . . I wanted to give the prize to David Lodge for *Small World*. It seemed to be a much more ambitious novel, breaking new territory as well as being hugely, hilariously enjoyable . . . I went on and on about it at that last meeting . . . but to no avail . . . in the end it was Fuller who said, "Well, you're not going to resign if we give it to Brookner." Put like that I had to admit I wasn't, and to Goff's relief I caved in, and we had a winner, *Hotel du Lac*.'

Naturally when I read this I felt grateful to Anthony Curtis for championing my novel. I also felt regretful that I never knowingly had a conversation about the matter with him. I say 'knowingly' because I did meet him and his wife in the 1990s at the annual *Sunday Times* Christmas books party, a large noisy gathering held in the library of the Reform Club. By this time I was suffering serious hearing impairment and reliant on hearing aids in both ears that could not cope with the volume of background noise. Readers of my novel *Deaf Sentence* will recall the opening scene in which the hero is in a similar plight. I remember that at one of those parties Anthony addressed me at some length, evidently expressing enthusiasm for my work, though I could not distinguish more than the occasional phrase, and was reduced to nodding and smiling and uttering phatic murmurs. When I read his memoir I wondered whether he had been telling me on that occasion of his part in the award of the Booker Prize in 1984.

Shortly after that event I heard from Mike Shaw that Tom Rosenthal had gone into partnership with André Deutsch, owner of one of the few remaining independent publishers in London, to form a new company with the same name. They were joint heads of the firm but it was understood that Tom would take it over when André retired. In fact the two men did not get on well and André sold out to Tom three years later. Tom worked hard to make the firm profitable in a publishing climate increasingly dominated by big conglomerates (Secker was soon acquired by the Reed Group, which was later swallowed up by Random House) and although he had some coups – getting Gore Vidal on his list, for instance, and publishing Penelope Lively's Booker winner, *Moon Tiger,* in 1987 – he was able to keep Deutsch going only by selling off backlist assets, and eventually he sold the business in 1998. I kept in touch with him after he left Secker, and whenever I published a new book he would send me a mint copy asking me to inscribe it. He said that he was building up a complete collection of my work to bequeath to his two sons, and I gave him some rare items from my early years which he received gratefully.

Tom made it plain that if I ever became dissatisfied with Secker & Warburg as a publisher of my novels he would welcome me with open arms at Deutsch, but I never contemplated such a move, and he respected my reasons. I'm sure he did the same with Malcolm, with the same result, but Deutsch did publish several of Malcolm's non-fiction titles, including the cod guidebook *Welcome to Slaka* (1986), a spin-off from *Rates of Exchange.* They wanted to have it printed on the kind of coarse, unbleached paper, with occasional fragments of wood embedded in it, characteristic of cheap books produced in East European countries at this time, but it proved to be unobtainable and, ironically, too expensive to manufacture for this purpose. In 1987 Tom published Malcolm's *Mensonge*, its full title being *My Strange Quest for Mensonge: Structuralism's Hidden Hero*. This began life as an April Fool's hoax printed in the *Observer* in 1984, a spoof report about a French literary theorist called Henri Mensonge who had anticipated the key ideas of the fashionable French exponents of structuralism and poststructuralism in a little-known book published years earlier, entitled *La Fornication comme acte culturel*, a discovery that was causing great excitement and controversy in the cafés and salons of Paris. The article apparently deceived a surprising number of readers, who failed to note the date on their newspapers or to recognise that *mensonge* is the French word for 'lie'. Malcolm proposed to extend this squib into a short book, writing as a British critic earnestly pursuing the truth about the mysterious and elusive *penseur*. Tom accepted it and asked me to write a foreword or afterword. I relished the challenge, and decided to do it in the persona of Michel Tardieu, the structuralist narratologist at the Sorbonne in *Small World*, whose contribution is 'translated by David Lodge'. Tom donated a photograph of his bald pate, taken from behind, as a portrait of Mensonge for the frontispiece. I enjoyed taking part in this parodic entertainment, which revived memories of collaborating with Malcolm in our younger days.

When Tom sold Deutsch, he did not retire completely from publishing, but set up a small firm called Bridgewater Press with the antiquarian bookseller Rick Gekoski, specialising in limited editions of new books for collectors, beautifully bound and printed on high-quality paper. In 1998 they published in this format a small collection of six stories of mine which had been published previously in several European countries but not in the UK,[3] and later my novel *Thinks . . .* simultaneously with the Secker edition in 2001. Though increasingly afflicted with various maladies, Tom

[3] This book, *The Man Who Wouldn't Get Up and Other Stories*, was eventually published in an expanded form by Vintage in 2016.

continued to live an active professional life and to pursue his many interests in the post-Deutsch years, and had an 'office' in central London as a concrete demonstration that he had not retired. He had started his career with the art publishers Thames and Hudson, was a keen collector of modern art, and used his release from the burden of commercial publishing to add to the lavishly illustrated books he authored on modern artists including Jack Yeats, Sidney Nolan, Paula Rego and L.S. Lowry – whose work he had studied and lauded long before its importance was widely recognised. He had a passion (which I did not share) for opera, and reviewed it for national newspapers. His office was a little flat tucked away behind Leicester Square, and I called on him there occasionally after I acquired a London pied-à-terre nearby. Like me he suffered from impaired hearing, and if we had lunch together he always stipulated that the table was booked for two o'clock so that the noise level in the restaurant had begun to decline by the time we took our seats. He was passionately interested in Test cricket, and when Edgbaston hosted a match he came up to Birmingham to watch it and we would give him dinner. I was a contributor to *A Life in Books*, a *liber amicorum* privately published in 2005 to celebrate Tom's seventieth birthday, in which I said truthfully that when he accepted *Changing Places* 'he rescued my career as a novelist from the doldrums and set it on a course that proved increasingly prosperous – for which I remain eternally grateful to him'. The long list of contributors to this book impressively demonstrated the number and variety of his friends, and the breadth of his interests. The most serious of his afflictions was kidney disease and towards the end of his life he required frequent dialysis, but with extraordinary fortitude, and the devoted support of his wife Ann, he carried on working and travelling and opera-going, until at the age of seventy-eight he gave up the struggle and stopped the dialysis. Tom had a great appetite for life and I admired his determination to persist until there was no drop of quality to be wrung from it.

## 11

In late 1984 I found myself in the enviable position of being wooed by producers in BBC Television and the ITV company Granada, each of whom wanted to option the rights to make a drama serial out of *Small World*. I met people from both organisations and listened to their ideas about adapting the novel. I was (and still am) a great admirer of BBC drama and detest the intrusion of commercial breaks in television programmes, especially dramatic ones, but I decided in favour of Granada. The BBC producer did not seem to have the sense of humour that I thought was requisite for the task, and when I questioned whether BBC2 (the channel for which it was proposed) could provide a budget that would be adequate for the variety of locations in the story, his plans to reduce their number did not reassure me. The executive producer at Granada, Mike Cox, convinced me that they had the means and the will to represent the international scope of the novel, and conveyed a personal enthusiasm for the project, so I favoured them. Charles Elton, who had taken over this aspect of my affairs at Curtis Brown, was in agreement, and negotiated an option contract with Granada.

Some famous names were approached to write the script, but declined in spite of their admiration for the book, one saying that he couldn't see how he could add anything to it. When I was asked if I had any ideas, I suggested Andrew Davies. Andrew had been an undergraduate in the English Department at UCL a year or two after me. He knew who I was then, but we had no contact and I didn't know him. After graduating from UCL Andrew became a schoolteacher and later moved into teacher training, where he introduced creative writing into the curriculum. We met for the first time in the mid-sixties when he invited me to give a reading to his students in a course of this kind at Coventry College of Education. It was the first time I had been asked to read to an audience and I was sufficiently intrigued and flattered to accept. He told me in the same letter that he had a television play coming on soon, called *Bavarian Night*, that I might find interesting – as I did, and wrote to tell him so. It was about tensions in a marriage between a couple who had met at university, set against a Parent–Teacher Association party with entertainment from a pseudo-Bavarian band. In a poignant domestic scene the husband reminds his wife of how he used to sit behind her at '*old Emslie's lectures, and try to will you to turn your head and look at me.*' That was a reference to MacDonald Emslie, the lecturer in the English Department of UCL who had supervised my MA thesis, as I described in *QAGTTBB*. I imagined Emslie, who had since moved to Edinburgh and was reputed to be an alcoholic, idly watching his TV one evening, sitting up suddenly in astonishment at the sound of his name and spilling his glass of malt.

After that meeting at Coventry I observed that Andrew was an increasingly successful writer of television drama, including a very popular series aimed at younger viewers about a rebellious schoolgirl called Marmalade Atkins. In October 1984 he wrote to me again. He was still teaching, but now at the University of Warwick which had absorbed the Coventry College, and he asked if he could give my name as a referee for his promotion there to Reader in Arts Education, a function I was very willing to perform. In the last paragraph of his letter he said: 'I'm currently reading and enjoying very much (for the second time) *Small World*. Actually I'd love to have a crack at adapting that and/ or *How Far Can You Go?* Has anyone bought options on either of them?' I replied that there had been nibbles, but no offers, and that I thought he would be a very eligible adaptor of *Small World*, but if *How Far Can You Go?* was ever optioned I would want to do it myself.

When I suggested Andrew for *Small World*, Granada were aware of his growing talents and agreed that he was eligible; but perhaps he hadn't yet done enough large-scale projects to convince them that he was the right person for the job, because they didn't offer it to him. Later, of course, he became an acknowledged master of adapting novels for television, of every kind, from *House of Cards* to *Pride and Prejudice* and *War and Peace*, and is constantly in demand. Granada commissioned Howard Schuman, an American who came to Britain in the 1960s and never left, to write the script for *Small World*. At that time he was best known for *Rock Follies*, a very successful series in 1976–77 about the struggles of a girls' band. I hadn't seen it, or any of his other work, and when I heard he was to write the script I wondered if Andrew, with his experience of academia, wouldn't have been a better choice. In fact Howard, who turned out to be a lovely man and a pleasure to work with, wrote a very good script, and that was not the reason why the eventual production was not entirely successful.

Knowing that I had no qualifications to show for such a task, I did not put myself forward as scriptwriter. I had written two draft scripts of *Out of the Shelter*, and had found the exercise interesting and instructive, but Channel 4 had withdrawn their offer to make this film, allegedly because Charles Elton was demanding an excessive fee. We presumed they had lost interest in the subject and were using this as an excuse. However by the following March the project was still in play, and I was in correspondence with David Rose, the Head of Drama at Channel 4, to say I would prefer to do another version of the script in collaboration with a director. I suggested Claude Whatham, who had done some well-received films and TV adaptations based on novels, most recently Beryl Bainbridge's *Sweet William*. I met Claude to discuss *Out of the Shelter* and found him sympathetic, but nothing in the end came of this proposed collaboration. Writing for film is like fishing – casting your baited hook into the water time after time, feeling an occasional tug on the line, but very seldom catching a fish. Nevertheless I persisted in trying for many years to come, mainly because it is very difficult to think of a story that is interesting and has not been told before, and having told it as a novel, it is tempting to present the material to a different audience, and to different effect, in another medium.

Film and TV rights play an important part in the economics of literary fiction for both writers and their agents, whether or not the author adapts his or her own work. A large proportion of films and TV dramas are based on novels, and the income from the sale of the author's rights can be considerable. (For publishers the main benefit is the second wave of publicity and sales which the film or TV serial of a well-known novel can generate.) Most novels that are optioned are never made in either form, in which case the financial yield is much smaller, but it is a useful supplement to an author's earnings without requiring any more work from him – especially if, as not infrequently happens when a film is 'in development', the duration of the option (usually set at 18 months or two years) runs out and is renewed. Eventually the producer may be asked to purchase the rights or relinquish them. This happened with my novel *Changing Places*. Otto Plaschkes, owner of a small independent production company called Ariel, who in 1966 had made a successful film called *Georgy Girl* based on a novel by Margaret Forster, took an option on my novel when it was published in 1975, and decided to purchase the rights in 1978 'in perpetuity', as was common practice then. Nowadays there is normally a time limit, after which the rights revert to the author. This sale brought me a very useful sum but, as in most film contracts, the full potential yield was tied to percentages of the budget and profits (if any) of the film when it was eventually made. Otto commissioned the playwright Peter Nichols to adapt *Changing Places*, and Michael Blakemore, who had directed several of Peter's plays for the National Theatre, was provisionally attached to the project in that capacity. They came up to Birmingham together to meet me, and I drove them around the city to give them an idea of Rummidge. I was particularly pleased to meet Peter, whose plays I admired. *A Day in the Death of Joe Egg*, about a married couple struggling to care for a severely handicapped daughter with the aid of wryly comic music hall routines, had been an unforgettable theatrical experience for Mary and me when we saw it in 1967, a year after Christopher's birth. Peter and I have kept in touch ever since that meeting in Birmingham.

I met Otto on a few occasions over the years and corresponded with him more frequently. I found him very likeable – courteous, cultured and articulate – but it was not until I read his obituary in the *Guardian* in February 2005, when he died suddenly from a heart attack at the age of seventy-five, that I fully realised what a very interesting life he had had, and wished I had known him better. He was a Jewish refugee from Vienna who came to England in 1939 as a child on the Kindertransport and was lucky to be later reunited with his parents in Wiltshire. He attended Bishop Wordsworth's School in Salisbury where he was taught by William Golding and is credibly reported to have been the model for Piggy in *The Lord of the Flies*, the tubby, bespectacled innocent victim of the savagery that breaks out among the schoolboys abandoned on their desert island. Otto fell in love with film as a student at

Cambridge and after graduating started his career as a runner at Ealing Studios, then worked his way up through the various levels of the industry until he became an independent producer. He worked with many famous directors, writers and actors, but produced few notable successes himself. Perhaps he was too nice a man to succeed in the film industry, or perhaps he was just unlucky. Once he had a fort built in the North African desert at the cost of a million pounds which had to be demolished when the epic film for which it was designed was cancelled.

To me Otto was mainly a source of letters at long intervals alternately raising and dashing hopes of *Changing Places* being made. He had useful contacts with some Hollywood actors, such as Walter Matthau, with whom he made his most successful film, *Hopscotch*, and entertained ambitious plans for casting *Changing Places*. There was a period when he was working on a dream cast of Matthau for Morris Zapp, John Cleese for Philip Swallow, Shirley MacLaine for Zapp's wife Desirée and Judi Dench for Hilary Swallow. If there is a heaven where deserving writers and producers frustrated in this world can view perfect versions of their favourite films which were never made, I would like to see that one more than any other. But Otto never managed to get all the pieces of the jigsaw together, and the longer he tried the more difficult it became. The novel is tied to its period setting in 1969, focusing on the student revolution and the counter-culture, and in the early seventies several American movies exploited this material. They were not very good but they took the gloss of novelty off *Changing Places* for potential backers. Later the big British company EMI, whose chief interest was music but who were diversifying into drama, expressed interest in developing the novel for television, and Peter Nichols was commissioned to write a new script. But in March 1985 Otto wrote to me: 'EMI don't want to go ahead on the present screenplay and they don't wish to spend any further monies on it.' It seemed like the end of the road.

When Granada heard about this, they became interested in acquiring the TV rights to *Changing Places* and combining the plot with that of *Small World*, which shared many of the same characters, but the terms Otto demanded were too high and the idea was dropped. I was in fact relieved when this project fell through, because it seemed to me that the two books were thematically distinct and structurally incompatible. After that, my agents periodically received enquiries over many years from TV and film companies about the availability of the rights and were referred to Otto, with the usual negative outcome. I sometimes suspected that he asked an unreasonably high price because he couldn't bear to part with a property on which he had expended so much time and effort, or risk seeing other hands botching it.

*Small World* was published by Macmillan in America in March 1985, and received the kind of reviews an author dreams of. At last I received an unqualified rave in the *New York Times Book Review*, which described it as 'an exuberant, marvelously funny novel', while the *Boston Globe* declared: 'It is hard to imagine a funnier book about academe. In fact it's hard to imagine a funnier book about anything.' It did not sell as well as might have been expected after this kind of reception, because Macmillan (like Morrow with *How Far Can You Go?*) had not strongly promoted the novel to the book trade before publication. They tried to compensate by auctioning the paperback rights, and the winner was Warner, an imprint of the Time Warner corporation which I did not associate with literary fiction. They published a large-format paperback, with three pages of review quotes at the front, which I assumed was photographically offset from the Macmillan hardback, and so I did not bother to check the text. Two or three years later I received a letter from a reader who admired the novel but complained about the number of gross misprints the Warner edition contained, citing some of them. I immediately sat down to read the book myself and found many more, which I reported to Warner. They were very apologetic and reissued a corrected edition, but it was another manifestation of the jinx that seemed to haunt my dealings with American publishers.

Meanwhile, back in Birmingham, I continued to maintain the academic side of my twin-track career, exploring the implications of Mikhail Bakhtin's literary theories in a series of essays on subjects like 'Mimesis and Diegesis in Modern Fiction', 'Dialogue in the Modern Novel' and 'Lawrence, Dostoevsky, Bakhtin', which would eventually be collected in *After Bakhtin* (1990). I was now experienced in getting the maximum mileage out of a single idea: I would for instance agree to write an essay for a journal, or as a contribution to a book to be published in the future, drafting it first as a lecture or conference paper at venues around the world whose audiences I could be reasonably sure would not overlap, and eventually collect the essays together in a book of my own. Sometimes this process would begin with an invitation to give a lecture on a topic of one's choice on some special occasion. 'Dialogue in the Modern Novel' had its first airing in 1985 at the Memorial University of Newfoundland as the Pratt Lecture – an unfortunate but unavoidable collocation, an annual event founded in honour of the distinguished Canadian poet and versatile prose writer E.J. Pratt (1882–1964), who was a native of the island and had been a professor in the University's English Department for a time in his long and varied career.

I went there for a week in April, enticed by the warmth of the invitation and the opportunity to see this remote, poetically named island (for me inextricably associated with the line 'O, my America! my new-found-land' in John Donne's famous erotic poem 'To his mistress going to bed'.) April in Newfoundland is not spring, but a continuation of winter. I was told that there are about two months in the summer when the place is idyllic, and I could believe it, but I arrived at night in the middle of a snowstorm and there was snow on the ground and intermittently in the air all the time I was there. Unsurprisingly the weather is a constant, obsessive subject of conversation. St John's, where the University is situated, is the chief city of the island, built around a natural harbour. Its clapboard houses are painted in various bright colours, no doubt to make up for a dominantly monochrome habitat during most of the year. Visitors to a community like this, in a place like this, where new faces are rare, are usually warmly welcomed, and I certainly was. The high point for me was a day-long party at the home of Christopher and Mary Pratt, a rambling white clapboard house beside a tidal salmon stream which flows into St Mary's Bay. He is related to E.J. Pratt, and one of Canada's most distinguished artists, painting and drawing common objects and domestic interiors in a meticulous fashion that goes beyond a merely photographic realism and endows them with a hypnotic fascination, so that you feel you have never really looked at and appreciated a window frame or an iron bedstead before. He does something similar with the softer shapes of nude and semi-nude female figures, and sometimes juxtaposes the animate and the inanimate to striking effect. Before I left the house, he kindly presented me with a beautifully illustrated book, *Christopher Pratt* with text by David B. Wilcox and Meriké Weiler. The first illustration is a long landscape-size painting spread over two pages, which depicts the artist seated on one side of a bare room of austere modern design, working with calm concentration on a picture of a nubile young woman who is standing on the other side, wearing only a pair of plain pink underpants. She has turned her head and glances suspiciously out of the picture at the viewer, as if warning us to keep our distance and not violate this private collaboration with a lascivious gaze. The picture is entitled *Me and the Bride*. Pratt's wife Mary is also an artist, with her own studio in the house beside the salmon stream.

*

Houses were very much on our own minds at that time. The three-storey semi-detached Edwardian villa in Norman Road, Northfield, had served us well for nearly twenty years, but the contours of the family were changing and it no longer met our needs or satisfied our desires. Julia was working on her PhD at Aston and had recently left the parental home to rent a bedsitter in the house of friends. Stephen was due to graduate in Politics at Newcastle University in the summer of 1985, and intended to save up enough money to travel extensively around the world by working for a time in clerical jobs in London. Only Christopher was living with us now.

Parents of children with mental and/or physical handicaps who will always require some degree of continuous care face a serious problem as these offspring approach the end of the education which the state provides according to their needs and abilities. By this time Chris was in his last year at the Victoria School in Northfield which had served him so well, and was going to attend the Bournville College of Further Education which provided courses suitable for him (though we had some difficulty in convincing the head of the relevant department that a Down's teenager was capable of taking them). But that extension of education would also come to an end after two more years. What then? What kind of adult life could he have that was as secure and satisfying as the one he had enjoyed up to now, as we ourselves grew old? Mary and I had addressed this question several years earlier. Some parents of such children are prepared to look after them at home indefinitely, but we were not, nor did we think it would be in Christopher's best interest to do so. What we wished for him was an adult life as independent as it could be while still keeping him safe, fulfilled and happy; and we wanted to ensure that this would continue if we predeceased him, without making him a burden on his siblings. After considering various options we decided in favour of placing him, when the time seemed right, in a residential community for mentally handicapped adults (as they were called then, a term later super-seded by 'adults with learning disabilities').

There were several charitable organisations that ran commu-nities of this kind in various parts of England and we investigated two: Home Farm Trust and CARE (an acronym for Cottage and Rural Enterprises). Both combined a sheltered environment with useful and fulfilling work – mainly agricultural in the case of HFT and a mixture of horticulture, crafts and domestic tasks in the case of CARE. We went first, with Chris, to look at the nearest HFT community to us in Gloucestershire, centred on a large country house with a working farm. The ambience of the place was friendly and the manager who showed us round sympathetic, but we observed that most of the residents had shared bedrooms, four to a room. Chris had always had his own bedroom where he pursued his hobbies and listened to his favourite music. That, and the isolated location deep in the country, very different from the urban environment in which Chris had been brought up, made us think it was not the right place for him. The nearest CARE community to us, at Shangton in Leicestershire, was also in the country, but it was not far from the town of Market Harborough and had a more modern ambience than the HFT one.

It owed its existence to a remarkable man who had once worked with HFT, Peter Forbes. He believed passionately that people with learning disabilities should be enabled and stimulated to lead fulfilling lives to the limits of their abilities, and he left HFT to put his own ideas for improving its model into prac-tice. He started by creating a community in Blackerton, Devon, and although he died at a rather early age, the organisation he founded thrived and there were now several other communities in various regions of the country. One feature of Shangton that particularly impressed us was that every resident had their own bed-sitting room, and we liked the variety of work and leisure activities that was available to them. A crucially important factor was that CARE undertook to look after its residents for life. We put Chris's name down on a waiting list for admission when he reached an appropriate age to leave home, and were encouraged to learn that CARE was planning to build a new community in the West Midlands, which would create more places in a location closer to Birmingham. In due course the Development Director of the organisation, Stephen Doggett, who himself had a son at Shangton, informed us that they had found a suitable site at Ironbridge, Shropshire, and asked me if I would be chairman of a fund-raising group for the new community, involving the families and friends of the residents. I agreed on the understanding that Chris would be offered a place when it opened. The first meeting was in our living room, but later we met in a Portakabin on the muddy site of the new village while it was being constructed.

The CARE communities were called 'villages' and the houses they lived in 'cottages'. This nomenclature went with the locations of most of them, based on an assumption, shared with HFT, that people with learning disabilities would be happier, and less subject to discrimination, in quiet rural settings. But as society became more enlightened this model fell out of favour, and some CARE communities relocated to places more typical of modern urban or suburban life, into which residents could be integrated. The Ironbridge site was ideal for this purpose, situated next to a large modern housing estate on the edge of a picturesque little town, known as the 'Birthplace of the Industrial Revolution' because Abraham Darby perfected the process of smelting iron with coke there. It attracts tourists all the year round to see the cast-iron bridge his grandson built over the Severn, and to visit a cluster of small museums dedicated to industrial history. It is also within easy reach of the new town of Telford, with many facilities and good rail and road connections, and is about an hour's drive from Birmingham. We prepared Chris to move there at some future date, using the departure of his sister and brother to go to university as a demonstration that this was a normal stage of growing up. He was already accustomed to spending short periods away from home without us, sometimes with relatives, and more frequently in a respite home called Charles House operated by Birmingham Social Services, where parents of children with learning disabilities could leave them in complete safety for short periods. It was a marvellous facility which allowed Mary and me to make many trips away together, but sadly it no longer exists – a victim no doubt of cuts in local authority funding. Chris took an interest in the development of CARE Ironbridge and seemed to accept the idea of living there eventually. He had already experienced a trial residency for a week at Shangton and enjoyed it.

Since it became clear to us that we were not going to move from Birmingham, Mary and I had been looking for a house which would be more suited to our needs, be easier to run, and enhance the quality of our lives: a modern house of pleasing design, with three or four bedrooms, two bathrooms and a room that would serve as a study for me, as well as a spacious living room, dining room and kitchen. I wanted to live in the part of Edgbaston where the University is situated, a green inner-city suburb whose unusual combination of attractive features I described in the first volume of this memoir. Property prices there were the highest in Birmingham, but with the money I was making from writing and a modest legacy from my aunt Eileen, I thought I would be able to afford something we liked. We searched for some time without finding it: the houses we saw advertised and occasionally viewed were either unsuitable or way above our price range. Then in the spring of 1985 a house came on the market which was distinctly promising, situated about ten minutes' walk from the University in an area that had been redeveloped in the late sixties and early seventies with a variety of detached houses, many of them uniquely architect-designed, as was the one that attracted our attention. We knew the location well because the house was near the Catholic Chaplaincy of the University where we usually attended mass on Sundays in preference to the Northfield parish church, and we knew the original owners, who were also Catholics. Its design was strikingly, even aggressively modern, with a steeply pitched roof on top of an assembly of brick-built cubes and wedges that were timber-clad in parts, and it had strong vertical features in the form of long narrow windows over the staircase. There was a two-car garage which was joined to the garage of the adjoining house, designed by the same architects in a different but compatible style. These two were flanked by huge modern houses with indoor swimming pools, and faced across the street a row of pleasant Victorian semi-detached brick houses of modest proportions, some of whose owners had lived there for a long time. I liked the idea of living in this interestingly mixed street in the house with the distinctive design, and made a prompt request to view it.

The interior, however, was something of a disappointment. The ceilings were low, and the rooms rather small apart from the master bedroom and the drawing room, and the latter was dominated by a disproportionately large open fireplace and chimney breast that squeezed the floor area into an awkward oblong shape. Although there were large windows in parts of the house, there was a lot of pinewood cladding and exposed brick inside which did not reflect light and gave a gloomy aspect to some rooms, especially the kitchen. The original owners had split up since we had known them at the Chaplaincy and moved away, selling the house to a man I shall call Mr R, who had owned a small company and was retiring to a newly purchased home in the country. He had neglected the property and it had a dispiritingly shabby appearance inside. Mary was less put off than I was by these first impressions, and I had to admit that both house and garden had possibilities for improvement. The room that was designated a 'study' in the estate agent's particulars was barely nine feet square, but there was a family room at the end of the house adjoining the garage which would make a decent study and could be extended into the back garden. The latter was a large but manageable square shape, mostly consisting of unkempt grass, partly bisected by a red brick wall, relic of the Victorian chapel of ease for Edgbaston Old Church which originally occupied the site, creating a paved patio overhung by chestnut trees. The wall badly needed repointing and the paving stones were relieved only by a patch of overgrown pampas grass and a sandpit in which no child had played for many years, but it was a space of which something could be made.

Mary was keen on the house, but I hesitated, partly because I was also hesitating about whether to leave academia to become a full-time writer. To buy it at the high price Mr R was asking without taking on a big mortgage would use up most of my capital; it was not the house I had dreamed of and to make it approximate to that vision would require a lot of expensive modifications. I made an offer considerably lower than the asking price, which was refused. I went back again to have another look, without overcoming my reservations. Weeks passed. Mary was convinced that the house would soon be sold, but it stayed on the market, which made me think my doubts were well founded.

I was not teaching in the summer term and we decided to go to the south of France for the spring holiday week at the end of May when Mary was also free. We flew to Nice, rented a car and toured along the Riviera and in the Languedoc *Parc naturel régional*, staying in comfortable hotels with pools. I was hoping that the change of scene would allow me to stop brooding on the house for sale in Birmingham, but in idle moments my thoughts would return to it. One afternoon towards the end of the holiday I was lying awake in our hotel room after a siesta and began to think of the rear garden of the house in Edgbaston, screened from neighbours by trees and high hedges, and its patio sheltered by the wall of weathered red brick, so superior to the side garden we had in Norman Road, which was exposed to the view of passing

pedestrians and the noise of vehicles. I had a vision of myself –
a kind of projection of the *ambiance* of the south of France on
to Edgbaston – reclining comfortably there on a lounger with a
book, enjoying perfect peace and privacy. At dinner that evening
I told Mary that I was going to make another offer for the house
when we returned home. 'Good,' she said. 'But it will be gone.'

It wasn't, but I found reasons to procrastinate and delib-
erate further until one evening, a week or so after we were back
in Norman Road, Mary answered a phone call, and came into the
living room to tell me: 'It's Mr R.' We stared at each other, wondering what this portended. I took the call in my study, watched
intently by Mary. Mr R did not beat about the bush. 'Look,'
he said, 'can't we come to some agreement about my house?
I know you want it.' 'Well, that depends on the price,' I said. I
realised at once that he must be getting desperate to sell because
he was anxious to complete the purchase of his new home, and I
had told him that I would be able to exchange contracts as soon
as a deal was done, without waiting to find a purchaser for our
own house. We bargained for a while, Mary watching me tensely.
He was asking £130,000, and I had offered £117,000, after getting
a surveyor's evaluation of £116,000. What would I offer him
now, he asked. With adrenalin surging through my veins I said,
'A hundred and ten thousand.' He said, 'I've already rejected
two offers of that amount. What about a hundred and twenty?'
I thought the rejected offers were probably not for cash. 'No,' I
said, 'a hundred and ten thousand is my limit. But with immediate
exchange of contracts.' After a pause, he said: 'You wouldn't go
up to a hundred and thirteen?' I said no. He gave a long sigh. 'All
right,' he said, 'a hundred and ten it is.' After a short exchange
about dates and other details, he closed the conversation by
saying, 'I take my hat off to you as a hard-nosed bargainer.'
Mary shrieked with laughter when I repeated this compliment to
her from the armchair into which I collapsed like a wrung-out
dishcloth as soon as I replaced the telephone receiver.

It was indeed most uncharacteristic behaviour on my part, and in retrospect it was foolish of me to jeopardise the deal by refusing to raise my offer by a mere three thousand pounds. But I knew that if I got the house for a hundred and ten thousand it was a bargain, and a decision I would never regret. I went forward confidently with the purchase and the move, and every stage of our occupation of the house confirmed the wisdom of our choice. We were able to have it redecorated and carpeted before we moved in towards the end of August, and its shabby rooms immediately became lighter, brighter and more spacious than they had seemed before. Over the years since we have improved the house in various ways, extending the family room into the patio to make the spacious study I had always dreamed of; increasing the size of the drawing room by building out into the garden; and enlarging the tiny bathroom adjoining the main bedroom into a luxurious en-suite. For all our extensions we employed an architect, John Price, who worked for the local firm that had originally designed the house. He had access to the plans and took a personal interest in making modifications which harmonised with the existing building, inside and out. Mary developed a gift for gardening that she was never able to exercise in Norman Road, partly because she was then too busy bringing up the family, but also because our patch of grass and stony earth there did not inspire her. At the new house she created over the years a thing of beauty, which has given her great satisfaction and both of us pleasure. We were extremely lucky to have had such a long time for me to overcome my initial doubts about the house. A couple of years later a boom in the property market began, people were scrambling to buy, and gazumping was rife.

It was some time, however, before my idyllic vision of lounging on the patio of our new house was realised. Whenever I lingered in the back garden I was bitten by tiny, almost invisible black flies that seemed especially attracted to my flesh and raised inflamed and itching bumps on it, while mostly ignoring Mary and Christopher. Eventually we traced their domicile to two festering compost heaps in the garden, and when these were removed the plague gradually disappeared. Considering it was less than two miles from the city centre, our garden was remarkably well populated by every kind of natural life. Most welcome were the birds who swooped in to perch on the wall and trees or probe the lawn for grubs and worms: pigeons, blackbirds, thrushes, robins, wrens, tits of several kinds, magpies (so elegant in gliding flight, so ugly strutting about on the lawn intimidating the smaller birds) and the occasional woodpecker and jay. Squirrels scampered among the branches of the trees; and although the house and its neighbours were built on a triangle between three roads, with a perimeter of not more than 400 yards, our garden was visited by foxes, sometimes in broad daylight. There was a foxhole in the middle of our lawn, beside which, we learned, the wife of the previous owner foolishly used to leave food. Mary blocked up the opening with bricks and stones, but we still had the occasional vulpine visitor for years afterwards. I remember being interviewed one afternoon in my study by a sophisticated New York journalist who nearly fell out of her chair in astonishment when a fox loped past the full-length windows.

## 12

At the end of August 1985, just a few weeks after we moved into the house, Dad phoned to tell me that he was in hospital. He had seen blood in the toilet bowl and went to see his GP, who referred him to Greenwich Hospital. They did some tests and told him he had to have an operation on his bowel without delay. I went down to London to see him shortly afterwards, and he seemed to be recuperating very well. With the Sony Walkman radio/cassette player and headphones I had given him as a Christmas present he was able to retreat into a private cocoon of music and information, blotting out the life of the ward. I felt that he was drawing on his wartime experience in the RAF to make himself as comfortable as circumstances permitted. He was in good spirits because he had been told that the operation had been successful: they had cut out a section of his intestine and sewn it together again, so to his great relief he would not require 'a bag'. His GP told me later that he had been diagnosed with cancer, and that it would probably recur, but wisely neither he nor the hospital medics told Dad since it would only have worried him, and in fact he lived for another fourteen years, enjoying good health considering his age, with no recurrence of the disease.

When he was discharged from the hospital he was transferred to a convalescent home on the south coast near Worthing for a few weeks, and Mary and I visited him there one weekend. It was familiar territory to him and he always enjoyed the smell and sight of the sea, but he was glad to return to the house in Millmark Grove. He managed to run it and look after himself with the assistance of a Polish home help supplied by the local social services, with whom he got on very well. I had persuaded him to let me pay for central heating in the house to make it more comfortable. He was dogmatically opposed to gas as a source of energy for a reason I never discovered, though the house was connected to it, and oil was impractical for several reasons, so it had to be an electric system and one that would not seem to him alarmingly expensive. He agreed to the installation of night storage heaters throughout the house, which accumulated heat in the night when electricity was cheaper, and gradually leaked it into the air during the day. He seemed content with this system despite its limitations, and at least it was completely safe.

In this kind of situation an elderly widow or widower will often go to live with a married son or daughter. It was a relief to Mary and me that Dad never showed any inclination to make such a move, because we both felt that we had enough to cope with, professionally and domestically, without taking on that additional responsibility. Dad for his part would not contemplate moving out of the house where he had lived contentedly for so long, in a part of London that he knew intimately. Birmingham always seemed to him like a foreign country, which he was glad to visit occasionally but could never belong to. So he and I settled into a routine of regular contact by phone and letter, with his occasional visits to us in Birmingham and mine to Brockley when business took me to London. He always spent Christmas with us, along with Mary's mother and other members of her family, and these were usually successful visits. When Dad set himself out to be sociable, drawing on his experience as a bandleader, he could be good company, and friends who got to know him at the parties we usually had at the festive season have warm memories of him. But there was always a gap between his domestic habits and ours which could produce friction, especially between him and Mary, as it had in the past between her and my mother, and the longer the visit lasted the more likely it was to occur. One of several reasons why I felt fortunate that chance led me to make my home in Birmingham for the greater part of my adult life, while keeping it to myself as a slightly guilty secret, was that it was close enough to London for me to see Mum and Dad quite often, but distant enough to ensure that most of the time we were able to lead our own lives without much involvement in theirs. Fortunately Dad didn't seem to suffer from loneliness after Mum's death. He had always been content to be on his own, a trait I recognise in myself to a lesser extent, and it may be something that comes naturally from being an only child, as we both were.

There were several strands to my life as a writer at this period. There was the prospective TV serial of *Small World* which I looked forward to being involved with, for Mike Cox promised to send me Howard Schuman's draft of the first episode for my comments. In September I went to Germany for a week to promote the edition of this novel published by List – the first time I had done anything of the kind with a foreign translation. The tour, taking in Cologne, Frankfurt and Munich, was sponsored in part by the British Council, though I presume my German publishers paid for the hotel accommodation for me and my editor, who accompanied me on the tour. She was an elegant and confident young woman called Erica who spoke perfect English and informed me early in our acquaintance that she was engaged to be married, perhaps to discourage any flirtatious behaviour on my part. She was obviously very intelligent but I thought rather young to be entrusted with total control, as it seemed, over the editing and production of *Schnitzeljagd* – for that was the title of the German edition. She had written to me soon after List acquired the rights to say that the literal translation of the English title, *Kleine Welt*, would not be appropriate since it would suggest that it was a book for juvenile readers, and she asked me to suggest some alternative titles. I did so, and from them she selected 'Paperchase', which I proposed as a concise metaphor for the hectic peregrinations of my academic characters around the globe. It was however an obsolete sporting event even in England and almost unknown in Germany, while the pun on 'paper' in the scholarly sense did not carry over into the German equivalent, *Schnitzeljagd*. Several German readers told me subsequently that they had never encountered the word before, and that *Kleine Welt* would have been a perfectly appropriate title for the novel. Erica's decision enabled her to use the very attractive illuminated 'S' on the cover of the English novel for the German edition, and when I saw the latter I wondered if that had influenced her choice of this dud title. In spite of that, the novel did well in Germany. Later editions issued by different publishers were called *Kleine Welt*, no doubt causing confusion to readers and booksellers.

More than a year had passed after *Small World* was first published but I hadn't started another novel, because I didn't have an idea for one. I did however have an idea for a stage play, and in the early summer of 1985 I decided to write it, prompted by seeing an advertisement in the *Guardian* for a play competition sponsored by Mobil Oil, for which the first prize was £5,000 and a guaranteed production at Manchester's Royal Exchange Theatre. I wanted to do something creative, and if it didn't work out I would soon know, and not waste much time on it. The idea had originated in an invitation from the novelist Deborah Moggach to partner her as tutor of an Arvon Course on writing prose fiction

In 1978 I interviewed Malcolm Bradbury about his novel *The History Man* in front of an audience of postgraduates and staff at Birmingham University, followed by their questions and comments. This is a still from a video recording of the event produced by the University's TV and Film Unit, directed by Paul Morby, whose idea it was.

Tom Rosenthal at the launch of a compendium of novels by George Orwell published jointly by Secker & Warburg and Octopus in 1976.

Paul Morby, a good friend for many years, also took this photo of me with a display of the first Penguin edition of *Changing Places* in Hudson's Bookshop, New St, Birmingham in 1978.

Young relatives visiting our home amuse themselves with polystyrene cut-outs of Morris Zapp and Philip Swallow, as caricatured on the cover of the Penguin *Changing Places*.

In Connemara, in the summer of 1979, with the Mirror-Class dinghy on the roof of our Cortina Estate.

Mum, sadly afflicted by Parkinson's in the late 1970s, at the front door of 81 Millmark Grove with Dad, Mary and Christopher.

When I visited the city of Lodz, Poland, in November 1981, as part of a British Council tour, temperatures were well below zero, and some kind person lent me this luxurious fur coat.

Mary and I enjoyed a memorable holiday in the Peloponnese in the spring of 1982, added on to another British Council-sponsored excursion to Athens and Thessaloniki.

My faithful Japanese translator and friend Susumu Takagi took me to the ancient city of Kamakura, near Tokyo, where I broke my journey round the world in 1982.

I took this photo of Eileen in Waikiki, on the same journey in 1982.

David and Goliath: I receive my consolation prize as a shortlisted candidate for the Booker Prize in 1984 from the towering figure of Sir Michael Caine.

From left to right, Robert Stone, me and Craig Raine, taking a break from the Wellington, New Zealand literary festival in 1986.

The rear garden of our house in Edgbaston, with the new study extension visible to the left. Late 1980s.

Malcolm and me in the garden of Frank Kermode's house in Cambridge, probably early 1980s.

Colin MacCabe, who tells me 'I bought the jacket in Shanghai in May 1984 and wore it constantly in the eighties. It was my perk from the People's Republic of China.'

A lone reader of Dostoevsky on the Caribbean cruise, summer 1988.

The nuclear family in 1989: Stephen, Chris, Julia, Mary and me.

Dad on the patio of our Edgbaston house. He could use a sewing machine and sewed breast pockets on shirts that did not have them, to keep his glasses in.

I make a suggestion to John Adams, director, during rehearsals for *The Writing Game* at the Birmingham Rep, spring 1990.

Recording a conversation with Melvyn Bragg at home in Edgbaston for 'The South Bank Show', in 1991.

On an unidentified beach, probably in summer 1991, wearing a T-shirt I bought from a store in Harvard Square earlier that year.

in the summer of 1984. In the late 1960s the Arvon Foundation pioneered the provision of short residential courses in creative writing of various kinds, open to all comers and tutored by professionals. Their programmes had since become extremely popular, starting several aspiring writers on the road to publication. Debbie was a client of the Curtis Brown agency, and I had met her for the first time at Graham Watson's retirement dinner, when I was seated next to her and much enjoyed her lively conversation. I was curious to see what an Arvon course was like, and seized the opportunity she offered me. She had tutored on several of these courses and briefed me in London one day about what to expect, some weeks before we met our students in a converted farmhouse at Totleigh Barton in Devon, which was the first of the three centres the foundation established in Britain.

At that time Arvon courses lasted for four to five days over a weekend, and there were usually up to fifteen students, who were admitted on a first come, first served basis without being vetted, so the level of ability was uneven and unpredictable. At Totleigh Barton they were accommodated in the main building and took turns to help prepare and cook the evening meal and wash up afterwards, under the supervision of the manager. The tutors occupied a converted barn which had a large living area, a bathroom and three bedrooms – one being for the 'guest writer'. Halfway through the course another professional writer was invited to stay for a night, to read from his or her work, chat to the students and generally offer some diversion and relief from what could become a somewhat intense and introverted communal life. The visiting writer on our course was Kazuo Ishiguro, a Japanese writer brought up in England since childhood and known then chiefly as the author of a highly praised first novel, *A Pale View of Hills*. He turned out to be charming as well as gifted. Tutors made their own arrangements for teaching, usually a mixture of group workshops and individual tutorials. Students could bring work in progress with them to show their tutor but were encouraged to write, or at least start, something new while in residence. On the last evening they gave readings from their own work, followed by a party. The tutors had also read from their own work after dinner on two previous evenings. That was how it was in 1984.

Our students were a mixed bunch as regards age, background and ability, and it was difficult to get them to bond. The best of those I tutored was herself a teacher and a veteran of Arvon courses, who had written one novel which was looking for a publisher, and brought with her the beginning of another. She wrote to me later to thank me for my advice and tell me that the first one had been accepted by Bodley Head, for which I could take no credit, but I congratulated her on the achievement. At the other end of the spectrum there were one or two students painfully lacking any literary talent, but Debbie and I did our best for them all, and the course went off reasonably well. One heard lurid stories on the grapevine of some Arvon courses that were total disasters, disrupted by heavy drinking, violent arguments and debauchery, but we were happily spared anything of that kind. Nothing very dramatic happened over our five days, but very soon it struck me that the set-up, bringing together a disparate group of strangers in an isolated location and putting them under competitive pressure, would be perfect for a stage play. It had the classical dramatic unities of time, place and action. One day, I thought, I might try writing a play about a residential creative writing course.

In writing a novel there are no practical constraints on what your imagination conceives and represents, but in writing for the stage there are several, and they affect the content of a story as well as the way it is told. A novel can be as long as you like, and if necessary split up into instalments of a *roman-fleuve*, but a play that lasts longer than three hours in performance is likely to test the audience's patience, and something like two and a half hours, including an interval, was the average in Britain at that time.

It has since become shorter. A novel can have a multiplicity of characters, but I was aware that my first attempt at drama would have a better chance of being staged if it didn't require more than five or six actors. This meant that the play couldn't present the students together as a group, but would have to be focused on the tutors, with one student who would interact with them. A feature of the Arvon course I wanted to exploit was that the tutors and the visiting writer all read from their work to the students. This seemed a natural way to translate the normally silent mental process of writing and reading prose fiction into performance; it also offered possibilities for arousing rivalry and anxiety on the part of the writers, and revealing the personal sources of their writing. In these scenes I envisaged that the actor, seated in a spotlight at the front of the stage with the set darkened, would read to the theatre audience as if they were the students gathered in the farmhouse. In reality such readings each lasted at least half an hour, and three of them would take up the larger part of a play's duration, so each one had to be interrupted and cut short in a different way – an example of how the formal constraints of drama can stimulate the invention of narrative content.

The main set would be the open-plan living room of the converted barn where the tutors are accommodated, with doors off to bedrooms and bathroom. The dramatis personae would be the three writers, the student and the manager of Wheatcroft, as I called the fictional establishment, and to create the drama there would have to be conflicts between them. The source of conflict between the writers would be professional and sexual rivalry; between them and the student it would be the quality of her work and the tutor–student relationship. I made this student a young primary school teacher called Penny who has brought with her the beginning of a novel she is writing. For one of the tutors I created a character called Leo Rafkin, an American writer currently in England on a Guggenheim fellowship, a last-minute substitute for an English writer who cancelled because of illness.

Leo is a kind of synthesis of Norman Mailer and Philip Roth, but less famous and successful, and has a low opinion of contemporary British fiction. He teaches Creative Writing to graduate students at an American university and is dismayed to discover on his arrival in the first scene that he will have to tutor beginners. To the consternation of the manager, Jeremy, he decides to leave immediately, but changes his mind on the arrival of the other tutor, Maude Lockett, an attractive woman in her forties who has written a number of bestselling novels of middle-class English manners, and is married to an Oxford don. Leo makes a clumsy pass at Maude on their first evening together and is rebuffed. Next day they quarrel about Leo's harsh criticism of the manuscript Penny shows him, which caused her to flee in tears. In the evening Maude reads from her novel in progress, and is interrupted by Jeremy bursting into the room to ask if anyone has seen Penny, who is missing and whose hat has been discovered beside a nearby lake. In the next scene Leo returns to the barn alone while the rest form a search party, and finds Penny asleep on the couch in the barn. As he supposed, she has not tried to drown herself because he told her what was wrong with her work, but now she wants him to tell her how to do it right. Disarmed by her sincerity, he makes some more constructive comments on her novel draft, and tells her how he solved a problem in writing a story of his own, based on the experience of making a visit to Poland and feeling, as a Jew, oppressed by its association with pogroms and Nazi extermination camps. At this point Maude returns to the barn from the search party, her shoes covered in mud, and makes some acid remarks on the pair's reconciliation before retiring to bed. On the following evening Leo reads his Polish story to the students. At its climax the Jewish central character sodomises a Polish prostitute with a bar of soap in a symbolic act of revenge for the extermination of Jews whose bodies were boiled down to make soap. Sound effects of a door slamming several times indicate that a number of the students walk out in disgust. Back in the barn afterwards, helping herself liberally to a bottle of wine, Maude tries to explain to Leo the hostile reaction of the audience, and the conversation becomes a discussion of the different ways in which male and female novelists write about sex. Maude evidently finds this conversation arousing, for she leaves the door of the bathroom open when she takes a shower before going to bed. Leo, looking up from the computer on which he is revising the text of his story, takes the steam coming from the bathroom as an invitation to join her. So ends the first of two acts.

On the following day the visiting writer arrives. He is Simon St Clair, a young Cambridge-educated Englishman who has published a scabrous novel called *Wormcasts* and a collection of his cultural journalism. His reading to the students that evening is a work in progress called *Instead of a Novel* which consists of a detailed description of the book's physical appearance and prolegomena – jacket, blurb, author's photo, list of previous publications, dedication, epigraph, acknowledgements, etc. – and when published will otherwise consist of 250 completely blank pages. Simon is disconcerted to learn that Leo is a late recruit to the course because he once wrote a very destructive review of one of Leo's books, but continues to goad him with sarcastic mockery of his career, to which Leo responds with scornful denunciations of the English literary scene. As Jeremy reveals to Leo, Simon is one of several young writers whom Maude 'collects', and the two writers become rivals for her favour in a war of literary words, which eventually turns to blows – or at least one blow, which gives Simon a nosebleed and turns Maude into his sympathetic nurse for the night. Next morning, in the last scene of the play, Simon has departed. Leo also intends to leave as soon as possible, missing the finale of the course, but sees Penny to return the revised text of her novel in progress. He is impressed and tells her it is a terrific improvement – that she has it in her to become a *'real* writer . . . But it's a hard lonely road, Penny. You sure you want to go down it?' Disconcertingly, she replies,

'No . . . Coming on this course has sort of cured me of wanting to be a writer.' Maude, who has overheard this conversation, tries to console Leo for the rebuff and persuades him to stay on for the final evening of the course. A kind of reconciliation occurs, but Leo disturbs her with his last line: 'I've just had a great idea for a play . . .'

I have described the action of this play in some detail because I will be recalling its varied fortunes in later chapters. My working title for it was 'The Pressure Cooker', a metaphor for the course invoked enthusiastically by Jeremy in the first scene to persuade Leo to stay, which actually has the reverse effect. I wrote the first draft in the summer of 1985 with what seemed to me surprising speed (little did I know then how much rewriting a play normally requires before it is performed) and with considerable enjoyment. I sent it off hopefully to the Mobil Oil competition, and a copy to Charles Elton who was then handling drama as well as TV at Curtis Brown. It wasn't until December that I heard I had been unsuccessful in the competition, in a kindly letter saying that 'The Pressure Cooker' hadn't quite made the shortlist of thirty-three plays selected from the two thousand which had been submitted, but the judges had enjoyed reading it. Meanwhile Charles had been showing it to London producers, and reported early in the New Year that Robert Fox, a well-known member of this fraternity, had found much to admire in it and described it as 'a near miss' for him, which I considered encouraging.


By then I had decided what my next novel would be about. Although *Small World* was a success, and elicited enthusiastic fan mail from an international academic readership, I was aware that some colleagues at Birmingham and elsewhere thought it was irresponsible to publish a satirical novel about academics swanning around the world to exotic locations at public expense in 1984, when British universities were reeling from drastic cuts in their funding under Margaret Thatcher's government. A few reviewers of the book who worked in universities, including Philip Larkin in *The Listener,* and Germaine Greer when she was on the critics' panel in the Booker Prize TV programme, took this line. Larkin described the novel as only 'fairly funny', while Germaine Greer found it not amusing at all, and at Christmas named it in the *Guardian* as the novel she had most disliked that year.[1]

There is always a gap between the time when a novel is written and the time when it is published, and one expects competent readers to take that into account. *Small World* is set explicitly in the spring and summer of 1979, just before and after the general election that brought Margaret Thatcher to power, and most of it was written before the effects of her government's policies on British society were fully felt. In any case it was not a novel about British university life but a novel about the 'global campus', and the international conference circuit which was part of that phenomenon was still in full swing in 1984. The novel was true to the milieu it represented, granted a degree of exaggeration that goes with its genre, but I had no intention of writing a sequel in the same carnivalesque mode. I was not oblivious to the effect of the Thatcher government's monetarist economic policies on British universities and on society at large. 'Sadomonetarism', as it was sometimes called by its critics, meant high interest rates, designed to make British industry more competitive by eliminating inefficient businesses, and drastic cuts in public spending. The effect of the first measure was a

[1] I met her for the first time some years later when we were seated next to each other at a Channel 4 Arts Awards lunch. I looked at her name card on the table before she arrived, and wondered how we would manage our conversation when she did. She took her place just as the meal was about to begin, and acknowledged that she knew who I was by declaring, 'I don't think I have been required to pass judgement on your work.' Before I could contradict her, she turned to speak to the guest on her other side and remained in that posture for the remainder of the meal.

steep rise in unemployment at all levels from the shop floor to management (in the West Midlands it reached 17 per cent) and one effect of the second was a substantial reduction in the funding of British universities, leading to the freezing of new appointments at many, including Birmingham. Our students were graduating without any confidence that they would find a job, and the prospects for the brightest ones to pursue an academic career were especially bleak.

These developments shaped my thoughts about a new novel. It would be about work – what their work meant to people in different walks of life and how it defined their identity. One of the attractions of an academic career was that for those in it their work was what most interested them intellectually. Of course there were aspects of teaching – 'marking', for instance – that could be tedious; but essentially one was paid to do what one would want to do anyway for personal pleasure and satisfaction – in my own case reading, discussing and writing about literature. It was obvious to me, however, that many people in other occupations were equally committed to their work, whatever it was, as a source of personal fulfilment and self-esteem, and could be devastated if they were suddenly deprived of it. I began to make notes for a story about a man who was the boss of a factory or similar business in a city like Birmingham, who had lived wholly for his work and was suddenly made redundant. How would he cope, rejected by the only milieu in which he had any expertise? What effect would it have on his personal life, his marriage and family? I thought he might have some kind of breakdown, until he met a woman with an academic background, whose career was also under threat but whose professional involvement in the humanities, which he would at first despise, gradually persuaded him that there was more to life than profit and loss. Originally I thought the novel would begin with the man being made redundant, but I realised that to make his character convincing I needed to convey what his working life had been like before he was deprived of it – and I had very little idea of what that might be. I would have to research it.

Fortunately I had a personal contact in the world of industry. His name was Maurice Andrews, known to his family and friends as 'Andy'. I had met him through his wife, Marie, who was one of several mature students who enrolled for degrees in English at Birmingham in the 1970s. They were bright women who for various reasons had left school without proceeding to higher education, got married and had children who no longer needed continual supervision, and then studied for the necessary exams to obtain the free university education to which they were entitled. They were a very welcome addition to the student body, highly motivated and bringing more experience of life to the study of literature than the average undergraduate. Marie Andrews caught my attention as a member of a seminar group I taught in a course for all first-year students called 'Close Reading and Composition', which included some creative writing exercises. One week I asked them to write a short autobiographical narrative and she astonished me with an account of having a baby at the same time and in the same maternity ward as her mother, who was giving birth to her twelfth child. It was written in a simple, direct style which made it all the more effective. I discovered that Marie belonged to a Catholic family who had come to England from Northern Ireland and settled in Birmingham. She had left school at sixteen and gone to work as a typist in an industrial firm where she met and married Andy, a native Brummie who had studied mechanical engineering at Birmingham University and was climbing the ladder of manufacturing management. They were practising Catholics, occasionally attended events at the Chaplaincy, and their eldest son Jonathan shared my Stephen's interest in astronomy, so our two families became friends. By this time Marie had obtained a 2.1 BA degree, followed by an MA in Old Icelandic, then did a law conversion course and became a solicitor. Andy continued to advance his career in industry, moving from one firm to another.

Andy may have deduced from our conversations that I had a very limited knowledge of life outside the university. Perhaps I made some ill-informed remark about the strikes that disrupted British industry in the seventies, especially in the local Longbridge plant then occupied by British Leyland. At any rate, one day he spontaneously invited me to sit in on a meeting he was due to have shortly with union representatives concerning a dispute at a factory he was running near Coventry that made Triumph cars. 'You might find it interesting,' he said, and I did. The issue over which shop stewards were threatening to call a strike was a proposed reduction in the number of men required to operate the paint shop – in Andy's view this factory, like many others in the car industry, was excessively overmanned. He gave me a quick tour of the plant before the meeting. Two shop stewards, representing different unions, came to his office and looked suspiciously at me sitting beside him, but seemed satisfied by his explanation that I was a writer, simply observing. After some discussion they retired to another room where their colleagues were gathered to report on the meeting, and returned with a revised set of demands. This procedure was repeated perhaps twice, until agreement was reached and the strike was averted. I was impressed by the orderly manner of the negotiations but also struck by the adversarial relationship between management and labour which they revealed.

It was this experience that emboldened me, at the beginning of 1986, to tell Andy that I was planning a novel about the boss of a factory, and to ask if there was any way I could observe him at work over a longer period in his current position, Managing Director of a firm manufacturing steel tubing. He said, 'Yes, no problem – you could shadow me.' This phrase and the activity to which it referred were new to me, but he explained that it was common practice in business and industry. For instance, if someone was leaving or about to be promoted, the person appointed to replace him would follow him about for a period to learn what the job entailed. The only problem was to devise some plausible explanation of why I was shadowing Andy without revealing my true motive.

By happy chance 1986 had been declared by the government 'Industry Year', during which there would be all kinds of initiatives to improve the efficiency and morale of British Industry. Universities were involved, and like all academic staff at Birmingham I had received a circular letter from the VC urging us to develop contacts and co-operation with local industry. This message was directed mainly at science and technology departments, but I saw how it could give me a plausible role as Andy's shadow at Tube Investments. Under my part-time contract I would be 'off' in the spring term of 1986. It was not unknown for humanities graduates to be employed in industry, and I could pretend that, as a project for Industry Year, I was devoting part of my study leave to discovering what sort of careers my students might find in this sector. It proved to be a perfect alibi. For two weeks in January I drove on every working day to the factory in Oldbury, one of the towns and boroughs that make up the urban-industrial sprawl north-west of Birmingham known as the Black Country, and followed Andy about, sitting in on meetings with his senior management team, touring the factory with him, eating in the staff canteen, and accompanying him on his occasional trips to do business with other firms. Only one of his colleagues recognised my name as that of a novelist, and he kept schtum. Andy also gave me introductions to other factories which I visited later on my own. At first I was shocked by the dirty, sometimes dangerous, and boringly repetitive nature of much factory work, and by the instrumental attitude of management to labour, as if they were a quantifiable source of energy rather than human beings. But I developed a respect for the foremen on the shop floor and the managers in their offices who were doing their best to keep companies going in an adverse economic climate, providing employment and contributing to the wealth without which universities, and the civilised way of life their workforce enjoyed, would not exist. I was struck by how little those who worked in one of these sectors of society knew about the other.

As soon as I started shadowing Andy I realised that the procedure was a perfect mechanism for driving the plot of my novel, with many more possibilities for development, especially in the form of comedy, than the rather sentimental scenario I had originally sketched. For my heroine I imagined a young temporary lecturer in English Literature at the University of Rummidge – I thought I would use this fictional version of Birmingham, and a number of characters who belonged to it, once again – who fears she may be 'let go' at the end of the academic year in spite of being a popular and dedicated teacher. She is a left-wing feminist and devotee of literary theory, and has never even peeped inside a factory till she is asked, as part of the University's contribution to Industry Year, to shadow on one day a week the managing director of a local foundry and engineering works, a man totally immersed in the macho culture of business and engineering, struggling to keep the firm in profit. The Shadow Scheme, as I called it, is at first an equally unwelcome distraction from their work for both of them, but she dares not refuse to participate because of her precarious position at the University, while he is similarly helpless to resist the pressure of his divisional chief in the corporation to which his firm belongs. I called them Robyn Penrose and Vic Wilcox. Her first name, communicated by telephone, causes him to expect a male shadow, compounding his resentment and dismay when she arrives at the factory.

As the novel developed I made Robyn the author of a book on early Victorian industrial novels such as Charlotte Brontë's *Shirley*, Disraeli's *Sybil*, Charles Dickens's *Hard Times* and Mrs Gaskell's *North and South*. These books dealt with the social unrest in England generated by economic recession and the Chartist movement: strikes, demonstrations and riots. There were analogies with events in Britain in the 1980s, especially the miners' strike. The Victorian authors were haunted by the memory of the French Revolution and sought to encourage reconciliation between the warring classes, often expressed through a love story. Mrs Gaskell's novel was particularly relevant to my project. Its heroine is an idealistic young woman who is compelled to move from a genteel milieu in the south of England to an industrial town in the North, where she gets involved in a dispute between the master of a factory and his workforce which arouses conflicting feelings in her. To help readers who might not be well versed in Victorian fiction I described Robyn lecturing on these novels, and used quotations from them as epigraphs for the chapters, beginning with a passage from *Shirley*:

> If you think . . . that anything like a romance is
> preparing for you, reader, you will never be more
> mistaken . . . Something real, cool and solid lies before
> you, something unromantic as Monday morning, when
> all who have work wake with the consciousness that
> they must rise and betake themselves thereto.

I hoped some readers would remember that *Small World* was subtitled 'An Academic Romance'.


I started writing the novel in February 1986 with a chapter that intercut between my two main characters as they rose on a chilly Monday morning in winter and went to their respective workplaces. The beginning of a new novel is always slow, because there is so much detail about the characters and settings to be decided; but I was pleased with how it was going and eager to continue. Unfortunately I had committed myself to another round-the-world tour in March, more extensive than the one in 1982. It had begun with a letter from Harriet Harvey-Wood, Head of the British Council's English Literature Department and a regular presence at the Council's Cambridge seminars, asking me if I would take part in a literary festival in Wellington, New Zealand in the spring of 1986. It would be the first such event mounted in this city at the southern tip of the country's North Island and the Council was anxious to support it with well-known British writers. At about the same time I received an invitation to be a Lansdowne Scholar at the University of Victoria, British Columbia. This was an endowed scheme to bring academic visitors there for a few days, to give a lecture or two and meet faculty. I thought I could conveniently combine this with the invitation to New Zealand, breaking up the long journey to the Antipodes, so I accepted both proposals. Over the next few months I added several other stages to the trip: a visit to Fiji, urged on me by an academic from that country who was spending a sabbatical attached to the Birmingham English Department, visits to Melbourne and Sydney, giving lectures or readings at universities, and a final stopover of a few days in Hong Kong. American Express eventually gave me an itinerary which listed sixteen flights in twenty-three days.

As the time approached I lost all desire to make this laborious and entirely unnecessary journey, and felt I had made a terrible mistake in planning it. What I really wanted to do was to stay at home in my term 'off' and get on with the new novel, but it was much too late to back out of my commitments. I succumbed to a familiar syndrome: regret for a decision triggering anxiety and depression. A friend suggested recourse to yoga, and recommended a retired teacher of Pranayama yoga, a gentle, calming form of yoga focused on control of breathing, who would sometimes take on beginners like me. Mrs F, as I shall call her, kindly agreed to help me. In the sitting room of her semi-detached house this elderly lady disconcertingly whipped off her long skirt to reveal spindly legs in grey tights. She looked frail, but was able to demonstrate the lotus position with ease;

I settled for the half-lotus. I got some relief from the exercises she taught me, and still use a few of them occasionally, but as the day of departure approached my dread of the journey ahead intensified. This of course was entirely irrational. However awful the trip turned out to be – and I had no reason at all to think it would be awful – it would only last for three weeks, and then I would be back home again. That didn't seem to make any difference to my state of mind. I didn't want to go. But I had to go – or suffer humiliation and disgrace.

Leaving home in the morning of the 3rd of March was a miserable experience. Mary had never really approved of the trip and was understandably unsympathetic to my tardy regrets about undertaking it. She saw Christopher off to college after breakfast, then discovered that he had left his bus pass behind and had to run after him with it, which would make her late for her own teaching job. My taxi was waiting to take me to the airport and our goodbye embrace was hurried. She was in tears as I left the house, which made me feel I could not have managed my departure worse.

I took the shuttle which existed then from Birmingham airport to Heathrow, transferring on to an Air Canada flight to Vancouver, all the time in a state of mental distress which became acute in the darkness over Alberta. I actually considered consulting a doctor in Victoria and indulged in fantasies of being declared unfit to travel further and sent home to recuperate. In my hand baggage there was a pamphlet on meditation which Mrs F had given me and I had packed on impulse that morning. She was a Christian and the little book had a Christian slant. I took it out and found it had an immediate calming effect. I also had with me a new notebook in which to keep a diary of my journey, and when we landed at Edmonton, with a long wait on the tarmac before continuing, I described the experience of reading the pamphlet. Thirty years later, while writing this book, I found the diary in my files, with a passage about this episode on the second page. I had forgotten reading the meditation pamphlet, and was astonished by the language in which I expressed its effect on me:

> What a Godsend (literally). What good luck (providential?) that I thought to put it in my flight bag this morning. It seemed to speak directly to my condition, and the first meditation was so apropos. *'Be still and know that I am peace within thee.'* Peace is exactly what I need. This meditation, undertaken as we descended towards Edmonton, certainly calmed me. It also made me for the first time in a long while think that I *do* believe in God, that without God I couldn't manage to carry on – or that perhaps I have been trying to carry on my life all on my own, and that is the source of my depression. The plane which had been a hateful symbol of alienation and pointless travel (cf. M. Amis) was suddenly redeemed, and the miracle of flight, sustaining these tons of metal in the air, became a symbol of God's sustaining presence in the world.

Apart from the reference to the plane and Martin Amis (I was thinking of John Self's joyless commuting across the Atlantic in *Money*) this passage might have come from one of the testimonies of born-again Christians in William James's *Varieties of Religious Experience*, a book I did not read until many years later. It was, I think, the only genuinely spiritual experience I have had in my life, for the foundations of my Catholic faith had always been essentially intellectual, cultural, familial, and continued to be for many years after this episode, until I felt free in old age to openly confess my agnosticism.

The epiphany I recorded on the tarmac at Edmonton did not fundamentally change me, or cure my malaise, but it did enable me to go on with my trip impersonating the person I was supposed to be, hotshot academic and successful comic novelist, and even to enjoy parts of it. I possess a photo of myself at the University of Victoria, laughing uproariously, from which one would never guess the stoical gloom with which I rose each morning in the University's Guest House to face the day's engagements – a mood not improved by the breakfast arrangements. There was no catering for guests except the means of making coffee and tea for oneself, and a toaster – but no bread, only muffins, the intolerably sweet cupcakes which go by that name in Canada and the USA. Later some members of the Faculty in whom I confided kindly gave me slices of bread in paper bags, which I was able to toast, sharing the excess with other guests. I met some very pleasant and interesting people at Victoria but there was too little time to get to know any of them well. They divided between a majority who found the mild climate and easy pace of life in British Columbia congenial, and those who felt as if they were on the very edge of civilisation and in danger of falling off it. I managed to do a little sightseeing in downtown Victoria, and spent some absorbing hours in the Museum with its magnificent displays of BC's wildlife and history, before I had to move on.

The shuttle from Victoria to Vancouver was delayed, and I nearly missed my flight to Honolulu, where I had to wait a couple of hours in the middle of the night for the flight to Fiji. Fortunately that plane was almost empty so I was able to stretch out and sleep fitfully for several hours. Whenever I woke, the elderly man across the aisle was in the same posture, sitting upright with his reading lamp on, staring fixedly at the card with emergency instructions for vacating the plane, which he held in both hands. It was not a good idea to think of the breadth and depth of water over which we were passing, and what might happen if the engines failed. Better to sleep, or read, or listen to music while looking out at the changing sky as dawn began to tint the clouds. The voice of the captain pointed out that Halley's Comet was visible near the sickle moon.

The international airport of Fiji is at Nadi on the opposite side of the island from the capital, Suva, another short flight away, where the University of the South Pacific is situated. Looking down from the plane I saw nothing but dense vegetation covering steep hills with summits that looked as if they had been pinched into shape by a giant hand. The man who had persuaded me to make this visit, Dr S, had informed me late in the day that he would not after all be in Fiji himself at the time, but would arrange for someone from the University to meet me. Nobody was at the airport, however. I had been given the name of Andrew Hook, a professor in the English Department, but no telephone number. I managed to obtain it by phoning the University from a public call box with the assistance of a taxi driver who explained how the phone worked, and a lady selling flowers who gave me change. All the Fijians I met subsequently were equally friendly and obliging. When he collected me Andrew Hook apologised and explained that he had been given the wrong time for my arrival. He drove me into the city and gave me breakfast at the Travellers Lodge overlooking the bay of Suva. Somerset Maugham had stayed at the hotel next door, and it seemed to me, when Andrew took me on a stroll along the waterfront later, that the whole city had the atmosphere of a Maugham short story. He briefly explained the social and political tension in the country between the native Fijian population and the wealthier, mainly Indian middle and upper class. He himself was American, but spoke with a British accent, and was married, he told me, to an African from Uganda.

He took me to my accommodation at the University Lodge, a large one-storey building with a pleasant veranda and lounge, and ceiling fans instead of air conditioning, looked after by a motherly Fijian housekeeper who cooked an excellent early dinner for me. I showered and rested in preparation for the meeting of the local Writers' Group scheduled for that evening. Dr S himself belonged to this group and introducing me to its members had been his main motive for proposing my visit to Fiji, so I was annoyed that he had absented himself for unexplained reasons. I could have done with some help in addressing a group who turned out to have very varied interests, abilities and ethnic identities. The first to arrive was a gigantic Tongan with a beard and a mop of woolly hair, wearing a long skirt and a T-shirt stretched over his beer belly, who said that he was writing a comic novel about a man who has a pain in the arse and tries various remedies without success. 'It is autobiographical,' he told me. The next was an Indian who said, 'I come early because I am interested in words, and in the beginning was the word.' Disconcertingly he picked up one of my own books without my permission, sat down and began reading it. I can't remember what I said when they were all assembled, but they seemed to enjoy the occasion and some stayed talking and drinking until well after midnight. Andrew Hook's wife Caroline came and did not stay late, but I had an interesting conversation with her before she left. She had given up a career in nursing to do a degree in English and Politics, taught at the University and was a fan of Terry Eagleton. She said Fiji was full of racism of a genteel, unacknowledged kind, based on shades of skin colour.

Next day, a Sunday, she and Andrew took me with their two delightful young children to Pacific Harbour, a famous resort near Suva, choosing a beach that epitomised the archetypal tropical paradise: a long, palm-fringed crescent of pristine, platinum-coloured sand, lapped by a turquoise sea. I was eager to swim, but soon after I entered the water I felt a tingling sensation like pins and needles all over my body. It was not painful, but rather unpleasant, and soon drove us all out of the water. There was no visible source, and we suffered no after-effects, but I thought it must have been caused by something – perhaps minuscule creatures that were biting us or discharging some kind of electricity. A friend who had the same experience in tropical waters

237

has recently told me I was being stung by tiny jellyfish. It was very frustrating, but we retired to a nearby hotel behind the beach which had a fine pool in which we enjoyed a swim, and afterwards I treated the Hooks to a barbecue lunch.

No arrangements had been made for me to visit the University the following day or to do anything else, which I attributed to Dr S's incompetence. References to him by the Hooks and others were guarded and ambiguous, and I inferred that he was embroiled in some kind of marital crisis and his whereabouts were unknown. With nothing to detain me in Suva I decided to fly back to the international airport at Nadi that afternoon and stay at a hotel there for a night instead of getting up very early the next day to catch my connecting flight to Auckland. I had flown to Suva in a Boeing 737, but the return flight to Nadi was in a small and fragile-looking propeller plane which was 'Delayed'. Out on the tarmac a couple of engineers were tinkering with its undercarriage, calling occasionally for new tools to be brought out. Time passed. Eventually the plane was cleared for take-off, and we passengers, a dozen or so in number, carried our bags out to be weighed on scales beside the plane. Then they weighed the passengers. I had never experienced this before, and it did not inspire confidence. By the time we took off it was evening, and very soon, in the way of the tropics, it was night. We were flying through clouds which entered the cabin through the ventilators in the form of vapour, and the little plane pitched and yawed in the turbulence. One could see nothing through the windows, but I knew what was underneath us: nothing but jungle-covered hills, with no place for an emergency landing. Fortunately none was required.

A representative of my publishers in New Zealand, a very nice man called David, met me at Auckland and gave me a lightning tour of the handsome city in his car and an excellent lunch at Sails restaurant, overlooking the marina, before taking me back to the airport to catch my plane to Wellington. David told me he had tried to read Keri Hulme's *The Bone People* three times without being able to finish it. This first novel by a writer of part-Maori descent, published by an obscure New Zealand press in a first edition of 800 copies, was the surprise winner of the Booker Prize in 1985, and a highly controversial choice by the judges. Although I managed to read it to the end I shared David's opinion of its literary merit. Its success had however given an enormous boost to New Zealand's cultural prestige, and David warned me to be tactful in discussing it while I was in the country. New Zealand writers are polarised between those who see themselves as belonging to an essentially English and European literary tradition and those who, motivated either by loyalty to their native roots or by post-colonial guilt, believe they have a duty to recognise, recuperate and integrate the aboriginal cultural tradition in their work. In a country with a relatively small population, where literary writing is heavily dependent on state subsidy in various forms, this is a contentious issue.

Wellington is very different from Auckland: smaller, quieter, perceptibly provincial. You could tell that the week-long Readers and Writers Festival was the first of its kind there, because the audiences filled most of the seats at every session and responded enthusiastically, but seemed rather shy of approaching the writers afterwards, preferring to smile from a distance. Most of us were accommodated in a hotel I came to hate. It was recently built and the lobby and public rooms were superficially chic, but the bedrooms were poorly designed and furnished. There were no drawers for clothes and no upright chair on which to sit and write at the desk, just a stool. The shower and toilet unit was open to the room, with a drain-hole in its tiled floor, but the floor sloped the wrong way so I had to paddle through half an inch of water to use the lavatory until the chambermaid mopped it up. The décor was beige wallpaper with a faint pattern that looked like patches of damp, and paintwork in a nauseous combination of lilac, pink and black. When I was alone in this room my depression returned so I spent as little time there as possible. I took part in various events, solo and with other writers, gave interviews to journalists, lectured at the University and went to receptions and parties. The local writers were very welcoming and hospitable, especially the poet Fleur Adcock and her sister who shared a house in Wellington. I shook hands with Keri Hulme at the Mayor's reception, but had no conversation with her. In my solo event I read from a scene in 'The Pressure Cooker' where Penny mentions the title of her novel in progress, 'Lights and Shadows', which elicited a few isolated laughs from the audience that puzzled me. Somebody told me later that it was the original name of Keri Hulme's first collection of stories, which was later republished with a Maori title. I went to a party for the doyen of the *nouveau roman*, Alain Robbe-Grillet, and his wife, who was rumoured to have written the notorious erotic novel *The Story of O*, published in 1954 under the pen-name of Pauline Réage. Emboldened by drink, I asked her if this was true. She gave a good-humoured ambiguous answer, and remarked that it was not a book for children. '*Et pas pour tante Agatha*,' I said in my appalling French accent. She seemed amused by the phrase and repeated it with a smile. Much later it was revealed that 'Pauline Réage' was the pen-name of another writer, Anne Declos. Catherine Robbe-Grillet published a novel in the same genre at about the same time under the pseudonym Jean de Berg.

A great enhancement of the week for me was the presence of the poet Craig Raine and the American novelist Robert Stone, who came straight from attending the Adelaide Literary Festival in Australia. They had had a good time there, but Craig was beginning to feel homesick – he carried a small tape recorder round with him everywhere to record his impressions and airmailed the cassettes back to his family – and Bob Stone had misgivings about a book tour of New Zealand he was committed to after the Festival, so I felt a kinship with them. I had known Craig only slightly before this time, but a proper friendship between us began then. Bob Stone I didn't know at all, nor his novels, though I read a couple later with pleasure, but he was an amiable and amusing companion with a wit he kept flowing with alcohol and pills. One day a local man took the three of us on an excursion along the spectacular coast of the South Island. We swam in a fast-running stream and drank beer and ate a picnic, and mocked the people at the Festival who had most irritated us. It was a rare interval of carefree pleasure for me. Later our escort drove us to a magnificent beach where I watched two young women galloping their horses through the surf, a stirring sight. But when you looked beyond them you knew that you were standing on the edge of the habitable world, with nothing for thousands of miles but cold seawater and ice. I was as far from home as I could be.

In spite of these diversions I would wake in the night in my horrible room and be unable to get to sleep again, oppressed by the knowledge that I was only halfway through my absurd itinerary, and wondering how much longer I could manage to give the impression of enjoying myself. I seriously considered cancelling the remaining stages of my tour, flying back direct to England, and even went so far as to enquire about flights. But I could not face the ignominy and shame of upsetting and inconveniencing the many people involved. Chief among these was Howard Felperin who had initiated the Australian part of my tour. I had only met him once, when he applied speculatively for the second Chair of English at Strathclyde University as he happened to be passing through the UK at the right time to be interviewed, and I was one of the external assessors recruited by the Head of Department, Colin MacCabe. We didn't appoint Howard – he seemed too flamboyantly exotic for this academic setting, and there was another strong candidate – but we enjoyed talking to him both before and after the formal committee proceedings.

Howard is American, and as he freely admits, his career was crucially shaped by his failure to get tenure after several years of teaching in the prestigious Yale English Department. He regarded the decision as unjust and set out to prove it by obtaining full professorships in Australia and publishing respected books on Shakespeare and literary theory. He was a great fan of *Small World*, and hearing that I was going to New Zealand persuaded me to go on to Australia, fixing up lectures at Melbourne where he taught for some years, and McQuarrie University near Sydney where he now lived. He was very hospitable, put me up in his house high up above the harbour, escorted me to my lectures, introduced me to many interesting people and even mended the handle of my suitcase. But all the time I had a dull ache in the core of my being, of longing to get home. I regretted having arranged to break my journey in Hong Kong, and fretted impatiently there for two days, having meals with expatriate academic friends, buying a silk dress as a present for Mary, and not doing much else. Almost the last passage in my diary, written in my hotel, is this:

So the last hours of this trip drag to their conclusion. I have never found myself wondering so often, 'What am I doing here?' However, there has been a certain deepening of knowledge I hope, of myself and of the world. What an extraordinarily small place it is. And how easy it is to detach yourself from a rooted position and become simply a floating body, not belonging anywhere, borne along on the tide like flotsam.

When I got home and embraced Mary and told her how miserable I had been, she said, 'Don't do it again.' I made many more long-haul journeys later, but never again went round the world in a single trip.

# 13

When I left England to orbit the globe at the beginning of March I had barely begun to write the novel that I called provisionally 'Shadow Work', and throughout that trip I looked forward to taking it up again when I was back home and recovered from jet lag. But I soon found that I had other pressing literary business to deal with. It is a common temptation for novelists, I suspect, especially in the early stages of composing a novel, when everything seems so difficult because of the number of decisions that have to be made, to put it aside and accept an invitation to do something else which seems interesting, rewarding – and easier. 'Displacement activity' is the psychologist's term for this phenomenon. I think I have been fairly disciplined in this respect in the course of my career, but at this time I had so many commitments of various kinds that had to be honoured, long-standing projects that unexpectedly matured, and new opportunities which couldn't be resisted, that it was well into autumn 1986 when I resumed serious work on the novel.

The first of these distractions was Howard Schuman's draft screenplay of Episode One of *Small World*, which I was invited to comment on. It began in the Chapel of St George at Heathrow, for Howard's plan was to frame the whole story as Persse's private confession to God in that location. I suspended judgement on this concept, but otherwise the script was a more faithful rendering of the first part of the novel than I had dared to hope for, and I offered only a few notes on it. That didn't take up much time, but very soon afterwards there was an exciting new development in the prospects of my play, 'The Pressure Cooker'. Charles Elton had sent the script to Patrick Garland, a well-known director of work on stage and screen with a special interest in theatrical adaptations of literary texts, and he had been favourably impressed by it. At this time he was directing and performing in his own *Conversation Piece*, a montage of poems, extracts from essays and recorded conversation by Philip Larkin, performed by the actor Alan Bates responding to prompts and questions from an anonymous interlocutor played by Patrick. It was on at the National Theatre in the Cottesloe, the smallest of its three spaces. I saw the show there at a matinee, enjoyed it enormously, and met Patrick afterwards, a friendly, intelligent and modest man whom I took to immediately. He told me that he had shown my play to a senior administrator at the NT, John Faulkner, who had read it at a sitting – 'always a good sign' – and proposed that it should be given a rehearsed reading at the Cottesloe with Patrick as director. This was the NT's way of trying out new plays in front of an audience of in-house personnel and invited guests, using available actors from the current repertory of plays in performance. I was lucky to have a quality cast for my piece: Jack Shepherd as Leo, Eleanor Bron as Maude, Greg Hicks as Simon, and Roger Lloyd Pack as Jeremy. Caroline Bliss who played Penny was then little known, but would soon become Miss Moneypenny in the latest James Bond movie.

A performance was scheduled for 16th June, Bloomsday, which as a devoted Joycean I took as a good omen. I had agreed to examine a PhD at Kent University that day, an appointment which couldn't be changed because the candidate was flying from China especially for the purpose and returning immediately. I despatched the business in her favour in the morning and drove quickly to London to attend the two o'clock dress rehearsal – so called, although there were no special costumes and only a minimal amount of movement by the actors, who had to read from the scripts in their hands. The Cottesloe was more than half full for the performance to an invited audience at seven in the evening. Mary was there, and my son Stephen and his girlfriend; also a few friends including Richard and Mary Hoggart, Tom Rosenthal and my former colleague John Russell Brown who had been a dramaturge at the National for a time after leaving Birmingham University. Charles Elton had brought along a new agent at Curtis Brown, Leah Schmidt, an American who had moved to the UK when she married an Englishman. She was to take over the handling of the play and all my future writing for theatre, television and film – another lucky break for me because she became one of the most respected agents in this field in London.

I learned an enormous amount from watching my play performed by first-class professional actors. On the whole it went well, aroused a good deal of laughter from the audience, and was warmly applauded at the end. Eleanor Bron was excellent as Maude, and Greg Hicks stole the show with his reading of Simon's 'Instead of a Novel', having obviously taken the trouble to learn it by heart. The scene that followed, however, which should have tightened the tension between the three main characters to breaking point, fell flat and clearly needed more work, as did other parts of the play. But Patrick was pleased with the way it had gone and hopeful of further developments. It was barely credible to me that I would become a National Theatre playwright with my first stage play, and I was astonished as well as delighted when, a few days later, I had a call from Leah to say that the National wanted to option it for one year. They offered an advance of £3,500 which seemed to me handsome.

I couldn't believe my luck, and in fact it proved illusory. No area of artistic endeavour is more susceptible to good and bad luck, to accidents of timing and the interaction of individuals, than theatre, unless it is perhaps film, and fortune turned against me at this point. Peter Hall had recently announced his intention to resign as Artistic Director of the National, and while the search for his successor proceeded, a new post of Executive Director was created and filled by David Aukin. One consequence of this reorganisation was that my original supporter, John Faulkner, was eased out of his position and eventually left the NT. When David Aukin read the play, he liked it and wanted to see it produced. But none of the resident directors at the National to whom he showed the script had bothered to come to the rehearsed reading, and David was unable to persuade any of them to take it on, so it was left on the back burner of the theatre's programming while the weeks and months of the option ticked away.

Meanwhile there were other projects I had to attend to. One was writing an introduction and other apparatus to an edition of Henry James's novel *The Spoils of Poynton* for the Penguin Classics series, which was due for delivery in the autumn. I enjoyed doing assignments of this kind because it was a way of thoroughly possessing a book in all its complexity, but they took time. As well as reading it carefully, and studying the history of its composition and any textual variants in different editions, I liked to read a wide spectrum of academic discussions of the book. This novel of James was the first of his 'late period', when his work became extremely ambiguous and therefore apt to provoke disagreement and controversy among critics. As in the case of *The Turn of the Screw*, commentators on *The Spoils of Poynton* divided sharply between those who regarded the main female character, Fleda, as a genuine heroine and those who saw her as a deeply flawed and neurotic character who is responsible for the tragedy with which the story concludes. My own argument was that both these readings oversimplify the meaning of the text, in which every crucial passage is capable of a double interpretation. The novel is *meant* to be irresolvably ambiguous, because James at this stage of his life was concerned to demonstrate the impossibility of arriving at a single, simple understanding of 'the truth' of any human interaction.

*The Spoils of Poynton* was also the first novel James wrote after the humiliating failure of his efforts to become a successful playwright, when his play *Guy Domville* was produced in London in January 1895 and he was booed by the gallery on taking his bow at the end of the first-night performance. This provoked a crisis in James's self-confidence from which he eventually recovered, partly by integrating the lessons he had learned from the theatre into the structure of his later novels – what he called his 'scenic method'. In the course of my research for the edition of *Spoils*, I read Leon Edel's account of the first night of *Guy Domville* in his biography of Henry James, an episode which I said in my introduction was 'as full of suspense, pathos, comedy and irony as any novel'. Those few pages made a deep impression on me, perhaps because of my own current involvement in theatre, and stayed in my memory. Some twenty years later I wrote a novel about Henry James, *Author, Author*, in which the events of that night made up the climactic chapter.

Another project was ripening which would occupy a good deal of my time in 1986 and into the following year. This was a television documentary about an international conference on 'The Linguistics of Writing' which was to take place in July at the University of Strathclyde, Glasgow's 'New' university created in 1964. It was the brainchild of two bright young lecturers, Nigel Fabb and Alan Durant, who ran a postgraduate programme in Literary Linguistics in the English Department headed by Colin

MacCabe. Their collective aim was to put the Strathclyde English Department on the international academic map with this conference. Its theme was cleverly chosen: examining the contrasts, conflicts and possible reconciliation of different approaches to the phenomenon of language in its written form. Through most of the twentieth century these approaches had been broadly divided between functionalist explanations of how language works using methods associated with linguistics and stylistics, and the more intuitive, discursive approaches of literary criticism. But recently this distinction had been complicated and overwritten by the rise of structuralism and poststructuralism and the various schools of thought within those categories. So really the title of the conference could incorporate almost any academic approach to the phenomenon of language. The prospectus promised a discussion between two academic stars in this large field with very different styles and temperaments: Jacques Derrida, the French *philosophe* and high priest of Deconstruction, who was then at the peak of his fame in America, and Raymond Williams, the Cambridge professor from a working-class background who had absorbed the influence of both Marx and Leavis in a committed engagement with the relations between Culture and Society and the Keywords that define and mediate them (those capitalised words being the titles of two of his most influential books). Other high-profile speakers from all round the world agreed to participate, attracted by the opportunity to hear and debate with each other, and the promise of a few days' rest and recreation prior to the conference at Strathclyde's Country Club on the shore of Loch Lomond. It was not surprising that the announcement of this event attracted a good deal of attention and it was soon oversubscribed. Some three hundred academics signed up, most of whom would be able to speak only from the floor in the Q&A sessions.

Colin had contacts and experience in film and television as well as academia, and made use of them to give the conference a longer and more public life than such events usually have.

He persuaded Mike Kustow, in charge of Arts programming at Channel 4 Television, to commission a 90-minute documentary about the Strathclyde conference to be written and narrated by me as both a participant and an observer of the event. My brief was to produce an accessible study of an academic conference, an institution unfamiliar to the general public, about a subject of fundamental human importance (language), but treated with an element of the satirical humour that characterised *Small World*. It was eventually given the title *Big Words . . . Small Worlds*. This assignment entailed going up to Glasgow several days before the conference began, being filmed arriving at the railway station, and then interviewing some of the principal speakers who had arrived earlier and were relaxing at the Country Club. The film would begin with a montage of their replies to my questions, put to them in this setting, about what had drawn them to the conference and what they expected to get out of it. Their responses were politely expectant and modestly unassertive. But soon the *mise en scène* shifted to a large utilitarian lecture room, deprived of natural light for the purpose of filming, inside the grey concrete mass of Strathclyde University where the conference sessions took place over three days, and the mood of the participants gradually became less genial.

An extra attraction of the conference for me was that Stanley Fish and his new wife Jane Tompkins were coming to it. I hadn't seen Stanley for several years and had never met Jane, whom he married after his divorce from Adrienne. I had looked forward to doing so in the days preceding the conference, but they did not arrive until the morning of the opening day and my introduction to Jane was when she chaired my own contribution that evening, a paper on Bakhtin. She turned out to be blonde, WASP, extrovert and feisty – very different from Adrienne, which I suppose was what had attracted Stanley. She had started out as a reader-response critic like him, but was now identified as a feminist revisionist critic of classic American literature and beginning to move in the direction of what she called a holistic approach to literary studies that would eventually lead her away from them altogether. They were a formidable couple and had recently moved from Johns Hopkins to positions at Duke University in North Carolina. This immensely rich institution was striving to rival the elite Ivy League universities by recruiting star professors, rather as the billionaire owners of British football clubs boost their performance in the Premier League by paying extravagant transfer fees and salaries for top players. As chairman of the English Department Stanley followed this policy and rapidly assembled a team of cutting-edge literary theorists who attracted bright graduate students. As a student himself, Stanley had been torn between studying English or Law, and he stipulated that his appointment at Duke should be half in the Law Faculty so that he could return to the subject he had been obliged to abandon. He was soon teaching students in Law as well as Literature, and publishing in law journals as well as literary ones, a rare and possibly unique combination of disciplines at this level.

Stanley's paper was entitled 'Withholding the Missing Portion: Power, Meaning and Persuasion in Freud's "The Wolf Man"'. In this case history Freud speculatively traced the source of the Wolf Man's neurosis to the trauma of observing in childhood his parents engaged in sexual intercourse, causing him to soil himself. As Stanley began to analyse all the rhetorical strategies and tropes that Freud used to make this theory plausible, it seemed that he was exposing Freud's bad faith; but in the conclusion of his paper Stanley produced a stunning reversal which exonerated him. Whether the primal scene postulated by Freud actually happened was irrelevant. 'Rather its credibility is a function of its explanatory power. It satisfies the need Freud has created in us to understand, and by understanding to become his partner in the story . . . The thesis of psychoanalysis is that one cannot get to the side of the unconscious. The thesis of this paper is that one cannot get to the side of rhetoric. These two theses are one and the same.' The second thesis is one that underlies all Stanley's work. He boldly admitted his 'relentless campaign against some of the so-called virtues that have already received pious endorsement at this conference – openness, flexibility, indeterminacy, generosity of mind, and the acknowledgement of difference. For all of these I would substitute the notion of persuasion, which I would define as a desire for mastery and closure.'

The opposition between 'openness' and 'closure' was central to several sessions of the conference, including my own. Bakhtin's 'dialogic' concept of discourse, in which every statement invites a response, seems to favour openness, but his own prose, like that of most scholars, is carefully composed to make his assertions appear irresistible. There is a similar, more basic opposition between speech and writing as media of communication, which was illustrated again and again in the conference by interventions from the floor, or responses to them by speakers, which were full of hesitations, qualifications and incomplete grammatical constructions, unlike the carefully crafted lectures that their authors had read out. That disparity is more or less inevitable unless, like Stanley Fish, you can speak extempore in perfectly formed sentences. He had developed a kind of realpolitik of discourse which he defended with great rhetorical skill, and it was regrettable from a dialectical point of view that some famous figures in the field who had enrolled for the conference and might have challenged him had withdrawn. Terry Eagleton, Fredric Jameson and Edward Said were all men of the Left and their absence unbalanced the event ideologically, contributing to the mutinous mood that developed in the audience later.

Another reason for discontent was that the unremitting succession of lectures left no time for rest and recreation. Anyone who had signed up for the conference hoping it might include the hedonistic diversions described in *Small World* would have been disappointed. Fredric Jameson had been scheduled to speak after dinner on the second evening, but in case anyone was tempted to take advantage of his absence to go out on the town, the organisers persuaded Derrida to plug the gap with a public lecture. Most of the conferees trooped off dutifully to hear it, some of whom discovered they had heard it before, at another conference. Entitled 'How to Avoid Speaking', it was about Negative Theology and lasted for two hours.

And so we came to the last day of our conference and the last session, which was to consist of Colin MacCabe's summing up of the event before we all dispersed. Half an hour had been allocated for general comments from the floor before he spoke. It was not enough. One person after another got to their feet to complain that the programme had been elitist, privileging the main speakers and leaving little opportunity for the audience to challenge what they said, or did not say. Others said that it was Eurocentric and politically reactionary. One hinted darkly that the absence of Fredric Jameson and Terry Eagleton seemed mysteriously convenient for the silencing of dissent. Another objected to the filming of the event as intimidation and asked for the cameras to be switched off while he was speaking. (The request was granted.) Another was so disappointed that he felt like asking for his money back. Plainly disconcerted by this barrage of complaints, Colin admitted that he was hesitating about whether to plunge into his talk. Jane Tompkins passed a note up to the podium, which he read out, suggesting that the discussion should continue. Someone suggested from the floor that they should take a vote on whether Colin should give his talk or not. This was done by a show of hands and he won by a humiliatingly small margin, but soldiered on.

The subject of the conference had become the conference itself. It was a disappointing conclusion for the organisers, but I saw at once that this episode would provide a dramatic climax for our film. It was useful to have that ending in mind as I set about the formidable task of turning the transcripts of some fifty hours of filmed discourse, formal and informal, into a coherent script. The sheer bulk of material was not the only challenge. There had been two cameras covering the whole event, but one of them turned out to have a focusing fault that the cameraman had inexplicably failed to notice. In consequence all the footage from this source was unusable, including Derrida's contribution to the conversation between himself and Raymond Williams, which was to have been the high point of the film. To be accidentally erased from it was an ironic fate for the great Deconstructionist, since one of his signature tropes was to visibly cross out words in his own text which were indispensable but in his opinion conceptually flawed, a device he called 'sous rature', usually translated as 'under erasure'. All we had of this encounter was a series of remarks by Williams which had to be turned into a monologue. In spite of this setback and other difficulties I managed to produce a rough draft script which pleased Mike Kustow at Channel 4. 'I can't wait to see it on the screen,' he wrote to me in October.

Like all scripts it went through several rewrites, and it wasn't until the spring of 1987 that I began to record my commentary which linked the various scenes and episodes. This was done partly as voice-over, and partly to camera in a studio set furnished like a large study, where I read the script from an autocue. Though I say it myself, I think I did a good job of explaining to a lay audience the concepts and issues the conference was concerned with. But Colin and his young collaborators, obviously unsettled by the Rebellion of the Proles (as I privately tagged the last session), thought my commentary was too cut-and-dried, too confident of its interpretations, too anxious to exert its authority – in short, too prone to closure rather than openness. Their proposal to avoid giving this impression was to disrupt my discourse in various ways. They staged a scene in which Colin, as producer, burst into the studio, interrupted my commentary and argued with me that it was too monologic, and that we needed to interpolate other points of view. This scene was incorporated in the finished film and proved only that neither of us was a very good actor. Also included was a cutaway from me making a joke on the podium to me laughing at it from the front row of the audience, a surrealist jape which, since it was not repeated, looked like a mistake. I did not have an opportunity to veto it. Later the first edited version of the film was shown to a number of intellectual and artistic celebrities who had not been at the conference, including the academics who had withdrawn after enrolling for it, and short comments by them were inserted in the final cut. Those who had withdrawn did not seem to regret their decision.

In spite of these problems, setbacks and disagreements, I had no regrets about my involvement in the film, for it had been an interesting experience. But a couple of months later I attended another ambitious symposium which was more successful and certainly less acrimonious. The subject was 'Images and Understanding', and the chief organisers were the distinguished neuroscientist Colin Blakemore and the polymath Jonathan Miller, co-creator of *Beyond the Fringe*, director of drama and opera, and a medical doctor with a mission to disseminate scientific knowledge of mind–body interaction through TV documentaries. The subject of the Symposium was how human beings process the images which present themselves to consciousness in a great variety of forms and media. It was hosted by the Royal Society, and the speakers were predominantly scientists, but Jonathan Miller's involvement ensured that the arts were represented. He himself spoke about film as a medium, the great art historian Ernst Gombrich talked about the history of textbook illustration, Margaret Drabble chaired a session entitled 'Images and Meaning', and the cartoonist Mel Calman chaired the session on 'Narrative' to which I contributed, sketching us as we spoke. I really didn't know enough science to benefit from most of the scientific presentations, and I was more interested in their form than their content. It was the first occasion I had seen and heard academic scientists doing their stuff, and I was impressed by the highly sophisticated visual aids they used to illustrate their talks, and the way this seemed to encourage a more informal verbal exposition than the typical humanities lecture. I felt underequipped in this company with no videos or slides to project, only a cyclostyled handout of passages from a few novels. Later all the speakers would submit written and revised versions of their contributions for publication in a substantial book.[1] In retrospect it is clear to me that this symposium heralded an international surge of research and publications on the phenomenon of consciousness across a wide range of academic disciplines which would peak in the next decade, and some of the leading contributors to that body of work, like Daniel Dennett, were present at the event. But it was not until ten years later that I became seriously interested in the subject myself and began to do some research in preparation for my novel called *Thinks . . .*

In August that year Mary and I had a touring holiday in Brittany with Malcolm and Elizabeth Bradbury. We took two cars to give each couple freedom to roam separately and avoid friction over issues like smoking, to which Malcom was addicted. It was an enjoyable trip which concluded with a reunion with the Honans, who were spending the summer as usual at St Brévin and crossed the Loire estuary to meet us for dinner at our hotel. We also made a new friend, Maurice Couturier, who would later play an important part in my authorial life. Professor of English and American Literature at Nice University, and the leading French specialist in the work of Vladimir Nabokov, he had spent a term as a visiting Fellow at East Anglia where he got to know Malcolm. He and his wife Yvonne usually spent August in Brittany to get away from the heat and crowds on the Côte d'Azur, and he had arranged to meet us at a hotel in the country, where we stayed for a couple of nights. We immediately felt at ease with him and Yvonne and passed a

---

[1] *Images and Understanding,* ed. Horace Barlow, Colin Blakemore and Miranda Weston-Smith, Cambridge UP (1990).

pleasant few hours in their company. He had some experience of translating and told us that he had made several efforts to persuade French publishers to commission a translation of *The History Man*, but without success. He had enjoyed some of my novels and asked me if any French publishers had expressed interest in them and I said that some had been approached, but I had received no offers. There seemed to be something about the kind of novel that Malcolm and I wrote which didn't suit French publishers' taste.

By the autumn of 1986 the cuts in university funding initiated by Mrs Thatcher's government began to really hurt. Student numbers had grown without a corresponding increase in staff. The size of tutorials and seminars was increasing and it was getting difficult to remember the names of all the students one taught. It was inevitable that soon all courses in the English Department would be taught in seminar-sized groups and lectures. I was not looking forward to my next teaching term in the spring. Birmingham happened to be without a Vice Chancellor at this time. One had recently retired, and his replacement, Professor Michael Thompson, was serving his last term as VC of the University of East Anglia and would not be arriving until January. In the meantime, the Vice Principal, Professor Mike Hamlin, was Acting Vice Chancellor. He circulated a warning to staff in September that 'unless action is taken during this current financial year to reduce expenditure . . . by the end of the year the University's current reserves will be totally exhausted'. It was estimated that the University would have to shed 140 academic and 100 technical and secretarial posts and would therefore be offering early retirement schemes to encourage staff to leave service earlier than they had intended. (This had to be voluntary because at the time most academic staff in British universities had tenure and could not be made redundant.) Retiring under such a scheme meant that you immediately began to draw the pension you would have received if you had continued working until the age of sixty. This was exactly the kind of financial life jacket that I needed to take the plunge into being a full-time writer, so I applied for it. Christopher was due to begin his residence at the CARE village in Ironbridge in the autumn of 1987, and I anticipated that I would have to 'top up' the cost of his fees there, which were in excess of the sum paid by central government through Birmingham Social Services under the system then in place. Early retirement would ease anxiety about keeping up such payments while pursuing the uncertain career of a freelance writer.

My application was rejected at first, but I accepted an invitation from the Acting VC to discuss the matter further, after which it was approved. The basis of the agreement was that I would have a continuing membership of the University as an Honorary Professor, making occasional contributions to its educational and cultural life, and my appropriate publications would continue to be listed in the University's annual Research Report – a document that had acquired new importance in the competition for funds in higher education. I made clear that it was my intention to continue living in Birmingham in close proximity to the campus. I was lucky that Mike Hamlin, who knew my writing and appreciated it, was Acting VC at this time. The previous VC would not have been so sympathetic, and Michael Thompson was coming from UEA where the MA in Creative Writing directed by Malcolm was a huge success. I had met Thompson socially at Norwich through that connection, and it was likely that when he arrived at Birmingham he would have asked me to head a similar programme, extinguishing any prospect of early retirement.

I felt some qualms of guilt at deserting the ship in which I had sailed for half my adult life at such a critical moment, and I admitted as much in the speech I gave at the customary farewell drinks party in the summer, which I shared with my colleague Joan Rees, a veteran of the Department who was retiring at the usual age. But as well as wanting more time to develop my various creative interests, and as well as finding teaching more and more difficult due to increasing hearing loss, I was becoming more conscious of difficulties in reconciling my persona as a senior professor with my identity as a writer. I had managed to separate these two roles by not performing as a writer on campus, but there had been something artificial about the pretence. The writer inevitably drew on his experience of the milieu he worked in, and I had managed to get away with that in *Changing Places* and *Small World* by using the licence of comedy. 'Rummidge' in those novels was a kind of caricature of Birmingham, a city that was used to being the butt of jokes, and could laugh at itself. Most of my colleagues had reacted to the novels in that spirit, well aware that the real University was a much more impressive institution than its fictional equivalent. But I was conscious that the novel I had nearly finished, though it contained comedy and humour, was a much more realistic and recognisable picture of both the city and its university than its predecessors, which would only make it more difficult to continue pretending that my lives as a novelist and as a professor were quite distinct. In retrospect I think that must have been one reason why I had applied for the Oxford chair; but now I was more grateful than ever that I had not been offered it.

# 14

I was to retire officially at the end of the academic year in September 1987, but as I was on leave in the summer term under my part-time contract, and that was followed by the long vacation, I was in effect a full-time writer by the end of March, free to devote myself to several projects I had in development. The most important was the novel, 'Shadow Work', but since I had not signed a contract for it or committed myself to a delivery date I put it aside when other projects demanded my attention. Chief among these were my play, 'The Pressure Cooker', and a script for a TV adaptation of *How Far Can You Go?* which London Weekend Television had optioned. But the first thing I did at the end of March was to head down to the Oval Rehearsal Rooms in London to observe the read-through and first rehearsals of Granada's production of *Small World*, clutching the thick type-script of Episode One which had been sent to me.

I had had very little contact with Granada since I was shown Howard Schuman's first draft a year earlier. It had probably taken him many months of writing and rewriting further episodes before the serial was green-lighted for production, and then he had been involved in auditioning actors with the Director, Robert Chetwyn, while the production team worked on a schedule for filming. This latter task was more than usually complicated because of the many foreign locations in the story, very few of which were faked in the TV serial. Persse's encounter with Miss Maiden in Hawaii, for instance, was filmed at the swimming pool bar of a luxury hotel at Heathrow with Polynesian décor; but more extended episodes of this kind were filmed on location, in Amsterdam, Lausanne, Istanbul and other exotic settings. The kind of expenditure this entails is more usually associated with major feature films than television drama. The serial also had an enormously long cast list, of some seventy actors with speaking parts, major and minor. Granada really splashed out on this project, and I felt that I had made the right choice between them and the BBC. Furthermore, they agreed at some point to increase the number of episodes from four to six to accommodate Howard's faithful adaptation. Everybody involved in the production was very excited and expectant as this show got on the road.

All drama, whether acted on stage or filmed or televised or broadcast on radio, is a collaborative activity, but the person with most responsibility for the character and quality of the finished product is the director. Bob Chetwyn, five years older than me, had started out as an actor but established himself as one of the most successful theatrical directors in London during the sixties and seventies, particularly in the field of comedy, working with a number of distinguished playwrights such as Tom Stoppard, Peter Nichols and Joe Orton, and actors such as Ian McKellen, Ralph Richardson and Flora Robson. More recently, like many theatre directors, he had moved into the medium of television, and had directed two very popular comedy drama series, *Private Shultz* and *An Irish RM*; but *Small World* was a more challenging project than either of those. Bob and Howard were both gay. They had shared a flat together in Eccleston Square, Belgravia, since the 1960s, and entered into a civil partnership in 2006, but temperamentally they were very different. I quickly established a warm relationship with Howard, who was cheerful, amusing, and obviously enjoyed his continuing involvement in the production. Bob was more reticent and saturnine, and sometimes I felt he was weighed down by the responsibility of his position.

As a complete novice in this milieu, I did not have such a thought during the few days I spent at the Oval rehearsal room, a large space like a school hall, with miscellaneous items of furniture lined up against the walls for use when needed, and white lines marked out on the floor. I was too excited by simply being there, meeting and chatting to actors, watching them at work, seeing scenes from my novel performed, and helping myself from the table in one corner laid with snacks, coffee, tea and soft drinks. Television rehearsals are less intensive than the theatrical equivalent, because there isn't time to do every scene. Their main purpose is to familiarise actors with their parts and get them used to working with the director and each other, by acting out a number of selected scenes. Inevitably some lines are queried by the actors and may be changed on the spot. I ventured to make a couple of suggestions, and felt disproportionately pleased with myself when they were adopted.

Because of his theatrical contacts Bob had been able to recruit a number of excellent actors willing to play supporting roles, for example Sarah Badel, who played Philip Swallow's wife Hilary and doubled as his mistress Joy, Sheila Gish, who played Fulvia Morgana and Désirée Zapp, and Rachel Kempson, matriarch of the famous Redgrave theatrical dynasty, who was a superb Sibyl Maiden, the retired Girton scholar. The actors in leading roles were in fact less well known, and the one who played the young hero, Persse McGarrigle, was not known at all in Britain. Finbar ('Barry') Lynch was an Irish stage actor whom Bob and Howard discovered in Dublin after a long search. He was perfect for the role: a newcomer to British television drama as Persse is to international academia. Morris Zapp was played by John Ratzenberger, an American actor who was known in the UK mainly for his role as the Postman in the enormously popular sitcom *Cheers*.

After the rehearsals in London the production team moved back to Manchester, where Granada's headquarters are situated, for filming in studios and on nearby locations, and I went up there for a few days to observe and eavesdrop. This is in fact a less interesting experience than watching rehearsals, since there is a lot of boring repetition of short takes with long pauses between them while technicians make adjustments to cameras and lighting. In the evenings I watched the 'rushes' – roughly edited sequences only a few minutes long filmed that day – and they too were slightly disappointing, but I was assured by the professionals that properly edited and with a good soundtrack they would come alive. I was however awed by the scale of the operation my novel had set in motion: the number of people besides the actors and director and writer who were involved, and the many different operations from casting to catering that had to be arranged and co-ordinated to move the film forward. Soon the production team and principal actors would set off again, like some great caravan of old, with the lighting cameraman and sound recordist, gaffer and clapper boy, make-up artists and wardrobe mistresses, set dressers and gofers, on a journey of several months' duration to new locations, acquiring and shedding members on the way. Before I returned home I left my own mark on the final product when Bob allowed me to make a brief appearance in one of the scenes, as a member of the conference at Rummidge University pausing in a corridor to examine a noticeboard.

Of the parallel projects I mentioned earlier the one that can be most briefly dealt with was the proposed adaptation of *How Far Can You Go?* as a four-part serial for London Weekend Television. I was originally encouraged to attempt this by Patrick Garland, who liked the novel, and he interested Nick Elliott, the Controller of Drama and Arts at LWT, in the idea. John Birt, who later became Director General of the BBC, was then head of LWT. He was a fan of my book, having had a Catholic upbringing in Liverpool similar to that of some of my characters, and he gave strong support to the project. Patrick had been scathing about my first attempt at a draft script of Episode One, but I improved on it and submitted it to Nick Elliott, who responded in July. His letter began promisingly, 'I really do like the script. I think you've done it very well. It moves along and delivers the book well.' But he continued: 'The trouble is that things have changed completely here at LWT. John Birt has gone to the BBC to be Deputy D.G. His replacement is a man called Greg Dyke who I don't think would want HFCYG for his schedule . . . He's very keen on ratings . . . best known for the invention of Roland Rat on Breakfast TV.' Nick Elliott didn't in fact dare even to mention my draft script to Greg Dyke. Instead he passed it to his equivalent at Channel 4, but that didn't come to anything either. I had never quite believed that a dramatisation of a novel all about Catholics would appeal to the largely secular TV audience, so I decided not to waste any more time on it. Greg Dyke became Director General of the BBC thirteen years later, after John Birt.

The history of 'The Pressure Cooker', later called *The Writing Game*, is more complicated, and a full account would fill a book as long as this one. It was a fascinating though often frustrating odyssey, which initiated me into a way of working entirely different from writing prose fiction. Composing a novel is an essentially solitary, silent process, over which the writer has more or less complete control up to the point of finishing it and submitting it for publication. Before and/or after acceptance there may be some feedback from editors, friends, and people with relevant special knowledge, which the writer is free to accept, emending the text accordingly, or reject (though that may have consequences). With a play this intervention of other minds in the creative process never ceases, because it does not consist entirely of words on a page. Every production of a play is different from every other because different artists are involved. It evolves through rehearsals which throw up new problems and new solutions, often until its first public performance and sometimes afterwards; and every performance of the same production is subtly different from every other one, as is the audience's reaction to each. (It is also true of course that every reading and re-reading of a novel is unique, produced in the silent theatre of the individual reader's mind.)

For a playwright even getting to the start of this collaborative process – i.e. having the play performed for the first time – can be a long and frustrating experience. I had a lucky start with the rehearsed reading of 'The Pressure Cooker' at the National Theatre, but their option on the play led only to a long period of inactivity. In the late spring of 1987 I made an appointment to see David Aukin about the stalemate, and was pleasantly surprised by the outcome. He had given up hope of persuading any of the NT's resident directors to take on the play. Instead he wanted to use it to test a new initiative of his own: getting provincial repertory theatres to produce new plays which if suitable and successful could transfer to the National. He had the Bristol Old Vic in mind, since he knew the Artistic Director there, Leon Rubin, and I agreed readily to sending him the script. Rubin responded enthusiastically, said it was the best-written play he had read in a long time, and that he wanted to direct it himself in the Bristol Studio. I was thrilled. But on 15th June I had a letter from David: 'Catastrophe! Leon Rubin has parted from Bristol, he had a bust-up with his Board, he tells me one of the issues was our co-production. He does, however, still want to direct your play and suggested that it now be mounted with Leicester, my old haunt.' David had been Artistic Director at the Leicester Haymarket Theatre before coming to the National, but he did not seem to think this would necessarily ensure a warm reception from the new management; and my own feeling was that if the play was going to be premiered at a theatre in the Midlands, it ought to be the Birmingham Rep.

The reason I had not approached the Rep before was that it didn't really have a suitable space for my play. The shabby but intimate and acoustically perfect theatre in Station Street where *Between These Four Walls*, the revue I co-authored with Malcolm Bradbury and Jim Duckett, was produced in 1962 had been supplanted in 1971 by a new one, a striking modernist structure more than twice its size at the end of Broad Street. It was largely financed by Birmingham City Council, and its scale was a typical case of civic ambition overriding theatrical common sense. The architect's brief was to design a theatre with nine hundred seats in the main auditorium, and his response, approved by the Rep's Board and several qualified advisers, was a steeply raked fan-shaped auditorium facing an enormous stage – bigger than Covent Garden's at that time. It is a spectacular space, and fine for epic plays and pantomimes, but much too big for most modern drama with small casts and realistic dialogue. If the actors project to reach the back rows their lines lose subtlety and nuance for the auditors in the front rows; if they play appropriately to the front rows the people in the back rows can't hear them well. It is a space in which it is very difficult to create a bond between audience and players, and it has broken several directors' hearts. It was also far too big for the potential audience in Birmingham for serious theatre, and often half empty for performances. It reached its nadir when a matinee of Shaw's *St Joan* had to be cancelled because only a dozen people had booked for it. (In recent years it has much improved in this respect by commercially astute programming, co-productions with other reps, and hosting touring productions, and it now has the use of a new 300-seat theatre embedded in the new Library to which it is joined.)

Having sat in this theatre many times I was sure it was unsuitable for my play, but the only alternative was a Studio theatre which was originally designed as a rehearsal room, and had been converted to make a space with flexible seating for about 125 people. Some outstanding productions were mounted there, but on very limited budgets, and they seldom attracted 'name' actors. Nevertheless I was willing to see my play premiered there and hoped that a more ambitious production might develop from it. The moment seemed propitious because a new Artistic Director had recently been appointed to the Rep: John Adams, who had come from the Octagon in Bolton where he had made a reputation for lively and innovative productions. Leah sent him 'The Pressure Cooker' and we heard that he was definitely interested and would like to meet me to discuss it. But when I went to have lunch with him at the Rep's restaurant his interest had cooled. Evidently he had been upset by hearing that the Leicester Haymarket was considering the play when he had supposed it was being exclusively offered to him – an unfortunate crossing of wires traceable to Leon Rubin. John told me that the Rep's budget allowed them to put on only one play a year in the Studio, and he planned to fill the rest of the programme with shows by touring companies appealing to a youthful audience. He doubted whether 'The Pressure Cooker' was suitable for the Rep's solitary production, and his last word on that occasion was not promising: 'Is it perhaps really a good radio play?'

I had in fact had a letter from a BBC Radio 3 producer who had been at the Cottesloe reading, offering to produce the play with some pruning of the language likely to give offence. But after talking it over with Leah I decided that there was no advantage in doing it first on radio. I had conceived it from the beginning as a stage play. It seemed to me that the force of the three readings was essentially theatrical, that they would gain much from the presence of a live audience; and that the tensions between the three main characters, compelled to be in each other's company by the circumstances of the course, would also gain from being acted on a single set. I recognised in retrospect the influence on me of Jean-Paul Sartre's play *Huis Clos* (*No Exit*), about the special hell of three mutually incompatible people who are trapped for ever in a French Empire drawing room. It had made a considerable impact on me in my youth, and I had seen it again on television not long before writing the first draft of 'The Pressure Cooker'.

The National Theatre's option ran out in July. David Aukin was willing to renew it, but I sensed that he was discouraged by our bad luck with the provincial reps. Leah and I decided to take the rights back and try to find a producer ourselves. She suggested the Royal Shakespeare Company and I thought it was worth my writing to its Artistic Director, Terry Hands, whom I had tutored in my first year as an assistant lecturer at Birmingham. Terry replied encouragingly: 'I am delighted you've written a play – though I must warn you that, unlike novels, you will have less control over the physical aspects of each scene. Could you send it in to us and we will take it from there.' The phrasing of this message might have implied acceptance sight unseen if I had not already become inured to disappointment in my first theatrical venture. Leah sent off the playscript, but neither she nor I ever heard another word about it from Terry or anybody else at the RSC.

Then my faithful friend Donald Fanger, Professor of Russian Literature at Harvard, hearing that I had written a play, offered to pass it to his friend Robert Brustein, a famously versatile man of the theatre – playwright, critic, producer, teacher and currently Artistic Director of the American Repertory Theatre in Cambridge, Mass., which is part of Harvard University but also a professional public theatre. I accepted the suggestion gratefully; Leah and I had talked about the possibility of launching the play in America, and she had already elicited strong interest from the Long Wharf Theatre which stood to Yale much as the ART did to Harvard. We sent the script to Bob Brustein, who replied, 'It's a funny, intelligent look at the whole notion of writing colonies, and I think it would do very well in Cambridge.' But he wanted to try it out with a rehearsed reading before committing himself. I was happy to agree to that and planned to attend it if possible.

Meanwhile Leah had shown the play to a young London producer, André Ptaszynski, who had been very successful in managing tours by the new generation of British comic actors and actresses like Rowan Atkinson, Victoria Wood, Mel Smith and Griff Rhys Jones, and was now looking to get involved in straight drama. He liked 'The Pressure Cooker' and optioned it for a year. The agreement included American rights, but Bob Brustein wasn't bothered by that. He proposed to stage the reading early in the New Year, and as André was going to be in New York at the same time, it was agreed that he would join me at it.

I was glad to put this play aside for a few months and to stop thinking and negotiating about it. I was now determined to finish 'Shadow Work' by the end of the year so that it could be submitted to Secker and included in their autumn catalogue for 1988, which would go to press some time in February. The spring and autumn catalogues are the essential means by which booksellers, literary festivals, literary editors of newspapers and magazines, and interested personnel in other media inform themselves about forthcoming books and plan their responses accordingly. If it missed the autumn catalogue, the novel would not be published until the spring of the following year, and I did not want to wait that long. I had been writing it, on and off, for nearly two years and like many authors I secreted an underlying anxiety that some other writer might have the same or a similar idea for a novel and publish it first. Also I felt that it was a timely book which might seem less pertinent if its publication were delayed too long. It treated not only the impact of monetarism on industry and universities in the 1980s, but also the deregulation of financial markets which was another of Mrs Thatcher's initiatives, colloquially known as the Big Bang. I gave my heroine a brother who was a product of the new aggressive financial culture, with a cockney currency-dealer girlfriend who handled sums equivalent to a small university's annual budget every week, and to give some credibility to these characters I managed, with the help of my accountant, to be a fly on the wall of a dealing room for a day in a London investment bank.

'Shadow Work' was a book that presented new challenges for me because the two main characters, or 'centres of consciousness', to use Henry James's term, through whom the story is filtered, were more different from me than characters of equivalent importance in my previous novels. One was a woman, and the other was the managing director of an engineering firm. Of course I was very familiar with Robyn Penrose's professional life and could easily represent it, and satirise it to some extent, but like any male writer I was dependent on intuition and imagination to represent her consciousness. For Vic's family life I was able to draw on my own relationship with my father, and to a lesser extent with my son Stephen in adolescence, but Vic's marriage is entirely different from mine. His professional life was wholly strange to me, and could only be portrayed by research, observation and the help of Maurice Andrews, without which I could never have written the book. The basic structure of the narrative – a man and a woman meet and are mutually antagonistic at first but gradually develop a respect for each other and for the work each does – has something in common with the classic heroine-centred love story, for example *Pride and Prejudice.* Clearly it could not end in the same way, for Robyn would never fall in love with Vic. But Vic could conceivably become infatuated with Robyn, a development replete with interesting and amusing possibilities. This led me to conceive a reversal of the plot towards the end of the novel whereby Vic arranges to 'shadow' Robyn at the University, pretending it is all in the spirit of Industry Year. The scene where he sits in on a tutorial discussion of Tennyson's *Maud* is one I particularly enjoyed writing.

At this stage I was grappling with the problem of how to tie up the various other strands in the narrative into a satisfactory ending. I decided to exploit the novel's subtext of allusions to the Victorian industrial novels on which Robyn lectures early in the book. She comments sardonically on their endings, which evade the political issues raised in the stories by the way the fortunes of the main characters are settled. 'All the Victorian novelist could offer as a solution to the problems of industrial capitalism were a legacy, a marriage, emigration or death,' she says. Death did not belong in this essentially comic novel, but when Robyn faces the imminent termination of her temporary lectureship, chance offers her in succession the other three solutions: emigration (to a job in America offered by Morris Zapp), marriage (to her boyfriend Charles) and a legacy (from a long-forgotten Australian uncle) which makes her financially independent. In the end she passes on all of them. She gets an unexpected last-minute renewal of her appointment at Rummidge and invests her legacy in a business venture that Vic, who has suddenly lost his own job, has long dreamed hopelessly of starting. I remember getting this idea and driving over to Maurice Andrews's house that evening to ask him to invent for me a plausible product for this enterprise. He came up very quickly with a spectrometer that could give an instant readout of the composition of molten metal in foundry operations, instead of having to send it to labs for analysis, and I inserted this idea into a conversation between Vic and Robyn earlier in the novel.

I did a final read-through and polish of the typescript in December and sent it off to Mike Shaw at Curtis Brown. It was now the season of office parties and Christmas lunch menus, and he was caught up in the obligatory socialising, so did not write to me until the 22nd to congratulate me on the book, which he had forwarded confidently to Secker. I was able to relax and enjoy our own family Christmas, but I had to wait till the New Year to discover what David Godwin, who had recently moved from

Heinemann to replace Peter Gross as head of Secker, and whom I had not yet met, thought of 'Shadow Work'.

Although 1987 was a year in which I concentrated mainly on creative projects, I did not disengage entirely from the world of academic literary criticism and theory. Towards the end of April I went back to Providence, Rhode Island, having been invited by Mark Spilka to give the keynote lecture at a conference he had organised to celebrate the twentieth anniversary of NOVEL, the journal that he and Park Honan had started at Brown University, where I had spent a semester as a Harkness Fellow in 1964–65. The lovely campus had not changed much in the meantime, and the tree-lined streets of frame houses around it had largely preserved their character, though the house in which we occupied a flat next to the Armenian shoe-mender's shop had gone. But I had little time to indulge in nostalgic musings because the conference had a crowded programme. Mark had suggested I might speak on 'Why the Novel Matters', the title of a well-known essay by D.H. Lawrence, but that was not my style. I offered a more neutral title: 'The Novel Now: Theories and Practices', which Mark resignedly accepted. I spoke in my dual role as novelist and critic and considered the widening gap between the two professions as a result of the saturation of academic criticism with theoretical discourse that was alien to most writers and readers of contemporary fiction, and ended by proposing Bakhtin's theory of the novel as something both sides could identify with and learn from.

The conference had attracted a large and interesting crowd and I met several friends and acquaintances from previous conferences, including Susan Suleiman and Robert Scholes – it was on this occasion that Bob revealed to me the subtext of the late-night conversation in Marilyn French's hotel room in Zurich in 1979. I was not the only novelist participating. Nadine Gordimer was the star of the occasion, though she had not yet won the Nobel Prize. I went to the 'Reading and Commentary' she gave one evening in a packed Baptist church, a tiny, elfin, almost girlish-looking woman in spite of her grey hair. We sat in pews, which seemed appropriate to the quasi-religious fervour with which she anticipated a coming 'revolution' in South Africa. I had read very little of her fiction – in fact, only a magazine extract from *The Conservationist*, in which a man of distinguished reputation on an intercontinental night flight, when the cabin lights are dimmed and blankets distributed, insanely risks disgrace by masturbating a silently acquiescent teenage girl in the seat beside him for hours on end. I thought it was one of the most brilliant feats of prose writing I had ever encountered: tense, precise, sensual but not pornographic, and totally convincing. Nadine Gordimer had the reputation of being a rather prickly person, and with only this specific tribute to her work to offer, I did not seek a conversation with her.

The most controversial speaker at the conference was Joseph Gold, who had written a book called *Read for Your Life*, and asserted that the function of the novel is to 'increase human self-awareness and cultural awareness . . . and to increase our chances of survival', which another delegate denounced as 'an arrogant and pompous usurping of a moral standard'. I discovered that Gold had been born and educated in England and studied at Birmingham University before moving to the USA and more recently to Canada. He told me he was a therapist as well as a professor and offered counselling in which he prescribed to his clients the reading of novels carefully selected to help them come to terms with their particular problems. It sounded unorthodox to me then, but I believe it is an approved item in the therapeutic toolbag these days. The conferee I was most pleased to meet was a young woman from the University of California who, improbably, had attended the reading of 'The Pressure Cooker' at the National Theatre and claimed it was the best thing she had seen in London during her visit, which was even more improbable, but I chose to believe her. I was also pleased to be seated at dinner on the last evening next to Marianna Torgovnick, a very smart lady who was in the English Department at Duke University, and described Stanley Fish's arrival in that institution as 'like a dream come true'.

I looked forward to relaying this compliment to Stanley himself, as I had arranged to spend the coming weekend with him and Jane in North Carolina before returning home. I found them occupying a luxurious house surrounded by flowering shrubs and trees, with four cars in the drive, one of them Jane's, the other three to provide Stanley with automotive variety. They gave a party for me to meet people from Duke, and the Southern spring evening was warm enough for drinks on the lawn. It seemed an idyllic way of life they were leading in the most salubrious part of the so-called 'Research Triangle', an area of North Carolina containing several universities, research institutes and hi-tech companies. Climate, environment, standard of living were all of the highest quality; it was just a little tame, I thought, compared to the Bay Area, and I wondered how long Stanley would stay there.

In June I attended another conference, though this time as a creative writer rather than a critic. It is an annual event known as the International Writers Reunion, at Lahti, in Finland. Every year, at the summer solstice in June, about fifty writers from all over the world are invited, with their travel expenses paid, to join a somewhat larger number of Finnish writers at a lakeside site in the middle of the country to discuss, over three days and numerous beers, an appropriate theme, which in 1987 was 'Literature and Exhibitionism'. Conscious of their marginal geographical position and a language which resembles only Hungarian and Estonian, educated Finns, and writers in particular, are fluent in English and other languages and crave contact with their counterparts in other countries. The Reunion is a way of facilitating this and they make the most of it. The event gets front-page coverage in the Finnish newspapers, and its proceedings are extensively reported on radio and TV. A regular feature in those days, and perhaps still, was a friendly football match between Finland and the Rest of the World, played by the light of the midnight sun and described live on radio by one of the country's top commentators.

The format of the Lahti discussions is simple: a panel of four or five writers speak on some aspect of the conference theme and then other participants take the roving microphone to comment. All speeches are simultaneously translated into five languages by a team of expert interpreters who compete eagerly for the work because it is much more interesting than the political and economic forums which are their usual assignments. The responses to the theme of Exhibitionism were predictably varied, but many focused on the confessional, autobiographical element in writing. J.M. Coetzee thoughtfully fingered the paradox that self-revelation is ultimately impossible because behind the self which is revealed there is always a hidden self that is doing the revealing. My compatriot Graham Swift claimed that the English writer was temperamentally afraid of doing anything that looked like 'showing off' and that it was only by reading literary exhibitionists like Borges, Beckett and Márquez that he had liberated himself from dull autobiographically based realism. As part of my own presentation I read an extract from Morris Zapp's lecture, 'Textuality as Striptease', in *Small World*. It provoked much laughter but often, it seemed to me, in the wrong places. It was only when I reflected on this on the flight home that I realised that the simultaneous translations would have been lagging a sentence or two behind my reading.

These sessions normally take place in the open air, but the weather was unseasonably cool and wet, and we spent a good deal of time in marquees. However, the rain held off to allow the football match to be played under a cloud-veiled midnight sun. I was enlisted as a substitute for the Rest of the World, and spent the game on the sidelines praying that I would not be called upon. Fortunately our side won the game 4–3 without my assistance, due mainly to the efforts of a Hungarian writer who I do not remember making any contribution to our discussions but was a brilliant dribbler of the ball in the style of Puskás. Graham Swift, a younger and fitter novelist than me, also played a useful midfield role in this victory. I took home with me a red shirt imprinted with the insignia of the Rest of the World team as a souvenir to impress the family.

The highlight of this conference for me was sampling a traditional Finnish smoke sauna, offered as a diversion one afternoon as an alternative to a tour of the town of Lahti, a kind of small-scale Milton Keynes. The only kind of sauna I knew at that time was a cramped wooden cubicle in Birmingham University's Sports Centre which I had tried once in preparation to write a scene in *How Far Can You Go?* The Finnish smoke sauna was a very different experience. It was like a large timber oven with bench seats, heated in advance by an open wood fire, until the required high temperature was reached, which imparted its smoky aroma and sooty deposits to the interior and thus on to the perspiring naked bodies of the writers (all male; the ladies had a separate facility elsewhere) who crowded into it. One emerged into the open air feeling mildly barbecued and plunged, with a shock of brief duration, into the nearby lake. After three such treatments I felt beatifically warm and relaxed. Later we lolled on the veranda, drank beer and ate sausages as swallows swooped through the pearly permanent dusk of the summer night. In the years that followed saunas of various kinds would figure frequently in my recreational life and occasionally in my fiction and drama.


My next experience of one came quite soon, as a result of looking for a suitable place to give our Down's son Christopher a summer holiday. He was now nearly twenty-two and had been at the CARE community in Ironbridge for two years. He had settled in happily there, and was doing well in the carpentry workshop, turning out elegant wooden bowls on a lathe. He came home to Edgbaston every fourth weekend. As he was well trained in using public transport he was able to take a bus on a Friday afternoon from near the CARE community to the Birmingham bus station where I met him, and to which I returned him early on Monday morning for the return journey. He also had seasonal holidays at home, including two weeks in the summer. As we no longer had annual family holidays with Julia and Stephen, it was difficult to think of one that would suit him and be tolerable for us. I had read in the newspapers about Center Parcs, a new type of upmarket holiday village originating in Holland, which had recently opened in Sherwood Forest and seemed promising for our purpose. The concept was a large secure area in the country with one-storey 'villas' built in the woods so as to be screened from each other, and a vast indoor swimming pool complex called a Tropical Paradise, plus other sporting facilities both indoor and outdoor, shops and restaurants, and an artificial lake for water sports. You parked your car on arrival, and after that moved around on bicycles or on foot.

It seemed ideal for our purpose so I booked a villa for a week in August for Mary, myself and Chris, and Julia decided to join us. The experiment was successful – so much so that since then we have spent either a week or a few days nearly every summer at Sherwood Forest or one of the other Center Parcs that have been created in England. It became a family tradition, supplementing the more exotic or luxurious holidays we severally arranged for ourselves. It was the perfect holiday resort for Chris, safe, friendly and predictable. He has always looked forward eagerly to the annual visit to Center Parcs, and in due course so did our three grandchildren from infancy right through their teenage years. Their parents came with them, and

Mary's mother and other members of her family joined us on several occasions. We got into the habit of booking two villas next to each other for large family parties, and shared evening meals together, al fresco in warm weather. After trying the other sites, we have in recent years remained faithful to the greatly improved Sherwood Forest one.

In a late novel called *Deaf Sentence* (2007) I wrote a somewhat prejudicial account of a fictional holiday village inspired by Center Parcs, called 'Gladeworld'.

> Gladeworld. What a strange phenomenon. Like a
> negative image of a place with properties, such as
> confinement and induced pain, that you would
> normally regard as being themselves negative, which has
> the curious effect of turning them into positives, or so
> it seems from the contented looks of the inhabitants.
> A benevolent concentration camp. A benign prison. A
> happy hell.

The narrator is Desmond Bates, a retired professor of linguistics, whose temperament has not been made sunnier by hearing loss, and who has been reluctantly persuaded by his wife to take a weekend break with two friends in Gladeworld. The barbed-wire chain link fence around the place reminds him of prisons and concentration camps; the crowds of bathers in the Tropical Paradise screaming as they launch themselves into the moulded fibreglass White Water Rapids, or down the twisting transparent tube which coils its way from the top of the geodesic dome to spit them out into a deep pool at the bottom, remind him of medieval paintings of Hell. I enjoyed writing this chapter and relieving myself of some of the negative feelings I developed from being condemned to repeat the same experience year after year. But there was one feature of Center Parcs that I genuinely looked forward to, which Desmond also admits to enjoying, and that was the sauna.

I observed on our very first visit to Sherwood Forest that there was a sauna for which one paid an entrance fee and to which children were not admitted, and it seemed an attractive alternative to the crowded and noisy Tropical Paradise to which it was attached. One afternoon, with memories of the Finnish smoke sauna still fresh in my mind, I went on my own to see what it was like. Pictures of the facility in brochures and posters at Sherwood Forest showed smiling men and women together, draped in towels, so naturally I put on swimming trunks in the men's changing room. But when I passed into the sauna proper I noticed a large sign, 'Swimming Costumes Optional', and to my astonishment I saw that about half the people in the pool and under the open showers that ran along one wall were naked. I made a quick decision to dodge back into the changing room, where I took off my trunks, put them in the locker with my clothes, and went back into the sauna with a towel wrapped round my waist. As I was taking a shower two beautiful young girls aged about seventeen, naked and wet from the swimming pool, came to the shower heads next to me and proceeded to wash off the chlorinated water of the pool, laughing and chattering in a foreign tongue, without giving me a glance.

Their unselfconscious nudity enchanted me, but how could such things happen in England? The foreign tongue was a clue. The founder of Center Parcs was a Dutchman, a Catholic who had conceived these holiday villages as places in which families could enjoy active holidays in the north of Europe, where the weather can never be relied on in summer and is freezing cold in winter. The sauna was historically a response to the same climatic challenge, and it is a standard feature of life in Holland, Germany and other countries in north-eastern Europe. No one there would dream of wearing a swimming costume in a sauna, for it cancels out much of the physical pleasure and health benefit of the experience, and mixed public saunas where everyone is naked are accepted. The first Center Parc in England was evidently being managed by people who had brought with them the sauna culture of Continental Europe, and it had probably attracted a good many visitors from there. When I offered to introduce Mary to the sauna at Center Parc, she hesitated, but having taken the plunge, metaphorically and literally, she enjoyed it and became like me a devotee of the baking heat of the wooden cabin, the icy shock of the cold douche and plunge pool, the luxurious sensation of swimming naked in a warm swimming pool, and the deep relaxation afterwards.

This carefree acceptance of 'optional' nudity in mixed saunas at Sherwood Forest Center Parcs didn't last long, and in fact it is hard to believe that it happened at all, for it constituted a charter for voyeurs and exhibitionists. After a couple of years the management, perhaps responding to complaints, catered for customers who preferred to be naked in the sauna by offering mixed 'Continental' sessions, and sessions for men or women only where costumes were optional. We took advantage of these while they were available. When the company opened new villages in Longleat and Suffolk, and redeveloped the Sherwood Forest one, they had large luxurious spas offering massage and beauty treatments, with a warm swimming pool open to the sky, surrounded on two levels by saunas and steam rooms of various exotic and specialised kinds, and areas for relaxation equipped with waterbeds, loungers and divans covered with blankets and artificial furs. Continental sessions in the evenings were particularly pleasant, lolling in the warm pool and gazing up at the sunset-tinted sky. Unfortunately neither these nor the single-sex option proved popular with Center Parcs' clientele, and they were gradually phased out. All now have the same dress code: swimming costumes must be worn.

As the years passed and I became more affluent we booked more expensive 'executive' villas at Sherwood Forest which had superior amenities, including a private sauna beside the patio at the back – a very small basic one, just big enough for two or three people, with a cold shower outside, or in some cases a tub of cold water suspended from a bracket with a dangling rope attached which you pulled to drench your heated body with icy water. Mary and I, and Julia and her husband Phil, with whom we usually shared a villa, would often use this facility in turns when it got dark enough in the evening to have a sauna and cool off outside without attracting peeping Toms. It was a sovereign way to ensure a deep sleep afterwards, though it inspired a comic set-piece in *Deaf Sentence* with alarming consequences for the central character.

The sauna became a habit for Mary and me, sometimes indulged in hotels, and more frequently at our local tennis club which has a small sauna and steam room next to its indoor and outdoor pools, but always clad in a swimming costume. For me there are two distinct kinds of euphoria produced by the full sauna experience. One is the relaxation and sense of physical well-being generated by the transition from hot to cold to warm, and the other is the sensation of swimming naked afterwards. The difference in pleasure between swimming wearing a costume of any kind and the sensation of swimming without one, the water coursing unimpeded round your loins as you move through it, cannot be exaggerated, and I first discovered it in Center Parcs.

We swam naked in the sea during a heatwave in Majorca one summer. The hotel we were staying at would drive us to an unfrequented rocky shore in the evenings where we bathed in caressingly warm water. But such opportunities were rare. Much later Mary and I several times rented an old Provençal house in the hills above the Côte d'Azur near Grasse belonging to a friend of my French translator, Maurice Couturier. It was much too big for just the two of us, inside and out, but we enjoyed its extravagant spaciousness and the privacy it afforded. The back of the house faced south and from the terrace where we breakfasted you looked down over the steep garden and the rolling hills beyond, towards the profile of Antibes and the Mediterranean horizon.

On the lower level of the garden there was a large rectangular swimming pool warmed by the sun, and a lean-to with loungers, parasols and other equipment. A gardener and handyman came in at prescribed times to tend the plants and check the swimming pool's water, but otherwise we were able to swim in the nude unobserved, drying off afterwards in the same state, and we usually did so twice a day. In my first memoir I described meeting Mary on what was for both of us our first day as students at University College London, initially attracted by her looks, and wrote that 'I remember thinking, if not at that precise moment, then not long afterwards, that Mary had a kind of beauty that would last – a rather extraordinary reflection for a seventeen-year-old, as if I were already sizing her up as a possible wife.' I was not wrong. In her seventies she still had a very fine body, and nothing pleased me more on those holidays, or did more for my libido, than to watch her from my deckchair sauntering round the margins of the pool, or removing insects from its surface with a long-handled net, wearing only a straw hat.

## 15

Shortly after Christmas 1987 I had a phone call from the Marketing Director of Secker & Warburg, who had read the typescript of 'Shadow Work' over the holiday and was very excited by it. He assured me it would appeal to a much wider audience than any of my previous novels, and he was going to make sure that the trade knew about it. Early in the New Year I received a handwritten note from the new Publishing Director of Secker, David Godwin, which simply said, 'I think the book is an absolute triumph.' John Blackwell, who had been on a skiing holiday, took a little more time to send a long baroque epistle of praise. The only reservation anyone at Secker had about the novel was the title, 'Shadow Work', which was thought to have slightly sinister connotations more appropriate to a thriller. I had conceived it as a variation on the phrase 'shadow play', but I took the point and luckily I had another title in reserve, 'Nice Work', which everybody approved. Like the suppressed working title of an earlier book, 'The British Museum Had Lost Its Charm', it echoed a song by George and Ira Gershwin, 'Nice work if you can get it', and perhaps it was the fear of getting embroiled in another copyright dispute with the Gershwin Publishing Corporation that had deterred me from choosing it initially, though in fact no one could claim ownership of the two-word phrase 'nice work'. It occurs with several different applications in the course of the novel, firstly on page 20 when Vic Wilcox remarks of the largely Asian workforce in his foundry, 'They do nice work.'

Secker & Warburg had an option on the book of course, but there were several weeks of bargaining before a joint offer from Secker and Penguin was accepted and the contract signed. It included an advance on royalties for hardback and paperback rights in the British and Commonwealth market which was several times bigger than the advance I had received for *Small World* and would relieve me of any financial anxiety for some time to come. This reflected not only the sales of *Small World* and expectations for those of *Nice Work*, but also an increase in advances paid for literary fiction generally which had developed in the 1980s and continued into the 1990s, reaching its apogee perhaps when Martin Amis, or rather his agent Andrew Wylie, succeeded in getting an advance of half a million pounds for *The Information* in 1995. There were several factors involved in this phenomenon: the deregulation of financial markets in the eighties, the formation of new publishing conglomerates eager to get fashionable authors on their lists, the publicity-creating power of the Booker Prize and its imitators, and the insatiable need of the upmarket mass media for news and gossip with which to fill their columns and programmes.

All this had an impact on the profession of novelist, especially on authors of what the trade called 'literary novels', who earlier in the century were motivated primarily by a desire to add something of value to the body of English literature, rather than to attract a large audience and sell a large number of books (though of course such an outcome was always welcome). Now there wasn't the same gulf between these two categories of fiction. The lists of top 10 bestsellers in the newspapers were still dominated by popular genre fiction, but occasionally a literary novel would get on to the ladder and even rise to the top. These lists became increasingly detailed as the computerised system Epos provided instantly available figures for bookshop sales of individual books down to the last digit. There were longer lists in the *Bookseller* and other trade magazines in which literary fiction made a better showing, and authors could see how they had fared in comparison with their peers. They could not be oblivious to the fact that they were operating in a market.

Success was rewarded with improved advances, but one was expected, and probably contractually obliged, to do one's bit to earn them, giving up a good deal of time to publicity, being interviewed by the press, on radio and TV, and doing events in bookshops and at literary festivals which usually took the form of a short reading, a conversation with a compère, and responding to questions from the audience, followed by a book-signing. Not all writers found this public exposure easy, and even those who enjoyed it, and the occasional breaks from the solitary life of authorship these events afforded, could weary of them. I was lucky that I never suffered from stage fright, but in later years increasing deafness made these occasions more challenging. In the late 1980s and '90s however, when the publicity merry-go-round was still something of a novelty to me, I was very willing to climb aboard.

Soon after the contract for *Nice Work* was signed I was invited to a meeting in David Godwin's office where people from all departments of the firm were arranged in a semicircle. David outlined to us an ambitious programme of publicity and promotion for *Nice Work*, and I kept my copy of the schedule he distributed:

*May*. Appearance at the Secker Breakfast at the Booksellers' Conference in Bournemouth. 180 signed and numbered proof copies to be given to the booksellers.
*June*. A special pre-publication champagne dinner at the

Groucho Club for 30 booksellers and 10 others. Each bookseller will receive a personal, signed and numbered copy of the book, bound in four-colour jacket and gift wrapped. At least 70 of the numbered proofs will be mailed to booksellers, accompanied by a personal letter from David Godwin. *July.* Four-colour bound insert in the *Bookseller.* Four-colour poster on front cover of *Publishing News. September.* Publication Day. Dinner at Claridge's for Literary Editors and writers.

There followed long lists of the TV and radio programmes, newspapers and magazines, hopefully earmarked for interviews, a proposed book tour of eight major cities, and appearances at the Cheltenham and Birmingham literary festivals which would take place shortly after the publication date. Not all these promises were kept – I don't recall a champagne dinner at Groucho's in June, for instance – but most of them were, and several events were added, such as a visit to Guernsey in May to address the Secker sales reps at their annual get-together, and a big drinks party before the dinner on publication day in the atrium of Secker's new home, Michelin House in Kensington. This kind of lavish expenditure on publicity was characteristic of the era, and seems a historical curiosity now, like the extravagant advances that were paid and never earned out.

While I waited for my publicity programme to begin, I interested myself in the four-colour jacket mentioned in the plan. Gill Sutherland, who conceived the brilliant design for *Small World*, had left Secker by now, but I had an idea of my own for the front cover of *Nice Work* which I sketched out crudely with a black felt-tip: two cars passing each other, with a front view of Vic Wilcox's Jaguar saloon, reg. VIC 100, and rear view of Robyn's well-worn Renault 5, with the slogan '*Britain Needs Its Universities*' in its back window. This concept found favour at Secker and was passed to Paul Cox, a gifted artist who straddles the boundary between commercial and fine art with a distinctive loose watercolour style, and has a gift for evoking people and their milieux with sympathetic humour. He produced a vivid evocation of the two main characters in their cars and the Rummidge setting, which Secker later had framed and generously presented to me. Paul provided the cover art for my next novel, and for several paperback editions of earlier and later ones over the next twelve years, including a lovely painting of the façade of the fictional Palladium cinema for the Penguin edition of *The Picturegoers*, the original of which I also possess and cherish.

Meanwhile the Granada serial of *Small World* was being transmitted every Sunday evening from the beginning of February. Bob Chetwyn and Howard Schuman had hosted a party in their flat in Eccleston Square towards the end of January to give a video preview of the first episode to the principal actors and other key participants who were able to attend, clustered around a television which was not quite big enough for the purpose and not exactly state-of-the-art. We all applauded loyally at the end of the show, but it seemed to me that the reception was slightly muted, with not as much laughter as I would have expected, and I could not suppress a feeling of slight disappointment myself, without quite being able to put my finger on the reason, unless it was the TV set. I was not totally surprised therefore that the reviews of the first episode when it was transmitted a week later were predominantly negative, especially in the posh papers; but this reception was a blow after the high hopes the project had generated in production. Unfortunately the reviews of a TV serial always focus on the first episode, and the critics refer only fleetingly, if at all, to subsequent episodes unless it is a phenomenal hit, which *Small World* certainly was not.[1] Therefore, although the

[1] An internet blogzine called 'Forgotten TV' which describes it as 'a smash [hit]' is in this respect, and several others, deeply misleading.

serial improved considerably as it progressed, containing many memorable scenes and sequences, and certainly had some enthusiastic fans, by the usual criteria of viewing figures and reviews it was not regarded as a success, and it had cost so much to make (something like £4.5 million, a huge sum in 1988) that anything less than success was failure. Granada evidently perceived it as such, for it was never transmitted again in the UK, and as far as I know only once abroad, in Australia. One reason for this, I was told, was that the contracts for the individual artists stipulated excessively generous payments for repeat transmissions, making the latter unacceptably expensive. Nor was the serial ever made commercially available as a videotape or DVD, and occasional plaintive appeals on the internet suggest that bootleg copies are also unobtainable.

So what went wrong? In my own opinion it was, as always in these cases, a combination of factors. While the production was in progress there was a euphoric mood on set and on location. Everybody involved thought it was terrific fun and was going to be a hit, and in consequence there wasn't enough critical examination of the work in progress. Even I noticed that the visual quality of some rushes from the first episode was disappointing. The serial was shot on film stock, and was often brilliant, but at other times it looked as if it had been recorded on the cheaper and less luminous medium of videotape. The casting was sometimes spot on, sometimes ill-judged. This was a drama all about academics, but I was unable to discover any member of the cast who had been to university, and occasionally this showed. Leonie Mellinger, for instance, who played both of the twins, was appropriately beautiful and desirable as Lily, but unconvincing as the ambitious high-powered intellectual, Angelica. John Ratzenberger chose to play Morris Zapp as a genial avuncular character without the sharp professional edge he has in the novel, which I missed. Of Bob Chetwyn, who died in 2015, I can say candidly that I thought his direction was erratic – sometimes inspired but sometimes lame. As examples of the inspired I would cite the magical street theatre enactment of T.S. Eliot's *The Waste Land* in Lausanne into which Persse unknowingly wanders, and the tableau in which Philip and his mistress Joy repose naked in post-coital languor, like figures painted by an old master, in a sunny bedroom overlooking the Bosphorus, and the ominous shape of a Russian tanker slides past the window like a repressed memory of his wife Hilary; and as examples of the lame, two crucial scenes of sexual intercourse in the story – Philip Swallow's first rapturous embrace of Joy in Genoa, and Persse's long-delayed possession of Angelica (as he supposes; in fact it is her twin, Lily) at the MLA convention in New York. Both of these scenes were filmed in bright, almost clinical lighting which deprived them of any atmosphere of sensuality and romance. This may have been the fault of the lighting cameraman; but Barry Lynch told me several years later, when I met him in Stratford-upon-Avon where he was playing in Shakespeare, that Bob gave him and Leonie no help at all with their scene, but simply pointed to the bed and told them to get on with it. My only reservation about Howard's script is that when I watch my tapes again I feel he was *too* faithful to the novel, especially in the first episode which would have benefited from some cuts and a quicker tempo; but that should have been spotted by others.

It was unfortunate for us that Channel 4 chose to rerun their drama serial *Porterhouse Blue* over the same period. This was Malcolm Bradbury's skilful adaptation of Tom Sharpe's comic novel about a Cambridge college, expertly directed by Robert Knights, who had directed *The History Man*, and starring two of the most popular actors on British television, David Jason and Ian Richardson. It was first transmitted in 1987 to deserved acclaim, but to repeat it at the same time as *Small World* had its first airing did us no favours. The two programmes were relentlessly compared in the press as academic satires, to the disadvantage of *Small World*, though the texts on which they were based were quite different. Tom Sharpe's novel was a clever farce about political intrigues and sexual indiscretions among the denizens of a fictitious Cambridge college and did not concern itself with the scholarly life of the institution. *Small World*, in contrast, though comic in tone, and containing some farcical and erotic elements, dealt explicitly with the intellectual preoccupations, arguments and rivalries of the academic characters. In April, after the show had run its course, I was invited to contribute an article to *The Listener* in a series by writers whose work had been adapted for television, in which I made the best case I could for *Small World*. I noted that however much one has been involved in the making of such a production there is something subtly different about viewing the actual transmission:

> It was not until I began watching *Small World* at 9.30
> p.m. every Sunday that I realised what a bold enterprise
> it was. Here after all, was a TV drama serial networked
> on the main commercial channel in prime time on a
> Sunday evening in which characters were arguing about
> Structuralism and analysing Keats' imagery and getting
> entangled in a street theatre version of *The Waste Land*
> and reciting *The Faerie Queene* and referring to the
> Grail legend and Freud and Frazer and Jessie Weston
> without condescension or vulgarisation, and managing
> to be funny and entertaining at the same time . . . With
> a few honourable exceptions the press did not, I think,
> give credit to Granada for the daring and difficulty of
> the undertaking, or the production team credit for their
> efforts to preserve the allusiveness of the original text.

One effect of observing the production, transmission and reception of *Small World* was to strengthen my desire to be much more deeply involved in the adaptation of any future novel of mine. The opportunity occurred much sooner than I could reasonably have hoped for, in the spring of this same year. One morning in March I was alone in the house, working in my study, when I noticed that some BBC vehicles were in the street, apparently filming a piece of drama action for which they had obtained the use of one of the houses opposite ours, or possibly just its front door. I recognised the man in an anorak who was watching an actor being filmed repeatedly knocking on the door and being admitted, as Chris Parr. Mary and I had met him for the first time very recently, with his wife Anne Devlin, as fellow guests at a dinner party hosted by David Edgar and his wife Eve. David I had known for a longer period, but for much of it only by reputation as one of the leading radical playwrights of the sixties and seventies. I had seen and admired several of his plays, notably the two-part adaptation of *Nicholas Nickleby* for the Royal Shakespeare Company, which was a global hit, and *Mary Barnes*, his powerful dramatisation of a woman's account of being treated for schizophrenia in R.D. Laing's controversial therapeutic community, which I saw in the Rep's tiny Studio theatre before it moved on to other stages. David and I had been aware of each other's presence in Birmingham for some time without actually meeting, and we recognised each other one evening in 1983 when returning home from London on the same train. I sat down opposite him and we had a conversation for the first time. He asked if I had a new novel on the stocks. I happened to have the bulky typescript of *Small World* in my briefcase, as I had spent much of that day going over the text with John Blackwell for a final review before the copy-editing stage, and I pulled it out to demonstrate that it was finished. We made a pact that he would buy my novel when it was published in the autumn, and I would see his next play when it was produced. That was *Maydays*, an ambitious work about the ups and downs and divisions of left-wing political factions over five generations, premiered by the Royal Shakespeare

Company in their London home at the end of that year. We both kept our promises.

David and Eve, who was a prominent Birmingham Labour councillor, were at the centre of a network of leftist political, intellectual and creative folk who mainly lived in the inner suburb of Moseley. They entertained frequently and gave a large Boxing Day buffet lunch party annually to which we were invited, but the dinner early in 1988 was the first occasion of its kind for us. Chris Parr and Anne Devlin were newcomers to Birmingham from Belfast, and new members of the Moseley circle. Anne was a writer of plays and short stories, born and brought up as a member of the Catholic Republican community in Northern Ireland, the daughter of Paddy Devlin, Social Democrat and Labour MP at Stormont. She had recently had a television play about the Troubles, *Naming the Names*, produced for the BBC in Belfast by Chris, who was of English and German parentage and had been Artistic Director of the Traverse Theatre in Edinburgh before moving into television. He was now a producer at Pebble Mill, the BBC's Midland regional headquarters, working under Michael Wearing, who had made his department a highly esteemed source of television drama with serials like *The History Man* and *The Boys from the Blackstuff*. We ate in the big kitchen of the Edgars' house and David cooked and served a tasty dinner while participating in the conversation, which became increasingly animated when he sat down and the wine flowed. Anne was a feisty young woman with strong opinions strongly expressed, while David liked to provoke people with elegantly composed ripostes coolly delivered from his great height, and between them they ensured a lively evening.

Cut to the morning when I observed Chris Parr in the street outside our house. Some time later he rang the doorbell and asked if he could come in for a brief chat. The BBC vans and crew had all departed. I led him into my study where he told me that he and Mike Wearing wanted to produce a drama serial which would do for Birmingham what *The Boys from the Blackstuff* had done for Liverpool: i.e. tell a story set in and around the city that would reflect its life truthfully, topically and entertainingly. They had looked at my two Rummidge novels and Chris had gathered from David that I had some experience of writing plays and screenplays. They wanted to know if I would be interested in writing such a script, and if so, would I think about a possible storyline and let them know so that we could meet to discuss it. Grinning all over my face I told Chris I already had the very thing, and gave him a copy of the typescript of *Nice Work* to take back to Pebble Mill. I had not mentioned this novel at the Edgars' dinner party, or indeed said anything much about it to anybody, as I am rather secretive about work in progress.

Chris Parr and Mike Wearing read the novel and liked it. After just one meeting, in April, I was commissioned to write the complete script, without first submitting a treatment or the draft of a first episode, as was customary then and is mandatory today. This was an extraordinary act of faith on the part of Mike and Chris (who was to be producer of the serial) in a writer who had had no success so far in this form of writing. It was only possible because regional drama departments had a good deal of autonomy in those days: they were given an annual budget and were fairly free to use it as they wished, exercising their own judgement. Today the script of every significant drama production has to be approved at a series of development stages and management levels until the man or woman at the top, usually in London, gives it the green light. The consequence has been a considerable thinning and narrowing of the range of television drama.

Another reason for Pebble Mill's rapid commitment to the project was that all concerned were aware that it was highly desirable that it should be broadcast when its picture of Britain under Margaret Thatcher was still recognisable. The winter–spring calendar of the story required that filming would have to start by the beginning of February 1989, or be postponed for another year and risk losing its topicality. This in turn meant I would have to produce a complete and approved script by the end of the present year. I was confident of doing that, but I did not begin work immediately. I waited until I had received and corrected the proofs of the novel, and seen the revises, so that the text was beyond my control to emend it before beginning the screenplay. I thought of the novel and the TV serial as two essentially different treatments of the same story and I wanted to be finished with the first before I started on the second.

I was surprised by how quickly the activities and preoccupations of the Birmingham English Department receded from my consciousness once I became a freelance writer. I had feared that I might miss the human contacts academic life provided, because writing novels is a lonely, introspective activity, but I found that other areas of my work, like the adaptation of *Nice Work* for television, and continuing efforts to get my play 'The Pressure Cooker' produced, had a collaborative dimension which compensated for the loss of academic collegiality. Also I now had several friends and acquaintances in or near Birmingham who were freelance writers, and in the spring of 1988 I conceived the idea of organising a regular lunch for such a group, like the one I knew existed in London which included Martin Amis, Julian Barnes, Craig Raine and others of that generation. When I sounded out the writers I knew well I got a very favourable response, and the project soon got off the ground. We had a trial lunch at the Chung Ying restaurant in Birmingham's Chinatown which specialised in Dim Sum (ideal for sharing) and had big round tables suitable for conversation between a dozen or more people, and we agreed to meet there every six weeks or so, on a Friday. I undertook to act as secretary and confirm the date of the next gathering. The pool of participants, some of whom travelled a considerable distance to attend, but not all of whom were at every lunch, grew quite quickly, and included in addition to myself: David Edgar, Anne Devlin, Andrew Davies, the novelist Jim Crace, the poet Roy Fisher, the playwright Joyce Holliday, the playwright Stephen Bill, novelist Richard Thornley, screenwriter Hugh Stoddard, and Mary Cutler, a regular scriptwriter for the BBC's seemingly eternal radio serial *The Archers*, which is produced in Birmingham. Spouses and partners were not eligible unless they were professional writers too, like Roy Fisher's wife Joyce. Later additions to the group included Vayu Naidu, an Indian storyteller, and the novelist and poet William Palmer. The lunches were always lively and sometimes contentious, lubricated by Chinese tea and numerous bottles of the house dry white. In due course we decided to invite a guest to the occasional lunch to add some variety to our gatherings, sometimes taking advantage of a visiting writer's engagement in Birmingham. Among the guests we entertained over the years were Fay Weldon, Will Self, Jonathan Coe (born and brought up in Birmingham, but based in London), Craig Raine and Malcolm Bradbury. Simon Rattle, charismatic conductor of the Birmingham Symphony Orchestra, also responded enthusiastically to an invitation. These lunches continued into the late 1990s, by which time several members of the original group had moved away from Birmingham and the attendance of the remainder began to fall off to a point when we decided the institution had come to the end of its natural life. But in its heyday it enhanced our individual lives, and several friendships formed through it survived its demise.

In June 1988 I was invited to take part in a big International Literary Conference in Dublin, one of several events celebrating the city's Millennium which the Irish Tourist Board had decided, on debatable historical evidence, was founded in AD 988. It was a distinguished gathering of writers from all over the world, including Derek Walcott, Susan Sontag, Chinua Achebe, Joseph Brodsky, Liz Lochhead, Les Murray and Craig Raine, as well as an impressive home team including Seamus Heaney, Brian Friel, Aidan Higgins, Thomas Kilroy and John Banville. There were three days of short papers by individuals on the theme (very loosely interpreted) of 'Literature as Celebration', with responses from the floor. The most contentious session was Chinua Achebe's denunciation of Conrad's classic tale *Heart of Darkness* as racist, which was robustly challenged by Craig Raine, stirring up a debate which rumbled on throughout the conference. I agreed with Craig that it is a mistake to read texts from an earlier era through the ideological spectacles of the present, and that by the standards of his own age Conrad was enlightened in his treatment of European colonialism, but this is a kind of argument which will never be settled. In my own slot I spoke about the difficulty of applying the word 'celebration' to literature in the modern period, when most great writers (including Conrad) were deeply pessimistic; but Joyce's idea of 'epiphany' and Bakhtin's concept of the 'carnivalesque', which applies perfectly to *Finnegans Wake*, helped me to reach a more positive conclusion and end with homage to the greatest of Dublin writers. The conference had been timed to coincide with Bloomsday, and I joined with several other Joyceans in the early morning of 16th June on the roof of the Martello Tower in Blackrock where the first episode of *Ulysses* is set. Standing in a circle we read passages from it aloud like a prayer group, before dispersing to find some breakfast.

The climax of the conference, on its last evening, was a collective reading by the visiting writers, chaired by Seamus Heaney, in the Royal Hospital Kilmainham, a magnificent seventeenth-century neoclassical building on the outskirts of Dublin modelled on *Les Invalides* in Paris, which had been beautifully restored and renovated very recently. The event was open to the public, and the great hall was packed. All the writers at the conference had been invited to read from their work, and were allowed a maximum of seven minutes each, with stern instructions to strictly observe this limit. Cynics among us argued about who would overrun by the greatest margin, and some made bets on the outcome. Susan Sontag turned out to be the biggest offender, going on for twenty minutes. I chose a passage from *Nice Work* which I thought would work well as a reading and with some judicious cuts would not overrun by more than a minute or two. It was from the chapter in which Robyn Penrose, accompanying Vic Wilcox in his Jaguar on a business mission, analyses a roadside advertisement for Silk Cut cigarettes which they occasionally pass (it was ubiquitous at that time) consisting of a flowing expanse of purple silk with a long slit in it. She uses all the most sophisticated methods of literary criticism, including the metaphor/metonymy distinction, to demonstrate the levels of subliminal persuasion, including sexual symbolism, encoded in the advertisement, to his outraged bafflement. It was the first time I had exposed this novel to a public reading, and I was elated by the laughter it drew from the audience. Craig Raine congratulated me afterwards and said he was going to put a pound on the novel for the Booker Prize as soon as possible.

I could not suppress private hopes of some luck with the Booker this year, but I kept them to myself and got on with the task of adapting *Nice Work* for television. Nearly all novels contain more narrative information than can be dramatised in a few hours on a screen; and although a serial adaptation, running to several hours, can do more justice to the original novel than a single film, the main task of an adaptor is always to decide what to leave out. The first things to go are passages describing the consciousness of the main characters – their private thoughts and emotions. Although these can be suggested in film by body language, facial expressions and music, or by interior monologue spoken in voice-over, the densely detailed rendering of consciousness we take for granted in the novel is not possible in the film medium. *Nice Work* contains many passages of that kind, but essentially it is about a relationship between two people who are continually interacting with each other, in dialogue scenes which express the differences of character and values between them, and it was therefore well suited to adaptation.

The characters of Vic and Robyn are introduced separately in the novel, in the first and second chapters respectively, with a detailed rendering of their thoughts as they get up on a chilly winter morning and leave their homes to go to work. In the screenplay this action is covered more concisely by cutting back and forth between the two characters and their interaction with wife or partner. When a director, Christopher Menaul, was appointed and read the first draft of my script, he suggested a further acceleration of the narrative tempo, a near-encounter between the two main characters in the first ten minutes, when Vic is held up in a traffic jam close to the University caused by a one-day strike of academic staff in which Robyn is a leading participant. She approaches Vic, fuming in his car, with a sheaf of leaflets in her hand and a winning smile on her face, and is saved from an angry confrontation when a cheer from the strikers (because a lorry driver has agreed to respect the picketing) makes her turn back. It's a nice moment, anticipating the combative relationship that will soon develop between them, and Chris Menaul added many other visually effective scenes to the script as it developed. I was lucky that he was chosen to direct the serial. He had been working in TV drama mainly on popular series like *The Sweeney* and *Minder*, for some ten years, and *Nice Work* was a new kind of opportunity to show what he was capable of.

Once the director is in place, the next stage in the process of producing a TV drama is casting. While I was writing the novel in

1987 Mary and I were watching, along with a sizeable proportion of the British population, a BBC serial called *Fortunes of War*, based on a sequence of six novels by Olivia Manning known as the Balkan Trilogy and the Levant Trilogy, which portrayed the experiences of a young British married couple in Romania and Egypt just before and in the early years of the Second World War. Guy and Harriet Pringle and their adventures were known to be closely based on the lives of the author and her husband Reggie Smith. He was one of the people I interviewed for my TV documentary *Birmingham Writers in the Thirties*, and for me an additional source of interest in the novels and the excellent TV adaptation. Guy was played by Kenneth Branagh and Harriet by Emma Thompson, two rising stars who became attached while making the serial and would later marry. I was quickly hooked on *Fortunes of War*, and enraptured by Emma Thompson's performance in particular. Her portrayal of Harriet as an intelligent, fearless, and attractive young woman in a strange and sometimes hostile environment made her seem perfect casting for Robyn Penrose, and I began to visualise my heroine as Emma Thompson as I wrote and brooded on the novel. When I made this suggestion to Chris Parr, he agreed and approached her agent. Emma expressed interest, and as it happened Ken Branagh had brought his Renaissance Theatre touring company to Birmingham at this time, the late summer of 1988, and she was there with him. I invited her to our house in Edgbaston for a chat and she came – not in a taxi, as I expected, but on foot, having walked from the nearest bus stop. It was a sunny afternoon, and we sat in the garden in deckchairs, discussing *Nice Work* over a cup of tea. She was calm, focused and candid. She admired the novel and was definitely interested in the role of Robyn, but said that if she were to play it she would have to find a way to make her sympathetic to the audience. 'She seems such a cold character on the page,' she said. 'I don't think she has ever had her heart broken.' The comment surprised me, but I saw that she had a point, and stored up the remark for future use.[2] Emma also told me that Channel 4 had proposed to produce a weekly TV show of her own, consisting of sketches and songs which she would write and perform with a few select partners. It was scheduled to be made in the same period of the coming year as *Nice Work*, so she would have to decide between them. I expressed a sincere hope that she would choose *Nice Work*, but I could understand the attraction for her of a show which she would write as well as perform in. I was not surprised when in due course that was the offer she accepted, though when the series, entitled *Thompson*, was broadcast the following spring it was generally found disappointing.

The first actor approached for the part of Vic was Bob Peck, who had established himself as a TV star in the BBC serial *Edge of Darkness* in 1985, and would soon play a leading role as the gamekeeper in the film *Jurassic Park*. Chris Parr and I visited him on the set of another TV drama and chatted to him about *Nice Work*. He was friendly but I sensed that he was not really drawn to the character of Vic – and I think he was right. Peck excelled at playing characters under extreme stress – on the edge of darkness, one might say – but I'm not sure that he had an equal gift for comedy, which was essential to the role of Vic. Casting the other parts was not a problem, and we ended up with a great team of actors, but it was a long time before Warren Clarke was cast as Vic and Haydn Gwynne as Robyn. I was disappointed when I heard this news, for although Warren Clarke was a versatile actor on stage, in films and on television, he was not an established lead actor, and Haydn Gwynne was almost completely unknown. In the event this turned out to be a great advantage, because they

[2] Towards the end of the novel the infatuated Vic pleads with Robyn to recognise his love for her and she responds with mockery. In the TV version he seems to recognise the hopelessness of his desire, and says sadly, 'I don't think you've ever had your heart broken, have you?' The remark takes Robyn by surprise and silences her for a moment. It's one which softens their parting and prepares for Vic's reconciliation with his wife.

both gave superb performances, and the fact that they were not instantly recognisable to the audience enhanced the realism of the drama.

The novel was published on 19th September, and received excellent reviews. The only notable exception was one in the *Sunday Times* by Craig Brown. The literary editor who had replaced Claire Tomalin after she resigned from the paper in 1986 told me that Brown had 'begged' to review the book, but he did not care for its combination of realism and playful intertextuality. A little later the Booker shortlist was announced, and *Nice Work* was on it, to the jubilation of myself and everyone at Secker & Warburg, Penguin and Curtis Brown. The banquet at which the result would be announced was on 25th October, which meant that, preoccupied as I was with the screenplay of *Nice Work*, I had to scan the competition rather hastily. Salman Rushdie's *The Satanic Verses* was an ambitious and challenging fabulation, taking Rushdie's brand of magic realism to a new extreme, but there was as yet no inkling of the global impact it would have. Peter Carey's *Oscar and Lucinda* was inspired by Edmund Gosse's autobiography *Father and Son*, but it too was a kind of fabulation, its climax the transportation and construction of a glass church in the Australian wilderness to settle a wager. The book that really gripped me was Penelope Fitzgerald's *The Beginning of Spring*, a fascinating evocation of a British expat family's life in Moscow in 1913, as the ice and snow of winter begin to thaw. The other novels were *Utz* by Bruce Chatwin, a very short book about a collector and dealer in fine porcelain living dangerously in Eastern Europe in the Cold War period, and Marina Warner's *The Lost Father*, a complex family saga set mainly in Italy, stretching back to the nineteenth century. *Nice Work* was the only novel of the six which dealt realistically with contemporary British life, though that didn't strike me at the time.

The chairman of the judges that year was the politician and author Michael Foot. I had spotted him one evening in the Tube on my way to a party in Hampstead, with a bulging book bag at his feet, reading what had to be one of the novels submitted for the Booker, but it did not look like mine. The other judges were the novelist Sebastian Faulks, the film critic Philip French, the poet and critic Blake Morrison, and the novelist Rose Tremain. They made a distinguished and well-qualified team. I had met Rose socially as a member of the Norwich literary community connected with UEA, but I didn't presume that this would bias her in my favour. On the night of the banquet I chatted briefly with some of the other candidates as we gathered in the Guildhall for drinks, telling Penelope how much I had admired her book, and exchanging compliments with Salman on our respective novels. Marina looked tense and complained that the event was 'so gladiatorial', which of course it is by design. Peter Carey was the bookies' favourite, and it was soon pretty obvious that he was the winner, because several reporters were clustered around him, indicating that the judges' verdict that afternoon had leaked out.

I didn't find my second Booker banquet as exciting as the first one. Apart from the absence of suspense about the result, there was a feeling of déjà vu in being a runner-up for the second time, sitting through Michael Foot's dutiful praise of all the candidates, stepping up to receive the bound copy of one's novel and a consolation cheque from Sir Michael Caine, accepting the condolences of friends among the guests, watching John Blackwell drink himself legless in disappointment again, and having to pour him into a cab to take him home to Clapham before returning to our hotel.

In a book called *Lives in Writing* published in 2014 I wrote an essay about my friendship with Malcolm Bradbury in which I described watching next day 'in a hungover and somewhat despondent mood' a videotape of the live television coverage of this Booker prize-giving at home, when he was one of the guests who 'as they arrived . . . were quizzed about who should or would win . . . Tall and handsome in his dinner jacket, Malcolm said with a smile, "For love and friendship I hope it's David Lodge", for which I blessed him, knowing that such an outcome would have revived the hurt of his own disappointment five years earlier.' But a reference I came across later in a letter suggests that it was at the 1984 Booker banquet, when *Small World* was shortlisted, that he said this. Not that it matters – his magnanimity would have been the same in either case – but my confusion shows how closely one Booker night resembles another. The only memory of the 1988 occasion I am quite sure about was a brief conversation with Michael Foot as the evening drew to a close, in which he told me that only three novels had been in contention at the judges' meeting that day, and he had personally wished to give the prize to *The Satanic Verses*, but his second choice was *Nice Work*. That was pleasing to know.

Earlier that month I had received news from Curtis Brown's Foreign Rights department which, in retrospect, was just as significant for my career as the success of *Nice Work* in Britain. A small but up-and-coming French publisher called Rivages had made a good offer for the rights in that novel, and an option on all my previous titles. For years Curtis Brown and their French sub-agent Boris Hoffman had tried to interest the leading Parisian publishers of literary fiction like Gallimard in my novels without success, but now at last they had a home there. I soon received a charming letter from Gilles Barbedette, the editor in charge of foreign fiction at Rivages who was responsible. 'I couldn't resist the charm, wit, intelligence and irony of *Nice Work*. You definitely could sit on the same bench as Alison Lurie, for instance, an author whom we publish very success-fully here, and I have a fantastically funny conversation with her. I actually just sent a copy of *Nice Work* to her for fun.' He added that Maurice Couturier had agreed to translate the novel. Maurice, whom I had met during our tour of Brittany with the Bradburys, would have been my own first suggestion as translator if I had been asked, but I wasn't: Gilles had chosen him through knowing his work on the Pléiade edition of Nabokov, in which both were involved. I had first met Alison Lurie when I interviewed her on stage at the ICA in London in 1985 to publicise her latest novel, *Foreign Affairs*, and began a friendship with her then which has been maintained ever since in correspondence, in her annual summer sojourns in London and occasional meetings in America. This web of personal associations which, unknown to Gilles, we had in common seemed a good omen for my relationship with him and Rivages, and so it proved in the years that followed.

My first novel to be translated into Italian also appeared in 1988, the fortuitous consequence of a personal friendship. Jeswyn Jones, wife of Martin, a couple who figured in *QAGTTBB* as friends of Mary and me at UCL and afterwards, had an Italian father who had immigrated to England, and an Italian cousin in Milan called Mariella Gislon, who translated English books in collaboration with a friend called Rosetta Palazzi. Early in 1987 Mariella wrote to Jeswyn asking her to suggest some contemporary English novelists whom they might propose for translation to their publisher Bompiani, Umberto Eco's publisher. Jeswyn suggested my name to Mariella, who wrote to me expressing interest, and I instructed my agents to send her copies of *Changing Places*, *Small World* and *Nice Work*. I recommended starting with the first one, since they formed a kind of sequence, though not by intention. The project prospered with what seemed to me unprecedented speed, and in little more than a year Mariella and Rosetta's translation of the first novel, called *Scambi*, was published, and they had begun work on *Il professore va al congresso*, published in 1990. Most of my fiction, and some nonfiction books, have been published in Italy, where they have been well received and mostly kept in print. Who knows whether I would have had the same success there without that connection between Jeswyn Jones and Mariella Gislon? It was a matter of luck.

Throughout this eventful year the prospects of getting 'The Pressure Cooker' produced waxed and waned intermittently. Robert Brustein had optioned the play and arranged to try it out in a rehearsed reading at the ART on Monday 18th January. I flew to Boston a few days earlier because Donald Fanger and his wife Margot had kindly arranged a dinner party for Seamus Heaney and his wife Marie, Bob Brustein and myself on the Saturday. Seamus was teaching at Harvard at this time, and the hospitable Fangers had become friends of the Heaneys. I looked forward eagerly to this occasion, but I was disconcerted to discover soon after my arrival in Cambridge that Ted Hughes would also be a guest. He and Seamus were co-judges of the *Observer* Poetry Competition, and he had come over from England to spend a few days going through the entries to decide the winner and runners-up. The opportunity to dine in the company of these two famous poets would normally have seemed a rare privilege – but not at this time and place. My play was a somewhat satirical account of a residential creative writing course closely resembling the courses run by the Arvon Foundation, which Ted Hughes had actively and publicly supported from its inception. It was an extraordinary coincidence that I should meet him in Cambridge, Mass. at an intimate dinner party just before the play was given a rehearsed reading there. Fortunately there was no risk of his actually attending it, as he was returning to England before the event; but it seemed to me that I would hardly be able to avoid explaining the reason for my presence in Cambridge and arousing his interest in my play; and that the more I – or Bob and Donald – told him about it, the less he would like what he heard. I had never met Ted Hughes socially before, though I had heard him read at a Birmingham Literary Festival several years ago, and bought a book which he signed for me. On that occasion he had struck me as a wonderful reader of his own poetry but a rather grim and intimidating person whom one would not wish to cross in argument. I approached the evening with a certain trepidation.

However, the dinner turned out to be a wholly convivial occasion. Ted Hughes was a good-humoured member of the party and displayed only mild interest when I told him the reason for my visit and something about the subject matter of my play. Seamus and Marie were charming and entertaining, and Donald as always a witty and attentive host. A grown-up daughter of the Fangers was also present. The food was excellent and a good deal of fine wine flowed. After the dessert, when there was a satisfied silence around the table for a moment, without preamble Margot began to sing a folk song in a strong melodious voice, and was warmly applauded by the rest of us. Then her daughter sang, followed in due course by Seamus and Marie and finally Ted Hughes. He sang the 'Ballad of Finnegan's Wake', which partly inspired Joyce's last great book. I was obliged to pass when it was my turn, mortified that I was unable to remember more than a few words of a single song, not even the riddle-song beginning, 'I gave my love a cherry which has no stone', which I used to sing to Julia and Stephen as a lullaby when they were infants. That Bob Brustein didn't have a party piece to contribute either was some consolation. All the guests were amazed and delighted by the spontaneous sing-song. Whether it was a tradition in the Fanger family I did not discover.

The next morning I went into the ART building for a rehearsal. The cast had already had a couple of read-throughs, and proposed some cuts to speed up the tempo of the play, and a certain amount of bowdlerisation. It seemed that American, or at any rate Bostonian audiences were more conservative than those in London, and the word 'cunt' just couldn't be spoken from a stage in the ART. In the play the word is used referentially, not as an expletive which would have been easy to replace. The American writer Leo and the British novelist Maude are arguing about the different ways in which men and women write about sex, and Leo says: 'Most women, in my experience, don't believe their cunts are beautiful. That's why they write about sex with their eyes shut.' Bob suggested the archaic 'quim' as a substitute, which I accepted, along with the other small changes they had made. The part of Leo was read by Bob Brustein himself, which I took as a compliment, and the part of Maude by Sandra Shipley, a British actress who had been working in America for some time. The casting of Jeremy, the manager in charge of the converted farm where the action takes place, was interesting. I had described him as a young gay man, but Bob had cast a middle-aged actor who he thought could do the part effectively and would make more of a contrast with the character of Simon, the young British writer. This worked so well that I later changed the character-description of Jeremy, and his lines to some extent, making him more neuter than gay, the kind of man sometimes described as 'a bit of an old woman'.

The reading that evening was performed on a platform in the spacious foyer of the ART on Brattle Street, attended by about 150 people who almost filled the chairs available. André Ptaszynski, who had the British rights under option, came from New York to join me, and we sat in the middle of the audience. The reading went extremely well and got a lot of laughs. At the end of it I went on to the platform to take questions and comments from the audience and there was a lively discussion. Numerous people came up to me afterwards to say how much they had enjoyed the evening. Although it was evident to me that the scene leading up to the fight between Leo and Simon still didn't work satisfactorily, there was no doubt that the evening had been a success. Bob Brustein said he would stage the play as soon as his commitments allowed and André's belief in it had been reinforced. He and I went off to have a pizza, well pleased on the whole, and indulged in 'dream casting', the favourite game of people involved in the making of plays and films. For Leo,

André suggested Dustin Hoffman, who was known to be looking for an opportunity to act on the London stage. If only . . .

Before approaching actors, André had to secure a director, somebody with a track record of successfully directing comedies in the West End. Such people are as difficult to engage as star actors, and I was thrilled when Mike Ockrent responded positively after reading the play, for he had an impressive list of hits to his credit, including *Educating Rita*, *Once a Catholic*, and Peter Nichols' *Passion Play* which I had particularly enjoyed. He also turned out to be a most engaging person, friendly, amusing and relaxed. The three of us had several meetings and in the late spring I started rewriting 'The Pressure Cooker' prompted by Mike's comments, which were always suggestive, not prescriptive. He said he would like the characters to have more to do on stage while they were talking – for instance, perhaps Maude could be trying to telephone people during some of the scenes. That gave me the idea of introducing an answerphone into the writers' living room. I had recently acquired one myself and was struck by the dramatic possibilities of this device, still something of a novelty at that time. I developed Maude's Oxford don husband, who up to this point was just a name that occurred in conversation, into a bumbling character who keeps leaving messages for her about farcical domestic disasters at their home which are overheard by the others. As these lines would be recorded, I had added a sixth character to the play very cheaply.

But the most important revision I made was in the 'fight scene'. Mike's vital suggestion was that the quarrel which leads to Leo punching Simon on the nose should arise out of their professional as well as their sexual rivalry – that Simon should provoke Leo by probing his most sensitive spot, his self-esteem as a writer, uncovering the fact that he is blocked on his big novel-in-progress about the Second World War, and mocking his allegiance to an old-fashioned kind of realism. I also used the answerphone to introduce some music and a little dancing to increase the sexual tension in the build-up to the fight. Another fairly new electronic device which figured in the play to heighten the contrast between the American and the British writers was the portable computer which Leo brings with him to the writing course (nothing like a modern laptop, but resembling an old-fashioned portable type-writer in a case, with a heavy monitor carried separately). It occurred to me that towards the end of the last act Leo might hoax Maude, who knows nothing about computers, by pretending that he is permanently deleting the text of his novel in despair, in spite of her earnest efforts to dissuade him, before revealing that it is all safely backed up on a floppy disk, thus preparing for a kind of reconciliation between them at the end. It seemed to me that the play had been immeasurably improved by these rewrites, and I was eager to hear it read by professional actors. This was arranged in a room off Shaftesbury Avenue with a group of actors mainly from the cast of the Sondheim musical *Follies*, which was having a successful run at the Shaftesbury Theatre, directed by Mike. The reading went extremely well, and clinched his commitment to the play. He and André agreed to aim for a production opening in the autumn.

The next step was casting. Mike was insistent that Leo should be played by an American, not an Englishman putting on an American accent, and André was equally firm in stipulating that it had to be someone with a recognised name in Britain. They knew that it would not be easy to attract such an actor, but at first it seemed as if we might be incredibly lucky. André had started at the very top of his list with Dustin Hoffman, and astonishingly the actor was seriously considering the offer. We were told that he had two close advisers, one of whom had told him he should do it and the other one that he shouldn't. Some tense weeks followed while he made up his mind. *Nice Work* was published at this time and Mike Ockrent came to the launch party, warning me that if Hoffman really did say yes he would make my life hell by his demands for rewrites, because he was that kind of star actor. In fact I had the impression that Mike himself rather dreaded the prospect of working with him. But neither of us had to worry about this for long because Dustin Hoffman decided to do Shylock in *The Merchant of Venice* instead, produced in London by Peter Hall for the Royal Shakespeare Company.

The search for an American Leo resumed with the help of a New York casting agency, but proved incredibly frustrating. It was difficult to get actors to even read the script. Real stars were understandably reluctant to risk their reputations in a new play by a writer with no track record as a playwright, and all suggestions of good but less well known actors failed to satisfy André. We were running out of time, because his option would expire at the end of the year, and although he was willing to renew it there was no reason to think he would have any more success in casting Leo, and Mike's availability to direct was shrinking. Leah's advice to me was that we should take the rights back and think about launching the play from a provincial theatre. This was a deeply disappointing conclusion to what had been a very exciting and creative collaboration with André and Mike, but I accepted Leah's realistic assessment of the situation. Not for the first time I was grateful that I was primarily a novelist, rather than a playwright totally dependent on the co-operation of other people to see his work into fruition. And I certainly couldn't complain about my fortunes in the former capacity. At about this time I at last acquired a publisher in America and had reason to hope that the partnership would last for more than one book. Viking-Penguin enthusiastically accepted *Nice Work* for publication in the summer of 1989, and soon afterwards obtained the US paperback rights to several novels in my backlist to add to the Penguin edition of *Changing Places* they had issued in 1978. From then onwards they published all my fiction, and some non-fiction, in America.

# 16

Early in December 1988 *Nice Work* was shortlisted for the *Sunday Express* Book of the Year, sometimes confusingly referred to as the *Sunday Express* Fiction Award. This was a new prize, founded the previous year, when it was won by the Irish novelist Brian Moore for *The Colour of Blood*. It was the first of several new literary prizes which were set up on the model of the Booker in the eighties and nineties, in the hope of bringing equivalent publicity and cachet to their sponsors, though none succeeded in that aim. The *Sunday Express* was a surprising sponsor, being a popular middlebrow paper, but its energetic Books Editor, Graham Lord, who had published several novels himself, was a vociferous critic of many of those that had won the Booker Prize, and he founded the *Sunday Express* one to challenge its primacy, rewarding novels which combined good writing with strong narrative content and subjects of general interest. To compete with the Booker for public recognition, he persuaded the paper to set the value of its award at £20,000, compared to the Booker's £15,000, and for some time it was in cash terms the biggest literary prize in the UK.

I wrote to Anthony Burgess in December, thanking him for nominating *Nice Work* as one of his 'Books of the Year' in the *Observer*, and mentioning that it had been shortlisted for the *Sunday Express* Prize, 'though it is inauspicious that one of the judges, Auberon Waugh, publicly announced in September that he hoped I wouldn't be shortlisted for the Booker and, when I was, that *Nice Work* wouldn't win it'. I have no memory of where Auberon Waugh made these statements, or what reasons he gave; but I had had a touchy relationship with him for some time past, conducted mainly by letter or in print. In 1971 I published a pamphlet on Evelyn Waugh in the Columbia Essays on Modern Writers series and sent him a copy. He wrote to me commending my critical appreciation of his father's work, but objected violently to a sentence on the very last page: 'Measured against the very great novelists, whether of the nineteenth century or the twentieth, Waugh falls a little short of the first rank', and he was not placated by the next sentence: 'But almost everything he wrote displayed the integrity of a master craftsman and much of it was touched with comic genius.' It still seems to me a reasonable assessment, which Evelyn Waugh himself would have agreed with. In his fictional self-portrait *The Ordeal of Gilbert Pinfold* (1957) he wrote that 'the English novelists of the present day will come to be valued as we now value the artists and craftsmen of the late eighteenth century. The originators, the exuberant men, are extinct and in their place subsists and modestly flourishes a generation notable for elegance and variety of contrivance . . . among these novelists Mr Gilbert Pinfold stood quite high.' What Auberon objected to in my words was the implied elevation of writers like James, Conrad, Lawrence and Joyce above his father, for he shared Evelyn's distaste for modernism. He was very much his father's son in literary and other matters. A few years later he gave *Changing Places*, probably the most Waugh-like of my novels, a favourable review, but was scathingly dismissive of *How Far Can You Go?* because of its sympathetic treatment of the post-Vatican II renewal of the Catholic Church, which Evelyn deplored in the few years he lived to observe it.

The *Sunday Express* Prize was announced and awarded early in January 1989 at a lunch in the Café de Paris in Regent Street. I must have put all the documents relating to this event in a folder which I have mislaid, and my efforts to glean information about it from other sources, including Express Newspapers, have failed. Graham Lord died in 2015, and it would seem that all data about the prize were lost with him. At this distance in time I can recall few details of the prize-giving lunch. Of the other shortlisted writers who were there, I can name only two. One was Justin Cartwright, who was sitting next to me and told me how much difference it would make to his career to win the prize, though he thought I would win it. I hoped he was right because I didn't relish being a runner-up yet again. Mike Shaw sat next to me on the other side, sharing the same thought. Another shortlisted author was Graham Greene, nominated for his last novel, *The Captain and the Enemy*. Though it is the best of his late fiction, it is a short and slight novel and was probably chosen by the judges partly in recognition of a lifetime's achievement, and accepted as such. His publisher Max Reinhardt was present at the lunch and passed me a very kind message from Graham saying that he thought I deserved the prize and hoped I would win it.

Among the judges present were Kingsley Amis and, I think, Ruth Rendell, but I can't recall any others. If Auberon Waugh had been there I would have recognised and remembered him, so perhaps he had dropped out of the judging panel. At the end of the meal someone, probably the editor of the *Sunday Express*, made a short speech and announced that I had won the prize, and I went to the head of the long table where photographers were grouped to record the handing over of the cheque. I asked the man who seemed to be master of ceremonies if I should say a few words afterwards and to my surprise he said 'No', and was quite emphatic when I queried this answer. So after receiving the cheque, with a brief thank-you to the presenter, I returned to my seat. It made a very anticlimactic conclusion to the event, and I felt it must have seemed ungracious to the assembled company. The party broke up fairly soon afterwards, and I was able to thank Kingsley Amis as he was leaving for his share in the verdict. It meant a lot to me because his novels had been an important influence on my own, and the subject of a good deal of my literary criticism. But I felt none of the elation that should have accompanied winning this substantial prize, only relief at not losing, and regret that I had not ignored the officious man who told me not to make a speech. This was prolonged by a report in one of the next day's papers that 'David Lodge collected his cheque and scuttled back to his seat without a word of thanks.'

I did however write to thank Graham Greene, with whom I had corresponded over the years and met on a few occasions, for his message and a similar statement he had made to the *Sunday Express*. I wrote: 'These remarks have done something to relieve me of a certain embarrassment at being pushed involuntarily into competition with you, whom I revere above all other living writers. I feel there is only one prize worthy of your achievement, and I hope that the award will not be frustrated by one silly man in Stockholm any longer.' It was well known that a member of the committee for the Nobel Prize for Literature had persistently vetoed Graham Greene as a recipient.


Soon afterwards I flew to Los Angeles to be Regents' Professor at the Riverside campus of the University of California. This was a two-week engagement, funded by the governing body of the University to bring distinguished academics to its several campuses for short visits. Riverside was the poor relation in this family of institutions, situated in an unfashionable suburban area on the southern outskirts of the vast sprawling conurbation, but it was keen to raise its profile. The invitation was instigated by Ruth apRoberts, the senior professor of English there, who had met me at Los Angeles airport and driven me to the Beverly Hills Hotel in 1982. She was a big lady in every sense – in stature, in enthusiasm, in generosity – who had published scholarly books on Trollope, Carlyle, Matthew Arnold and literary criticism of the Bible, but was also well read in other periods, and a fan of my novels. Ruth was Jewish but, as her surname declared, married to a man of Welsh extraction, Bob apRoberts, who was Professor of Medieval Literature at one of the campuses of California State University.

I had declined similar invitations from more prestigious institutions in America than Riverside, but I had a particular reason, apart from Ruth's involvement, for accepting theirs. With *Nice Work* published, and the TV adaptation finished and accepted, my thoughts were turning towards my next novel, which was to draw on the experience of going to Hawaii in 1983 to help Eileen when she was terminally ill. I had only a vague idea of the characters and plot of the book at this point, but I knew that thematically it would juxtapose the commodified version of paradise disseminated by the tourist industry with the promise of a transcendent paradise after death which gives comfort to religious believers but is losing credibility for many in our sceptical age. In the preceding November I had attended a seminar on 'The Anthropology of Tourism' at the ICA in London which gave me a number of useful ideas, and I was doing a lot of reading in liberal theology, but I felt a need to refresh and increase my knowledge of Hawaii before I started writing. The visiting appointment at Riverside was an ideal opportunity to return there, paying travel expenses which would cover two thirds of the cost of flying from London to Honolulu and back, with an honorarium that would more than cover the cost of an extra week in Hawaii.

My duties at Riverside were fairly light: to give three lectures (which I had already prepared for other occasions and had not published), to be available in an office at certain hours for anyone interested in talking to me, and to make other incidental contributions to the cultural life of the campus. I had suggested to Ruth in advance that I might direct a rehearsed reading of 'The Pressure Cooker', if actors could be recruited. I sent her the play, and she embraced the idea enthusiastically. When I arrived she already had a cast in place, mostly staff and graduate students from the English Department. One was a British expat who had once been a professional actress, and made an excellent Maude. For Leo, Ruth had enlisted a seventeenth-century specialist because he was Jewish and from Chicago, like the character, but unfortunately he had no natural talent for acting. However, the ex-actress gave me a very good tip which served me well with all the cast: telling them to breathe in just *before* their cue lines are delivered – it helps to eliminate the heavy, monotonous pauses between lines that are typical of amateur theatricals. I found directing an interesting experience. My priority immediately became not doing justice to the subtleties and integrity of the text but ensuring that the audience didn't get bored and switch off. I cut many lines and left out whole scenes, summarising their content myself, so that the reading didn't take more than 90 minutes. The audience seemed to enjoy it.

The apRobertses were very helpful and hospitable during my stay, taking me for a long drive in the desert as far as Palm Springs, and giving a party in my honour in their home, but I didn't want to impose on them for company. Fortunately there were a number of friends living in the LA area who had cars to pick me up, otherwise I might have felt rather lonely. I was boarding in a bed & breakfast, with a spacious room that had huge windows, giving a splendid view of the Pacific Ocean but with no curtains, only flimsy paper blinds, which I found vaguely discomfiting, imagining I must be silhouetted against them at night. One evening I received a telephone call in this room from Martyn Goff, chief administrator of the Booker Prize, asking if I would be chairman of the judges in the current year. It was not entirely a surprise, as Malcolm had told me he was going to recommend to the Committee of Management that I should be invited to act in this capacity. Nowadays the chairman is always appointed first, but Goff had already conscripted three other judges: Maggie Gee, Edmund White and David Profumo. Of these Maggie Gee was the only one I knew personally, though I hadn't been in touch with her for several years. Goff told me that he wanted to find a woman for the fifth judge, and was hopeful of getting Doris Lessing to act, which I thought would be interesting. I asked him to give me time to reflect, and then call me back. I didn't hesitate for long. I knew it would mean reading over a hundred novels, or enough of some of them to be confident of eliminating them, and re-reading the best ones. But I thought it would be an interesting experience which I would want to have at some time, and it might as well be this year. By the time the Booker was done and dusted I would be ready to begin writing my new novel. I seldom phoned Mary while I was away on long trips, because she found it rather upsetting; but I made an exception in this case, and told her about the invitation and that I was going to accept. She told me I would regret it. She was right.

I flew to Honolulu on my fifty-fourth birthday, 28th January. My aim was to soak up as much detail as I could in one week about the location of the new novel, and in particular about the dominance of its social and economic life by tourism. I took with me a stoutly bound A4 notebook I had dedicated to the work in progress, and the first thing I wrote in it that day was the name of a free newspaper, *Paradise News*, which I plucked from a rack in the baggage hall of the airport, adding the comment: 'Could this be the title for my novel?' I did not find a better one, for it seemed to incorporate all the themes I had in mind: religion, death, the afterlife, tourism, and discovery of the unexpected.

I had arranged to write an article about my trip for the *Evening Standard*'s travel pages, which gave me a pretext to contact in advance various people in the tourist industry in Hawaii, and brought me a complimentary upgrade of the room I had booked at the towering Hyatt Regency Beach hotel in Waikiki, with a splendid view of the beach and the ocean. I also had some very useful contacts at the University of Honolulu. One was Nell Altizer, a poet and teacher of American Literature who had done an exchange with UEA and was a friend of the Bradburys. Alerted by them to my visit, Nell had arranged for me to give a talk on campus, and there I met one of its most venerable figures, the seventy-six-year-old Ruel Denney, also a poet but perhaps best known as one of the three authors of a classic work of sociology, *The Lonely Crowd*. He introduced me to the Dean of Travel Industry Management, who was slightly defensive about the academic status of his subject, but usefully informative. Ruel also gave me his own pragmatic take on the exploitation of Hawaii as a tourists' paradise: that its commercialism was justified by the contribution it made to the local economy, and to funding education in particular. But he urged me to try and see more than Oahu, the most developed of the Hawaiian islands, where Honolulu and its beach resort Waikiki are situated. To that end he arranged for me to visit a friend of his, William Merwin, a very distinguished poet, twice recipient of the Pulitzer Prize for Poetry and American Poet Laureate in 2010, who lived with his wife in an unspoiled part of the island of Maui. Before I made that trip, I hired a car and drove to Sunset Beach on the north side of Oahu, where the biggest waves pound the shore, to watch the surfers at their spectacular sport, and swam cautiously in the shallows myself. On another day I took a tour of Pearl Harbor which was extremely interesting, though not very relevant to my novel. I also wrote down all the names of all the businesses in the Honololu Yellow Pages that began with the word 'Paradise', from *Paradise Antique Arts* through *Paradise Dental* and *Paradise Pizza* to *Paradise Yacht Sales*. There were more than fifty of them.

The head of PR for the Hyatt Regency, who was very helpful throughout my stay, booked me into the Hyatt hotel on Maui and drove me to the airport to take the short flight to the island. My first impressions were that it was at an early stage of the same kind of tourist development as Oahu had undergone, but still had much unspoiled natural beauty. The main problem in accessing the latter was the density of traffic on the two-lane highways. I hired a car for the day and, following the directions I had been given, drove along narrow twisty rural roads to the far side of the island where William Merwin and his wife Paula had their home. I eventually found it, hidden in a small plot carved out of dense vegetation on the side of a hill. Merwin and Paula, who had been an editor of children's books, were very hospitable in a laid-back, low-key way. They gave me a welcome gin and tonic on arrival, a simple meal cooked by Paula, and afterwards we sat on their porch and talked.

It turned out that William had worked for the BBC in London for a time in the late forties or early fifties, and knew Henry Reed and Reggie Smith, two men who figured in my TV documentary *Birmingham Writers in the Thirties*. That was about the only link between us. I hadn't had time to read any of his poetry, and he didn't know my novels. Though still writing, he had opted out of the professional literary life, while I was still making my way in it. As a couple they lived simply, were dedicated environmentalists, used solar power, and despised their neighbours for linking up with cabled electricity. Europe – even New York – seemed incredibly distant to them. In effect they had exiled themselves from modern America. When I raised the topic of the tourist industry's appropriation of the Paradise myth, William said it was an invention of the hotel trade between the wars, and Paula said the word didn't misrepresent Hawaii as it was *then*. She was probably right, but he was quite wrong. I later discovered *The Hawaiian Guidebook*, by Harry Whitney, published in 1875, which declared on its title page: '*The earthly paradise! Don't you want to go there? Why of course!*' I made this the epigraph to my novel.

I returned from the sunshine and balmy trade winds of Hawaii to chilly and overcast England on Monday 6th February, and had barely recovered from jet lag before I was on my way to Cambridge on the following Friday to deliver a lecture I had tried out at Riverside, 'The Novel as Communication'. It was in a series sponsored by Darwin College, published the following year as *Ways of Communicating*, with Noam Chomsky and Jonathan Miller among the contributors. It seems common sense that novelists communicate something to their readers, but this assumption has been questioned by various modern theorists: Wimsatt and Beardsley for instance, with their 'intentional fallacy';[1] Roland Barthes' announcement of the 'Death of the Author', which follows from recognising that the meaning of a text is produced by its reader; and Derrida's argument that the nature of language itself makes it impossible to fix the meaning of an utterance. As a critic I recognised that these ideas had some force, but as an author I was not willing to give up the idea that I was involved in a communicative activity. In my lecture I said:

> To write a novel is to conduct imaginary personages
> through imaginary space and time in a way that will be
> simultaneously interesting, perhaps amusing, surprising
> yet convincing, representative or significant in a more
> than merely personal, private sense. You cannot do this
> without projecting the effect of what you write upon an
> imagined reader. In other words, although you cannot
> absolutely know or control the meanings that your
> novel communicates to its readers, you cannot *not* know
> that you are involved in an activity of communication.

The complexities of this process, and the unpredictability of the interpretation of texts, were very soon demonstrated in a dramatic and alarming way, when the Ayatollah Khomeini, Supreme Leader of Iran, issued a fatwa on the 14th of February calling for the

---

[1] This is summarised in *QAGTTBB*, pp. 323–24.

killing of Salman Rushdie for blasphemy against the Islamic faith and the Prophet Muhammad in his novel *The Satanic Verses*, and for the same punishment to be meted out to those who assisted in its publication. There had been a number of protests against the book by Muslim individuals and communities in Britain and other countries towards the end of 1988, and in January 1989 there were significant demonstrations in Bolton and in Bradford where the book was publicly burned. But the fatwa was a wholly new phenomenon, and very shocking to all writers and readers of literary fiction in Britain and other secular democratic states. In retrospect it heralded a new age of anxiety for the whole world, which was ramped up to a new level of terror by the destruction of the Twin Towers in New York on the 11th of September 2001.

With a few exceptions most writers were shocked by Rushdie's plight in 1989, and protested against the fatwa in the media. Several of his friends generously offered him refuge from pursuit by the press and intimidation by outraged Muslims. Fay Weldon declared that she was prepared to die for Salman Rushdie. I can't say I was, but I signed a declaration by an impressive list of writers deploring the fatwa and its consequences. On the day of its publication I was asked by the BBC if I would be interviewed about it on *Newsnight* that evening, by a link with a studio at Pebble Mill, and I agreed. The interviewer indicated the kind of questions I would be asked: for instance, did I think the declaration would change the minds of the protestors? I would regretfully answer 'No', but affirm that if you were offended by a book, you shouldn't kill the author, but instead write another book, or article, opposing it. When Mary came in from work at Handsworth College of Further Education and I told her about the interview, she was not pleased. There was a large Muslim element in the student body at the college, and she was aware of the feelings the Rushdie controversy had stirred up. She was afraid some students would know that she was married to me, watch or hear about the programme, and that this would affect her relations with them and possibly lead to some unpleasant incidents. I didn't feel I could put her in what she regarded as jeopardy without her agreement, so I phoned the BBC to explain the circumstances and pulled out, though with deep regret.

Salman Rushdie has written his own detailed memoir of the history of *The Satanic Verses*, entitled *Joseph Anton*, one of the pseudonyms he used while he was in hiding. That he has not only survived his extraordinary ordeal, but managed to go on writing and publishing until the fatwa was withdrawn, is testimony to his courage and resilience. Several people connected with the publication of the novel in other countries were not so fortunate, and events like the massacre of the staff of the Parisian satirical magazine *Charlie Hebdo* in 2015 have shown that the threat to the principle of free speech remains. What the *Satanic Verses* affair demonstrated unignorably was that the increasing permissiveness of Western culture and society from the 1960s onwards, in which virtually nothing is forbidden which does not harm people and nothing is sacred in the realm of discourse, is alien and offensive to a large section of the human race. Very few of the Muslims who demonstrated against *The Satanic Verses* from Bradford to Bangladesh had read it, or would have understood it if they had tried to do so. It was enough to be told by an ayatollah that it was blasphemous. The speed and reach of modern communications contributed to this phenomenon. Salman Rushdie, who in an earlier era would have been an avant-garde author with a fairly small, highbrow audience, was propelled to global fame by winning the Booker Prize with *Midnight's Children*, which became an international bestseller. Its successor *Shame* attacked political figures on the Indian subcontinent under a thin cover of magic realism, and they reacted angrily, but he survived unscathed. In *The Satanic Verses*, however, he took liberties with the religion of Islam, which brought down on him a kind of condemnation not heard of in the West since the seventeenth century. The global village has been a more dangerous place for writers and artists ever since. Which is not to say that he is to blame for it.

## 17

Rehearsals for *Nice Work* began in mid-February 1989 at Pebble Mill, and I looked forward eagerly to being involved in them – too eagerly, as it turned out. The very first session I attended, sitting on a chair at the back of the room, began with a short scene in which Robyn's yuppie brother Basil is speaking to her on the phone, expressing suspicion of the friendly relationship Robyn's boyfriend Charles has formed in London with Basil's girlfriend, Debbie. The part of Basil was played by a young actor called Patrick Pearson. It seemed to me that the way he delivered his lines betrayed much more emotion than was appropriate to the character, and when he paused at the end of a line I could not restrain myself from saying, 'Oh, no, that's not the way to do it!' He turned round and looked at me with angry astonishment, and the others in the room also stared. I gave an embarrassed explanation of my comment, and the rehearsal continued. In a coffee break later the young production assistant came over to me and said, 'Professor Lodge, you must never criticise an artist in rehearsal like that, you know.' I apologised, and promised not to do it again, my mortification increased by the fact that he had been one of my brightest tutorial students a few years before. His name was Gareth Neame and he had a successful career later as a producer in television and film.

This was a bad start to my participation, but I managed to recover from it. Shortly afterwards Chris Menaul sent me a hand-written letter saying that the actors found my presence disturbing while they were working on scenes, so instead he would invite me in at the end of each week to see a run-through of what they had done. He would listen carefully to my comments afterwards, but I should try to find something encouraging to say to the actors, because 'they're all congenitally paranoid. Like directors. And writers?' This system worked well, and I developed a good relationship with Chris and with the actors, including Patrick Pearson whose portrayal of Basil got better and better. It was immediately obvious to me that Haydn Gwynne was perfectly cast for Robyn. Tall and slim, with expressive eyes and long auburn hair that could be worn in a variety of ways, she looked like a more beautiful young Germaine Greer, and she had the advantage of knowing something about academic life, being a graduate of Nottingham University who had taught English Language at an Italian university. Warren Clarke was physically the antithesis of Vic Wilcox as described in the novel, for I had made him small in stature in order to prevent any identification of the character with my friend and guide to factory life, Maurice Andrews, who is tall and burly. But Warren Clarke was also tall and burly – a physique in fact more typical of industrial bosses in the West Midlands, and therefore excellent casting for Vic. Andy never made any secret of his input to my novel and was rather chuffed when he was enlisted as an adviser to the television production and given a credit for it. Before rehearsals started he had shown Warren the inside of a factory or two, while I gave Haydn a tour of Birmingham University.

The BBC had obtained permission to film[1] a lot of scenes on the campus in the four-week Easter Vacation. When this was announced it caused concern to some academic staff, and I heard there was a protest in Senate about the arrangement, on the grounds that the satirical elements in the story would reflect badly on the University. I wasn't entirely surprised by this reaction, and it made me all the happier that I was no longer employed there. The Administration did not yield to these protests however, and were vindicated when they commissioned market research after the serial was transmitted which showed that 60 per cent of viewers thought it gave a very positive image of the University. But it was a strange experience for me to observe the recreation of my fiction in the place where I once worked. One morning I left my house and went to watch the filming of the scene mentioned earlier, when Robyn almost meets Vic, who is held up on his way to work by a demonstration of striking staff and student supporters at the entrance to the University. When I arrived, there before me was the scene I had imagined more than a year ago, brought to life with astonishing accuracy: a large delivery lorry surrounded by demonstrators blocking the entrance, wielding banners and chanting slogans. A young woman with a briefcase came up to stand beside me. 'Oh dear,' she said, gazing at the crowd. 'Is the campus closed? I need to use the Library.' 'No, it's just a television programme being made,' I reassured her. She had not noticed the large signboard to one side of the entrance with the legend 'University of Rummidge'.

A little later the crew filmed the arrival of Philip Swallow, to be challenged by the pickets guarding the entrance. This character was played brilliantly by Christopher Godwin, one

[1] Strictly speaking the action was not 'filmed' on celluloid, but 'recorded' on videotape, using Outside Broadcast equipment when on location. Most TV drama was recorded on tape in those days because it is cheaper than film. But the methods used with each medium are essentially the same, and it seems less confusing to use the verb 'film' for both.

of several excellent supporting performances in the series. I was surprised to see him approaching at the wheel of a swish new car, immaculately polished by the rental company from which it had obviously just been obtained, which seemed to me inappropriate to Philip Swallow's character and lifestyle. I mentioned this to Chris Menaul and he immediately called for a replacement vehicle, a compact saloon some years old which, to save time, was borrowed from its owner, one of the technicians. Because *Nice Work* was being made on my doorstep, so to speak, I observed far more of the process than most screenplay writers get to see, both in studios and on location. I developed a very good working relationship with Chris Menaul, often sitting beside him as he watched the action on a monitor, and occasionally making a comment which he sometimes acted on. He often had new ideas of his own to improve the script and would ask me to write a few new lines at short notice, which I took some professional pride in supplying to his satisfaction. He also executed some of his ideas without telling me and I didn't discover them until I saw the first, roughly edited tapes – usually with approval.

Two major crises arose in the course of filming. There is an episode in the novel in which Robyn shadows Vic on a visit to a trade fair in Germany, where he plans to order a new coreblower to improve the output of his foundry. Chris Parr had discovered very early in the development of the project that the biggest foundry trade show in Europe, which only takes place every four years, would open in Düsseldorf in May 1989, just when we would want to film this episode. The organising body, GIFA, readily agreed to let us film inside the exhibition hall and a participating company were willing to let us use their stand for a few hours. I accordingly wrote a scene showing Vic and Robyn making their way through a crowded hall between massive machines in simulated operation. It promised to be a stunning spectacle. But soon after filming in Birmingham began, GIFA abruptly withdrew their permission for us to film in or anywhere near the Düsseldorf show. Apparently someone had sent them not only the script of the scene at the trade fair, but the following scene in a restaurant, in which two German businessmen, unaware that Robyn understands German, try to deceive Vic about the specification of the machine he wants to buy. Alerted to this by Robyn, Vic is able to turn the tables on them. It is this collaboration in an unfamiliar setting far from home, and their celebration of it later in a luxury hotel, which make it plausible that Robyn should indulge Vic, and perhaps herself (for she is disaffected with her boyfriend Charles at this point) with a one-night stand. But to GIFA this twist in the plot was an unacceptable slur on the honour of German businessmen which called for our banishment from the trade show.

We pleaded that our story also showed British businessmen indulging in deception – but to no avail. We appealed to GIFA's sense of humour – but it evidently didn't exist. Desperately we offered to make the offending characters Swiss-German. No dice. In the end I had to rewrite the sequence so that Vic visits a German *factory* to buy his core-moulder. It was filmed in a factory in the Black Country town of Stourbridge which made machinery of this type, with German actors and appropriate signs on the walls. It was much less visually interesting than the original setting, but it stimulated me to improve the script. With Andy's help the technical discussions were made more convincing, and the comedy of Robyn pretending to be Vic's bimbo girlfriend, with a Rummidge accent that could shatter glass, so that she couldn't possibly be suspected of understanding German, and the unprepared Vic's astonishment at this transformation, was hilarious. It helped me to write this scene that by now I had a good idea of the way the two lead actors could play off each other. It was such discoveries of new possibilities of comedy and drama in my own story, arising out of the collaborative process of adaptation, that made the whole experience so interesting for me.

The second crisis also had a connection with the German episode in the story. At this stage of my life I still took an interest in popular music, listened to it on my car radio or *Top of the Pops*, and occasionally bought albums or tapes of this kind. When writing *Nice Work* it occurred to me that if I gave Vic a similar taste, which he indulges only in the privacy of his Jaguar, it would indicate a sentimental vulnerability not apparent from his outward persona, and prepare for his infatuation with Robyn. I wrote:

> He favours female vocalists, slow tempos, lush
> arrangements of tuneful melodies in the jazz-soul
> idiom. Carly Simon, Dusty Springfield, Dionne
> Warwick, Diana Ross, Randy Crawford and, more
> recently, Sade and Jennifer Rush.

A song called 'The Power of Love', sung and co-written by Jennifer Rush, was a worldwide number one single in 1985 and remained popular for some time afterwards. The words express a woman's passionate commitment to a vaguely defined affair, and urge the man to surrender to the power of love. When Vic begins to feel an amorous attraction to Robyn,

> he played Jennifer Rush a lot on the car stereo . . . her
> voice – deep, vibrant, stern, backed by a throbbing,
> insistent rhythm accompaniment – moved him
> strangely, enclosing his daydreaming in a protective wall
> of sound.

It is by dancing with Robyn to this record in the German hotel's discotheque that Vic finally gets to hold her in his arms, sheds his inhibitions, and is willingly led upstairs to her bed.

The dance was therefore a crucial scene, and we were all delighted by how well it worked when we saw it on video. But it was necessary to apply for permission to use the music, and this had been left rather late. Imagine our dismay when a letter from Jennifer Rush's agents was received, saying that Miss Rush understood that her song was used in the story as 'an aural aphrodisiac', and permission was refused. If the scene had to be shot again, we would never be able to find an alternative song with appropriate lyrics whose rhythm would match the movement of the dancers' limbs; and if we had to commission the composition of a new one, it would have nothing like the same effect on the audience as the well-known original. Summoning all my rhetorical skills, I composed a letter to the agents assuring them that in my screenplay the song served to express a sincere, romantic and chivalrous attraction between the man and the woman. After a suspenseful interval, to our immense relief permission to use it was granted.

As spring turned into summer, my time was more and more occupied by reading the submissions for the Booker Prize, which were arriving in the house in Jiffy bags almost daily. In April Martyn Goff had entertained us five judges to lunch at the Athenaeum and explained the procedure. Employed at times in the rare book trade, currently Head of Book Trust, a charity dedicated to the promotion of reading and writing, and himself the author of several novels, he was admirably qualified to administer the Booker Prize. Part of his job was to sit in on all our discussions to ensure that they were properly conducted, without himself contributing except to answer questions about the rules. One of these was not to talk about our proceedings to others, either publicly or privately. In spite of that prohibition, ever since the prize became newsworthy juicy morsels of information invariably appeared in the press in the run-up to the announcement of the winner, and it was only after Martyn Goff's death that it became clear he was the source of most of these leaks. I was mildly shocked by this revelation, which was perhaps naïve of me. His instinct for publicity was one of his qualifications for the job.

Part of the purpose of the lunch was for the judges to get to know each other. Maggie Gee I had met before on several occasions, but some time ago. She had a BA and B.Litt. in English from Oxford and in the late 1970s she obtained a research fellowship at Wolverhampton Polytechnic to write a PhD thesis on 'Portraits of the Artist in Contemporary Fiction: critical selfconsciousness as a characteristic feature of 20th century writing'. Wolverhampton Poly was hopeful of attaining University status and had established a number of such fellowships to support its case, but it lacked a qualified member of staff to supervise Maggie Gee's thesis. John Fuller, who had supervised Maggie at Oxford and thought highly of her, wrote to me on her behalf asking if I would be her 'external supervisor', and I agreed to see her. She was obviously very bright, so I took on the assignment, for which I was paid, seeing her at longish intervals, reading and commenting on her thesis, and acting in due course as one of the examiners who approved it for the doctorate. In 1981 she sent me a copy of a novel she was about to publish called *Dying, in Other Words*, a quirky metafictional tale centred on the mysterious death of a young woman whose naked corpse is found on the pavement beneath her fourth floor bedroom in an Oxford lodging house. I was impressed by its energy and originality, and provided a few lines of commendation which were printed on the back of the jacket in due course. Two years later I received a proof copy of *The Burning Book*, which combined similar postmodernist tricks with an earnest polemic against nuclear weapons. On the strength of these books Maggie Gee was included in the 'Best of Young British Novelists' showcased in the magazine *Granta* in 1983, but my memory of them was dim when we met at the Athenaeum, and I hadn't read her latest, *Light Years* (1985).

Two of the other judges I had never met before: the American writer Edmund White, then based in Paris, whose semi-autobiographical novel *A Boy's Own Story* (1982) is a classic of gay writing; and David Profumo, son of the former

Cabinet Minister, a novelist and regular book reviewer for the *Daily Telegraph*. The fifth judge was Helen McNeil, who taught American Literature at the University of East Anglia, where I had met her previously. Martyn Goff had been turned down by Doris Lessing when he approached her to be a judge, and he appointed Helen in her place when I was in Hawaii, without consulting me, which I regretted and resented. She was a second American on the panel, which seemed one too many for a prize restricted to novels by British, Irish and Commonwealth writers. My misgivings deepened when I discovered that Maggie Gee had held a Creative Writing Fellowship at UEA and formed a friendship with Helen McNeil, and that David Profumo was also a good friend of Maggie's. Such personal friendships between members of a committee can affect independent thinking and inhibit debate, and I thought it might seem to outside observers who discovered these facts that the judges, myself included, had too many associations with each other and the University of East Anglia for comfort.[2]

We dispersed after the Athenaeum lunch to resume the task of reading. I enjoyed it on the whole, especially when the hay fever season was over and I could read in the garden, for the summer of 1989 was a good one. It was fascinating to sample such a huge number of literary novels published in the same year instead of cherry-picking as usual, and to see what trends in form and content could be discerned. I say 'sampled' because it would have been impossible to read from cover to cover every one of the 120-odd novels that had been submitted by their publishers, who were allowed two titles each. I found that after fifty or sixty pages it was pretty obvious whether a novel was a contender, and

[2] The journalist Helen Fielding (not yet famous as the creator of Bridget Jones) made exactly this point two years later in an article about the Booker Prize in the *Sunday Times*, 27th October 1991, with the strapline 'You Scratch My Hardback . . .'

if you discovered that other judges greatly admired one of your rejects you could go back and give it further consideration. A meeting was scheduled in June for us to draw up a provisional list of 'possibles', and another early in September to agree on a more stringent list of eligible candidates (later known as the longlist, and published). The meeting to select a shortlist of six would be held on 21st September, and we would decide on the winner in the afternoon before the banquet on 26th October.

At the June meeting we drew up a list of forty-seven novels which were deemed worthy of serious consideration, and at the first September meeting we whittled these down to seventeen to be considered for the shortlist. During that time I had phone conversations with both Maggie and Helen. Maggie wanted an assurance that the shortlist would not be decided by a numerical majority of only 3 to 2. I could not give it, but reiterated what I had said at the beginning of the process, that I hoped we could reach a consensus by discussion. In the course of my conversation with Helen she listed her criteria for a good novel, and the last of them was, 'It must be ideologically correct.' I was so startled by this declaration that I did not challenge it, as I should have done. At this time the phrase 'politically correct' had not yet reached Britain from America, and when it did so it carried the scare quotes which allowed it to be used ironically by sophisticated left-wingers as well as scornfully by outraged right-wingers. 'Ideologically correct' was a much more inflexible concept which one associated with Stalinist Russia or Mao's China. In my view a responsible literary critic should always try to suspend his or her ideological principles and prejudices when reading a text to assess its literary merit.

I prepared carefully for the shortlist meeting, and had a folder with my notes on all seventeen books, arranged alphabetically by author. The first of these was Amis, Martin. As mentioned earlier, I thought his novel *Money* had been unjustly excluded from the shortlist by the judges in 1984. I was pleased when I heard that he had a new novel out this year, called *London Fields*, and looked forward eagerly to reading it. Having done so I described it in my notes as:

> Notable for dense, imaginative and expressive use
> of language, summoning up a wasteland vision of
> urban and global entropy. Brilliant metaphors and
> similes. Often blackly funny. Cunning interweaving
> of motifs and symbolism. MA's preoccupations with
> pornography & Swiftian relish of disgusting behaviour
> manifest in earlier work continue here, but much more
> under control. Keith is an extraordinary creation –
> totally loathsome, yet credible and weirdly vital . . .
> The flatness and unchangingness of the other main
> characters is the only arguable flaw in this generally
> brilliant achievement, and perhaps it is a little too long
> for its own good. But a frontrunner.

The shortlist meeting took place in the utilitarian premises of Book Trust in south-west London. We sat at a rectangular Formica-topped table with myself at the head, Martyn to one side and slightly behind me, the two men to my left, and the two women on the right. I began by proposing that we should get an idea of our collective preferences by going through the seventeen novels one by one, each person classifying them as 'shortlist', 'hold' or 'eliminate', and I had prepared a chart to record these responses, but Ed suggested that instead we should each simply say what our current six choices for the shortlist were, and this won support from the others. At the end of the first round everyone had chosen Kazuo Ishiguro's *The Remains of the Day*, and Rose Tremain's *Restoration*, and they were accordingly shortlisted. Both Ed White and David Profumo had nominated *London Fields*, though they were less enthusiastic than I in giving their reasons. I pointed out that no other novel in the remainder we were now considering had achieved three votes in the first round, and proposed that it should therefore be shortlisted.

At this Maggie launched a fierce attack on the book as morally and formally flawed: seriously confused, banal, unconvincing on nuclear catastrophe and pollution, and irredeemably sexist. It sounded like a prepared speech, lasted for ten minutes or more, and was remembered later by Martyn Goff in an interview as 'the time when Maggie Gee handbagged David Lodge'. She was supported unreservedly by Helen McNeil. The import of the telephone conversations I had had with each of them was now clear. I did my best to defend Amis's novel, but Maggie and Helen were adamant. Ed said that as I was chairman they should accept my casting vote in Amis's favour, at which Maggie looked distressed and said she would be very unhappy if *London Fields* went through. David Profumo said that he didn't think we could shortlist a novel to which the two women judges were so strongly opposed. It was 12.30 and we still had only two books on the shortlist. I put *London Fields* on hold and suggested we considered Margaret Atwood's *Cat's Eye*, which had been commended with some qualifications in the first round, and it was agreed that it should be shortlisted. With that accomplished, we broke for lunch.

At the heart of the 'sexism' accusation against *London Fields* was that the plot turned on the murder of the central female character, who is by implication complicit in the crime, and Amis underlined this theme by stating in a prefatory note to the novel that originally he had intended to call it *The Murderee*. Some days later, when I was still brooding on the meeting, I recalled that Maggie's own first novel had been based on a similar idea, which I confirmed from the copy in my possession. At the end of the novel it is revealed that the dead woman left in the room from which she apparently threw herself, or was thrown, the complete text of the novel we have been reading. Had I remembered this fact at the time of the meeting I would have been tempted to use it against Maggie, but it was just as well I didn't. During the lunch break David Profumo quietly informed the other judges that Maggie had recently had a very upsetting experience and was in a fragile psychological state, so should be treated sensitively. He was right to tell us, but it inhibited me from making any attempt to revive the case for *London Fields* in the afternoon session. Had I put it to a vote, David would certainly have voted against, or abstained and left us with a 2:2 deadlock.

I felt I had lost control of the meeting as the discussion swung this way and that, with a number of new candidates being proposed and opposed for the three remaining places. John Banville's stylish and noirish novel *The Book of Evidence*, which had been on my own first-round list, was added to the shortlist. Michael Frayn's witty epistolary novel *The Trick of It* had also been one of my original six, and had been enjoyed by most of the others, but was deemed too slight. Then we seriously considered a book we had 'called in'[3] – James Hamilton-Paterson's *Gerontius*, a biographical novel about the composer Elgar and the voyage he took to Brazil in old age, which we had all read recently and been charmed by. I was tempted by it, but I was concerned that so far we had no novel on the list which reflected contemporary life in Britain, as *London Fields* did. I had been very impressed with *A Disaffection*, by the Scottish writer James Kelman, a novel about a few days in the life of a disillusioned young schoolteacher in Glasgow, written in a stream-of-consciousness style which managed to be different from Joyce or Woolf, and gave a vivid if depressing picture of Glaswegian working-class life. I had described it in my notes as 'very impressive – a serious contender'. Apart from me, only Ed had named it as one of his six titles in the first round, and the

[3] The rules of the Booker allow the judges to request copies of a book not submitted by its publisher if they think it may be worthy of consideration. This was some compensation for publishers who specialised in literary fiction but were allowed to submit only two books.

others were not enthusiastic when I brought it forward at this late stage. And now Ed proposed *Jigsaw* by Sybille Bedford, a venerable literary figure born in 1911, who had not published a novel since 1968. *Jigsaw* was in fact a memoir of the author's early years in France and Italy, with names and minor details fictionalised. It was gracefully written, but not in my opinion a novel. Ed spoke eloquently of the pleasure it had given him, and which its lesbian theme was sure to give to many gay readers, subtly drawing our attention to the heterosexual orientation of the other contenders, and he won the support of Maggie and Helen. It looked as though *Jigsaw* and *Gerontius* were going to fill the last two places on the shortlist, which to me would have been a dismayingly bland outcome. Martyn Goff was getting restive because we were approaching the deadline for relaying the result in time for the next day's newspapers. (It was in fact the longest shortlist meeting in the history of the prize to date.) There was no time for further discussion, only for a deal. I said: 'If we can have Kelman on the list instead of Hamilton-Paterson, I'll accept *Jigsaw*.' The others agreed. Martyn hurried off to phone the media, and we slumped in our seats, drained of energy, and silent for quite a long time, as we wondered how the result of our deliberations would be received. When Martyn returned Maggie put that question to him. He said we would be blamed for the books we had left out, but not for those we had chosen. I suspected he said that to every panel of judges.

In fact we were blamed on both counts by the press. Admirers of Martin Amis deplored the omission of *London Fields*, but *A Disaffection* was generally perceived as a large indigestible lump of Scottish miserabilism. Ishiguro's nomination was expected, and John Banville's was approved by those who had read his novel, but Sybille Bedford's name meant little to all but some elderly literati and Rose Tremain's novel had not yet been published so elicited little comment. The passage of time justified our choice of authors: Atwood, Banville and Kelman all won the Booker Prize later, and Rose Tremain won that year's *Sunday Express* Prize for *Restoration*. At the time, though, our shortlist was generally described in the press as very disappointing, and I felt I had mismanaged the judging, especially in failing to get *London Fields* included. In fact I succumbed to a period of deep depression and longed for the whole charade to be over. But there were several weeks before the prize was awarded and no respite from obsessional brooding about it. We judges had to re-read the contenders in preparation for our final meeting, and I had to prepare two speeches for the final ceremony in the Guildhall. One was the ritual complimentary description of the shortlisted books before I announced the winner, and the other was a speech to the assembled guests after a comfort break, in which the chairman of the judges was asked to address a topic of his choice related to the prize (a custom which I think has since been discontinued). Furthermore I was committed to attending a weekend conference at the University of East Anglia totally dedicated to the Booker Prize in this year of its twentieth anniversary. One of the participants was Antonia Byatt, who had been a judge in the past and was to win the prize herself in the following year with *Possession*. In a panel discussion about the judging process she said, 'One judge cannot ensure that a particular novelist wins, but they can stop someone from winning.' True – and two judges are probably irresistible.

Our final meeting on the 26th of October to decide the winner of the 1989 prize was something of an anticlimax after the passion and dissension of the shortlist meeting. We met in a hotel in the afternoon before the banquet, and the proceedings took little more than an hour. All of us chose *The Remains of the Day* as the winner except for one person who argued for *Restoration* but gracefully accepted the majority verdict. So in the end we had the consensus I had aimed at, for a book that I had always regarded as the likely winner and described in my notes as 'a near perfect execution of an original and intriguing concept'. We then had tea and retired to change into our evening clothes before being driven to the Guildhall, where I met up with Mary. Because it was the twentieth anniversary of the Booker several previous winners had been invited, but not Salman Rushdie, who was still in hiding under police protection. Kazuo Ishiguro was a popular winner, and got a long round of applause when at the end of his acceptance speech he referred sympathetically to Rushdie's 'alarming plight'.

For my own second speech of the evening I delivered some thoughts on the novel as both commodity and work of art, and the impact the prize had had on this duality:

> The Booker Prize is now situated on the dangerous, glamorous interface between the two sets of values. The judges do their best, debating the merits and comparing them according to the criteria of literary criticism. But media interest, and therefore public interest, is focused on its lottery-like nature, the known fact that the book which wins automatically becomes a bestseller. This has tended to generate a certain amount of hysteria around the event, and certainly produces considerable psychological strain for writers, publishers, agents and, not least, judges.

Two years earlier Julian Barnes, who had been shortlisted for *Flaubert's Parrot* in 1984, but would not be again until 1998, expressed the same sentiment more forcefully in the *London Review of Books*:

> The Booker, after 19 years, is beginning to drive people mad. It drives publishers mad with hope, booksellers

mad with greed, judges mad with power, winners mad with pride, and losers (the unsuccessful shortlistees plus every other novelist in the country) mad with envy and disappointment.

When I am asked what I think of the Booker Prize as an institution, I always reply that it has been good for the Novel, but bad on the whole for novelists. It has been good for the Novel because, together with other literary prizes that were later established on a similar model, it made literary fiction a subject of wider public interest than ever before, it got people buying and reading books they would probably not otherwise have heard of, and contributed to the proliferation of 'Readers' Groups' which has been a generally benign social and cultural phenomenon. But there has been a downside to the Prize Culture which the Booker engendered. It has warped the evaluation of new fiction by measuring success as if it were a competitive sport. There is only one winner of the Booker Prize each year,[4] and a few runners-up who derive some positive benefit from the outcome, but behind them a long tail of losers. Salman Rushdie told me that when one of his novels was not awarded the Whitbread Prize for that year's best novel it was actually reported by the *Guardian* under the headline: 'Rushdie Loses Whitbread'. Before the advent of Prize Culture the reputations of literary novelists were formed by a vague consensus among readers of such fiction, derived mainly from exchanging views within their peer group and reading and comparing reviews, whose writers were obliged to give specific reasons for their assessments. Now these reputations are made by small committees who by convention express only the most general praise of the prize-winning books, and some committees

[4] In 1974, very early in the history of the prize, it was shared between two writers, Nadine Gordimer and Stanley Middleton, and between Michael Ondaatje and Barry Unsworth in 1992, after which judges were told they must choose a single winner.

include people who have no qualifications as literary critics what-soever. Everything that gets into the public domain about the award of these prizes confirms that the results depend crucially on the personalities of the judges and the chemistry between them. Or, in other words, on luck. The majority of ordinary readers do not perceive the Booker and similar prizes in this way, and tend to attribute to their judgements a kind of authority which they do not and cannot possess.

The competitive nature of Prize Culture has produced new kinds of stress for novelists by giving them an opportunity to fail which did not previously exist. Even novelists who have won the Booker Prize, or came near to doing so, may feel snubbed if their subsequent books are not shortlisted or longlisted. The publication of the longlist, which was adopted by the Booker in 2001, created a new kind of humiliation for such writers. For a book not to be chosen as one of the best six novels of a whole year's crop is no disgrace, but not to make the cut of a dozen or more is less easy to shrug off. If you detect a personal note in that sentence you would not be mistaken: none of my novels was shortlisted or longlisted for the Booker after *Small World* and *Nice Work*. But I was very lucky to be shortlisted twice in this competition when its influence was at its peak.

It was a pity that I allowed myself to become so obsessed with what I regarded as my failure as chairman of the Booker Prize committee because it prevented me from fully enjoying the success of the television serial of *Nice Work*, which began its weekly transmission two weeks before the banquet at the Guildhall. The reviews were excellent, and praised both the acting and the adaptation. Reviewers of TV drama, unlike film reviewers, rarely mention directors, and Chris Menaul was not given the credit he deserved, but his next commission was the first series of *Prime Suspect*, with Helen Mirren as DCI Jane Tennison, which raised the Police Procedural genre to a new level. Because *Nice Work* was shown on BBC2, and had no famous stars, it did not attract a huge audience, but it was greatly enjoyed by fans of the book who watched it, which is not always the case. It aroused some controversy on account of its sexual explicitness, which was as much verbal as visual. I received a call from somebody at the *Daily Mail* who had been shocked by this and said accusingly, 'Do you realise this is the first time the word "clitoris" has been used on prime-time television?' I didn't know how he could be so sure, but if it was true I regarded it as a feather in my cap. One of the things in the TV adaptation that gave me particular satisfaction was the way it managed to capture the interplay in the novel between people belonging to two different social groups with distinctive vocabularies. Among the messages of congratulation I received, one I particularly valued was from Debbie Moggach, herself an experienced screenplay writer, saying, 'The characters in it looked and sounded as if they actually did their jobs – rare on TV.'

Another good thing that happened in this period, and did something to lift my spirits in the aftermath of the Booker, was finally getting an offer to produce my play – from the Birmingham Rep. Leah Schmidt had taken maternity leave to look after an adopted baby, and Charles Elton was handling the play in her absence. We had had a number of approaches during the summer from provincial and touring theatre companies, none of which came to anything for a variety of reasons, some of them bizarre. (One producer offered to do it if I would cut out all three readings, which are essential to the plot and arguably the play's most original feature.) I decided to offer it to John Adams again because the script had been substantially revised, and I thought much improved, by the work I had done on it with Mike Ockrent. Early in September I rang John and briefly described the history of the play since he had read it, and he said he would like to see the latest script. After a few weeks' delay, and one impatient enquiry from me, I received a call from John, who was in London. He had read the play on his way down, and loved it. He didn't know what I had done to it, but it worked. The question was not whether the Rep would do it, but when; and he saw it as a main house play.

After so much frustration and so many rejections I was delighted by this enthusiastic acceptance, and pleased when I heard that John intended to direct the play himself. It demonstrated his commitment to the piece, and his production of Tom Stoppard's *The Real Thing* in the main house of the Rep had shown me that he could make a play of talk and ideas work in that challenging space. But when he said in another telephone conversation that he planned to put the play on perhaps in the autumn of 1990, but more likely in the spring of 1991, I was dismayed at the prospect of having to wait for at least a year to see it on the stage. I told him that my adaptation of *Nice Work* for the BBC was soon to be shown and was likely to generate interest especially in the Birmingham area, so it would make sense to exploit that by bringing the play forward, and he quickly came back with a proposal to mount the production in May of 1990. He was not happy with the title, saying that 'The Pressure Cooker' might suggest it was a 'kitchen sink' play, and I sent him a note suggesting as an alternative 'The Writing Game', a phrase that occurs in the dialogue. Without further discussion it turned up in the contract that was sent to me for signing, and I decided it was a better title, and let it stand. Henceforth it was *The Writing Game. A Comedy.*

# 18

Gilles Barbedette had invited me to come to Paris for a few days in January 1990 for the publication of the Rivages edition of *Nice Work*, and I was looking forward to meeting him for the first time. But the meeting was unexpectedly brought forward when he told me he was coming to Birmingham shortly before Christmas to stay with a friend. Naturally I invited him to call on us while he was there, which he did one morning, and we talked over coffee in my study. He was thirty-four, with the same birthday as me, and the same slight build as mine, though his dark hair was more abundant and curly. He spoke English as fluently as he wrote in it. We chatted about *Jeu de société*, as the French edition of *Nice Work* was called, which he explained meant a board game such as Monopoly. I didn't love the title, but Gilles thought it was perfect so I concealed my doubts. He said how much he was looking forward to the book's publication, but there were signs of tension in his body language and a hint of anxiety in his eyes which I didn't understand until he spoke about the friend he was staying with in Birmingham. It was a young man who was a lecturer at Birmingham University whom he had met recently in Paris at a conference of some kind, and fallen in love with. He looked at me intently as he said this, obviously wondering how I would take the information that he was gay. It had not occurred to me that he might be, but I reacted calmly and he became more relaxed. I did not ask him about the young man, though when he mentioned his academic subject area I thought I knew who it was. Our conversation reverted to literature and I discovered that he was a writer himself and had published memoirs, novels and essays under the prestigious Gallimard imprint.

In January I went to Paris as planned and Gilles seemed more at ease there, confident and debonair, though he had a persistent dry cough which made me wonder why he walked about the cold streets without a topcoat, just a long scarf around his neck. He introduced me to his colleagues at Rivages, and to Curtis Brown's French sub-agent Boris Hoffman who had sent *Nice Work* to him: a gentle, rumpled man of about Gilles's age, stroking a large white cat on his knee in a one-room office heaped with books and manuscripts. I now had a copy of the finished *Jeu de société* which had a stylish if enigmatic cover design, a detail taken from a painting of an unoccupied office interior. Like nearly all French books it had lightweight flexible covers, a format I greatly prefer to British hardbacks, which are heavy to hold if they are long books, and stiff to open. Established French publishers still favoured matt covers without illustrations at that time, but Rivages, a small independent firm that punched above its weight, shrewdly differentiated their books by giving them laminated covers with colourful illustrations. Rivages arranged some press interviews for me but I have no memory of them. I was not known at all in France outside the academic world, but Gilles was confident that *Jeu de société* would be well received. The reviews, when they appeared, were indeed excellent, and he planned to bring out *Changement de décor* later that year, translated by Maurice Couturier and his wife Yvonne. At about the same time Mariella Gislon wrote to say that she and Rosetta had delivered their translation of *Small World* to Bompiani, and that Umberto Eco had offered to write an introduction to it for the Italian edition, something he had apparently never done before.

The success of the televised *Nice Work* gave a further boost to sales of the novel in Penguin's 'tie-in edition' with a still of Haydn Gwynne and Warren Clarke in hard hats on the cover. In fact this title was almost continuously in the long bestseller lists from the autumn of 1988 well into 1990, thanks to a succession of helpful events: the Booker shortlisting, the *Sunday Express* prize, and the television serial, which itself received two further awards in 1990. The first of these was a 'Silver Nymph' (a small statuette) for Best Adapted Screenplay at the Monte Carlo International Television Festival in February 1990. The BBC flew me out to the south of France to receive it, with a couple of other Brits. We transferred from Nice airport to Monte Carlo by helicopter, skimming the waves in a rather thrilling way, and were accommodated in a luxurious hotel near the Casino. The whole episode was a brief immersion in the kind of glamorous showbiz event that I had previously only observed on television.

I felt my freelance career was going well. It was certainly giving me a life of rich variety and interest as well as a considerable income, and my decision to retire from university teaching seemed thoroughly vindicated. Nevertheless I was still vulnerable to anxiety and depression provoked by the setbacks and disappointments which are inevitable in the kind of life I was leading. I had made regular visits over the past few years to a counsellor, a lady in Bromsgrove who specialised in the control of stress, and I had two projects for the year ahead which ensured that I would continue to need her support. One was *Paradise News*, which I hoped to finish by the end of the year, and the other was the Birmingham Rep's production of *The Writing Game* which was due to open in May.

*

As the play was being produced near my home, I was able to observe and participate in every stage of its development up to its public performance. I had enjoyed an unusual amount of access to the making of the TV serial of *Nice Work* for the same reason, but the writer of a stage play has a contractual right to be involved in casting, rehearsals and matters of design, and so feels more personally responsible for the end result. John Adams, like every producer I worked with subsequently, began the casting process at an unrealistically ambitious level, 'offering' the major parts to star actors, and was eventually forced to audition less well known ones who liked the play and were willing to spend eight weeks in Birmingham on the very limited pay the Rep's budget allowed. John Adams, sharing Mike Ockrent's view that Leo ought to be played by an American, tried several American actors with Broadway reputations at first, predictably without success. I accompanied him to the auditions, which usually took place in London, either at the premises of *Spotlight* (the indispensable reference guide to actors) or at the Actors' Centre, situated over a store in Tottenham Court Road called the Reject Shop, which must have been disheartening to the hopeful actors who made their way up its bleak stone staircase to the third floor. I found the auditioning process fascinating and exhausting, because so much was at stake for everyone concerned. Eventually we cast Lou Hirsch as Leo and Susan Penhaligon as Maude. Lou was a Jewish American working in England, more of a character actor than a lead actor, but we thought the authenticity he would bring to the part would compensate. Susan was a 'name' people would recognise, best known for her work in TV drama, but with considerable theatre experience. We were lucky to get her, because she had been taking a break from acting to look after her young son, but the play intrigued her as it offered something different from her usual roles. For the third main character, the flamboyant Simon St Clair, I suggested to John that we should audition Patrick Pearson, who played Robyn's yuppie brother

Basil in *Nice Work*. He did an excellent reading for us, and was signed up. Patrick became enraptured with the part and I was glad to have finally made amends for our unfortunate first encounter. The two minor roles of Jeremy the administrator and Penny the young aspiring novelist were filled very satisfactorily by John Webb and Lucy Jenkins.

The cast assembled at the Rep for the first read-through on 17th April, four weeks before the first previews. John sat at one end of the table and I at the other, with the designer Roger Butlin and the Assistant Stage Manager also present. We had a tea break after Act One at which John looked thoughtful. 'There are times,' he said to me, 'when you know after the first read-through that all you need do is refine and polish it; and times when you think, "Hmmm."' This occasion was evidently one of the latter kind. He proposed that instead of starting rehearsals immediately the cast should read through the text using a method devised by the director Max Stafford-Clark called 'Actions', in which the actor prefaces each line with a statement of what the character is trying to do to another character. For example, the first line of the play, 'Here we are!', when Jeremy leads Leo into the converted barn from outside, has to be prefaced by the actor with some formula like '*Jeremy shepherds Leo.*' This exercise fascinated me with its similarities to speech-act philosophy and pragmatics in linguistics, and it definitely enhanced the actors' rendering of their lines once we got into proper rehearsals. It also made each of them question me about their character's behaviour and motivation. Susan for instance wondered how Maude could be as coolly promiscuous in her sexual life as I had made her appear, and it prompted me to rewrite some lines in the play to give more definition and complexity to her character.

Words spoken in a public space are much more potent than words read silently on a page, and I was concerned that Lou's reading of his Polish story in Act Two should treat the subject of the Holocaust sensitively. The reading has to be shocking, because it provokes some of its imagined audience to walk out, but acceptable to the real audience. I spoke to John about this and he relayed it to Lou, encouraging the actor to draw on his own Jewishness to get the right tone. When we rehearsed the earlier scene in which Leo tells Penny about his story, and says of the main character, 'He's Jewish, you see, like me', he gave a little shrug which was immensely expressive. Lou's performance seemed to deepen from then on. Another sensitive issue was the wordless ending of Act One, when Maude leaves the door of the bathroom open while she is showering. Leo, looking up from his computer, shows that he is wondering whether this is an invitation to join her, prompted by a conversation they have had earlier about such situations in their own fictions. He decides that it is and enters the cloud of steam coming from the open door. John was anxious to avoid giving the impression that Leo was taking advantage of Maude. The debate about this came to a head during the last dress rehearsal, on the day of the play's first public performance, when it became evident that the bathroom door was a problem.

Roger had designed a sliding door of frosted glass that was opaque in daylight but provided a blurred image of the occupant when lit from within, so when Susie went in and switched on the light it was obvious that she was undressing. John had directed this scene so that Leo approaches the slightly open door tentatively, then throws it open and enters the steam. The sound of the shower is amplified to a crescendo and the act ends with a blackout. This was dramatically effective but too heavy for the play – too much Marlon, not enough Woody, to use one of John's own favourite phrases. Susie wasn't happy about it and mentioned that her contract hadn't required her to take off her clothes. John ordered the technicians to put a layer of opaque plastic on the glass door, but when we tried the scene again next day at a second dress rehearsal, it gradually unpeeled and the stagehands had to stick it back while the action continued. There was a heated discussion afterwards. In the script the telephone in the barn rings just after Leo goes into the bathroom and closes the door, and since all the calls before have been from Maude's husband Henry, the audience were meant to laugh. I suggested it would be more effective if the phone rings just as Leo, halfway across the room, moves towards the door; he hesitates, looks back at the phone, and gives a shrug as if to say, 'Tough luck, Henry', and then enters the bathroom. John liked this but wanted to keep his heavy sound effects. I pointed out that then the audience wouldn't hear the phone ring. The cast supported me, and John became angry. 'All right, *you* direct it!' he said to me. I declined. Gradually John calmed down, and when we ran the scene in 'Woody' style he approved it. I went home to have a meal and freshen up before the first preview that evening, relieved that a crisis had been averted at the last possible moment.

The Rep usually has two previews, on a Saturday and Monday, before the Press Night on Tuesday. John had warned us that there would probably be only about 300 people in the audience for the first preview, but in fact there were 500, which bolstered the cast's confidence and created an atmosphere conducive to comedy. The audience laughed a lot in the first act, and applauded in the blackouts between scenes, something that in my experience happened very rarely at the Rep. Leo's entry into the bathroom worked well, and got just the amused response we wanted. The technicians had managed to make the bathroom door permanently opaque, and Susie had added a useful bit of business – she closed the door behind her and then opened it again an inch or two, unobserved by Leo, making her intentions clear to the audience. At the interval John was generous enough to tell me, 'You were right and I was wrong.' All three readings went well, Patrick's rendition of 'Instead of a Novel' being now polished and sharpened to a fine edge, but I was particularly pleased with Lou's performance throughout. I realised that because Leo was an American, and played by one, his language was less shocking to the audience than it would be if uttered by an English actor, and they could laugh at it. Laughter is the oxygen of comedy for actors and, inhaling confidence from it, the cast enjoyed themselves. There were several curtain calls and morale was high backstage afterwards.

By tradition the Rep's staff are invited, with their families and friends, to the second preview. The theatre was nearly full on Monday night – an awesome sight – and the audience was as enthusiastic as Saturday's. Both previews had inevitably revealed some minor flaws in both text and performance to John and me, but we thought we had fixed them in time for the Press Night. Basically we were convinced that the play worked and could hold its own on a stage anywhere, including London. But John did drop one word of warning: that actors were sometimes intimidated by the presence of critics, so did not give their best performance, and this unfortunately turned out to be the case. The first scenes didn't get anything like the number of laughs as in the previews, and this unsettled the actors. My agent Leah, who had come up to see the show, told me in the interval that this sometimes happens at Press Nights because the audience feel they are under examination too, and restrain themselves. Certainly the lady sitting beside me was continually quaking with suppressed merriment. The cast gradually recovered their confidence and were warmly applauded at the end, and the evening was by no means a disaster, just somewhat disappointing after the heights of the second preview. Now we had to wait for the reviews.

They were, as the saying goes, 'mixed'. During the week there were negative ones in *The Times* and *Independent*, but a favourable one in the *Telegraph* which said the play should move to London. On Friday there was a rave in the *Guardian*, but the *Birmingham Mail*, the local evening paper which had an influence on ticket sales, carried a damning review by their populist drama critic who, John told me, had never given him a good one. The two

Sunday papers which we took at home cast a pall over breakfast with Mike and Marian Shaw, who had seen the previous evening's performance and stayed with us overnight. John Peter was harshly dismissive in the *Sunday Times* ('wobbly motivations, arthritic dialogue and plodding stagecraft') while Irving Wardle in the *Independent on Sunday*, though impressed by the dialogue, found the narrative structure old-fashioned and unconvincing. But on my way home after putting Mike and Marian Shaw on their train to London, I bought the *Observer* and was greatly cheered to find Michael Coveney predicting that 'with some fine tuning and smart recasting it will become a West End hit'. When we totted up all the reviews later they were almost equally divided, pro and con. There was still a possible future for the play in London.

I went to see it numerous times during the run, partly because I was fascinated by the slight variations in each performance and in the audience's reactions; and partly because a number of friends and relatives and people who had been involved in its development, like David Aukin, Mike Ockrent and André, came to see it. One night a large party of the Writers' Lunch regulars came and we had a jolly supper afterwards at a nearby Spanish restaurant. Dad came up to see the show and enjoyed the experience, especially when I took him backstage afterwards to meet the actors, though he found the play hard to follow because of his deafness. Mary's sister Margaret brought their mother to Birmingham for the same purpose, and I was apprehensive that this devout Catholic widow of eighty-eight years would be shocked, but fortunately she nodded off for most of the play's duration. Malcolm and Elizabeth had arranged to stay with us and see the play on their way to the Hay Festival, but unfortunately the date clashed with the Royal Television Society's annual awards ceremony at the Grosvenor House Hotel in London. *Nice Work* had been nominated for Best Drama Serial, and I didn't want to miss the event. The Bradburys were very understanding, and Mary accompanied them to the theatre, while Chris Parr and I were driven down to London in a limousine. As Mary was not available and Anne Devlin was abroad, we invited Haydn Gwynne and Janet Dale (who played Marjorie Wilcox perfectly in the serial) to be our guests. Happily, *Nice Work* won the award, and we managed to celebrate victory with them and have a brief whirl around the dance floor before we were driven back to Birmingham, arriving at about 3.30 a.m. Mary had accidentally locked me out, and I had to throw gravel up at our bedroom window from the back garden to wake her without disturbing the Bradburys.

In those weeks I lived in a state of perpetual excitement, and found it difficult to sleep. The play was always in my mind, even when I abstained from seeing it. I had to go to the last night, of course, and the cast gave their best all-round performance of the run to a wonderfully responsive audience. After they had taken their curtain calls and the house lights came up, a man in front of us rose from his seat and said loudly to his companion, in the kind of accent Vic Wilcox would have had, 'Well, I really enjoyed that. It was in English, and you could understand it.' I was not sure what plays he was, by implication, comparing with mine, but I appreciated the compliment. There were drinks with the cast but no party afterwards, since most of them were anxious to get back to London, so it was a slightly melancholy farewell between a group of people who had been closely involved for two months in a common endeavour. I wrote in the diary I kept at that time, 'It is no exaggeration to say that participating in the production of *The Writing Game* has been the most intensely interesting experience of my literary career to date.'

For the Rep it was their most successful production of the past twelve months in terms of audience figures, apart from the Christmas show, and the most successful new play in the main house for many years. Several producers came up from London to see it, and one of them, Nathan Joseph, who ran a small company called Freeshooter, expressed interest in moving the Rep production, suitably recast, to London, and eventually optioned the play. He then began the same frustrating search for suitable star actors that had hampered previous attempts by others. I let him get on with it while I turned my attention back to *Paradise News*.

At this point I had the essential elements of the story and a narrative structure in place, and had written drafts of the first few chapters. The main character is Bernard Walsh, a forty-year-old member of a London Irish family, who had been a Catholic priest but lost his faith and left the priesthood and the Church following a disastrous sexual relationship. At the beginning of the story he is leading a depressed and solitary life as a temporary teacher at a liberal theological college in Rummidge, when he receives a telephone call from his aunt Ursula, who lives in Hawaii and has been out of touch with the family for years. She is terminally ill and in hospital, and begs him to come to her help, if possible bringing with him her brother Jack, Bernard's father. Her motive for the latter plea is revealed later. Bernard agrees and persuades his reluctant father to accompany him. He finds that the cheapest way to travel is to take a package holiday, and the first chapter describes father and son checking in at Heathrow with a number of more typical tourists who cross Bernard's path knowingly or unknowingly throughout the novel, and an anthropologist studying tourism called Sheldrake who regales Bernard with his theories on the subject during the journey. Ursula is in a care home so Bernard and Jack stay in her apartment in Waikiki, but on the morning after their arrival Jack is knocked down by a car when he steps into the road looking the wrong way for American traffic, and is taken to hospital with a fractured pelvis. Bernard must spend the rest of his time in Honolulu shuttling back and forth between his two incapacitated elderly relatives. The driver of the car is a woman of Bernard's age called Yolande, whose reaction to the accident is confrontational at first, but becomes friendlier when Bernard admits that it was Jack's fault. Soon afterwards she invites Bernard to supper at her home in the hills above Honolulu to assure herself that he does not intend to sue her, and he learns that she is separated from her husband who has left her for a younger woman. After some initial awkwardness a relationship develops between them.

Although I had a full notebook about my previous research trip to Hawaii, it didn't contain the kind of information I needed to fill out this scenario. Would the police be involved, and if so how? What would be the procedure for calling an ambulance for Jack and admitting him to a hospital? What kind of treatment would he require, and would the package holiday insurance cover it? Would he have to prove ability to pay for it before being admitted? What kind of life would Yolande, a permanent resident in Hawaii, live? What kind of job would she have? And so on. I had one source of information near at hand: I discovered that a professor of banking, Max Fry, recently appointed to a new chair at Birmingham in the Faculty of Commerce, had come from the University of Hawaii and was living very near us in Edgbaston with his wife and family. I made contact with them, and they quickly became friends. Celia Fry was very helpful in answering my questions about domestic and family life in Hawaii, but it was inevitably an expat's view. I felt I needed more – and luckily an opportunity to revisit Oahu arose just at the right time. My publicist (and later, editor) at Viking, Paul Slovak, wrote to propose that I did a book tour in September to promote the US Penguin edition of *Nice Work*, beginning in San Francisco and Berkeley, then proceeding to Chicago, Washington, Boston and New York. I agreed readily and arranged to spend five days in Hawaii before the tour began.

At the start of the journey from San Francisco to Honolulu a member of the cabin crew welcomed us over the intercom to 'this Delta flight to Paradise'. On arrival I checked into a cheaper Waikiki hotel than last time, and set about my research. I took notes on ambulances and interviewed hospital administrators and lawyers, quizzed friends like Marian Vaught and Nell Altizer about 'Rock fever' (the feeling of entrapment that sometimes overcomes people living on an island two thousand miles from the nearest land mass) and other aspects of life on Oahu, looked at some of the sites and sights I had missed on previous visits, and made a day trip to the island of Kauai which I sent Sheldrake on in the novel. One day I walked the length of Waikiki's main drag with a pocket cassette recorder and muttered into it names and descriptions of the hotels, shops, restaurants and other features my characters might notice. I had decided to make Yolande a therapist specialising in helping couples, and investigated how and where she might practise. I wanted to work some themes from the history and culture of Hawaii into the novel, so visited the Bishop Museum, a rich source of such information; and from there I drove straight to a bar with topless go-go girls on a catwalk, where I intended to send one of the British minor characters. I discovered later that I was still wearing a 'Bishop Museum' sticker on the lapel of my jacket, probably a first for patrons of that establishment.

It was unusual to send an author on a book tour with a paperback edition of a novel, but I had not been invited to America for Viking's publication of the hardback in August 1989, and they wanted to exploit its very favourable reception, beginning on the front page of the *New York Sunday Times Book Review* and maintained in nearly every other major newspaper and magazine. There are two kinds of American book tour: one, which I never experienced, gives the author a bundle of travel tickets and three-star hotel vouchers and sends him or her off, often unaccompanied, on a long circuit of provincial cities to speak to journalists and radio interviewers who probably haven't read the writer's book. The other kind, which I was fortunate to enjoy, has more select itineraries, provides a driver to meet you at each destination and ferry you to your engagements, and accommodates you in first class hotels. My programme was a mixture of radio, TV and press interviews, bookshop readings and signings, and lectures. I had a lecture called 'Novel, Stageplay, Screenplay: Three Ways of Telling a Story', which served very well for this purpose. In New York I met Paul Slovak for the first time, a tall, quietly spoken man who impressed me with his calm efficiency and the absence of bullshit from his conversation. He and several of his colleagues took me to a fabulous dinner in a private room at the Trattoria Dell'Arte on Seventh Avenue after my lecture at the New York Public Library, and put me in a cab to take me back to my hotel afterwards. While the cab was halted at a red light two gaudily dressed and giggling prostitutes opened the car door, climbed into the back seat and tried to persuade me to take them wherever I was going. Even the cab driver was taken aback by their effrontery, and threatened to summon a cop, upon which they debouched and disappeared into the night.

Paul told me that Viking were very pleased with the feedback from my tour and were going to reward me with an upgrade to Business Class for the flight home from Boston, the last point of my tour. There I caught up with Cambridge friends and had dinner with Bob Brustein, who was looking forward to putting on *The Writing Game* at the ART in March, and wanted me to come out for the later stages of rehearsals. ART would pay my expenses, and he had a friend with a spare room in a house near the theatre where I could stay. I was glad to agree: the chance of seeing another professional production of my play was irresistible, and with luck it might lead to an off-Broadway production in New York. I went home to find that Nathan Joseph was no nearer to getting a viable cast in place for a London production, but that did not bother me, as I wanted to concentrate on *Paradise News* and finish it by the end of February 1991, in time for publication in the autumn of that year.

*

I met that deadline, and on 10th March I returned to Cambridge Mass., to see the final week of rehearsals, the previews and the first night of *The Writing Game*. It was directed by Michael Bloom, who had experience of directing British plays in major American theatres and also teaches and writes about drama. Phone calls we exchanged suggested that we would get on well together, which proved to be the case. My plane arrived in Boston at 1.30 p.m. local time and I was anxious to get to the theatre immediately as I knew there was a rehearsal that afternoon. It was my misfortune to draw in the taxi-rank lottery a small, sallow-faced, rather despondent young driver, crouched behind the wheel of an enormous estate car. He set off hesitantly and immediately lost his way inside the airport. He was communicating with his control all the time in a foreign language, which I thought was probably Russian, though I could only understand words like 'Harvard Square' as we roamed around the airport's perimeter, ending up in dead ends beside derelict warehouses. When I protested he apologised and said I was his first fare, and he wouldn't charge me for the detour. Eventually I told him to take me back to the terminal to get another cab, but this accidentally led him to the airport's exit and he delivered me eventually to the theatre. As I paid him off I said, 'I hope you don't expect a tip,' and he seemed grateful to receive any money at all. It made a good story to amuse Michael Bloom and the cast when I found them in the basement rehearsal room of the Loeb Theater. I was soon immersed in the same kind of experience, though shorter in duration, as I had had at the Rep: camaraderie and conflict, tensions and tantrums, inquests and rewrites.

The principal actors were David Margulies as Leo and Christine Estabrook as Maude. Both had impressive CVs which would be further enhanced in the future by performances in theatre, TV and film. David was probably best known for his role in *Ghostbusters*, and Christine later appeared in hugely popular series like *Mad Men*. She was an engaging, effervescent actress with a gift for comedy who led the production in that direction, teasing Margulies's rather dour Leo, playfully pinching him, throwing things at him, etc. At first I was disconcerted by this performance but I gradually warmed to it. She did what I called the Shower Scene at the end of Act One almost as farce, by making Maude get drunk during the conversation with Leo before she goes up the spiral staircase to the attic bedroom, which is open to the audience's view. There she made a hilariously bungled attempt to change into a dressing gown before her shower, followed by a controlled sliding fall down the staircase which I watched at a dress rehearsal with tears of laughter running down my cheeks.

There was a danger that this take on the play would distract attention from its more serious content to do with writing as a vocation and profession, and the kinds of stress it produces, which make Penny at the end of the play tell Leo that the experience of the course has cured her of any wish to become a writer. But it was hard to object to this interpretation of the play when its audience was obviously having such a good time, as they were at the second preview. The first one had been badly affected by the collapse, in the first scene, of a member of the audience in the front row who had to be carried out while the cast stumbled through their lines, and they never entirely recovered their poise. But the second preview went like a dream and Michael and I kept exchanging glances of amazed delight as the audience rocked with laughter at everything that was designed to be funny, and seemed to understand and appreciate every literary reference. I guessed there were a lot of people from Harvard and other universities in the area present.

The official opening night went almost as well, though the audience was more mixed, and different sections laughed at different things at first. David Margulies told me later that the actors had to work hard to unify them, but they succeeded sufficiently for the evening to be declared by Bob Brustein and others 'a triumph'. Several people came up to me after the final curtain to say that it was the best thing the ART had done in years. Overall I thought it was a more successful production than the Rep's, inasmuch as it *continuously* amused and engaged its audience whereas in Birmingham there were always flat spots, though not in the same places.

The next day was a Sunday, when there were two performances, a matinee and another in the evening, a common practice in America. I did not attend either of them as there was a party for me in the late afternoon and early evening at the Fangers' house. Bob Brustein came to it and reiterated his satisfaction at the way the play had been received. I said I had been delighted it had gone so well, but recalled my experience at Birmingham, of a euphoric preview followed by a very mixed set of reviews of the Press Night performance. He said, 'That can happen, of course, because reviewers hate intelligent plays.' I had heard from several sources that the *Globe* had been giving ART productions a hard time lately, and when I mentioned this, Bob admitted that there was some truth in it, but said, 'I have a feeling that Kevin Kelly will like this one.' Kevin Kelly was the chief drama critic of the *Boston Globe*, which has a large circulation in the state and some influence as far away as New York. He had interviewed me in advance of the first night by telephone and sounded friendly enough, so I hoped Bob's prediction would be fulfilled.

I had arranged to meet Michael Bloom for breakfast at the Au Bon Pain café at nine o'clock next morning, and picked up a copy of the *Boston Globe* in Harvard Square on my way. Standing on the sidewalk, I opened the paper and soon found Kelly's review, headed 'An Unamusing Writing Game'. It was hardly necessary to read any further. Kelly was complimentary about Christine Estabrook, but otherwise was entirely negative about both the play and the production. I found Michael in the café gloomily perusing this humourless dismissal of a show that had consumed so many hours of our lives and hugely entertained its audience. Michael gave me some background to the *Globe*'s vendetta against the ART which he had not revealed before, perhaps to avoid depressing me, namely that it had been provoked by an article Bob had imprudently published in the *New Republic* some time in the past, criticising the newspaper for its cultural coverage in general and its theatre reviewing in particular. Later that day I learned that another local paper, *The Phoenix*, carried an enthusiastic review, but the only one that might have had some useful influence on the play's future was a stinker.

It was a downbeat conclusion to my visit, but by now I was inured to such disappointments. I had enjoyed my involvement in the production and my faith in the play was unshaken. As I returned to England Nathan Joseph left to see it at the ART, and I called him as soon as he got back. I had anticipated that he might have reservations about the style of the production, but I was taken aback by the vehemence of his reaction. In a word, he hated it. He thought the ART had turned a witty, intelligent play into something like a Ray Cooney farce, and took particular exception to Christine Estabrook's performance. He grudgingly conceded that she had done Maude's reading well, and said that all three readings had been excellent because the actors had to rely on the words alone to make their effects without added business. He also agreed that there was an energy about the production that we would do well to incorporate in the Rep's, if and when it transferred to London. He had sent the play to Prunella Scales, and she had expressed an interest in playing the part of Maude if the actor cast as Leo was someone she would be happy to work with. This was an exciting prospect for me as she was an actress I adored, and I had enjoyed a very successful collaboration with her and her husband Timothy West, when they performed a set of readings about travel which I compiled and compèred for the Birmingham Literary Festival a few years earlier. We entertained them at our house, and afterwards Pru sent us a thank-you note with a red rose named after her which we planted in our front garden, where it still blooms every year. It was through that connection that we got Tim West to do the voice of Maude's husband in *The Writing Game* at the Rep. But once again the search for a suitable American or plausible British actor for Leo proved immensely difficult, with hopes being raised and dashed in a familiar rhythm. Eventually Nathan gave up and pulled out. 'I'm sad and frustrated about it,' he wrote to me in June, 'but finally I think it's the only sensible decision.' I too felt sad, for he was a sympathetic, intelligent and fundamentally decent man whom I had enjoyed working with, but I was not surprised. He wanted to take out an option on my next play, but since it didn't exist except as a vague idea in my head, I thought that would be premature. Some weeks later I had a postcard from Prunella Scales: 'Very sorry INDEED that a Leo was not forthcoming . . . Do hope we work together ONE of these days.' Alas, that never happened.

I had one more opportunity to test *The Writing Game* on an audience. I had been invited to do something in August at the 1991 Edinburgh Literary Festival, which is part of the larger festival and takes place under canvas in Charlotte Square. I didn't want to talk about *Paradise News* as it wouldn't be published till the end of September, so I suggested an edited reading of my play, if possible by actors from the Birmingham Rep production. The festival organisers were receptive to the idea, Susie Penhaligon and Lou Hirsch were available and willing, so it was scheduled for a session in the Spiegeltent, an antique marquee imported from Germany which serves as a café-bar and auditorium for performance events, seating about 300. I was to act as presenter, summarising the action of the scenes that were omitted and describing stage directions where relevant. The only scenes to be read were those between Leo and Maude and Leo and Penny, Susie doing the latter role with a Cornish accent. I sent them marked-up copies of the text just published by Secker, and we had one rehearsal in the afternoon before the evening performance, which was sold out. It went extremely well, and once again demonstrated the play's capacity to engage and amuse an audience. We got a lot of applause at the end and some interesting questions. Lou and Susie were delighted with the event and we celebrated afterwards with supper at an Italian restaurant. The next day I bumped into Susie in the Bookstore tent, and chatted with her for a while. In a slightly embarrassed way she confided that she had been writing poetry for years, and a friend had suggested she should ask my advice about getting it published. I said I would be glad to get a poetry editor to look at her work, but warned her about the pain of rejection. She took the point and admitted she had written the poems mainly for herself and that they were 'very private'. I never heard from her subsequently, but it was poignant to discover so late in the day that she had concealed this personal stake in the subject matter of *The Writing Game*. Her impassioned delivery of Maude's speech in Act One, scene 3 about how writing courses can help people who keep novels they have written in drawers, afraid to show them to anyone, suddenly acquired a new significance.

I was shocked and sympathetic when Susie told me that, after she had paid for childcare for her son and frequent travel between London and Birmingham, her participation in *The Writing Game* had left her out of pocket. She had certainly given her all to my play, and I was very grateful to her, but we might easily have had a bigger star. Early in the process of casting Maude the script had been sent speculatively to an actress, X, well known for her role in a very popular TV sitcom, who had also made her mark in the theatre and feature films. Early in 1990, on my return from a trip abroad, I received a phone call from John Adams. 'Good news,' he said. 'X is very interested and I think we can get her if we want her. I'm meeting her in London tomorrow. Her agent said can you come too, but I think it's best if I meet her on my own this time, because she's talking about possible rewrites and perhaps it would be better if I find out what she wants, or what she's proposing, so that you don't have to react instantly.' As I was still new to this business, and unfortunately had seen very little of X's work and therefore did not fully appreciate what an asset she would be, I deferred to John's advice, which was quite wrong. I gathered later from his account of the meeting that he didn't get on terribly well with X. She didn't, in fact, have any demands for revision except a tentative suggestion for an extra scene between Maude and Penny; but after being evasive for a week or so her agent told the Rep that she had decided to withdraw. She sent a letter to me saying she had always admired my books and enjoyed reading the play, but for reasons she wouldn't bother me with she'd decided not to do it. I had little doubt that John was one of the reasons. As time went on X's career on stage and screen became more and more distinguished, and she is now a Dame. I often think that the fortunes of *The Writing Game* might have been very different if I had accompanied John to that meeting in London and taken advantage of X's familiarity with my work to persuade her. She would have shone in the part of Maude and, paired with a male leading actor of equivalent status, greatly increased the chances of a London transfer. A golden opportunity had been missed; but I did not reproach John for his misjudgement. He had given my play its first professional production, and I would always be grateful to him for that.

I had other interesting projects in hand in the summer of 1991. One was preparation for the publication of *Paradise News* in September, which included some filming for an edition of *The South Bank Show*, the flagship of ITV's arts programming, presented by Melvyn Bragg, which usually profiled the life and work of a single person. He had wanted to do one in 1988 tied to *Nice Work*, but that book was published before the programme began its autumn season, so it was postponed till my next novel was out. Melvyn came to Birmingham to interview me, and invited Malcolm to join us, and a conversation was filmed in our sitting room. There was also some filming in Brockley, in and around the house where I grew up, which caused a stir among the neighbours and gave Dad an opportunity to boast about his TV experience to the very amiable production team. After the programme was broadcast in September he wrote to me: 'It was a magnificent show in my opinion, and a very happy experience for me to sit and watch it, and I shall never forget it.' For me there were some cringe-making moments when viewing it, but I was pleased that it gave him such pleasure.

There was another event around this time which greatly assisted me to keep in regular contact with Dad. I was coming to London frequently on literary or theatrical business now, and it was tiring to go there and back on the same day, especially at a time when the rail service between Birmingham and London was notoriously prone to breakdowns and delays. I sometimes stayed overnight at a hotel, or the Groucho Club, which I had joined after investing in some shares when the project was first launched in the mid-eighties, but that required travelling with pyjamas and other accessories. I was always welcome to stay overnight with Dad in Brockley, where I could have stored such things, but it was a tedious extra journey to make, and I didn't find my old bed and bedroom very comfortable, so I developed the habit of meeting Dad for lunch when I was in town at the BFI's cafeteria on the south bank of the Thames, which he could get to from Brockley by bus with his senior citizen's pass. He always liked to be beside 'the River' as he referred to it, as if there were only one, and enjoyed these excursions. To have chosen a posher restaurant would only have worried him with the prices on the menu, irrespective of my ability and willingness to pay them.

The sales of my books at home and abroad had by this time given me a healthy bank balance, and it occurred to me that I could afford to buy a small flat as a pied-à-terre in London, which would be a good investment as well as a great convenience, and a place to meet Dad in comfort. I began checking the *Sunday Times* property pages, and looked at a couple of flats in Bloomsbury and Fitzrovia without being impressed by what I could get for my money. Then one Sunday I saw a small advertisement in the paper for a new block of eight flats in WC2 which seemed promising, and I arranged to view a one-bedroom flat on my way home from a conference in Exeter later that week. The address was almost miraculously ideal, very near Leicester Square Tube station, a few minutes from Euston on the Northern line, and within easy walking distance of almost everywhere I would want to get to: theatres, cinemas, book-shops, libraries, galleries, my literary agency and the Groucho. The price for a 120-year lease was more than I had intended to pay, but as soon as I got inside the flat on the second floor where the estate agent was receiving potential buyers, I knew it was exactly what I wanted.

It was very small, but the space had been cleverly used, a galley kitchen open to the living room creating an illusion, enhanced by high ceilings, of greater space than the actual dimensions. Double-glazed windows subdued the noise of the traffic from the busy thoroughfare below, and the fixtures and appliances in bath-room and kitchen were of high quality. The agent was a pleasant lady who obviously regarded me as a desirable leaseholder and promised to reserve the flat for me for 24 hours. I phoned Mary, telling her to come up to London next day with Christopher to see it. She had been sceptical of my plan all along but she agreed immediately that the place was perfect for my purposes and had some attractions for herself. So I committed to buying it there and then and handed over a substantial cheque as a deposit. It was a quick, effortless decision about which, uncharacteristically, I never had second thoughts.

I got the keys to the flat in mid-June, and began accepting furniture and utensils which I had ordered, mainly from Heal's and John Lewis. I brought very few items from Birmingham, apart from pictures. There was a special pleasure to be derived from furnishing a completely new living-space, pristine and empty like a painter's blank canvas before he makes his first marks, where one could express one's taste undistracted by the traces of previous occupants. For the living room I bought a folding table of lacquered black ash that could serve as a desk or for dining, two tubular chrome upright chairs with black leather seats, a tan leather Italian sofa concealing a fold-out bed, a matching armchair, a matt black ash coffee table and a low cabinet with drawers, bookshelves and in due course a slim Bang & Olufsen music centre on top. The floor was already fitted with a grey speckled carpet which I later replaced with strips of maple wood. A modification I made more quickly was to install air conditioning, since the windows could not be left open for long periods without letting in a great deal of dirt with the London air. The living room faced east and was flooded with sunlight in the morning, and I never passed into it from the tiny front hall without feeling blessed by my ownership. It was another kind of writer's luck that had led me to that inconspicuous ad in the *Sunday Times* at a propitious moment. Although I rarely use the flat for sustained writing, for which I require all the resources of my study at home, I keep a laptop and printer there for email or when copy is needed at short notice, and use the space for uninterrupted thinking, reading and note-taking, and for professional business such as interviews with journalists, meetings with visiting foreign publishers, TV, radio and theatrical producers, and even on occasion auditions. It also gave a new source of pleasure and interest to Dad to come up by train from Brockley to Charing Cross and have lunch with me in comfort. He was amazed when he made his first visit. That I could afford to buy this light, airy and commodious flat in the heart of the West End, territory he knew so well from his days as a musician, finally convinced him that I was not only successful but well off, and made him feel a little more secure himself.

# 19

In the summer of 1991 I began work on a new project which had been proposed to me by Blake Morrison, at that time literary editor of the *Independent on Sunday*. Over the previous twelve months the poet James Fenton had contributed a weekly column to the paper called 'Ars Poetica', the title of a famous treatise by the Roman poet Horace. Each week he selected a short poem, or part of a longer poem, and wrote a few hundred words of commentary to bring out the meaning and felicity of the text and to throw light on some aspect of the art of poetry in general. Blake called me to say that Fenton was coming to the end of his stint, and to ask me if I would be interested in doing a similar column on the art of prose fiction. I said yes almost before he had finished his pitch, because I knew this was something I could do, and would enjoy doing, drawing on many years of teaching and writing about the techniques of the novel and the short story, as well as experience of writing prose fiction myself. I submitted a couple of trial contributions which Blake was happy with, and a contract was drawn up. 'Ars Poetica' had been tagged 'James Fenton's Masterclass' in the newspaper and Blake wanted to apply the same description to my column, but I vetoed that, aware that it would be an inviting target for a hostile reviewer of my forthcoming novel.

I began with a piece called 'Beginning', juxtaposing two opening paragraphs, one from Jane Austen's *Emma* ('Emma Woodhouse, handsome, clever, and rich, seemed to unite some of the best blessings of existence . . .') which is classically lucid, measured and objective, its ironic implications concealed beneath the elegant style; and the other from Ford Madox Ford's *The Good Soldier* ('This is the saddest story I have ever heard . . .'), an irresistible ploy to get the reader's attention which is soon infected by a characteristically modernist obscurity and ambiguity, conveying the narrator's despair of ever discovering the truth about other people's inner lives. I continued with weekly instalments on the Intrusive Author, Suspense, Teenage *Skaz*, The Epistolary Novel, Point of View, etc., each beginning with one or two short extracts from classic and modern fiction. I planned to end the series, which was entitled 'The Art of Fiction', a year later with a piece on Ending. These little essays went down very well with readers of the *Independent on Sunday*, and soon the *Washington Post*, the Melbourne *Sunday Age* and Milan's *Corriere della Sera* contracted to publish selections from the series. I realised that when it was finished I would be able to turn it into a book, extending the tight word-limit of the original commentaries.


This weekly task (though I always wrote two or three instalments ahead of the publishing schedule) was a good way to occupy myself while waiting for the publication of a new novel. I felt reasonably confident about the reception of *Paradise News*, which was to be published on 30th September. Dan Franklin, who was now head of Secker, described it as 'the work of a novelist at the top of his form'. Mike Shaw wrote to me: 'It really has done the spirit so much good to have such a joyful book and one which is so readable, well-constructed and beautifully written.' My publicist Serena Davies thanked me for making two hours trapped on a broken-down train pass in a pleasurable trance. These were all readers predisposed to like the book, but I felt they expressed genuine enthusiasm. It was also reassuring that Penguin had promptly bought the paperback rights, and the foreign rights had been acquired by Viking and several European publishers. But in September I observed some less encouraging portents. Critics and literary editors were speculating in the press about likely candidates for the Booker shortlist and I noticed only one reference to *Paradise News*. Then a few weeks before the novel's publication date two magazines, the *Literary Review* and the *London Review of Books*, published reviews which were, in different degrees, negative. These two magazines were published monthly and fortnightly, respectively, and used this as an excuse to ignore the customary request of publishers when sending out advance copies to the press, that reviews should not be printed before the date of publication. Weekly and daily journals also frequently ignored it, eager to publish their verdict on a new book of interest before it was swamped by a deluge of rival commentary. I (and probably most other writers) do not object strongly to papers jumping the gun if the review is on the whole favourable. But to publish a dismissive review of a book before potential readers can get their hands on it, or compare the review with others, may prejudice them against it and affect the tenor of reviews still in preparation. I always deplored this practice.

Graham Coster's review in the *LRB* was long, conscientiously detailed, and negative by default. That is, there wasn't a single statement in it that could have been quoted by my publishers to recommend the book, and it referred frequently to my previous novels and other novelists to measure its disappointment. David Sexton's piece in the *Literary Review* (then edited by Auberon Waugh) was openly hostile, attacking not only *Paradise News* but my work as a whole. He had evidently read the new novel in a proof copy with a cover designed for the book trade, which quoted the sales figures for my previous novel. He began: 'Waste not, want not. David Lodge is a dab hand at make do and mend. His previous novels have done nicely for him – *Nice Work* sold over 300,000 copies in paperback – so why change a winning formula? They don't do it in Hollywood, do they? . . . This year's model has exactly the same plot as its predecessors – a weedy academic from "Rummidge" goes to the New World and has his eyes opened and his wick dipped.' It ended: 'Lodge is aiming at an audience more attuned to Hi-de-Hi than Henry James. He is good at what he does and doesn't skimp his task. *Paradise News* will be a great success, the holiday paperback of 1992, the TV series of the year after that. The product he is flogging though is formulaic.' There was also an aside about 'his appalling little classes on "The Art of Fiction" in *The Independent on Sunday*'.[1]

Every novelist's work has its own DNA, a tendency to favour certain narrative structures and rhetorical devices which reappear in different contexts and to different effect in their work. I am, for instance, drawn to binary oppositions in my fictions between different cultures, professions and mind-sets, and had acknowledged that in print. *Paradise News* contained such contrasts, but to allege that its plot was 'exactly the same' as those of its predecessors, and that these replicated each other, was absurd. *Paradise News* was in fact the only one of my novels since *Changing Places* in which the central character goes from Rummidge to America, and its story was new fictional territory for me, having an ex-priest as the central character, dealing with dark family secrets and with death. This was subject matter that required considerable departures in form from my recent novels – for instance, a long

[1] In describing these articles as 'classes' Sexton was echoing, consciously or unconsciously, the term 'Masterclass' attached to James Fenton's series in the *Independent on Sunday*, which I had wisely prevented Blake Morrison from applying to mine. In 1992 these appalling little articles were collected and published as *The Art of Fiction*, which has remained in print in Britain and the USA ever since, and has been translated into fourteen foreign languages.

autobiographical narrative by Bernard, a method which I had not used since *Ginger, You're Barmy* thirty years earlier. But when *Paradise News* was published other reviewers seemed to take their cue from Sexton. Both Anthony Quinn in the *New Statesman* and Tom Shone in *The Spectator* accused me of recycling themes and narrative devices from previous novels with an eye to television serialisation. Zoë Heller (not yet a published novelist herself) trashed the novel comprehensively in the *Independent*, with occasional ejaculations like 'Intimations of Mortality in Paradise! Freaky Deaky!' She concluded, echoing Sexton: 'As always, Lodge works hard to make everything fit together . . . his mistake is to assume a pitifully lazy reader.'

Heller described Bernard's father as 'bog-Irish', though the text states that he was brought up in a suburb of Cork and emigrated to England with his family as a teenager, and she confused the names of Bernard's aunt Ursula and Yolande more than once, misattributing dialogue and garbling the story in the process. I listed these and other inaccuracies in a letter, not for publication, to the literary editor of the *Independent*, saying that I did not assume a pitifully lazy reader, and certainly didn't expect to meet one in the review pages of the *Independent*. I also questioned the jeering tone of the review. The editor replied, apologising for the mistakes and saying that Zoë Heller was 'devastated' to discover that she had perpetrated them. As regards tone, he said that when an author had had a run of successful books there was a journalistic tendency to re-examine the reputation robustly.

That is certainly a familiar phenomenon. Since 1975 I had published four novels in succession which were received with critical approbation and increasing sales figures. There comes a point when the media get tired of praising a successful writer and seize an opportunity to bring him or her down a peg or two – or three or four, and the culture of British literary journalism is probably more aggressive in this mode than that of any other country. Where else would there be a literary prize for 'Hatchet

Job of the Year'?[2] It is often younger critics, like those cited above, who lead the attack since they have nothing to lose and something – i.e. attention – to gain by it. But the comment which most disturbed me was made by a seasoned reviewer, Max Davidson, in the *Daily Telegraph*. '*Paradise News* is more than disappointing, it is shoddy: a hotch-potch of different themes and different styles thrown together so carelessly that the kindest interpretation is that Lodge's publishers and/or accountants are breathing six-foot flames down his neck.' I had spent two years researching and writing this book. It was Max Davidson's prerogative to express his low opinion of it, but if he couldn't discern that it must have required considerable compositional effort, then clearly one of us was in the wrong profession; and for about ten minutes after reading his review, I thought it might be me.

As more reviews appeared it became clear that they were not unanimously damning, but split about 50/50 pro and con. There were some very good ones, and sales seemed unaffected by the bad ones, for the book figured somewhere in the top 10 bestsellers until December. There were enough quotes from the favourable reviews to put on the cover of the Penguin edition, which did almost as well when it was issued next summer as Sexton had sarcastically predicted. Nevertheless I had to ask myself if there was any truth in the negative reviews, especially the repeated accusation that I had contrived an artificially happy resolution of all the issues which afflict or divide the characters in the course of the story. I had seen my novel as generically akin to Shakespeare's late plays, sometimes called tragicomedies, which invite the audience to take pleasure in the unexpected twists of the plot that bring about reconciliation and reunion of the alienated and separated

[2] This prize for 'the writer of the angriest, funniest, most trenchant book review of the past twelve months' was founded by a group of journalists in 2012. In its short life span Zoë Heller has been shortlisted once, and David Sexton twice.

characters; and the tropical island setting of the story allowed me to weave allusions to *The Tempest* into the text, the significance of which was picked up by the more sympathetic reviewers. But in one respect I think the criticism of the authorial manipulation of the plot was justified. Bernard's sudden discovery that Ursula is much wealthier than she was aware of is I think made plausible, but the amount of money involved is unnecessarily large and the diversion of some of it to Bernard in Ursula's will, in spite of his insistence that it should all be left to his sister Tess who has a severely handicapped child, was a mistake. It diminishes the essential goodness of his character, and I regret it. It was a case of the author becoming too attached to and protective of the character he invented.

While I was coming to terms with the very mixed reception of this novel I was also physically in pain. Mary and I played 'social tennis' regularly at the Edgbaston Priory Club on Saturday afternoons, when you just turned up and played doubles sets with whoever was available without the bother of arranging games and booking courts in advance. We played all through the year unless it was raining. The age range ran from teenagers to senior citizens, and ability varied similarly, but we usually managed to balance the pairs. Mary and I were not outstanding players, but we held our own and enjoyed the exercise. For my age I was agile and quick off the mark, and I compensated for my technical deficiencies by chasing apparently winning shots and returning them. It was probably some extreme effort of this kind that caused an acute intermittent pain in the right knee joint, unpredictable in occurrence and strong enough to make me cry out. It became most distressing at the very time when the worst reviews of *Paradise News* appeared. My excellent physiotherapist Barry Maddox, who is an expert on sporting injuries, was for once unable to diagnose exactly what the problem was, but after X-rays had been obtained a consultant orthopaedic surgeon determined that it was 'plica', a type of tissue around bones which can get torn due to wear and tear in the knee joint, and then gets pinched by movement. He proposed to perform an arthroscopy – keyhole surgery to clean up the knee joint – and an operation was scheduled for 2nd January in the New Year. With the aid of elastic bandages around the knee, and a growing awareness of what kind of movements to avoid, I managed to hobble though the remaining weeks of 1991.

After the operation my right leg swelled up into the shape of a Zeppelin and recovery took much longer than I had been led to expect. In March, halfway through this tedious process, I was stunned by the news that Gilles Barbedette had died. I knew he had been unwell, but had no idea that it was so serious. He died of AIDS, though this was not public knowledge until some time afterwards because he had made his family and closest friends promise not to divulge his condition, as one of the friends explained to me later in a letter. I recalled his persistent dry cough and his habit of going out in winter with no topcoat and just a scarf round his throat, and wondered in retrospect whether this had been a kind of denial that he was sick.

I had lost a friend and brilliant editor before I got to know him well, and I was hugely indebted to him for introducing my work to France – much, much more than I realised at that time. Though I recovered from the critical battering *Paradise News* received, and subsequently maintained a respectable position in the notional league table of British novelists, my later novels never made quite the same impact as they had in the previous decade. In France however my reputation grew astonishingly in the 1990s, and as I cannot be sure that I will write a third memoir I will conclude this one with a brief summary of the phenomenon.

English paperback editions of new novels are usually published within a year of first publication, but the French equivalent, *livres de poche*, are (or were in those days) not normally published until three years after the first publication. Therefore anyone eager to read your latest novel had to buy it when it first came out, and the French were increasingly eager to buy mine. The third translation to appear, *Un tout petit monde*, sold 58,000 copies within a few years, and as Rivages issued other titles from my backlist between the new ones there was a snowball effect of accumulating sales and fans. The books were reviewed widely and favourably, and for each new one I would spend a week in Paris, accompanied by Mary, doing an intensive programme of interviews for various media, photographic sessions, bookshop signings and occasional events with a mainly English-speaking audience. For TV and radio interviews I was dependent on simultaneous translation through an earpiece, which the French media are used to providing for foreign visitors. I managed pretty well in spite of my impaired hearing, though I was always anxious about live broadcasts, which could not be edited. At the signings I relied on Mary to chat with the punters in her fluent French when necessary, while I plied my pen. She told me after one such event that a young woman had said to her, 'You are so lucky to be married to David Lodge!' and she replied, 'I think he is lucky to be married to me.' Which is true.

These visits to promote my latest book in France were exhausting, but worthwhile. By the turn of the century sales of the Rivages first editions of my novels were several times greater than those of their English equivalents. In 1998 my second play, *Home Truths*, was premiered at the Birmingham Rep. I sent a copy of the Secker edition of the playtext to my new editor at Rivages, Françoise Pasquier, as a gift, and I was pleasantly surprised when she proposed to publish it. I suggested that instead I should try turning it into a novella, and she jumped at the idea. Secker were also receptive, and so it went ahead. The Secker edition was published in 1999, received mixed reviews, some as dismissive as the early ones of *Paradise News*, and struggled for several years to reach sales of 9,000. The Rivages edition, entitled *Les quatre vérités*, published a year later, sold over 90,000. In 2002 *Pensées secrètes*, the French translation of *Thinks . . .*, was number one in the bestseller list of *L'Express* immediately after publication, a position no book of mine ever reached in Britian, and it stayed there for three weeks.

In effect I enjoyed a second, accelerating career as a novelist in France while the first one in my own country began inevitably to slow down. Few writers can have had such luck. There are other British novelists, such as Julian Barnes, William Boyd and Jonathan Coe, who have large French readerships, but they belong to a younger generation and their success in France developed in parallel with their British careers. My late success in France was as surprising to me as it was gratifying, given the resistance of French publishers to my work before Gilles acquired *Nice Work* for Rivages. Why French *readers* responded so differently and in such numbers when the books were made available to them is an interesting question, which I often pondered myself, and sometimes put to French friends.

One common view was that French literary fiction was going through a very flat period – that it was introverted, humourless and lacking in narrative energy. What the French liked about my novels, and fiction by other British and American writers, was the combination of comedy and humour with serious themes and engaging plots. In a sense this contrast has always existed between French and English fiction. The former tends to make a clear generic distinction between 'serious' and 'comic' fiction, whereas it is hard to think of the work of any classic English novelist (apart from Samuel Richardson, who was hugely influential on French writing) which does not contain an element of comedy. But it is also true that whereas French writers like Sartre, Camus and Françoise Sagan were widely read in Britain in the 1940s and '50s, in the 1980s and '90s French novels rarely made much impression in Britain until the advent of Michel Houellebecq.

Another factor in the popularity of my novels in France is probably that two principal sources of their narrative and thematic material are academic life and Roman Catholicism. A large proportion of readers of literary fiction in any country are university graduates, and the Anglo-American campus novel, with its tendency to a comic-satirical treatment of this milieu, has a peculiar attraction for Continental European readers because there is no equivalent in their own cultures. To write a campus novel you need to have experience as a teacher and scholar to draw on, and the combination would be unacceptable in the ethos of most European universities where the dignity of the professoriate is sacrosanct. The genre therefore has a kind of transgressive fascination for their staff and students. Teachers of English literature in French universities who read my literary criticism also enjoyed my novels and would sometimes teach them in their courses, and graduate students would write theses about them. This probably helped to disseminate my work in society at large.

As in other western European countries the number of practising Catholics in France has dropped steeply in recent decades, though estimates vary considerably. It seems that about half the population still identify themselves as Catholic in polls (down from 80 per cent in the early 1990s) but only about 5 per cent of them are *pratiquant* as measured by weekly mass attendance. Private education in France is however predominantly Catholic, and has left its mark on many who left the Church in adulthood. France today is culturally more of a Christian country than the UK, and its Christianity is Catholic. A very much larger proportion of my French readers than British ones would therefore have a Catholic background, and be interested in fiction which treated Catholic experience without any didactic or devotional agenda, and with humour. I receive letters from French Catholic readers which confirm this.

The success of my writings in France owes much to the skill and dedication of my translators, especially Maurice and Yvonne Couturier, Suzanne Mayoux and Martine Aubert in fiction,

Marc Amfreville in criticism, and Armand Eloi in drama. I am profoundly grateful to all of them. The experience has given me great pleasure and satisfaction, marred only by regret that I am unable to converse with my readers and interviewers, when I meet them, in their own language; and that Gilles Barbedette, who started the whole phenomenon, did not live to fully enjoy the vindication of his professional judgement.

Reviewing the balance of good luck and bad luck recorded in this memoir I have no doubt that the former outweighed the latter. This was largely a matter of fortuitous timing. I happened to hit my stride as a novelist when the going was good for literary fiction in Britain, energised by a new generation of novelists younger than me, and by an entrepreneurial spirit in publishing and the book trade which extended the audience for new writing and made freelance authorship a viable profession. This eventually overreached itself in the abolition of the Net Book Agreement in 1997, which most people in the literary world now regard as a grave mistake. It allowed books to be sold as cheaply as the seller wished, putting power into the hands of chain stores and supermarkets, who pressured publishers for discounts, diminishing the yield for writers, and devaluing the book as a cherishable artefact by offering two or three for the price of one, like punnets of strawberries when there is a glut. Within a short time the digital revolution in communications, and in particular the rise of Amazon, first as a distributor of discounted books and ebooks, and then as an instrument of self-publishing, further increased the cheap availability of new writing but reduced the profit derived from it by publishers and their authors. It is significant that France, having abolished retail price maintenance for books shortly after Britain, quickly restored it when the disastrous effect of abolition on traditional bookselling was perceived. This was to my advantage as my French readership grew.

It was never easy to make a living as a full-time writer, but it is now extremely difficult in the UK, and even well-established authors have had to accept greatly reduced advances for their work. In consequence many British writers who began successful independent careers soon after graduating from university in the 1970s and '80s have returned to academia to supplement their declining incomes by teaching Creative Writing in the many universities and colleges which now offer this popular subject, thus encouraging new aspirants to a more and more crowded profession. This is almost exactly the opposite career path of myself and other writers of my generation and the previous one (Kingsley Amis and John Wain, for example) who adopted university teaching as their primary source of income until they felt confident enough to go freelance. This reversal was the result of changing social and economic conditions over time. Looking back I feel no regrets about the pattern of my own career, and no doubt that for me 1935 was quite a good time to be born.

# ACKNOWLEDGEMENTS

I am grateful to the following persons and institutions for permission to quote from unpublished letters: Ben Bergonzi, extract from letter by Barbara Wall; Curtis Brown on behalf of the Estate of Malcolm Bradbury, extract from one letter; Catherine Michaels, extracts from letters by Leonard Michaels; The Random House Group Archive and The Random House Group Ltd., extracts from letters by Tom Rosenthal and John Blackwell. For information received on request I am indebted to Maurice Andrews, John Archer, Paul Slovak and Anthony Thwaite.

The dedication to this book expresses deep gratitude to my literary agent, Jonny Geller, who has supported and encouraged me throughout the writing of this memoir and its predecessor, expressing his enjoyment as a reader while giving the occasional subtle hint of what parts might be usefully reconsidered. My editor Geoff Mulligan made many helpful suggestions for improving the text I finally delivered. An anonymous copyeditor, and a proof-reader, Alison Rae, contributed further refinements and saved me from making some embarrassing errors of fact. Liz Foley, Publishing Director of Harvill Secker, and her assistant

Mikaela Pedlow worked hard to satisfy my somewhat pernickety concerns about the production of the book and to incorporate my numerous late inserts and deletions. My wife Mary was an invaluable source of facts and memories for this book, its first reader when it was completed, and frequently called upon to give her opinion of various passages about which I was uncertain. Usually I decided she was right.

D. L., October 2017

# INDEX

penguin.co.uk/vintage